ERDOĞAN

Edinburgh Studies on Modern Turkey

Series General Editors: **Alpaslan Özerdem**, Dean of the School for Conflict Analysis and Resolution and Professor of Peace and Conflict Studies at George Mason University, and **Ahmet Erdi Öztürk**, Lecturer in International Relations and Politics at London Metropolitan University and a Marie Sklodowska-Curie Fellow at Coventry University in the UK and GIGA in Germany.

Series Advisory Board: Ayşe Kadıoğlu (Harvard University), Hakan Yavuz (University of Utah), Samim Akgönül (University of Strasbourg), Rebecca Bryant (Utrecht University), Nukhet Ahu Sandal (Ohio University), Mehmet Gurses (Florida Atlantic University), Paul Kubicek (Oakland University), Sinem Akgül Açıkmeşe (Kadir Has University), Gareth Jenkins (Institute for Security and Development Policy), Stephen Karam (World Bank), Peter Mandaville (George Mason University).

Edinburgh Studies on Modern Turkey is an outlet for academic works that examine the domestic and international issues of the Turkish republic from its establishment in the 1920s until the present. This broadly defined frame allows the series to adopt both interdisciplinary and trans-disciplinary approaches, covering research on the country's history and culture as well as political, religious and socio-economic developments.

Published and forthcoming titles

Policing Slums in Turkey: Crime, Resistance and the Republic on the Margin
Çağlar Dölek

Islamic Theology in the Turkish Republic
Philip Dorroll

The Kurds in Erdoğan's Turkey: Balancing Identity, Resistance and Citizenship
William Gourlay

Peace Processes in Northern Ireland and Turkey: Rethinking Conflict Resolution
İ. Aytaç Kadioğlu

The Decline of the Ottoman Empire and the Rise of the Turkish Republic: Observations of an American Diplomat, 1919–1927
Hakan Özoğlu

Religion, Identity and Power: Turkey and the Balkans in the Twenty-first Century
Ahmet Erdi Öztürk

Electoral Integrity in Turkey
Emre Toros

Erdoğan: The Making of an Autocrat
M. Hakan Yavuz

edinburghuniversitypress.com/series/esmt

ERDOĞAN

The Making of an Autocrat

M. Hakan Yavuz

EDINBURGH
University Press

Edinburgh University Press is one of the leading university presses in the UK. We publish academic books and journals in our selected subject areas across the humanities and social sciences, combining cutting-edge scholarship with high editorial and production values to produce academic works of lasting importance. For more information visit our website: edinburghuniversitypress.com

© M. Hakan Yavuz, 2021

Edinburgh University Press Ltd
The Tun – Holyrood Road
12 (2f) Jackson's Entry
Edinburgh EH8 8PJ

Typeset in 11/15 Adobe Garamond by
IDSUK (DataConnection) Ltd, and
printed and bound in Great Britain

A CIP record for this book is available from the British Library

ISBN 978 1 4744 8325 4 (hardback)
ISBN 978 1 4744 8326 1 (paperback)
ISBN 978 1 4744 8327 8 (webready PDF)
ISBN 978 1 4744 8328 5 (epub)

The right of M. Hakan Yavuz to be identified as author of this work has been asserted in accordance with the Copyright, Designs and Patents Act 1988 and the Copyright and Related Rights Regulations 2003 (SI No. 2498).

CONTENTS

List of Abbreviations	vii
Introduction	1
1 The Formative Years of Erdoğan	29
2 Erdoğan's Worldview	77
3 Erdoğan as a Mayor and the 2002 Elections	116
4 Erdoğan and the Secular Resistance (2007–12)	139
5 The *Annus Horribilis* (2013)	172
6 The Existential Clash: Erdoğan versus Gülen	206
7 Erdoğan's 'Seduced Coup' and the Presidential System	230
8 Erdoğan's Kurds: Allies and Enemies	258
9 Erdoğan's Neo-Ottoman Foreign Policy	282
Conclusion	314
Bibliography	328
Index	355

ABBREVIATIONS

AKP	Justice and Development Party (Adalet ve Kalkınma Partisi)
ANAP	Motherland Party (Anavatan Partisi)
AP	Justice Party (Adalet Partisi)
BDP	Peace and Democracy Party (Barış ve Demokrasi Partisi)
CHP	Republican People's Party (Cumhuriyet Halk Partisi)
CUP	Committee for Union and Progress (Ittihat ve Terraki Cemiyati)
DP	Democrat Party (Demokrat Parti)
DSP	Democratic Left Party (Demokratik Sol Parti)
DTP	Democratic Society Party (Demokratik Toplum Partisi)
DYP	True Path Party (Doğru Yol Partisi)
ECHR	European Court of Human Rights
HDP	People's Democratic Party (Halkın Demokrasi Partisi)
MHP	Nationalist Movement Party (Milliyetçi Hareket Partisi)
MGH	National Outlook Movement (Milli Görüş Hareketi)
MGK	National Security Council (Milli Güvenlik Kurulu)
MSP	National Salvation Party (Milli Selamet Partisi)
MTTB	National Turkish Student Union (Milli Türk Talebe Birliği)
PKK	Kurdistan Worker's Party (Partiya Karkeren Kurdistan)
RP	Welfare Party (Refah Partisi)
FP	Virtue Party (Fazilet Partisi)
SP	Felicity Party (Saadet Partisi)

TRT	Turkish Radio and Television Corporation
TSK	Turkish Armed Forces (Türk Silahı Kuvvetleri)
TÜSİAD	Association of Turkish Industrialists and Businessmen (Türk İşadamları ve Sanayiciler Derneği)
YAŞ	Supreme Military Council (Yüksek Askeri Şura)

To those Turkish citizens
Berkin Elvan, Adem Huduti, Mümtaz'er Türköne and Bülent Yavuz

INTRODUCTION

The founding fathers of the Turkish Republic, who emulated the governing model of the French Republic, sought to build a modern, secular, nation state out of the ashes of the multicultural Ottoman Empire. Mustafa Kemal Atatürk and his followers embarked upon a comprehensive, profound modernisation project predicated on secular Western precepts to displace every vestige of the Ottoman-Islamic legacy. The project would be focused on integrating the pulse of Western modernity into an independent Turkey, but it also expanded to incorporate an invented tradition borrowed from Central Asia and the ancient Hittites. Atatürk's authoritarian regime and his political entity, the Republican People's Party (Cumhuriyet Halk Partisi (CHP)) were the principal architects. However, the dilemma for this nascent republican elite became overcoming the repercussions from the new leadership's attempts to rebuke the traditional Anatolian majority identity that encompassed pious Muslims – Turkish and Kurdish – as well as the *muhacir*, who were post-Ottoman refugees from the Balkans, Crimea and the Caucasus. Atatürk and his deputies feared their propensity for rebellion.

The traditional Muslim majority, supported by a small group of conservative intellectuals, converted the Islamic and Ottoman heritage into an oppositional identity, suffusing it with a new political language to resist the coerced reforms of modernisation in the young Republic. Although this new oppositional Islamic identity echoed the anti-colonial and pan-Islamic language of the Ottoman Empire's last ruler, Abdulhamid II (r. 1876–1909), it would only officially enter into the Turkish political domain in 1950, with constitutional reforms allowing multiparty participation in elections. The cultural struggle (*Kulturkampf*) between secular and Islamic sectors of society shaped the axes of Turkish politics during the Cold War. The 1950 electoral victory of Adnan Menderes' Democrat Party opened a tentative détente between the two sectors, permitting some breathing space for the conservative Turkish Sunni majority to take public pride in their faith and Ottoman heritage. The modus vivendi, however, ended in 1960 with the Kemalist/military coup against Menderes, who was seen as becoming too powerful as he strayed from republican principles. When Prime Minister Menderes and three cabinet ministers were hanged on the Marmara Sea island of İmralı by military authorities, the unhealed wound was reopened, aggravating the underlying tensions between the Anatolian Muslim majority and the Kemalist military–bureaucratic establishment. The 1960 events signalled to the silent majority that a scrupulous administrative process for elections was insufficient to bridge the chasm between the republican establishment and the Turkish populace. Traditional voters regarded the centre-right parties collectively, including Süleyman Demirel's Justice Party (Adalet Partisi, AP), as a surrogate to represent their values and identity.

This political adaptation would evolve into political and cultural voices for the Anatolian Turkish Sunni majority, which gradually gained autonomy and eventually became a potent political movement under Necmettin Erbakan's leadership in the early 1970s. With the 1980 coup, the military, fearing Soviet inroads to the country, moved to blend Islamism with nationalism (which became popularly known as the Turkish-Islamic synthesis) to counter threats from Soviet-aligned communists and radical leftist groups. They also sought enhanced national integration by easing up on the widely unpopular Kemalist *Kulturkampf* campaign against preserving and acknowledging the country's Ottoman Islamic heritage. When Turgut Özal won the first democratically held elections in 1983, three years after the coup, he opened wider channels for Muslim activism and representation in politics, economics and education to modernise the country alongside its Muslim heritage and not against it, as had previously been the case. As a result of Özal's neo-liberal economic policies, which combined a moderate dose of Islamism, a new pious economic and cultural counter-elite emerged with the purpose of creating an Islamic modernity on their own terms. The neo-liberal policies of Özal, combined with the weakening of statist sentiments, nourished the rise of Islamic sociocultural movements. Under liberalised market conditions, broad concepts such as self-actualisation, individual achievement, wealth accumulation and work ethics were infused into Anatolian society, formulating a more liberal friendly Islam. Atasoy writes:

> Islamic ideology is fundamentally shaped by political choice made by state managers and political elites in response to domestic and international political and economic pressures. After all, following the 1980 military coup, it was the decision of civilian and military bureaucrats to restructure state organs and institutionalize neoliberal policies in Turkey while promoting Islam as a panacea to contain the Left.[1]

The seeds of Islamic modernity, as Özal had sown, blossomed in the 1990s, when Erbakan's avowedly Islamic political movement won a string of municipal elections. In 1994, Erbakan's Welfare Party (Refah Partisi (RP)) won major municipal elections, including Istanbul, where Recep Tayyip Erdoğan became the mayor of the country's largest city.[2] The RP gradually expanded its support to a level where it could form the coalition government after the national elections of 1995. This crossed a critical threshold in republican history, since for the first time an Islamic-oriented politician (Erbakan) became the prime minister of a republic that had been founded primarily on the traits of a secularised modern identity with a distinct nod to Western ideals. This political shift was too much for the Kemalist military-bureaucratic establishment, the Republic's self-declared guardians, which soon after mobilised against the newly elected Erbakan government. Eventually, the military-led campaign resulted in Erbakan's resignation and the military sought to cleanse the public sector of its Islamic presence.[3] The campaign was known as the February 28 process. The Turkish Constitutional Court, a secular Kemalist bastion of the Republic, banned the RP in 1998, not because it had actively sought to undo secularism but because of its appeal to the religious sentiments of the traditional Muslim majority.

After the RP was banned, its Islamic-oriented political leadership re-engineered itself into the Virtue Party (Fazilet Partizi (FP)).[4] Its existence was short-lived, as it was banned in 2001, acknowledging that despite its new name, the party essentially was the same as its predecessor. Several splinter groups within the FP accused Erbakan traditionalists of being too confrontational and not tactful in political rhetoric. This divided internally the Islamic movement and two separate parties were created as a result. The more conservative and confrontational faction established the Felicity Party (Saadet Partisi (SP)). The younger, more modern-oriented, and pragmatic group formed the Justice and Development Party (Adalet ve Kalkınma Partisi (AKP)) with Erdoğan, the former charismatic mayor of Istanbul, at the helm. However, the secular military-bureaucratic establishment, and its allied business elite were sceptical of the AKP's Islamic orientation. In 2001, following one of the worst economic and political crises of the Republic's history, the AKP decisively won the national elections in 2002 to gain power. Although AKP won six consecutive elections (2002, 2007, 2011, 2015, a run-off in 2015, and 2018 national and presidential voting), the Kemalist establishment never let up, aggressively deploying diverse tactics to retain power and resist what they saw as the gradual Islamisation of the state. Before the 2007 presidential elections, the Kemalist opposition mounted a fierce resistance via the parliament and the Constitutional Court along with political rallies in major cities, asserting that the historical foundations of the secular Republic were in danger. The secularist opposition was defeated in the 2007 national election in which the AKP won a landslide and elected Abdullah Gül as president of the Republic.

Politics in modern Turkey have revolved around three sociological fault lines: the secular elite versus religious masses; Turks versus Kurds; and Sunnis versus Alevis. The most consequential line has been Kemalist secularism versus traditional Turkish Islam.[5] Turkey, as Samuel Huntington (1993) argues, is a 'country torn' between rival constructs of Western and Islamic civilisations. The fact that these constructs often are ideological caricatures doesn't mean that they cannot take on real cultural and political saliency. Çarkoğlu and Toprak explain that in Turkish society, 'clearly distinguishable groups oppose one another on almost all important issues'.[6] The politics of Turkish society has been based heavily on the axis of religious versus secular, though it also should be underscored that these two orientations do not always clash against each other. They share national aspirations of economic development and modernisation and Turkey's globalised orientation, along with the desire to make Turkey powerful again but in following different strategies. Also important, the Kemalist secular conceptualisation was not more democratic, liberal and tolerant than its religious counterpart. Although some secularists believe that they have been besieged by conservative religious groups, the Kemalist secular elite failed to construct a credible alternative political platform fostering a liberal-democratic and pluralistic state and society. Şerif Mardin argued in 2005 that secular and religious Turks often swim in the same direction and at the same pace but, in the light of their differentiated values, he also highlighted the dangers of Islamist mob politics in the neighbourhoods of Turkey.[7]

This book chronicles the transformation of the Turkish state and society by critically examining President Erdoğan's place as the seminal leader of a new Turkey, which signifies the end of the Kemalist secular hold over state and society, the fragmentation of Kemalist state institutions, its neo-populist character as exemplified by a charismatic, yet divisive, leader and the ascendancy of a new economic elite closely allied with the AKP's political fortunes. More bluntly, New Turkey is defined by Erdoğan's kleptocratic practices, the collapse of the rule of law mindset, internalised fears about speaking out against the authoritarian practices of Erdoğan, and a nested network of Muslim Brotherhood organisations committed to restructuring how Arab countries should be governed. The New Turkey is neither ensconced in the East nor West, neither fully democratic nor dictatorial, neither fully Islamic nor secular. It is a hybrid political entity with multiple identities and orientations. However, one also must be careful not to place too much emphasis on the electoral rise and fall of specific Islamic political parties, because doing so ignores the widespread and deep cross-fertilisation of Islamic and European ideas and practices in the daily life of Turkish citizens. The formal Islamic political movement represents but one sector of such activities, but it also is important to recognise that it has changed the national agenda, introducing new modes of being modern, which also has brought Muslim identity and ideology to the public sphere.

The roots of polarisation in Turkey are not just political but more emphatically sociological in nature – ethnic, religious and lifestyle cleavages. Since the mid-1990s, identity-based polarisation has deepened in Turkey and the social distance among identity-based communities has widened. The current polarisation is rooted at the societal level and manifested at the elite level, which, in turn, is reflected in the parliament's composition. The only issue that brought these hostile identity-based communities together was based on their mutual feelings of revulsion against Erdoğan's policies, the charges of corruption against the AKP and, in particular, against his desire to establish a Turkish-style presidential system. It was the AKP and its arrogance in procedural moves to cover up corrupt activities connected to four cabinet ministers that generated near-unanimous reservations, if not negative feelings, about Erdoğan and his leadership performance. The current president, seen as Turkey's most consequential agent of change since the Republic's founding, ironically epitomised the status quo that he had vowed to overturn in his early political campaigns.

This book examines the complex account of the challenges of sustaining modern Turkish democracy under Erdoğan. His biography echoes and parallels the fault lines that have complicated the desire for national unity and collective purpose and which eventually burst forward into the political arena.[8] This book seeks to explain Turkey's recent authoritarian turn and the encroaching Islamisation of the state by focusing on Erdoğan's role along with how he cultivated his ideological character and the inevitable clash with the Gülen movement. Thus, this book constitutes more than a political biography of Erdoğan. It is also a biography of a Turkish society that has evolved and diversified dramatically since the 1923 founding of an independent Republic. The key actor in this biography unquestionably is Erdoğan. Now more than a quarter of a century since he emerged on the country's central political stage, he remains an enigma or a paradox because there is an Erdoğan for every occasion, event or political shift, with the prime goal always being to enhance and sustain his leadership position. Sometimes, he is an Islamist, nationalist, anti-nationalist, sultan, Köroğlu (the Turkish version of the Robin Hood character), *kabadayı* (bully or tough guy), *reis* (manipulative political strategist or a Turkish persona of Machiavelli) or a *başyüce* (a Turkish Il Duce). Often, he assumes several of these roles simultaneously, befuddling critics and supporters about how to sort out what he sets out to accomplish. At the core, Erdoğan is an Islamist populist. He stresses personalism in relations, as almost all personal engagements for Erdoğan are transactional (give and take), his understanding of democracy is plebiscitarian, and he believes that he is the one who represents the people; and those who vote for him constitute the people, not the opposition supporters. He seeks to exercise power without any mediating institutions or check and balances; he believes in direct connection with the masses. He realises that social benefits and direct food provided to his grass-roots supporters are instrumental in maintaining his power base.

Erdoğan's resiliency as Turkey's leader makes for an extraordinary political study of longevity, charisma and strategic decision-making. Turkey's problems are as vexing and intersecting as in any other nation, yet Erdoğan remains a broadly popular, even if autocratic, leader. Erdoğan's appeal for many Turkish citizens has always outperformed that for his party or cabinet ministers. Thus, the AKP's identity and ideological profile are secondary to Erdoğan's charismatic personality. To rely solely on the Western media in print and broadcast, and the immense output of blogs and digital content that varies widely in standards of veracity and factual precision, one might easily envision Turkey as one of the worst countries in the world as a measure of its commitment to freedom of media, speech and human rights. Moreover, one might be persuaded that Erdoğan has overthrown a vibrant democracy and is building an authoritarian system modelled on Vladimir Putin. Some of these perceptions are based upon facts and justifiably are more than troubling. Turkey leads on unfortunate measures. It ranks among the worst in press freedom, jailing more opposition journalists in 2017 than virtually every other country. It has banned more than 180 news outlets. Hundreds of scholars were among the more than 40,000 people who have been arrested or purged in Turkey since the seduced coup of July 2016. Turkey's counterinsurgency war against the Kurdish militants also has led to serious abuses on both sides. Yet, Erdoğan's popularity rating continues to outperform that of rivals in Turkey overall and among more religious Turkish Kurds. His approval numbers consistently fall within the range of 40 per cent to 52 per cent.

With sharp irony, Erdoğan, who has reviled social media access for his critics and has tried to censor it, took to iPhone's FaceTime app on 15 July 2016, the night of the attempted coup, to rally Turkish citizens against the aggression. He likely had no other choice at the time – but it was a serendipitous testament to the potency of social media reach, a feature that he previously had tried to suppress. However, social media alone did not save Erdoğan, who also benefited from legacy broadcast media disseminating information that the president was safe and ready to continue as leader. In one interview, a CNN-Turk journalist held a mobile phone to broadcast Erdoğan's statement via the iPhone's FaceTime app. The broadcasts, also disseminated in similar ways by other Turkish media, proved crucial in rallying the public.

Erdoğan's popularity can be explained in several ways. His positive image is perpetuated by media channels either controlled by him or those close to him. Any viewer of Turkish television will see broadcasts of Erdoğan's speeches, which are accompanied by presenters who avoid criticising the president. However, considering the history of Turkish media, which once was dominated by the Doğan Holding Group, censoring critical accounts of the country's most prominent politicians, including Erdoğan's predecessors, is nothing new. The Doğan Holding enterprise, which once owned *Hürriyet* and CNN-Turk, dutifully established and followed this tradition, in exchange for access to government resources.[9]

Many journalists and scholars also have sought to explain Erdoğan's popularity in terms of Turkey's authoritarian cultural values by stressing memories of a powerful sultan. Despite these culturally essentialist claims that Muslims (and Turks) favour authoritarianism, public opinion polling consistently indicates that the majority of Turks support democracy and democratic values. A 2015 Global Attitudes opinion survey by the US-based Pew Research Center, conducted in the spring before the June elections of that year, indicated that while a majority of Turkish citizens (56 per cent) believed a democratic government is the best model for resolving their country's problems, a growing minority (36 per cent, as compared to 26 per cent in 2012) believed that a leader with a strong hand is better suited to improving their lives. This, while in 2012, 68 per cent had indicated a preference for a democratic form of government when given this choice – the highest level reported since Erdoğan became prime minister after the 2002 elections.

On the other hand, the 2015 Pew Research survey indicated a deep divide over the country's political direction. Nearly one-half (49 per cent) said they were satisfied with the way democracy is working in Turkey, with an equal share (49 per cent) responding that they were dissatisfied. However, almost twice as many Turkish citizens said they were not at all satisfied with the current state of Turkish democracy (27 per cent) compared with the 14 per cent who were very satisfied. The divide is further demonstrated along religious and political lines. Turkish Muslims who seldom pray said they are much more likely to prefer a democratic form of government (78 per cent) compared with those who pray five times per day or more (44 per cent). Additionally, a mandate majority (61 per cent) of sympathisers with Erdoğan's AKP support a strong leader versus a democratic form of government (36 per cent). Meanwhile, the Republican Peoples' Party (CHP) supporters portray a mirror image: 68 per cent prefer democracy, while 27 per cent say they want a strong leader.

Many of the reductionist cultural arguments attempt to embody the rise of Islamophobia in Western media and policy circles. This mode of thinking becomes troublesome, as some seek to explain Erdoğan's popularity by otherising and essentialising Turkish political culture while ignoring the country's democratic legacy, which is still supported by many citizens. The most fallacious arguments come from Orientalists and Islamophobes who shamelessly argue that Turkey's political culture is inherently incompatible with democracy and instead facilitates the convenient rise of authoritarian tendencies. Erdoğan's popularity cannot be explained accurately by a presumed authoritarian culture in Turkey. Many Turks recognise the increasing danger of such authoritarianism as in the centralisation of power, media censorship and the restraining of civil society. However, they regard these as critical measures to cope with the severe security challenges Turkey is facing today, whether they be neutralising those who collaborated with the July 2016 coup attempt, the conflict with the militant PKK (Partiya Karkeren Kurdistan or Kurdistan Workers Party) fighters or threats by the Islamist extremists (ISIS and others) infiltrating from across the border in Syria and Iraq.

Turkish public opinion is often a compounded phenomenon, as the Pew Research poll suggests. While 49 per cent say they have a negative opinion of the European Union, 55 per cent favour joining the EU and 54 per cent say Turkey should be better respected in the global community than it currently is. The question is how democratically minded Turks can staunchly support an 'authoritarian leadership' model in the form of Erdoğan. That said, the majority of Turks do not consider Erdoğan's actions as authoritarian or in conflict with their understanding of democracy.

Some political scientists see Erdoğan as an avatar of '*caudillismo*' (an elected authoritarian leader with Latin American flair); it also means the art of maintaining political power through a coalition of forces by distributing (and disrupting) the resources of the state.[10] David Close defines elected *caudillismo* as 'government by a single, usually charismatic-leader, driven by personal ambitions and with little interest in building any institutions bedsides his own perpetuation in power'.[11] One could also see the form of delegative democracy emerging as Turkey's political landscape evolves. According to O'Donnell, delegative democracy

> [r]ests on the premise that whoever wins an election to the presidency is thereby entitled to govern as he or she sees fit, constrained only by the hard facts of existing power relations and by a constitutionally limited term of office. The president is taken to be the embodiment of the nation and the main custodian and definer of interests. The policies of his government need bear no resemblance to the promises of his campaign – has not the president been authorized to govern as he (or she) thinks best?[12]

Erdoğan embodies the political character of a *caudillismo* who undermines political institutions to build himself as a new 'father' of the country. Early in his tenure, he asserted civilian supremacy over the military and while many critics have been especially alarmed at his use of the judicial branch of government to squash political opponents, many Erdoğan supporters also have been encouraged by his willingness to take on once untouchable forces in Turkish politics. Erdoğan also has presided over the country's strongest economic performance in its history – an annual average of 4.5 per cent growth – particularly within the last decade as Turkish manufacturing and export sectors have flourished. Improvements have been made in national health care and welfare policies, accompanied by economic support for elderly and poor families. The country's infrastructure for domestic and international travel has been expanded significantly. However, since 2013, the successes of the Turkish economy have been largely negated and today's Turkish economy is defined by widespread corruption, tax evasion, favouritism, a growing income gap and institutionalised kleptocratic practices. Nearly all of the gains made between 2002 and 2013, which should be credited to the prudent economic leadership of Ali Babacan, have lost their lustre. As the economy worsens and little cash is available because of the COVID-19 pandemic, Erdoğan has tried to create distractions, such as invoking religious–nationalist emotions of the Turkish population by announcing his decision to remake the Hagia Sophia museum into a mosque or by intervening in Libya with military force. As with his American counterpart, who left office in 2021, Erdoğan wants to 'make Turkey great again'.

While many Islamic-oriented conservative Turks believe that Erdoğan has worked successfully at making Turkey into a respected, potentially formidable world power both in terms of the economy and geopolitical impact, many secular-oriented Turks portray a leader who cracks down on personal liberties and is deeply involved in corruption. Western reporters and editorialists have raised alarms about how Erdoğan has Islamised the state and society. However, his supporters are convinced that Erdoğan's intentions and policies are focused on improving the economy and enhancing political stability. A small shop owner in Istanbul told me during a visit after the 2016 coup attempt, 'Erdoğan is not trying to dismantle democracy but rather enhance it through the presidential system to serve the people and Islam.' So, in the mindset of Erdoğan's conservative grass roots, his policies serve for the populist interests, especially when they are set in Islam. There is a deepening sense that, under Erdoğan's leadership, Turkey, indeed, is restoring its true greatness for the first time since the Republic was established. Simply, it is seen as a mandate that Turkey can act unilaterally without worrying about critics or concerns from the West.

Erdoğan's selective persecution of some establishment figures such as Aydın Doğan, who once owned major media outlets and had used them in the past to support anti-democratic coups, has bolstered the president's charismatic image as a man who sincerely understands the predicaments of ordinary Turks, especially the marginalised. Erdoğan's periodic attacks on secular intellectuals are likely to be praised by the man in the street while the international media have regarded his attacks on the Doğan Corporation as an authoritarian's act to silence the free press. Doğan had no option but to 'sell' his media empire to a pro-Erdoğan businessman.

Doğan has openly meddled in government policies and has leveraged his media power to extort concessions from the government to benefit his businesses. Erdoğan's attacks on these media outlets are usually welcomed by the public. A Turkish citizen in Tübingen, Germany, told me that 'the more German media attack and try to dehumanise Erdoğan the more I become pro-Erdoğan. I am critical of some of Erdoğan policies but these dehumanising attacks have made me pro-Erdoğan'. I listened to similarly expressed sentiments in Turkey, as echoed in public rallies for Erdoğan that have been motivated by citizens angered by displays of European racism and the EU's exclusion of Turkey. Many American and European journalists and think tank experts contend that Erdoğan's high approval ratings are an outcrop of latent illiberal values among Turks, who carry the culture of Islamism and Ottomanism. The results of some public opinion surveys suggest that while many Turks define democracy within the frames of economic development and political stability, many also have been receptive to Erdoğan's transformative politics that have elevated their country's prestige and profile. Erdoğan followed an aggressive policy to build relations with Western countries to demonstrate his country's commitment to being a productive, meaningful member of the EU. To wit: he passed more laws than any other Turkish leader to fulfil the EU's membership requirements. In the period 2003–14, Erdoğan visited more than 100 countries in approximately 300 official state visits on five continents.

Turkey's process reversing democratisation is unique, as the country barely has a sustained tradition of a strong liberal democracy. One could argue that until 2010, Turkish politics were dominated by the military (an institution that remains one of the most widely approved in Turkish society), having defined itself as guardians of Turkey's secular state and society. In contrast, as the 2015 Pew Research study shows, 51 per cent of Turks see the media as a negative influence, compared to 38 per cent who see it otherwise. Reiterating an earlier point, Erdoğan's style of governance has been more populist but it also is unprecedentedly more authoritarian and kleptocratic.

The right-wing shift in the EU and the chaotic events around Turkey had a direct impact on the country's domestic politics. Erdoğan's populism is anti-Western, pan-Islamist, and anti-elite and favours state-run social services. With a series of events beginning in 2013, such as the Gezi Park protests, the coup against the democratically elected government in Egypt that Western powers tacitly accepted, and the corruption probes by the Gülen-led police and judiciary, a majority of the Turks have been suspicious about the true motives of foreign critics, as evidenced by Pew Research. Only 29 per cent have a favourable view of the US and just 23 per cent have a positive opinion of NATO. Faring even worse in the eyes of the Turkish public are China (18 per cent favourable), Iran (17 per cent) and Russia (15 per cent). Erdoğan, who has forged a powerful, personal connection with millions of Turks, also has leveraged deftly the anger that is predicated on the recently formulated historic victimisation of Turkey at the hands of major European powers.

Many of my interviews have challenged the broader spectrum of the scholarly literature and I would argue that there are socially oriented reasons explaining why public support for Erdoğan runs deeper than what has been portrayed in the domestic media, especially with different reports coming from external observers. Since 2013, major Western news outlets have frequently referred to Erdoğan either as an authoritarian Islamist or a dictator. He certainly has intensified his identity as an ideological Islamist and as a dictator, as these media outlets assert. He can be described as an amalgam of present and past authoritarian figures, including, for example, Mussolini, Putin and Modi (India's democratically elected Hindu nationalist prime minister who has been held responsible for the mass killings of thousands of Muslims in Gujarat). Depending upon the occasion, Erdoğan is a populist pragmatist with a benevolent vision or a vindictive politician who would not hesitate to humiliate his rivals or even neutralise and imprison them.

Erdoğan's supporters, nevertheless, have real social and political grievances that cannot be easily ignored, but paradoxically they also sit at the centre of Erdoğan's consolidation as a political and popular figure. Rather than focus on resolving and reconciling the social and political grievances, some Islamophobes and Turkophobes have abdicated the complicated path of critical analysis in favour of convenient caricatures of Erdoğan as a fascist and Islamist. These descriptions ignore the social roots of authoritarian impulses as well as the sociological causes behind Erdoğan's position in politics. Erdoğan's popularity is based on the social and political discontent of a large sector of the Turkish population. As domestic polls indicate, his supporters come from Turkish society's most marginalised sectors – people who seek the privileges of social and economic mobility, especially religiously oriented groups who want to be comfortable in bringing their Islamic identity to the public and political spheres. These groups have found their leader in the persona of Erdoğan who speaks their language and understands as well as empathises with their sentiments. Even if Erdoğan cannot solve their problems, he appears genuinely to dignify them and treat them as equals who legitimately own the rights and privileges in a New Turkey.

Erdoğan's popularity has arisen individually and collectively from his rhetoric, actions and capacity to connect with ordinary Turks, a trait which became evident in the 1990s during his first term as Istanbul's mayor. İhami Güler, a leading theologian at the divinity faculty of Ankara University and a leading critic of the politicisation of Islam, explains that

> he is a pious Muslim who confronts death and, with his bravado culture, is not cowed by it. Erdoğan sees death as the soul returning to its Creator. The daring position he has taken on a number of issues makes him the 'hero they've been waiting for' who will bring an end to the humiliation of the Muslims.[13]

Erdoğan's rhetorical skills are amplified by his use of emotion-laden language that moves crowds of his most loyal adherents. Pious, but not a particularly deep thinker, Erdoğan demonstrates a shallow understanding of the complex interactions between Islam and society, unlike Muslim reformers and political leaders such as Alija Izetbegovic of Bosnia or Rached Ghannouchi of Tunisia.[14] Güler argues that Erdoğan is not an intellectual in their mould, but rather he is grounded in political tactics that have permitted him to know how to manipulate emotions, especially of constituents who support him the most. His emotionally visceral comprehension about the intersections of religion, society and politics means that he is more comfortable with the pithy emotional verse of poets such as Necip Fazıl Kısakürek (1904–83), the quintessential literary ideologue of the Turkish Islamist movement, who promulgated a nativist, anti-Semitic discourse in lieu of the intricate arguments and nuanced analyses one would expect from a political theorist or technocrat with such a strong appeal.

Moreover, Erdoğan's popularity coincided with the collapse of Turkey's economy in 2001 and amid the continuous partisan clashes of the country's political leaders. Erdoğan's rise was as serendipitous as it was an astute political calculation. In 2002, Erdoğan told a *New York Times* reporter that 'I changed . . . it was necessary to catch up with developments, the modern age.'[15]

Erdoğan's rise is also rooted in history – most particularly, the victimisation of Anatolian conservative Muslims. Erdoğan emerged as the hero candidate capable of lifting the country to its rightful position of geopolitical leadership while resolving the cultural segregation between the secular White Turks and the conservative pious Muslims (aka Black Turks).[16] Erdoğan always has presented himself as a Black Turk and once he said: 'In this country, there is segregation of Black Turks and White Turks. Your brother Tayyip belongs to the Black Turks.'[17] This sense of exclusion was quite widespread among conservative Anatolians and Erdoğan's statement echoed their deep feeling of alienation. According to Binnaz Toprak, White Turks belong to a secular and westernised lifestyle, but neither money nor power alone is crucial in constituting the category of White Turks.[18] It means a status group as defined by Victor Turner:

> a collection of individuals who are organized to maintain or expand their social privileges by mechanism of social closure to protect existing monopolies of privilege against outsiders, and by usurpation to expand benefits by reference to proximate or superior status groups. The existence of status groups inevitably involves social conflict and social struggle, although these forms of social struggle may be frequently disguised or hidden.[19]

Unlike many other Muslim political movements in the Arab world or Pakistan, supporters of the AKP in the majority, support democratic values, back Erdoğan and believe that society can be simultaneously democratic, modern and Islamic. The perplexing perspective is reconciling this worldview with a conflicting one prevailing abroad in which Erdoğan is viewed as an Orientalist despot seeking to impose Khomeini-style sharia. The question few international media can answer sufficiently is how can so many Turkish citizens, who still see democratic government as the sole legitimate political option, continue to support Erdoğan.

My interviews in Istanbul and elsewhere with Turkish citizens echo what major public opinion surveys indicate. However, what must be explored in greater detail is why and how a majority of Turkish citizens do not characterise Erdoğan's governance as autocratic. There are other questions: How do Turks comprehend and define democracy? How do they envision Erdoğan's policies (related to public services and economic mobility) and his style of governance as conducive to democracy? What are the values that Turks connect with their perspective of democracy and how does Erdoğan communicate those values? This book probes the reasons for Erdoğan's popularity and why many Turks remain committed to democracy but simultaneously support the authoritarianism of Erdoğan, despite the growing fears that his leadership is the most foreboding existential threat to the country's commitment to democracy. For many Turks, democracy encompasses effective government, social mobility, an expanding economy and, more significantly, a restoration of Turkey's global image as a regional power. It also represents a deep longing to heal the cultural and identity rupture between modern Turkey and Ottoman heritage.

The following was a common sentiment I heard among the 250 open-ended interviews I conducted for my research (2015–20): 'Erdoğan has raised the Turks up from their knees; he made Turkey respected and feared by rivals.' The younger generation of Turks are more nationalistic and they express the following feelings:

> This anti-Erdoğan campaign in the Western media is irrational. The issue is not about Erdoğan but rather the potential of Turkey to become a regional power and to be in control of its own destiny. The roots of European hostility go back to the heydays of nineteenth century colonialism and also their longing for the Sèvres Treaty in which a defeated Turkey was forced to become a rump state.

Many recounted the humiliating collapse of the Turkish economy in 2001 and the renewed European desire to partition Turkey as was attempted at the end of World War I with the Treaty of Sèvres, and many cited Erdoğan as the only leader capable of forestalling predatory imperialism in the heart of the Muslim world.

In order to comprehend the origins of anti-Western sentiment in Turkey, one must acknowledge the trauma caused by a century of Christian European invasions and the genocidal ethnic cleansing of Ottoman Muslims, culminating with the Sèvres Treaty in 1920. One of the most acute critical symptoms of the Sèvres syndrome still found in Turkey is the suspicion of imperialist designs, especially by European countries, the US and Russia, along with their perceived internal agents – Kurds, Alevis or Christian minorities – to weaken, partition and dismantle the sovereign Turkish state. The Sèvres Treaty not only ended the political sovereignty of the Ottoman state but also carved out large parts of the Ottoman territories amongst the European powers and created new Kurdish and Armenian states on territories where the majority of the population had long been Turkish and/or Muslims. The treaty reduced to a small rump in Central Anatolia a Turkish homeland. The humiliating articles of the treaty became the rallying point for Anatolian Muslims to mobilise for the War of Independence under the leadership of Mustafa Kemal Atatürk. The local resistance movements which were unified under Atatürk annulled the Sèvres Treaty following their victories in the War of Liberation and replaced it with the less onerous Treaty of Lausanne in 1923, which secured the sovereignty and the current borders of the Turkish Republic.

The perpetual referencing of the Sèvres syndrome in Turkey's political discourse signifies an existential insecurity tied to recent traumatic events, ranging from the Bosnian Muslim genocide to devastating American-led wars in the region which directly fuelled both the Kurdish-PKK insurgency as well as that of ISIS. In this vein, there was a systematic attempt by the pro-Erdoğan media to compare European criticism of Turkish domestic and foreign policy as an attempt to revive the spirit of the Sèvres Treaty. The revived or reimagined collective memory of European colonialism plays an important role in consolidating the identity of Turkish nationalism around the leadership of Erdoğan. This has especially been true since the shift to full support of Erdoğan by the Nationalist Movement Party (Milliyetçi Hareket Partisi (MHP)) in 2017. Today, Erdoğan has auspiciously become the dominant leader of both Islamic Turkish nationalist movements.

Erdoğan's domineering role in the AKP is a norm for Turkish politics. Party leaders preside over a rigorous, centralised decision-making process in which they determine the list of candidates and establish their respective policy platforms. Due to his deeply internalised authoritarian tendencies and intolerance towards diverse lifestyles, it would be prudent and proper to call him a dictator. His confrontational style, blunt talk, a personal aversion to criticism and evidence of his charismatic leadership exist alongside a genuine desire to represent the long-marginalised pious Anatolian Turkish and Kurdish majority.

Erdoğan is arguably the most popular Turkish politician in Turkish history after Atatürk. He handily became the major planner and coordinator of Turkey's economic and political policies after coming to power in 2002. Yet, his extraordinarily powerful and charismatic personality has also isolated him as a politician and the side effects of that isolation have disturbed the expected routines of a democratically functioning government.[20] He represents a most severe threat to Turkey's institutions, including state entities, business groups and several Islamic groups such as the Gülen movement.

The key concept in comprehending Erdoğan's blend of autocratic governance and illiberal tendencies is populism. Although the concept of populism is applied in different contexts to signify the gap between the elite versus the masses or us (the people) versus them (the elite), I will define it as the ideological frame as well as a political strategy for the purposes of this book.[21] As an ideological frame, populism means an attempt to mobilise the traditionally marginalised sectors of the population against the government, elite, and their hegemonic discourse. Populist politicians usually define what they are against more than what they are for, with their platforms.[22] Cas Mudde, a leading scholar of populism, explains:

> In short, populism is an illiberal democratic response to undemocratic liberalism. It criticises the exclusion of important issues from the political agenda by the elites and calls for their repoliticisation. However, this comes at a price. Populism's black and white views and uncompromising stand leads to a polarised society – for which, of course, both sides share responsibility – and its majoritarian extremism denies legitimacy to opponents' views and weakens the rights of minorities.[23]

Populist politicians are perceived to be against the elite, institutions and the rich (at least in their public rhetoric although their actions typically contradict and undermine their public sentiments). They also typically believe that social and political goals could be realised not through political compromises or gradual institutional designs but rather through direct political action of the masses such as referenda or plebiscites. It defines the 'real people' (Turks/Muslims) against the 'alien' (westernised elite/bureaucracy/intellectuals). Populist politicians, in short, may enhance democracy while diminishing liberalism and minority rights.[24]

This is the most consequential paradox to be analysed. On the surface, Erdoğan appears to have enhanced democracy but actually has undermined liberalism and social cohesion through a majoritarian approach to politics. In Turkey, journalists are routinely jailed and the country's most popular daily, *Zaman*, was taken over in 2013 by government forces in the aftermath of the corruption probes and links to the Gülenist representatives in the police and judiciary. Nearly all opposition websites and newspapers linked to the Gülenists or pro-Kurdish nationalist political outlets have been shuttered while others not linked to terrorism (as perceived in the eyes of the Erdoğan government) are pressured aggressively to curtail their activities. These serious breaches of democratic values, which continue to intensify in their punitive means, must be analysed in tandem with Erdoğan's actions in the period after the seduced coup of 2016. In times of emergency, a chief executive's constitutional actions and prerogatives occasionally appear as more congenial in analysis to legal scholars than to historians. For example, as scholars have noted, many contemporary critics of Abraham Lincoln's suspension of the writ of habeas corpus and the use of other war powers during the US Civil War often tended to be superficial, unrealistic and erroneous. In 1862, Horace Binney began his long peroration on the American president's authority, by explaining that

> the power to suspend the privilege is supplementary of the power to suppress or repel. It is a civil power to arrest for privity or supposed privity with rebellion, as the military power is to suppress by capture for overt acts of rebellion.[25]

Lincoln's acts were controversial, completely opposed by the Democrats at the time and often questioned vigorously by members of his own Republican Party. In the end, the public and the US Congress backed the president, who won in a landslide against the Democrats in 1864. It would be a generation before the Democrats regrouped sufficiently from the political humiliation they suffered during the Civil War years. Lincoln today is, of course, viewed by many historians as among the greatest American presidents; in many rankings as second only to George Washington.

This is not presented to characterise Erdoğan as particularly Lincolnesque but to suggest that effective leaders in extraordinarily challenging times wisely acknowledge that the best way to justify their expansive powers of authority is to ground the explanation in a comprehensible act of power. Another reason for the disjuncture between Turkish public perception of Erdoğan and that of Western critics is that the latter have failed to comprehend the true state of emergency Turkey has faced since 2013 with charges of Gülenist coup plotting and the creation of a parallel state structure alongside the emergence of a terrorist insurgency by both the Kurdish PKK and ISIS. The latter two, for example, emerged directly from President Obama's failure to secure the promise of the Arab Spring in Libya, Egypt, Syria, Yemen and Bahrain, despite repeated Turkish entreaties to do so.

As he is neither constrained by humility or self-doubt, Erdoğan's tenure has been marked by both comprehensible and incomprehensible expressions of executive power. In the first five years of his tenure (2002–7), Erdoğan often quickly stepped back if his controversial initiatives were criticised, especially when pushback came from the military, judiciary and universities. For instance, he gave up his education initiative to enhance the status of İmam Hatip schools (a religious seminary to train Muslim preachers). Erdoğan also had to contend with the two other members of the AKP triumvirate: Abdullah Gül and Bülent Arınç. The first five-year period of AKP governance was punctuated by pro-EU policies, collective leadership which enhanced civil rights and a commitment to liberal democracy.

In the second period (2007–13), Erdoğan closely allied with the Gülen movement to defeat revanchist Kemalist forces in the military and bureaucracy who sought to repeat the 'soft-coup' of 1997. The AKP even let the Gülenists run the bureaucracy, and Erdoğan consolidated his political power when he rebuffed the military and Kemalist judiciary when his partner Abdullah Gül was elected president with the support of the plurality of the population. The AKP called for run-off elections in 2007 and were returned to power with nearly 47 per cent of the vote, up from 34 per cent in the November 2002 vote. The election results, which signalled a major defeat for the military and the opposition parties, gave Erdoğan the leverage to select parliament members and to purge liberal MPs in the AKP who had criticised his policies. Moreover, by electing Gül as the president, Erdoğan freed himself from the constraints of the AKP triumvirate, becoming the party's unchallenged leader. In 2008, the nation's chief prosecutor asked the Constitutional Court to ban the AKP on the basis of its alleged anti-secular policies and activities. In July of that year, Turkey's highest court narrowly voted to censure the party, for having become a focal point of anti-secular activities. The court decision made Erdoğan more vulnerable and he in turn depended on the Gülen movement in order to govern the country and constrain Kemalist coup plotting within the bureaucracy, judiciary and military. However, the court stopped short of decertifying the party, and the AKP managed to consolidate political power in what was a critical juncture in the history of the Turkish Republic long dominated by an unelected Kemalist version of a deep state.

During this second period, the first circle of the AKP elite were distinguished by their class aspirations in becoming conspicuously wealthy while engaging in an inner struggle in moralising the wealth they had amassed. Their resentment against the Kemalist establishment is at least, in part, related to their frustration of not being able to internalise all aspects of modernity and becoming outwardly modern and market oriented while also feeling guilty about this development and professing traditional forms of piety and abnegation.

The third period of the AKP (2013–present) has been shaped by a series of seismic events from the Gezi Park demonstrations and the anti-democratic coup in Egypt to the corruption probes of the Gülenist police and judiciary and, finally, the seduced coup in July 2016. These events profoundly changed Erdoğan's worldview of politics, to the detriment of his credibility and reputation as a democratic leader. More consequentially, his transformation has become detrimental to the whole of Turkey. This has worsened, as Erdoğan has become more combative towards opponents whom he suspects of seeking to unseat him in undemocratic ways. Over the last eighteen years, the country has witnessed the AKP's transformation from a peripheral political entity into the establishment party of the Turkish Republic. In short, we have witnessed dual transformations in the last decade: that of both Turkey and the AKP. The transformation has not improved Turkey's lot. The result, in fact, points towards a disturbing realisation that has worsened for the potential damage being inflicted upon the Republic of Turkey, its worst crisis since independence was won nearly a century ago. The figure at the centre of this calamitous downward turn is Erdoğan.

Outline of the Book

In this book, I outline the inner life and professional struggles of Erdoğan. I particularly focus on the interaction between his inner and outer worlds as well as how his political struggles shaped his personality and vice-versa. The story of Erdoğan's life is one of self-invention. Thus, there is a continuously evolving Erdoğan in different contexts. My work is based on interviews, focus-group discussions, and readings of first-hand memories and documents. In my attempt as an embedded constructivist to understand Erdoğan, I focus on the origins of his emotions and behaviours. To this end, I draw on psychology (self-images, memories and shared narratives), as well as the history of Islamic ideas that shaped Erdoğan's social imaginary, a set of ideas and practices that enabled him to make sense of his policies and actions. It is important to identify the conditions under which these shared beliefs transform into collective action. My key assumption is that we are in a hermeneutic age where the critical interpretation of competing narrative is essential to establishing the truths of history and politics. Thus, my narrative is one of the many possible interpretations of the events and personalities in Turkey. The best possible way of deciphering the events and making up a reliable narrative is to shuttle between and among particular events, theoretical concepts and interpretations.

The first chapter chronicles Erdoğan's formative period. This includes his early years in the cities of Kasımpaşa/Beyoğlu and Rize, along with his educational experiences, such as the İmam Hatip schools and his interactions with the anti-communist movements and the influences of Islamic leaders such as Mehmet Akif Ersoy and Necip Fazıl Kısakürek. Later, his first political experiences with Necmettin Erkaban, the founder of the National Outlook Movement and the country's first explicitly Islamic political parties, are examined.

The second chapter summarises Erdoğan's evolving worldview and socio-political beliefs on numerous topics. These include religion; the rise of nationalism; the politics and cultural practices of history and memory; the role of the state; the cultural clashes of modernity and tradition; the salient value of institutions at the community, individual and family levels; and democracy in the context of human rights and the rule of law.

The third chapter chronicles the emergence of Erdoğan's political career, first as the chairman of the Welfare (Refah) Party's branch in Beyoğlu and then as Istanbul's mayor (1994–8). After recounting Erdoğan's rise within the Welfare Party machine, I will explore how Erdoğan mastered working with the grass-roots levels of Islamic networks to translate their activism into voting blocs in the municipal elections of 1994, when he became the first Islamic mayor of Istanbul. As mayor of Turkey's largest city, Erdoğan gradually rose in the ranks to become the national Islamic leader. The third section will detail the 28 February soft military coup (1997) and its implications, such as the imprisonment of Erdoğan, which advanced his cause for becoming the leader of Turkey. The fourth section will explore the split within Turkey's leader-based Islamist movement and the establishment of the AKP. The final section examines the 2002 elections as the first wave of the tsunami to transform the old Turkey and the beginning of the 'New Turkey'.

The fourth chapter will examine the events that sharpened sociocultural cleavages leading to an increasingly polarised Turkish society. The events such as the 2007 presidential crisis, the EU's reluctance to accept Turkish membership, the closure decision of the constitutional court in 2008 and the 2010 constitutional referendum, played a critical role in the gradual radicalisation of Erdoğan. The main conflict between the secular and religious sectors of the population climaxed with the presidential election in 2007. In the second section of this chapter, I will examine the 2007 political crisis, along with the national elections, and the political consequences. The third section examines the closure case against the AKP and the Gülenist-cum-AKP move to intimidate and reduce the role of the military through a series of controversial court cases in 2009. The last section of the chapter will examine the 2010 constitutional referendum and the impact of these changes. The cumulative impact of the confrontations with the military and the Constitutional Court on the policies of Erdoğan are examined as the most important political developments between 2007 and 2013, when Erdoğan heavily relied on the Gülen movement against the secular establishment.

The fifth chapter is titled *Annus Horribilis*, and describes 2013, Erdoğan's worst year, for numerous reasons. The chapter will examine three events and their respective impacts on Erdoğan's political views and the gradual process of his authoritarian radicalisation. The first event was the Egyptian military coup which ended with the removal and jailing of Mohamed Morsi, a close friend of Erdoğan. Then, the Gezi Park demonstrations confirmed Erdoğan's fears that a confluence of domestic and international factors were seeking to overthrow him. Finally, the extrajudicial corruption probes of the Gülen community deepened his sense of being besieged. As I describe the sociological fault lines in Turkish society, I seek to explain the social origins of contemporary politics and gradual polarisation of the country after the 2013 Gezi Park demonstrations. This book argues that Erdoğan's popularity is girded, in part, by a begrudged majority, which has been repressed for a long time by a politically and economically dominant minority, also known as the White Turks. Erdoğan's supporters envision democracy as a way to wrest power away from and even to settle scores with this ancient regime. They also seek to redistribute the country's wealth and resources.

The sixth chapter focuses on the rise and fall of the symbiotic relations between Erdoğan and the Gülen movement. This chapter comprises three subsections. In the first, I will examine the Gülen movement, a former ally of the AKP, now officially referred to as the Fethullah Gülen Terror Organization (FETO), by focusing on the transformation of the Gülen movement from a pietistic–education focused movement to a network of business organisations and then eventually into a secretive religious political configuration. After examining the factors that played a key role in the movement's transformation, I will analyse the causes, the nature and the political consequences of the conflict between the two Islamic movements (the AKP and the Gülen movement).

The seventh chapter will examine the seduced coup of 2016 and then its consequences. The first section explores the social and political reasons for the coup and the role of the Gülen movement. It will also focus on the domestic and international consequences of this the coup. The seduced coup marks a turning point and the end of military tutelage in Turkey, but this does not guarantee that civilian democracy will be consolidated as Turkey also faces a severe institutional crisis. The second section examines Erdoğan's pursuit of an executive presidency. This section will examine his motive to shift from a parliamentary to presidential system, along with the counter argument of the opposition against the change in the political system. Although Erdoğan claims that a parliamentary system is less democratic than a presidential system, the main goal of this shift is (1) to complete the Islamisation of the society through top-down process and redefine Turkey as a Muslim, opposed to secular, Republic; and (2) to unite the country under strong executive leadership. His model of 'the Turkish style of executive presidential system' is different from the US or France. The main characteristic of the 'Turkish-style' presidential system is that there will be no checks and balances in the face of such a strong executive. The last part of the chapter will examine the political and judicial context of the April 2017 constitutional referendum and its political implications on the society.

The eighth chapter will first examine Erdoğan's political framework for dealing with the Kurdish question and then the rationale as to how he has continuously shifted his stance towards the Kurds within the most recent two decades. After summarising the historical origins of the perception of the Kurdish issue among the public, I will examine Erdoğan's ideological framework of understanding Kurdish identity claims and his understanding of this issue. The second section will focus on Erdoğan's understanding of the Kurds as Muslim brothers and the Kurdish question as the by-product of Kemalist secularism in addition to recounting his first attempt to resolve the issue by weakening the Kemalist system and bringing Islam into the public sphere. The third part explores the reasoning that drove Erdoğan's peace initiatives (2009–15) and why they failed. This section will focus on how and why Erdoğan reverted to the nationalist, state-security paradigm by examining the collapse of the ceasefire, the civil war in Syria and the internationalisation of the Kurdish issue. The last section of the chapter will summarise how Erdoğan has managed to portray himself as the saviour of the Turkish state by invoking victimhood memories of the partition of Ottoman Turkey in the hands of major European powers and the manipulation of the minorities.

The ninth chapter deals with Turkish foreign policy and the country's pivotal position in the international system between East and West. The domestic transformation in Turkish politics and national identity has had a profound effect on Turkish foreign policy as well. The rise of neo-Ottomanism has also led to aspirations of Turkey bringing order to a broader region still suffering from the fragmentation of the Sykes–Picot–Sazanov division of the Ottoman Empire. So far this has played out with very mixed results in the wake of the Arab Spring and the ongoing fallout of the Syrian and Iraqi civil wars.

The conclusion focuses on the potential success or failure of Turkey emerging as an effective polity and model that synthesises Islam and modernity alongside democracy. I will also conclude the discussion by examining how Erdoğan's desire for authoritarianism and kleptocratic practices compels a critical analysis of five political myths in Turkey related to Kemalism, secularism, the role of the military, and the moral and ethical dimensions of Islamism. I will summarise three possible scenarios in a post-Erdoğan Turkey and their respective likelihood of occurring, given specific factors. A post-Erdoğan period is more likely to lead towards disintegration than reintegration and potentially see Turkey become another Middle Eastern country with dysfunctional institutions and competing pockets of regional groups.

Notes

1. Atasoy, 'Cosmopolitan Islamists in Turkey', p. 139.
2. Yavuz, 'Political Islam and the Welfare Party', pp. 63–82.
3. Yavuz, 'Turkey's fault lines', pp. 33–9.
4. Yesilada, 'The Virtue Party', pp. 62–81.
5. Abbas, *Contemporary Turkey in Conflict*, pp. 34–46.
6. Carkoğlu and Toprak, *Religion, Society and Politics*; Toprak et al., *Being Different in Turkey*.
7. Mardin, 'Turkish Islamic exceptionalism', pp. 145–65; Mardin, 'Mahalle Havası Diye Birsey', 15 May 2007.
8. For the most detailed interview with Erdoğan about his life and activities, see Aksu, 'Kasımpaşa sokaklarından başkanlık koltuğuna'. The best book in Turkish is written by Dindar, *Bi'at ve Öfke: Recep Tayyip Erdoğan'ın Psikobiyografisi*. There are several other relevant books: Besli and Özbay, *Bir Liderin Doğuşu: Recep Tayyip Erdoğan*; Kaplan, *Recep Tayyip Erdoğan*; Pamuk, *Yasaklı Umut: Recep Tayyip Erdoğan*; Çakır and Çakmak, *Recep Tayyip Erdoğan*.

9. The Doğan Holding Company, which is owned by Aydın Doğan, has turned the media into a weapon of intimidation against perceived opponents of the Kemalist establishment as well as to promote its own narrow commercial interests. Due to its past hostility against pro-Islamic elected governments, Doğan Holding has been the main target of the AKP, and its leader Erdoğan. In 2009, the company was hit with huge tax bills due to tax evasion and decided to sell the newspapers *Milliyet* and *Vatan*. Today, the company owns a collection of newspapers, magazines and TV stations, along with a number of companies in energy, tourism and finance. For more on the modern history of Turkish media, see Finkel, 'Captured news media'.
10. Taş, 'Turkey – from tutelary to delegative democracy', pp. 776–91. Taş argues that Turkish democracy under the leadership of Erdoğan has turned into a delegative democracy by undermining institutions, shrinking the spaces of political debate and compromise, and promoting a client-focused majoritarian democracy.
11. Close, *Undoing Democracy*, p. 4.
12. O'Donnell, 'Delegative democracy', pp. 55–6.
13. Interview with İhami Güler, Ankara, 14 July 2018. Güler, 'İslamcı muhafazakârların ahlaki performansının teolojik-politik kökenleri üzerine', 26 June 2019.
14. Tamimi, *Rachid Ghannouchi*; Izetbegovic, *Islam Between East and West*; Binder, 'Alija Izetbegović', 20 October 2003.
15. Fisher, 'Turkey waits and wonders how closely bound to Islam', 7 November 2002.
16. The axis of White versus Black Turks was coined by Ufuk Güldemir in 1992 to describe the cultural and economic gap between the establishment and the marginalised Anatolian conservative masses. In his popular book entitled *Teksas Malatya*, he criticised the secular elite and their distance from the conservative masses and the supporters of Turgut Özal. For more on the conceptual debate about white versus black Turks, see Demiralp, 'White Turks, black Turks?', pp. 511–24.
17. Sontag, 'The Erdoğan experiment', 11 May 2003.
18. Toprak, 'Who are these White Turks?', 15 November 2010.
19. Turner, *Concepts in Social Thoughts*, p. 5
20. Özdenören, 'Yalnızlık: Erdoğan'ın Kaderi', 25 June 2015.
21. Laclau, *On Populist Reason*, pp. 10–23. Laclau explains the process in which the 'construction of the people' takes place. In this book, Laclau engages with the legacy of Kemalism, along with Peronism in Argentina. He treats populism as

an often-positive force for enhancing democratic politics. For more on populism and the application of Laclau's ideas, see Panizza, *Populism and the Mirror of Democracy*.
22. Mudde defines populism as a 'thing ideology' which sets up the framework of the people versus the corrupt elite; see Mudde, 'The populist zeitgeist', pp. 542–63.
23. Mudde, 'The problem with populism', 17 February 2015.
24. Müller, *What is Populism?*, pp. 1–6.
25. Binney, *The Privilege of the Writ of Habeas Corpus*, p. 8.

1

THE FORMATIVE YEARS OF ERDOĞAN

1.1 Introduction

> According to them we don't understand politics. According to them we don't understand art, theatre, cinema, and poetry. According to them we are uneducated, ignorant, the lower class who has to be content with what is being given, needy; meaning we are a group of negroes [Zenci] . . . In this country, there are Black Turks and White Turks. Your brother Tayyip belongs to the Black Turks.[1]

Erdoğan's core identity and the framework of his geopolitical understanding are shaped by two coinciding forces: his ongoing sense of victimhood and sustained perceptions of his marginalisation by the Kemalist secular system that also is connected to his Islamism. His rage and revenge provide a context for comprehending how he has constructed Islam as a legitimate ideology justifying the means of taking revenge upon and eliminating his opponents. There is a revealing paradox regarding Erdoğan as the most popular politician in Turkey and in the broader Muslim world where his appeal and legitimacy easily eclipse that of many the region's Western-backed kings, generals and presidents for life. However, in the West he is categorised as an autocrat often compared to Vladimir Putin or Roderigo Duterte. The views of an elderly Turkish woman in her late sixties, as relayed to the author are typical: 'Erdoğan is not only our *reis* [paternal leader] but, more importantly, he is the national mirror in which we see ourselves.' A young man from Konya also describes Erdoğan in similar terms: 'He is the second Atatürk. He cares for the people and is fearless.' For a Turkish immigrant woman at Tübingen University in Germany, this East–West paradox is explained by the fact that 'Erdoğan is covered negatively in the German media because in his persona, he, according to the media, represents Muslimness. The key problem here is the prevailing Islamophobia in Europe and this, in turn, leads to the demonisation of Erdoğan.' Yet, a retired military officer described Erdoğan as follows:

> He represents the historical revenge of the Islamists and accompanying conservative forces whom the Republic tried so hard to bury and leave in the past. He does not want to just replace the old elite with his own circle of Islamists but rather he also wants to extract the revenge of the Anatolian conservative masses. Therefore, the destruction of the Kemalist institutions is part of his political objectives and he has succeeded.[2]

To the consternation of many European officials and media commentators like Jochen Bittner, this is a prevalent view amongst the Turkish diaspora in Europe accounting for their overwhelming support for Erdoğan in the most recent presidential referendum. Erdoğan's struggles and triumphs are enmeshed in the broader societal transformations experienced by the Turkish state and society over the last fifty years. His biography and political career comprise a prism reflecting the broader centre in Turkish politics versus the periphery; religious versus secular; and Black Turks versus White Turks struggles which have cleaved modern Turkey. It is essential to analyse critically the formative development of Erdoğan's personality and character in order to make a proper assessment of the historical significance of his policies, ideology and his intellectual engagement with others in his long, transformative rise to becoming Turkey's most consequential leader since Atatürk.

Any discussion of contemporary Turkey must begin with Erdoğan, because since 2002 he has had the decisive vote over all major domestic and foreign policy decisions.[3] Although he now sits atop the executive presidential system for which he advocated strenuously, for the last decade, Erdoğan has overshadowed all rivals within his own party as well as the opposition at the national level. This has been due to both his personality and electoral dominance, facilitated by particular institutional features of Turkish politics. How did he manage to become the most popular leader in today's Turkey? Why has he eclipsed fellow rivals in the AKP and how has he managed to retain the loyalty of both party cadres as well as most of the leaders of the Republican military and bureaucratic establishment which bitterly opposed and sought to overthrow him in the AKP's first term in office? How culpable is Erdoğan for the current political crisis confronting Turkey? Will Erdoğan's installation of a strong presidential system consolidate or weaken Turkish democracy? How will his vision of a Turkey returning to her historical role of providing leadership and cohesion to a crisis-ridden Middle East evolve? As a pivotal state poised between East and West, what will Turkey's future orientation be in a rapidly transforming international system? In answering these questions, it is imperative to be acquainted with the foundations of Erdoğan's worldview and how it has matured and shifted.

The book's research includes numerous interviews and focus groups, such as one at Mulkiyeliler Birligi in Ankara. Respondents there identified two major negative views of Erdoğan that animate his critics in Turkey and can be summarised in the following quote-s taken from this focus group: (1) 'He is corrupt to the point that he is the national thief of the country', and (2) 'He is an Islamist dictator who wants to concentrate power in his own hand and transform a secular republic into an Islamic theocracy'.[4] In fact, President Erdoğan 'is now plainly a one-man hate figure for a large segment of Turkish society and wider international observers. He personifies for many everything that is wrong with Turkey, everything that is suspicious, corrupt and vengeful'.[5] Conversely, in another focus group at Gazi University, his proponents saw a positive mirror image. One student identified Erdoğan as 'a Robin Hood who defends the poor and marginalised sectors of the population; a populist-authoritarian leader who brought economic growth and fostered the rise of a dynamic Anatolian middle class in the country'.[6] Many of his supporters also saw him restoring Turkey's role of leadership in the region after two centuries of defeat and humiliation as well as healing the trauma caused by the early Kemalist leadership's radical efforts to deracinate the nation from its rich Seljuk and Ottoman Muslim heritage.

Paradoxically, Erdoğan balances between these opposing poles.[7] On the one hand, he and the newly minted AKP establishment are the new White Turks, representing the political and socio-economic leaders of the country. However, he and his inner circle still perceive themselves as Black Turks, yet to fully overcome the *ezik ruhlu* (inferiority complex) and resentment felt at the now-subordinated republican *ancien régime*. One sees the portrait of a man with multiple identities, torn between religious and secular aspects, as well as his primed self-confidence and his inferiority complex. He springs from the poorest neighbourhood of Istanbul but he is also the richest Turkish politician, holding shares in virtually every major company in the country.

Because he knows how to play to several constituencies, he often adopts multiple incongruent roles: one for his traditional Turkish Sunni Muslim supporters, and another for his secularist domestic and international audiences. He calls the fighters in Iraq alternatively 'martyrs' and 'terrorists', and labels Israel as a 'terrorist state', and yet he still desires to maintain a strategic relationship in his role as a statesman in order to maintain good relations with the US. He has also been genuinely committed to achieving the long-sought membership of the EU before souring on it after what he believed was implacable anti-Turkish and Muslim hostility on the part of Western leaders. He is a man with diverse loyalties and torn fantasies, who embodies Turkey's intricately bifurcated national persona where internal and external identities do not always seem to be consistent or reconcilable. At the core, he is a committed Islamist with deep desire for economic and political power. He learned at a young age that the political path is the best and shortest one to economic wealth. That lesson has come at great expense in unsettling millions of Turkish citizens who once believed and supported his efforts to stabilise and grow the national economy.

Any study of Erdoğan must be balanced according to the demands of a dispassionate analysis of a complex man with deep sources of inner contradictions that manifest themselves in controversial decisions. He is a natural charismatic leader, inspiring sincere connections with his constituencies, advocating for them and diligently following up with his subordinates to make sure they are responsive to their socio-economic needs. On the other hand, this expression of loyalty, for the purposes of defending and serving his supporters, goes beyond the proprieties of ethics and altruism as it entails elaborate patronage which also enriches his inner circle of friends, many of whom have become wealthy through state construction contracts. This has been particularly worrisome because of his aloof personality and tendency to surround himself with sycophantic individuals along with inferior and even incompetent advisers. One of the most trenchant criticisms of Erdoğan's leadership has been his failure to appreciate the centrality of creating vital state institutions and checks and balances, as opposed to the personalised and informal 'great man' style of leadership which has long plagued polities in the developing world.

In this vein, Erdoğan epitomises the personality-centric dynamic that has been a staple of Turkish political culture. Political parties with policy-centred platforms are created on a weekly basis in Turkey. Leaders commonly outlast their respective political parties, meanwhile aging in the public spotlight through cycles of new parties being born and buried in a metaphorical graveyard. These political characters supersede the ideologies, policies and national programmes that were supposedly the *raisons d'être* of their respective parties. These modern-day sultans view fellow politicians as subordinates rather than as colleagues. One of the reasons why Turkish party leaders tend to evolve into authoritarians is the lack of intra-party democracy. Instead of voters choosing candidates for national elections, party leaders typically dictate their slates of candidates. In such a scenario, the candidate's allegiance and obedience are owed more to the party leader than to the voters. Attributes of education, probity and strength of character, therefore, are discounted.

As the mayor of Istanbul in the 1990s and during the AKP's first two terms (2003–11) at the head of the national government, Erdoğan established a reputation for clean and efficient governance. This proved crucial for the substantial level of support he enjoyed even amongst the secular-liberal and Kurdish segments of society. Early in his career, Erdoğan lived in a small apartment and even when he assumed the AKP leadership, he refused to move to the state-owned prime minister's mansion but instead took up residence in an apartment in the middle-class neighbourhood of Keciören in Ankara. However, as Erdoğan's power grew so did his appetite for grandiosity, as seen in the controversy surrounding his mammoth presidential palace known as Aksaray. After the 2011 elections, and partly in response to the Gülenist formulation of a 'parallel state', the trend for ethical backsliding and state corruption began gradually and accelerated throughout the remainder of the decade. As perceived rivals like Abdullah Gül and Ahmet Davutoğlu were purged, the standard merit has been replaced by sycophancy masquerading as loyalty.[8] There is a dearth of expertise and ability amongst members of his inner circle as well as the broader AKP cadres. Precisely the kind of well-educated technocrats and policy experts who could provide the basis for Erdoğan's vision of a modern and dynamic Turkey increasingly see themselves as unwelcome in the corridors of power. Therefore, it should come as no surprise that since the Gezi Park disturbances and the Gülenist challenge for political power, state institutions and the rule of law have deteriorated at an accelerating rate.

Curiously, Erdoğan had not defined himself first and foremost as a Turk but rather as a Muslim from the Black Sea of Georgian descent and as one more sympathetic to the Ottoman legacy as opposed to the republican version. Only after the renewal of the PKK insurgency and the seduced coup in 2016, did he overtly identify with Turkish nationalism. Nevertheless, Islam and the Ottoman heritage for Erdoğan always has been at the core of his identity. Erdoğan sees the present post Sykes–Picot nation state system in the Middle East as a disastrous outcome of Western imperialism and its desire to divide and rule the region. He argues that the Muslim masses are presently exploited by their Western-backed despotic elites. Initially, he was an avid backer of the Arab Spring. Erdoğan's enormous popularity throughout the Muslim world stems from his deep and genuine concern for persecuted Muslims around the world – from Bosnia to Syria, Palestine, Kashmir, Somalia and Myanmar. However, he abhors his Muslim opponents, especially Muslim Kurds who disagree with his oppressive policies. While modern-day Turks always have felt a close affinity to Ottoman kin, such as Bosnian Muslims or Crimean Tatars, Erdoğan has expanded this vision to include diverse Muslim populations who were never part of the Ottoman domains.

Before delving into Erdoğan's current political challenges, however, it is important to look back to his formative years, which comprise a significant phase in his ideological evolution. It began in a rough neighbourhood of Istanbul, where his temperament and character were forged by four institutions of socialisation: his family and the Kasımpaşa neighbourhood where he grew up, the conservative-religious İmam Hatip school system where he was educated, the ethno-religious (MTTB; National Turkish Student Union) student union where he became familiar with the anti-communist ideologies and the writings of Kısakürek, and the National Outlook Movement of Necmettin Erbakan through which he became involved in Turkish politics. The next few sections discuss the imprint of these sociocultural environments in the development of Erdoğan's character and worldview.

1.2 Kasımpaşa and Erdoğan's Formative Years

Erdoğan was born on 6 February 1954 to 'a Georgian family who had migrated from Batumi, Georgia to the north-eastern Turkish city of Rize'.[9] Erdoğan's grandfather, Tayyip, was killed by the villagers of Dumankaya (formerly named during the Ottoman Empire as Plihoz) because of fears that he was going to claim domain over the village's common land and property. Erdoğan's father, Ahmet (d. 1988), was known by his neighbours as the Reis Kaptan (ferry captain). The family was poor with limited acreage to farm for their livelihood. This meant that men in the village either would go to different parts of the country as seasonal labourers or to Istanbul for work. Ahmet was only one or two years old when Tayyip was murdered. After reaching puberty Ahmet was married but had no children from his first wife. As a result, it was arranged that he would marry a woman, Fatma, whose husband had not returned from the battlefield and was presumed missing or dead. From her, Tayyip's stepbrothers Hasan (b. 1929) and Mehmet (1930) were born. After the divorce from his second wife, Erdoğan's father married Tenzile in 1952. From this marriage, Tenzile had two sons (Recep Tayyip and his brother Mustafa) and a daughter.

Erdoğan was born in Kasımpaşa, a tough neighbourhood of Istanbul but he spent some of his childhood in Rize, a city on Turkey's eastern Black Sea coast. His grandparents had migrated from Batumi. Erdoğan's father had been a member of the coastguard for forty-three years (1925–68) and so they moved back and forth between Rize and Istanbul. Erdoğan was the youngest child. His father, a ferry captain, was known as a religious man but also as a harsh, abusive disciplinarian. Erdoğan relates that his father once punished him for swearing by hanging him by his arms from the ceiling. Erdoğan told a journalist:

> We had to be home before it became dark. We had a neighbour called Sister Müşerref opposite our home. Since I was a kid, I often cursed at her and, in return, she slapped my bottom every time. She complained to my father and

I was, of course, unaware of this. My father entered the room – may he rest in peace – and he grabbed me and hanged me from the ceiling. Whether or not he tied my hands or arms, I do not remember. I must have been hanging there for fifteen to twenty minutes until my uncle came and rescued me. From that day onwards, there was no more swearing.[10]

In interviews, Erdoğan regularly complained about his father's oppressive, abusive and authoritarian behaviour. However, Erdoğan has exhibited many of the same character traits about which he criticised his father. Examining Erdoğan's relations with his father would remind one of how Franz Kafka described his relationship to his father. In a letter to his father, Kafka wrote: 'What was always incomprehensible to me was your total lack of feeling for the suffering and shame you could inflict on me with your words and judgments.'[11]

Kafka explained that the hostile relationship with his father shaped his character along with the fear-driven search for authority and power. The similarities with Erdoğan's experience are nearly as striking. Just like his father, Erdoğan has desired from his followers and loyalists a demonstration of unconditional fealty without question or scepticism, and the urge to seek revenge and retribution against those who criticise or disparage his leadership and governing authority. Erdoğan remains haunted by his father, even more than thirty-two years after his death. Therefore, one can comprehend how Erdoğan views the AKP as his personal property and the government ministers as his children, who risk being disciplined and punished should they stray from his agenda. The scars of his formative years manifest themselves in ways that become latently comprehensible to those observing and critiquing Erdoğan's performance in power.

As a teenager, Erdoğan sold lemonade and sesame buns, referred to as *simit* in Turkey, in order to support the family's livelihood. Erdoğan was close to his mother, who always remained protective of her youngest child. According to one journalist who has covered Erdoğan extensively, the only instance where he has seen the leader let his public guard down is when he visits his mother's grave. There are indications to the effect that he has perceived his mother as a protector or shield against the rage of the father. His father was a grumpy man; when he got mad, no one at home could approach or communicate with him. However, Erdoğan knew how to deal with his father. When the father of the house was angry, it was up to Erdoğan to calm him down. He would immediately snuggle with his father who would no longer be in bad spirits. When his father was sad, he would do something unbelievable: 'He would go kiss his father's shoes. This would calm the Captain down, who would start crying together with the rest of the kids.'[12]

He attended the Kasımpaşa Piyale primary school, starting in 1960. One day in class, the teacher placed a newspaper on the floor and asked the young man to demonstrate to his classmates how to pray, but the boy refused, explaining that because there were printed photos on the newspaper page, he could not kneel and pray.[13] His teacher, impressed by his religious convictions and knowledge, asked Erdoğan's father to send him to a İmam Hatip school. Young Tayyip had escaped from Reis Kaptan's smothering, strict storm of fatherhood when he attended the İmam Hatip high school. He strolled the streets of Kasımpaşa, played football and eventually was married, entered politics and did his military service as a reserve officer.

He was active in sports and played football for sixteen years, juggling this with school and political activism. Between 1969 and 1982, he played football and when he was sixteen, he transferred to a competitive amateur league. During that period, he also played for his neighbourhood team, Kasımpaşa, where the former stadium is now named after him. For years he kept his sporting activities a secret from his father, who did not approve.

Erdoğan's childhood and teenage years were marked by the conflicts, coups and widespread ideological violence between left and right-wing groups across the country. He grated under the Kemalist brand of secular-authoritarianism with its anti-Muslim Jacobin *Kulturkampf* directed against the values and identity of the Anatolian conservative religious masses. The coercive Kemalist modernisation project planted the seeds for clashes between the secularised elite and the religious masses. Erdoğan's personality and political identity were shaped by these struggles between the secularised and religious sectors of Turkish society that paralleled the circumstances occurring in the political left and the political right in the sixties and seventies.

Like many peers of his social class and generation, Erdoğan was alienated by the prevailing economic policies of the sixties and seventies, having been forced to live in the slum neighbourhood of Kasımpaşa. This was where the young Erdoğan was educated about the realities of life for a poor Turkish family. It was a cosmopolitan but economically lower–middle-class district of Istanbul with a distinct neighbourhood identity. Kasımpaşa was rough and notorious for its gangs, gypsies and criminal elements. Yet, Erdoğan waxes nostalgic whenever he speaks of those early years. His rosy-lensed reminiscing has the feel of a successful American politician speaking of a tough upbringing in New York City's Bronx, Harlem or Lower East Side or the south side of Chicago or the east side of Los Angeles. 'I was shaped by that mud, not like the poor kids of today who are surrounded by asphalt.'[14] The Kasımpaşa neighbourhood sustains a strong conservative moral ethos and a deep sense of solidarity among its poorest dwellers. Its inhabitants always have been envious of the rich and powerful whose lavish fortunes and modest abodes were often in plain view.[15]

He received his religious education in the neighbourhood summer school that operated at a local mosque.[16] Few would suggest that Kasımpaşa was conducive to an easy-going attitude. The neighbourhood residents believed in close relations among families even to the extent that many of them acted as if they were members of one large family. Kasımpaşa incubated a culture of bravado and machismo, and Erdoğan was not immune to it. In one interview he stated that 'my manliness, bluntness, and principled conduct derive from my roots [in Kasımpaşa]'.[17] When he was forced out of his job as mayor and on his way to jail, he told the chanting crowd outside:

> I am always telling with pride about where I was born; which kind of school life I had. They couldn't take that somebody raised in Kasımpaşa, graduated from İmam Hatip, to be a mayor. But, no matter if I am the son of a sea captain or a baker, I will never desist serving my nation [*millet*]. Nobody will be able to finish my political career. I am just having a break. This song will not end here.[18]

Later in life, when Erdoğan became involved with the National Salvation Party's (Milli Selamet Partisi (MSP)) youth organisation, some of the party members told him to give up football, a demand which he defied. He was blunt with critics from within the MSP's stand against allowing and encouraging women's participation in political activities and even registering them as members. Erdoğan always was a pragmatic Muslim, desiring an expression of Islam that was compatible with capitalism, secularism and electoral democracy. Erdoğan often went against conventional wisdom in his political circles, emphasising that an individual from a neighbourhood like Kasımpaşa could, in fact, become successful and widely known. He hardly regarded social background as a major hurdle in the way of achievement.

Erdoğan's pride in his Muslim identity grew steadily after he attended the İmam Hatip school. Kasımpaşa's close-knit character became an essential element in his ideological crucible. He recognised that many of those he had known so well in his early years had been unjustly relegated to the periphery of Turkish society. While other rising stars in Turkish politics preferred European tailored suits and relied on personal shoppers, Erdoğan continued to have his hair trimmed and face shaved at the same barbershop he frequented in his youth. Even while Necmettin Erbakan, one of his most important mentors in politics, enjoyed expensive brand-name clothing, Erdoğan preferred a less ostentatious appearance. It was a demonstration of the significance of the internalised Kasımpaşa values and attitudes he was exposed to during his formative years. When the Turkish government asked World Bank economist Kemal Derviş during the February 2001 economic crisis to recommend measures to rehabilitate the country's economy, Erdoğan said, 'I myself do not have an American passport. My mother is not a German. I am 100 per cent a citizen of this country. I am not an import commodity.'[19] His late teens and early twenties were shaped in the 1970s by his experiences in the Kasımpaşa and Beyoğlu districts of Istanbul. The tough, poor conditions of Kasımpaşa shaped his sociological perspective and reinforced his spiritual identity, but his aspirations also were determined by the images of economic wealth and ample welfare found in Beyoğlu, the Manhattan-like counterpart in Turkey.

1.3 Erdoğan's Education and İmam Hatip School

Years later, Erdoğan would talk about these schools which had an important impact on his psychosocial development:

> My İmam Hatip period means everything to me. I have attained my life path over there. İmam Hatip High School taught me to love the country and the people serving this country, to worship, love just for the sake of God, not to

oppress, environmental consciousness, socialisation, solidarity and the pleasure to want the same things for others as I wish for myself. This love, this pleasure to work day and night, often neglecting the family and myself have all come from that school. İmam Hatip has made me the man I am today.[20]

Erdoğan attended the İmam Hatip school in Istanbul until 1973. These schools were established to train imams following the closure of madrasas (Islamic seminaries) by the state. He also graduated from Eyub Lisesi, a secular high school, having taken some courses there in order to qualify for the university entrance exams. Even before his primary school teacher in Kasımpaşa encouraged the young student to attend the İmam Hatip school located at the opposite side of the Golden Horn from his hometown, Erdoğan already had learned the proper standard of Islamic prayers.

In the İmam Hatip school, Erdoğan studied Islamic sciences along with the regular curriculum. The İmam Hatip schools were established under Article 4 of the Unification of Education Law No. 430 with the goal of training personnel to carry out religious services. In 1973, the objectives of these schools were expanded under Article 32 of National Education Law, No. 1739 to offer programmes within the secondary school system that also prepared students for higher education. They were no longer simply vocational schools to train government-employed religious functionaries, as these schools also prepared the students for higher education. At İmam Hatip, he 'became known as a fiery orator in the cause of political Islam and he start to read Necip Fazıl's poems'.[21]

The mainstreaming of these schools in the national education system signalled the evolving process of compromise between religious and secular actors in the political system. The İmam Hatip schools were built by private donations and staffed by representatives of the Ministry of Education. Even though these schools were under the authority of the Ministry of Education, they presupposed and legitimated particular forms of religious authority, community and history. These schools became a hotbed of religious conservatism and regularly challenged the secular education system and the principles of Kemalism. What is important to remember here is not the subject matter being taught in these schools, but how conservative teachers introduced the material to their students. These schools provide a 'hidden' curriculum that includes extracurricular activities, student interaction and the role of disciplinarian teacher.[22] According to Roger Dale, hidden curriculum refers to the unwritten body of shared understanding that shapes the conduct of the classroom. In these schools, echoing Dale's definition, the classroom atmosphere surrounding the courses matters more than their content in terms of moulding character. Socialisation involves the inculcation of Islamic norms and values and behaviour patterns, augmented by teachers who criticise alternative lifestyles, gender and sexual identities and other characteristics they associate with the problems of secular modernisation.

Erdoğan's political identity was influenced by his religious upbringing and experience in the İmam Hatip school system. He joined his school's debate programme and participated in competitions where he recited poetry with religious and nationalistic themes and debated with students on social issues. He loved the verse of Kısakürek, a poet, playwright and the most important Islamic ideologue of modern Turkey. He became Erdoğan's intellectual muse. Another favourite was Mehmet Akif Ersoy (1873–1936), the author of the Turkish national anthem and a leading literary intellectual of his time (the impact of these two authors will be examined in the next section). In Turkey, religious parents sought out these schools. In Erdoğan's case, he credits his successes to his religious education: 'The period of İmam Hatip schools means everything to me. I obtained a framework, an orientation, and for my entire life . . . İmam Hatip schools have given myself to me.'[23] Although he was only a below-average student in high school, he was admitted to Aksaray Economics and Business School, which would eventually be integrated into Marmara University in Istanbul, where he studied economics and commerce.[24] In 1981, he graduated with a baccalaureate degree in business management.

His education did not delve into the humanities or sociology. Nor did he ever learn a foreign language. In his school years, it might be argued that his greatest passion was football. He devoted much time to the sport, and even participated in a professional league at the age of twenty-one – an experience which exposed him to the value of teamwork – and his successes there emboldened his self-confidence and ambitions for status and influence. Insomuch as the value of teamwork transferred to his political life, he has stressed the role of teamwork in that domain too, albeit as long as he is the coach. Football proved to be nearly as impactful as religion in the development of Erdoğan's character. He learned to cooperate with teammates for a common objective, as well as how to properly handle defeat or victory.

In order to understand Erdoğan's worldview, it is instructive to unpack the salient dynamics of morality that would have influenced a typical İmam Hatip student in the 1970s. Their moral worldview was inspired and directed by their resistance to accepting the Kemalist reforms of modernisation. Teachers and students believed that these reforms dismantled and nullified their power, making them feel alienated in their own country. They were alarmed by those trying not to suppress but also eliminate entirely the vestiges of Ottoman sociocultural practices and community Islamic institutions. Their moral worldview relied more on politics than an ethos or moral credo. The totality of a political morality echoed the terminology as Carl Schmitt had defined it: a political morality strictly draws an impenetrable line between 'us' Muslims, who are marginalised, versus 'them' who are secular and espouse the elements of westernization.[25] More specifically, it can be labelled in this instance as a manifestation of an İmam Hatip morality (*ahlakı*), arising from the dynamics of an imagined trauma revealed and laid bare by the impact of the Kemalist reforms, and which could only be soothed by an intense nostalgia for the Golden Age of Islam. This sense of nostalgia, which is ironically a production of modernist reforms started in nineteenth century and later reinforced by the Kemalist disruption, nourished and expanded the moral imagination, as translated into the educational programmes for İmam Hatip schools.

The İmam Hatip youth in the 1970s thus were conditioned to avoid diversifying their perspective through sources that would have espoused a different perspective. They relied on appropriately ideological broadcasts of TV or radio programmes whenever available, although the options were limited at the time, along with access to some Islamist magazines, a daily newspaper (*Milli Gazete*), and some free community theatres with ideologically driven creative missions that resonated with them.[26] Meanwhile, the main trend in the Turkish movies at the time invited stories of the rich and spoiled youth who were 'over-westernised', and rejected any authentic traditions of their homeland and upbringing. Therefore, as many Islamists came from middle- and lower-middle-class family backgrounds, their rage and resentment suggested a major socio-economic class dimension, the frustration of which was expressed in Islamic vocabulary and rhetoric.

The dominant view during this period emphasised that a pious person is a moral person. One's moral world then was limited to the experiences of religious rituals without gaining any deeper philosophical understanding of Islamic ethics. The youth were then motivated to be religious by way of engaging rituals of their faith while at the same time polishing their skills to find the path towards accumulating wealth and eventually gaining the political power to overthrow the Kemalist secular system. The İmam Hatip youth of the 1970s would never identify with the existing sociopolitical system, so they argued that Turkey is a part of *dar al-harp* and the state and the system should be regarded as non-Islamic. Thus, given that the state was not Islamic, the youth understood that they would have to fight to achieve the right Islamic state and political order. This perspective was simple, but it also was a potent inspiration and influence. They believed the state and prevailing bureaucracy were illegitimate, which convinced them that they could justify breaking the norms, engaging in corrupt practices, avoid paying taxes, and cheating and gaming the system (even in school exams). These actions then, in their eyes, became morally permissible and defensible because they were a part of the struggle between Islamic citizens and those who were not Islamic. This conceptualisation of morality (*İmam Hatip ahlakı*), which also was cross-fertilised by the leftist struggle and anti-capitalist sentiments, rejected the Kemalist reforms while calling for a restored Islamic Golden Age, as Kısakürek had envisioned.

These immoral acts are morally justified and normalised on the basis of their understanding of the existing system as illegitimate. Yet there also has been an uncompromising and disenfranchised understanding of personal morality in terms of controlling women's somatic freedoms, offering doctrinal explanations for rigid sociocultural rules, and creating informal networks of solidarity to stem any sense of social and cultural isolation. As the movement for public morality deliberately destroyed a previously accepted propriety for private morality (that is, decisions and practices confined to family affairs, especially gendered displays such as the headscarf), the rules, rites and practices only became more austere and strict. As a capitalist mentality also found its parallel in the community's social life and interactions that stressed one's self-interests and pursuit of self-enrichment in urban centres, other newcomers to the country's urban centres relied on religious rituals and private morality more often to preserve and strengthen their way of life.

There was a sense in the 1970s that Turkish citizens were in the midst of a struggle between the good and bad – that is, Islamic and non-Islamic. In Kasımpaşa and other districts of Istanbul, newcomers to these urban areas constructed a simple binary moral world: us versus them; rich/corrupt versus poor/moral Muslims; secular versus pious; and good versus bad. This moral worldview is based on sharp distinctions against the Kemalist reforms establishment. It compels believers to be patient and work closely with each other to accumulate wealth, even if means stealing and not paying taxes, as long as they are part of building and supporting Islamic institutions. While the Islamists imagine the rich and secular Turks as devilish and non-Islamic, they have desired to have their advantages including consumer wealth and consumer behaviour. They have rationalised the moral basis that controlling these tools of the devil can be justified through any means so long as the objective is achieved. Wealth and political power are good only when they are in the hands of Muslims who adhere to the tenets of their faith. The senses of alienation and feeling of being in a struggle within the *dar al-harp* emboldened the İmam Hatip youth to justify breaking every norm of public morality. Erdoğan is a product of this system: be pious not moral; morality is merely a by-product that can be adjusted as the means dictate and the ends identified.

The students of İmam Hatip in the 1970s and 1980s were expected to read the Qur'an, learn Islamic prayer rituals, develop their sermonising skills of explaining Islam and remain anti-system and support Islamic activism. Meanwhile, there were several centres of utopian ideology that attracted their attention. Leftist youth embraced communism, nationalist youth followed the concept of Turan (that is, unification of the Turkish national disapora), and Islamic youth yearned for the restoration of an Islamic Golden Age, which was connected to reimagining the early period of the Ottoman Empire. The blending of the Islamic Golden Age and the Ottoman Empire appealed to the conservative masses of Turkey. During the same period, the books of Muslim Brotherhood leaders motivated the İmam Hatip youth against their leftist and nationalist peers. To conclude, for the İmam Hatip youth, the Republic represented the worst anti-Islam and anti-Ottoman worldview. For them, the West was inherently anti-Islamic, imperialistic and materialistic with the goal of destroying Islam through the efforts of westernised local agents (Kemalists). The Republic epitomised the immoral capitalism and materialism of the West which was imposing a soulless world of reckless, rule-free competition and the consequential social isolation and economic disempowerment for those who did not follow the Western path.

As an İmam Hatip student, Erdoğan signified the common observations of the school attendees, who came from marginalised families and belonged to the lower-middle-class conservative family structure. The people who sent their children to İmam Hatip schools were not usually fully integrated into enjoying the fruits of modernisation in Istanbul and sought harbour in the conservative education system to protect their children from realities that might embarrass them socially. Moreover, a young man at an İmam Hatip school acknowledged the cultural and social peer pressures because the state regarded these schools as poor. His feelings as a marginalised Black Turk were tied to his accurate understanding of the consequences of being an İmam Hatip student. Thus, his intense animus towards the Kemalist and westernised sector of the population was reinforced by these circumstances. Also, Erdoğan's cognitive map is driven by an Islamic framework of identity, is based on oral culture, legends, stories of Ottoman history and the political slogans of Muslim Brotherhood. His comprehension of events within and outside of Turkey has always been filtered through an Islamist worldview, which is simplistic, absolute without nuance and conspiratorial in sentiment, as he believes Jews, Freemasons and Kemalists constituted the Other and, therefore, was the enemy of Islam. Coinciding with Erdoğan's education, there were active leftist worldviews based on classical Marxist writings as well as nationalist movements, known as *ülkücüler*, whose members were anti-communist and carried hybrid Turkish-cum-Islamic worldviews.

With this experience, Erdoğan cultivated virtues such as courage, patience and perseverance and vices such as vengeance and greed. Such virtues and vices were visible during his campaign for mayor of Istanbul, when he took private courses on problems concerning municipalities at Istanbul University and Istanbul Technical University. According to Hüseyin Besli, a close friend and speech writer of Erdoğan, who has written the most comprehensive and sympathetic biography of Erdoğan to date, Erdoğan's belief in education extended to municipal employees in Istanbul:

> Employees in both the metropolitan and district municipalities attended such courses as comparative history of municipal administration, aesthetics, history of art, urban affairs, planning and zoning, protection of the environment, infrastructure engineering, construction techniques as well as morals and ethics.[27]

Later, in 1999, when he was sentenced to prison (because he recited a popular patriotic poem that was considered anti-secular, a topic which will be discussed later), he explained that he wanted to expand his knowledge of economics and politics as well as work on his English. His understanding of education is instrumental and practical rather than reflective.

Erdoğan's devotion to Islam was a central tenet in his socialisation. He always prayed before playing football, and, when he had to choose between football and shaving off his beard, he gave up the sport. During the 1980 military coup, beards were banned in all public institutions and Erdoğan then was playing football for the Municipality of Istanbul team, a public institution, and was asked to shave off his beard. He refused to do so and had to leave the team. This was yet another example where the 'marginalised' religious people felt repressed by their own state. The state's intolerant attitude towards how religious people dress and follow some religious rituals and lifestyles angered conservative Muslims, and they converted their religious identity into an oppositional movement against the state and its Kemalist ideology. As he entered his adult years in the late 1970s, Erdoğan attended a *dergah* (seminary) where the teachings of the Nakşibendi Shaykh Mehmet Zahir Kotku were disseminated. A leading sect of Sunni/Sufi morality, the Nakşibendis harkened back to the early days of the Ottoman Empire. However, Shaykh Kotku encouraged adherents to embrace modernity as well. In another divergence from traditional seminaries, Kotku did not require members to wear traditional Islamic clothing. Erdoğan visited Kotku's seminary in 1976, when he was twenty-two – just once though, as he did not like to obey the requirements and be subjected to the control of any person. Moreover, the expression of Islam he encountered in the Sufi lodge did not meet his expectations. He aligned himself with the more didactic, ideologically oriented and confrontational expression of Islam of Kısakürek. The editor of an Islamic publication, known as *Islam*, published by the same order, told me that 'Erdoğan stayed away from the *dergah* because his vision of Islam was different than what he found in the lodge'.[28]

The Sufi liberal interpretation of Islam contradicted Erdoğan's interests in political Islam and his embrace of religious didactic poetry and associated politically oriented literature. It would be precisely his love of political poetry that brought him trouble in Siirt in 1998, but it also revealed a sentimental, even vulnerable aspect of his childhood personality that belied the veneer of bravado he would display as an adult.

1.4 The Influence of the MTTB and Necip Fazıl Kısakürek

Öz yurdunda garipsin, öz vatanında parya!

Necip Fazıl Kısakürek[29]

Another major influence in Erdoğan's critical development was his membership in the Milli Türk Talebe Birliği (MTTB, or the National Turkish Student Union).[30] Although the MTTB emerged as a secularist national student association, and later as a branch of a top-down Kemalist reform organisation, it transformed its mission and leadership in the late 1960s under the leadership of Rasim Cinisli, a lawyer who became a member of parliament, and İsmail Kahraman, who would eventually become the minister of culture in the Erbakan government (1996–7) and speaker of the parliament (2015–18). Under their direction, ethno-religious (Islamo-Turkish) nationalism encompassed the primary ideology for the Turkish state and the foundational core of Turkish identity. This resonated during the Cold War and was taken to combat the challenges and strong appeals of socialist ideas. Conservative intellectuals saw Islam as an antidote to the leftist appeal and one could begin to glimpse the ideological evolution of Islam in the hands of Kısakürek, certainly the most consequential influence for Erdoğan and his eventual move towards his self-identity as Turkey's indispensable counterpoint to the shortcomings of Kemalism.[31]

To truly understand Erdoğan, it is necessary to trace the intellectual roots of his cognitive map (*zihniyet*) about religion, history, politics and westernisation, which starts with Kısakürek, a leading anti-leftist and Islamist ideologue. Kısakürek's Great Eastern Movement (Büyük Doğu Hareketi) sought to synthesise Islamism, Turkish nationalism and conservatism.[32] Kısakürek went to the country's naval school for his high school education, and the irony cannot be missed that one of the sharpest critics of the Kemalist intelligentsia was taught in precisely the same French-model schools that had served an essential modern bureaucratic purpose of secularisation. The young Kısakürek enjoyed a bohemian lifestyle in Paris for several years. He apparently enjoyed the diversions enough to fail to complete his university education in France. He returned to Turkey, where he worked in banks for nearly a decade after which he completed two years of intermittent military service. By 1934, the way that Kısakürek viewed the world changed dramatically in his interactions with a new intellectual class that included Shaykh Abdulhakim Arvasi (1865–1943), a prominent Nakşibendi leader, as well as other Islamists, including instructors from the naval school and conservative intellectuals who taught philosophy at Istanbul University.

Kısakürek published his poetry during the Republic's initial constitutional period, which lasted from 1923 to 1960, when most Islamists still lacked strong political passions:

> Kısakürek's intellectual mind was formed by both the sorrows of the collapsed empire and the republican enthusiasm of the Kemalist intellectuals. This setting provided enough fertile ground for his experience with a metaphysical/intellectual crisis which he regarded as the foremost condition of being a true intellectual.[33]

His poetry often emphasised themes of aimlessness and the void of spirituality in a rapidly transformed society that had yet to fully come to terms with the collapse of the old empire.

Kısakürek, who was also a playwright, expounded on these themes, such as in *Bir Adam Yaratmak*, completed just as World War II had begun. The play follows a lead character – a Turkish intellectual – who is dismayed at the pace of westernisation that is occurring in his community and wonders how his fellow citizens will express their religious beliefs and spiritual needs during crises of life and death. In a period of less than a decade, Kısakürek had been transformed from a frustrated bohemian and republican poet into a smouldering, incisive intellectual who saw a certain rejuvenated form of Muslim spirituality and solidarity as the antidote to Turkey's deracinating and alienating embrace of westernisation as radical secularisation.[34]

In 1939, he published an article, '*Ben Buyum*' ('This is Me'), where he meticulously defined the major pillars of his ideology, that would precisely parallel Erdoğan's own ideological evolution. By stressing both Turkish nationalism and the Ottoman legacy, Kısakürek played an important role in the nationalisation of Islam. He was an iconic public intellectual who rose up during the 1950s and 1960s against coercive westernisation, the political hegemony of the Kemalists, especially the secular CHP (Republican People's Party) and other leftist movements. Crafting a political rhetoric infused with religious and Ottoman symbols and references, he presented perorations of his thinking in his periodical *Büyük Doğu* (1943–75) with the purpose of encouraging a new political philosophy – or, more precisely, a public theology – that was steeped in Islam and Ottoman history to retrieve and reconstruct a previously dismissed memory and heritage. Kısakürek's writings posited Turkey's historical experience and national mission in Islamic terms, which paralleled other ideological movements elsewhere in the world, such as the Muslim Brotherhood in Egypt and the Islamic Community (Cemaat-i İslami) in India (and subsequently in Pakistan).

Kısakürek remains largely unknown outside of Turkey since his ideas hardly travelled outside Anatolian conservative circles. However, it was Kısakürek who pioneered the publishing and dissemination of these Islamic ideals long before translations of the classic texts from the Islamic Diaspora would be made widely available. Carrying on the legacy of the Young Ottomans, Kısakürek envisioned literature – especially, poetry – as the most compelling, motivating source of societal change and individual enlightenment. He also leveraged the appeal of popularly published publications on arts and letters – most notably, *Büyük Doğu*. It was this journal that sowed the seeds of the first phase of the political evolution that would culminate in Erdoğan's emergence as the leader of the AKP. Kısakürek's literary ambitions were no idle assertions, as the government acknowledged by periodically trying to censor him and force him to cease publication. This occurred both in 1944 and in 1946, when Kısakürek was tried and convicted for insulting Turkishness (*Türklüğe hakaret davası*). He was in prison when the moderately right-wing Democratic Party (DP) came to power in 1950 and he was one of the first political prisoners to be released.

His vocabulary was not particularly elegant or nuanced, but rather it was marked by its populist tone. One can discern the similarities in Erdoğan's rhetoric, particularly as they have been amplified in his quest for a strong executive presidency. Kısakürek's unabashed criticism of Kemalism was easy to grasp and apply strategically. His ideas sparked the youth (for example, Erdoğan) in the 1970s to embrace their socioreligious identities in a broad moment of political activism and grass-roots participation. His writings formed the basis for the right-of-centre position in national politics as Kısakürek persuaded citizens that it was possible to belong to the newly forged Turkish Republic, as both proud Muslims and Turks realised that they did not have ro reconcile themselves with ideology from leftists and Kemalists that they saw as derisive and untenable in their own cultural and social experiences.

After the 1960 military coup, Turkey experienced a rising wave of leftist movements propelled by extensive intellectual debate and the appeal of the Marxist revolution. As a reaction to leftist ideology that was associated with renunciation of faith and atheism, one of the better-organised anti-leftist organisations was the MTTB student union movement, which closely aligned with Kısakürek. It provided channels to spread his writings via Anatolian networks. Kısakürek's ideology rested on a foundation of three pillars, one of which was premised on how contemporary Turkish-Muslim society had lost its 'ties' with the past by shedding its definitive language, morality and historical memory as a result of westernisation. The second pillar indicated that the Kemalist reforms had deliberately sought to destroy the inner spiritual power of the Turkish nation. The third was that this project of de-Islamisation could be reversed with the rise of a new ruling elite (*yönetici sınıf*) committed to espousing a Turkish-Islamic synthesis (*zihniyet*) of revival.

By the 1970s, Kısakürek emerged as the MTTB's most prominent ideologue. The main feature of Kısakürek's ideology was its totalitarian nature, which he often expressed with more impassioned emotion than with dispassionately argued ideological considerations.[35] He targeted readers whom he believed were aggrieved and looking for someone who empathised with their feelings of exclusion and marginalisation. He rejected the westernising efforts – the 1839 Tanzimat and the Kemalist modernising reforms of 1920s

– of Turkish society and persistently called upon believers to take revenge on the westernising elite. He believed that Islamic law should organise the public and private life of Muslims and there must be one man (*başyüce*) who should impose Islamic order on society. He insisted that the state should control the education system to create a pious (*dindar*) generation in the service of Islam. However, within this framework, he also articulated a deeper justification for revenge and detest within the context of being a part of one's religious duty, especially if such actions were directed towards those who behaved and acted particularly as un-Islamic.

One might summarise Kısakurek's ideology in the following way. He was an Islamist, but a Turkish-Islamist, who claimed that the Ottoman Turks understood and defended Islam more effectively than other Muslims. He espoused the aims of a Turkish-led Islamic unity while he was fiercely anti-Kemalist and anti-Western. He criticised the Tanzimat reforms of westernisation, convinced that there are two discrete nations: 'Muslims and non-Muslims'. Finally, he advocated hatred and revenge, justifying those sentiments throughout his life's writings.[36] No Turkish Islamist has been as influential as Kısakürek because he always articulated his ideals in a straightforward, unmistakable manner and consistently defined the Other as the enemy. The Other encompassed the communists, Jews, Kemalists and Westerners. What made him popular were the emotional connections found in his poetry and his impassioned calls for revenge and resentment against the establishment. His intellectual legacy is deeper and more effective than that of any other Turkish Islamist. He has been Erdoğan's most important muse and likewise for those who are in Erdoğan's innermost circles of cabinet ministers and advisors.

As embodied by Erdoğan's path of leadership, Kisakürek's ideal Islamic state, which he referred to as the *başyücelik*, means rule by a powerful leader who knows Islam and the actions serving the best interest of Islam. He rejects popular sovereignty and insists that sovereignty belongs to God (*hakimiyet hakkındır*). He laid out his Islamist state in his controversial *Ideolocya Örgüsü*. In his conceptualisation, the state must be led by the most exalted leader (the *başyüce*). *Başyüce* represents the perfect man, as derived from the understanding of Islam. Kısakürek's model of this exalted man was Abdulhamid II, and he wrote a very popular book about the former Ottoman leader (*Ulu Hakan*).

For Kısakürek, Abdulhamid II worked hard to defend the empire and Islam against Jews, Freemasons and Western imperialists, to name some of the most significant adversaries. These enemies used the opportunity of the empire's collapse to exploit the Young Turks to get rid of Abdulhamid II, and later under the Kemalist reforms they tolerated the existence of Turkey so long as the new Republic continued to distance itself from Islam.

Erdoğan's presidential system is shaped by Kısakürek's idea of *başyücelik*.[37] In an interview with one of Erdoğan's advisors, he said, 'Necip Fazıl's idea of *başyücelik* is an inspiration in creating the new presidential system. It must emerge from our culture and tradition.' Just as with the *başyüce*, Erdoğan rules the country without any checks and balances. He thinks and acts in ways indicating that he embodies the state, thereby manifesting the culmination of Kisakürek's ideals. Erdoğan always has been quick to remind his associates that the poet's life and published works constitute an essential guide for himself and should be so for future generations as well. In one interview, Erdoğan proudly connected his admiration of Kısakürek to his own comprehension of Turkish history, saying 'the master and his ordeals helped us, like none other, to make sense of history and the present'.[38] In 2014, when Erdoğan presented the first series of art awards named in Kısakürek's honour, he told the gathering:

> Necip Fazıl Kısakürek was a one-man school that prepared hundreds and thousands of young men and women for the world and the afterlife. I would like to draw your attention to the fact that he did not have a predecessor. You may say 'What about Mehmet Akif Ersoy?' Mehmet Akif was one of the last intellectuals of the Ottoman Empire. Unfortunately, he did not have the convenient environment to express his ideas freely and build a new intellectual atmosphere during the Republic.[39]

In 2015, Erdoğan stated that Kısakürek 'raised his voice and said "I am here, too" when only certain thoughts certain ideologies were allowed. This fact clearly shows that what a sound heart he had. Necip Fazıl emerges as a resistance, a revolution within a revolution'.[40]

Kısakürek's reputation as the leading anti-leftist polemicist had grown throughout the 1960s and into the early 1970s. Kısakürek closely allied himself with the National Outlook Movement of Necmettin Erbakan (1926–2011) but then withdrew his support when Erbakan agreed to form a coalition government with the centre-left CHP of former Prime Minister Bülent Ecevit (which lasted for only ten months during 1974). Kısakürek then flirted with the far-right Nationalist Movement Party (MHP) led by Alpaslan Türkeş. Due to his radical criticism of the Kemalist status quo, Kısakürek spent most of his time either in the courts under police questioning or in jail. Presented as the 'oppressed' (*mazlum*) savant of Anatolia, his civic struggles engendered a major sympathetic following in conservative Anatolian cities such as Kayseri. By the time of his death, Turkey's political landscape had changed significantly, as the secularists saw their political power and influence wane through a series of coalition governments. The turning point came in 1980 with the military coup, which opened the door for Islamist-affiliated parties just as economic reforms generated a newly wealthy class of Muslims. However, the 1980 coup was also fodder for reactionaries and conspiracy theorists who aroused the spectre of anti-Semitism and Freemasonry to present Turkey as being besieged by sinister foreign powers.

Kısakürek wrote several books of popularised history to disseminate alternative accounts of the past that were not considered in the history curriculum used in the Kemalist-focused educational system. He helped to create a new generation of amateur and semi-professional historians who developed a new narrative reclaiming the Seljuk and Ottoman Islamic heritage. Kısakürek, however, was not above relying on conspiracy theories to foment a sense of Turkey's hidden, repressed and forgotten history while offering explanations that relied on the seemingly implacable and malign intentions of the West. In these books, he gradually developed a Turkish-Muslim self-portrait that prides itself on its anti-communist, nationalistic and sacrificial themes.

As a young man, Erdoğan already was deeply influenced by his ideological mentor. In 1976, at twenty-two, Erdoğan, who was president of the Istanbul youth activist arm of Erbakan's National Salvation Party (MSP), directed and played the main character in the play *Mas-kom-Ya* (short for Masonic, Communist and Jew) which lambasted the deleterious influences of outside forces.[41] For Kısakürek, the mission of the Turkish nation is to defend Islamdom and become its 'sword and shield' against Western imperialism. Kısakürek was undeniably anti-Salafi and critical of the Wahhabi understanding of Islam.⁴² He cast Turkish anti-Semitism not in a Muslim context but rather within the same European Christian impulses that propelled anti-Semitism across the continent. Likewise, the youthful Erdoğan's *Mas-kom-Ya*, a play that was staged frequently by Erdoğan and his close friends throughout the 1970s, played an important role among the conservative-religious youth of Istanbul.⁴³ In fact, in 1977, Erbakan joined the audience and watched the play in which Erdoğan was the main actor. Erbakan was impressed by Erdoğan's acting and personally congratulated him.

For many reasons, the young Erdoğan strengthened his allegiance to Kısakürek's body of work. The MTTB student union was a useful conduit to proselytise and expand the impetus that had drawn many students to Kısakürek's writings. Erdoğan also looked forward to the student union's annual commemoration of the Gallipoli Campaign, which led to a historic Ottoman victory over Allied forces in 1915.⁴⁴ Islamic-oriented students visited the cemeteries annually to pay their respects to those who had died in the battle, and for those looking to embrace their Turkish-Islamic roots, the Dardanelles Campaign was given even greater significance than the War of Independence that led to the founding of the Turkish Republic. During this campaign, Istanbul had been successfully defended by Ottoman Muslim soldiers from all corners of the empire. The result of being a close follower of Kısakürek, Erdoğan's political identity took hold, casting many Kemalist reforms as destructive while believing that one could rightly espouse pan-Islamist beliefs and regard the Ottoman legacy as the true foundation for an authentic Turkish national identity. It is through Kısakürek that Erdoğan would eventually regard the long-running Kurdish question as a negative reaction to the severing of Muslim bonds by Kemalist authoritarianism. Erdoğan's appreciation for Kısakürek:

> Necip Fazıl [Kısakürek] is a tremendous blessing and is a model person even today for the young generations, those fighting for justice and for Turkey . . . When there was no one else, Necip Fazıl was there. He drew all the attacks onto himself and repelled them. He stood up tall in front of the young generations who needed a brother, a guide, a mentor, who were hungry for ideas. Necip Fazıl stood alone against those aggrandising themselves under the shadow of the status quo. Necip Fazıl preserved his national values against those exploiting the local and global ideologies for their own reputation.⁴⁵

The MTTB evolved into an anti-communist, anti-Kemalist, anti-establishment student organisation where individuals with strong religious and conservative beliefs could debate topics and cultivate social networks for advancing their careers and bolstering their social status.[46] Erdoğan, who joined the union in 1969, generally participated in activities reserved for men.[47] He was there more so because of his conservative upbringing rather than out of ideological conviction, but his MTTB ties helped him to expand his circle of friends that also became the crucible of an ideological brotherhood. After graduation, Erdoğan landed a job with the Istanbul public transport authority. And, it was his MTTB associations that crystallised Erdoğan's worldview against the Republic and its authoritarian Kemalist establishment. Through MTTB, Erdoğan entered into ideological world of Turkish politics and he start to develop his own ideological worldview.

Another individual who shaped Erdoğan's understanding of the role of Islam in modern society was the renowned poet Mehmet Akif Ersoy. A late Ottoman-Islamic intellectual, he was of Albanian descent and was a prominent modernist Muslim thinker. Ersoy was a sentimental poet originating from a traditional Muslim family, who had studied veterinary sciences. He became involved in the political debates of Istanbul and joined the Committee of Union and Progress Party (Ittihat ve Terakki Cemiyeti) and staunchly supported the 1908 revolution that resulted in the restoration of the First Constitution of 1876. During the Balkan Wars, he began publishing *Sırat-ı Mustakim* in 1908 and then changed its name to *Sebi-ül Reşat* in 1912. It was the main pro-Islamic periodical at that time.[48] He was both a patriot and pious poet and sought to fuse Islam and nationalism in his verse.[49] The traumatic defeats of the Balkan Wars and large-scale atrocities and ethnic cleansing against Balkan Muslim civilians by Christian forces had a profound effect on Ersoy, which was manifest in his writings. He called upon the Muslims to keep their desire for revenge alive. He wrote:

> Even if we do not take our revenge upon the foe,
> God, who has written your name in the ledger of the righteous and unrighteous,
> Will one day call down from these mountains, for sure,
> A hale and hearty nation that will take its revenge![50]

The Balkan Wars, which were only peripheral to Europe, were important to the Ottoman Empire. They converted the thinking of many Muslim intellectuals to the notion that pan-Islamic resistance was the only way to save their empire and the people from a genocidal Western/Russian imperial onslaught.

Ersoy was a modernist Islamic intellectual, who translated the highly influential essays of the Egyptian modernist Muslim thinker Muhammad Abduh (1849–1905) and Jamal al-Din al-Afghani (1838–97). He believed that Islam must be purified of its incorrect developments while still welcoming the adoption of Western technology and science for the improvement of the conditions of Muslims. Ersoy's Islamism was a resistance movement against Western imperialism. He called upon Muslim scholars to comprehend the zeitgeist of the Prophet Muhammed's time in order to see Muhammed's efforts to improve the social, political and economic conditions of Muslims:[51]

> Doğrudan doğruya Kur'an'dan alıp ilhâmı, (Taking the inspiration directly from the Qur'an)
> Asrın idrâkine söyletmeliyiz İslâm'ı (We need to let Islam speak in order to understand the century).

Ersoy was a popular late Ottoman poet, known for his patriotic verses and his defence of pan-Islamism, and he eventually penned the words for what would become the Turkish national anthem. However, due to his resistance to Mustafa Kemal's secularising policies, he abandoned the country to settle in Egypt in October 1923. Ersoy returned to Turkey in 1935 and died in Istanbul in 1936. His epic poems were praised for their realism. He focused on the Ottoman military defeats in the Balkan Wars of 1912 and the successful military resistance in Gallipoli in 1915. The anguish of the wounded and dying Ottoman soldiers was a common motif for sacrifice and patriotism for the Ottoman homeland. When the Ottoman sultan signed the Treaty of Sèvres, Ersoy relocated to Anatolia where he visited local mosques to encourage the Muslims to arm themselves in order to protect their religion and homeland against imperial powers.

In his poetry, the Turkish nation becomes an organic being, with a living personality and a firm Islamic identity based on the collective memories of the shared sufferings that constitute a timeless nation. In the *National Anthem*, Ersoy wrote:

> I have been free since the beginning and forever shall be so.
> What madman shall put me in chains! I defy the very idea!
> I'm like the roaring flood; trampling and overflowing my dyke [weir],
> I'll tear apart the mountains, fill up the open seas and still gush out![52]

Ersoy stresses faith in God as the source of heroism and as the bond of social integration. In his poems, he explains the victories of national independence as God's reward for having faith. For instance, at the end of the second stanza of the *National Anthem*, he wrote: 'For freedom is the absolute right of my God-worshipping nation.' Ersoy assumes a Turkish nation that is God-worshipping and compares the homeland to Paradise. He encourages Turkish Muslims to protect this Paradise to the very end. Again, he was fiercely opposed to the predations of Western imperialism in the Muslim world, as the following in the *National Anthem* indicates:

> The lands of the West may be armoured with walls of steel,
> But I have borders guarded by the mighty chest of a believer.
> Recognise your innate strength! And think: how can this fiery faith ever be killed,
> By that battered, single-toothed monster you call 'civilisation'?

The key is the metaphor of 'single-toothed monster', which indicates the Western imperialist powers and their justification for subduing and exploiting the rest of the non-Western world in the name of bringing 'civilisation'.

In one of his poems, a young man named Asım is introduced as a model individual. He signifies various characteristics: patriot, Muslim, just, hard-working, scientist, comfortable with technology, proud of his heritage, and connected with his culture and religion. Yet, Asım also is a fighter; if necessary, he is a Robin Hood character, and avenger to defend his homeland, values and sovereignty. Asım wants modernity with Islam, not without it. Erdoğan frequently cites this poem and even calls upon young people to emulate Asım,[53] who Erdoğan says 'represents justice, conscience, mercy'.

In his 2008 lecture at a scholarship award ceremony, Erdoğan insisted: 'We did not import the sciences and arts of the West. Unfortunately, we imported its immoralities that contradict our values. We should have raced to import its arts and sciences [instead].'[54] In this speech in which Erdoğan praises Western technology, art and science, he cites verses from a poem written by Ersoy in 1912. Erdoğan's admiration of European technology and science and his rejection of European amorality, Jacobin secularism and the marginalisation of religion comes from this modernist Islamic perspective that dominated the intellectual life of the late Ottoman period.

1.5 Erbakan as an Admired Role Model for Erdoğan and the Evolution of Turkey's Islamist Parties

Having been schooled in conservative religious networks, Erdoğan's Islamic identity emerged during his formative years as a young student. Erdoğan always valued his identity more than the accuracy of ideals and information. The İmam Hatip school and the MTTB indoctrinated Erdoğan within a world of political information relevant to the surrounding social and political environments of both entities. This, in turn, shaped his political ideology and activism. Because of his Islamist identity, he decided to join the MSP, a profoundly consequential choice for anchoring his political identity and how he would filter and distil the precepts, facts and social norms of his political process.[55] He became the chairman of the youth branch of the Beyoğlu district MSP in Istanbul in 1975. In fact, he met with Erbakan in 1977 when he staged and acted at the famous anti-Semitic play, *Mos-kom-ya*.[56] Although founding leaders of the MSP were more shaped by Nakşibendi Sufi tradition, Erdoğan's Islamism is shaped by Kısakürek and the Egyptian leaders of Muslim Brotherhood, such as Hasan al-Banna and Seyyid Qutb.[57]

The MSP emerged and evolved as an anti-establishment Islamic party to bring forward the voices of the marginalised conservative Islamic masses into the political arena. The MSP embodied a communitarian nature with a clear ideology and a charismatic leader – Erbakan. The party functioned to translate the resentment of the conservative Muslims into political rhetoric and to create a partisan community with its own party newspaper, its vision of history and auxiliary institutions engaged in diverse spheres of sociocultural life. The MSP always relied on face-to-face channels of communication or secondary associations to its ideological influence. For instance, Erbakan likened the electoral process to a census for counting the Muslims. The workings of secondary institutions along with the volunteered services of members during election campaigns were important. The MSP goal was to maintain a communal network with the ambitious goal of seizing power and radically transforming the state. It demanded the full commitment and unquestioning obedience of its members to the party and its leader (Erbakan). It was a party of religious devotees who remained partially loyal to democratic norms while advocating for an Islamic moral system and criticising the foundations of secularism.

In 1970s Turkey, a young man in Istanbul had access to various sites of political and ideological activism in which he could feel secure and build informal networks: Sufi and neo-Sufi (Nurcu) orders, football clubs, and political factions and parties. The political Islamic movements were nourished and fed by networks such as the İmam Hatip schools, Sufi orders, the MTTB and Islamic publishing houses. When the 1980 coup banned all secondary Islamic-oriented associations, including the MTTB, the only place where the conservative youth could safely socialise was the new Islamic organisation of Erbakan (the Welfare (Refah) Party). Erdoğan started at the grass-roots level and moved up the ranks of the party while learning all of the formal and informal avenues of Turkish political engagement. His party work brought home a regular salary, his main source of income.

While an active member within the MSP, Erdoğan was married, at twenty-four, to Emine Gülbaran, a young woman from the town of Tillo in the Siirt province. Her parents came from Istanbul and she was also active in the Idealist Women's Group of the MSP. Emine was invited by a friend to a town meeting in Tepebaşı, Istanbul, where she met Erdoğan. Wearing a white suit, Erdoğan cut an appealing figure, and his eloquent, passionate oration resonated with the young woman. The same day, she told her friend: 'I had a dream last night and a holy man with a white beard told me that this is the man I would marry. That man was Erdoğan.'[58] Her appearance also captured Erdoğan's attention at the town meeting. Emine would attend any meeting or event either organised by Erdoğan or at which he spoke. As they became more acquainted, both discovered how they shared many experiences from their social class backgrounds as well as their worldview on politics and morality. They were married 4 July 1978 in Istanbul. In the first two years of marriage, they had two daughters, Esra and Sumeyye, and then two sons, Ahmet Burak and Necmettin Bilal. The children have been visible in public politics and nepotism is obviously encouraged within the immediate family. Many conservative Muslims do not seem to be concerned about this, as they view this as right in the sphere of a loving father who cares for the welfare of his children. All of the children received their formative education at an İmam Hatip school.[59]

Having started in politics in Istanbul, Erdoğan was provided with new opportunities. He could cultivate his media, political and economic networks, as Istanbul stood as the country's centre of economic and media power. Erdoğan was an accomplished networker, mastering the power of money in party politics in his early years when he joined the MSP and extending his hands-on practice in political strategies and tactics. He realised the political party is a powerful network and an equally formidable source of income and enrichment. His experiences in the MSP would reinforce his attitude not to let anyone else control the AKP. He treated the AKP as his personal enterprise and the party's staff as employees who served at his pleasure. He removed any politicians he did not like and hired anyone whom he believed could be useful, even if they had criticised him in the past. For instance, he recruited Numan Kurtulmuş and Süleyman Soylu, both of whom had previously accused Erdoğan of being a thief.

Erdoğan's personal objectives also were advanced through legal loopholes. Turkey's Constitutional Court had banned nearly every previous Islamic party, taking possession of their assets and depositing them into the national treasury. However, Erbakan always kept two books: one formal register to detail the income and spending of the party, and the other, an informal record that, strategically, was more important for the party's activities. The practice of keeping an unofficial book, which actually represented the financial status of the party, served a party leader's desire to enrich his purse as well as those of his most loyal adherents. This, of course, fostered entrenched corruption. When Erbakan died, most of the party's wealth was under his name and his family went through several court cases to decide how the estate should be distributed.

In the earliest phases of his political leadership, he came to appreciate the value of party unity in achieving his goals, recognising that bridges were needed between younger and older Islamists, rich and poor, modernists and traditionalists – precisely what Istanbul has always provided. He tried to embody both old Ottoman and new republican Turkey. Erdoğan and Erbakan are different, but one critical aspect linked the two men: both are imperious leaders who are unimpressed by sceptical intellectuals. While Erbakan attained national status by focusing on national and international issues and mostly staying away from local issues, Erdoğan has focused almost obsessively on micro-managing politics even at the local level.

Despite being the nation's most powerful politician, Erdoğan would prefer confrontation over seclusion, always in search of a compromise if the cost of confrontation is much higher. In short, where Erbakan urged incrementalism and caution, while promoting religious nationalism, Erdoğan, before 2013, had pressed for dynamic change in seeking to pursue pro-EU policies through conservative democracy. Erdoğan's strategy was based on action and communication, manifested by his energy and body language. In this post-ideological world, before the Gezi Park demonstrations, Erdoğan was initially closer to Tony Blair and Bill Clinton in style and goals. He preferred inventive and tailor-made solutions over big ideas and grand ideological visions. He was a hard-core pragmatist who relied comfortably on feelings and popular emotion in order to project and magnify his power and achieve his concrete socio-economic goals. For Erdoğan, party politics has always been about loyalty and obedience to the leader in order to maintain stability and produce tangible results for the nation. That loyalty took on a more ominous intent during the 2010s.

It is a curious slight that Western media analysts often have not considered the complicating dimensions of Erdoğan's worldview in the way recent American presidents have been assessed in terms of their ideological commitments, faith and style of governance. Barack Obama's 1995 book *Dreams from My Father* introduced millions of Americans to his humble family life and to the unique aspects of the forty-fourth president's character. In 1994, *The Washington Post*'s David Maraniss wrote about the formative influences of Virginia Dell Kelley, the mother of Bill Clinton, who died a year after her son had assumed the presidency. Maraniss wrote:

> Most of Clinton's defining characteristics came from his mother. A clear line can be drawn back from his perseverance in the political world to her resilience in the face of personal tragedy and trauma. If he lost an election or an important legislative battle or she lost a husband or suffered from breast cancer, they kept going in similarly relentless, seemingly indefatigable fashion.[60]

Other writers have mentioned Erdoğan's father as a significant influence, but because of his work schedule, it was the young boy's mother who inculcated the emotional core in Erdoğan, which explains in part his policy towards refugees, which is unlike many countries that have treated refugees as terrorists or pariahs who should be shunted back to their war-torn lands.

From a critical perspective, his early political experiences played an important role in shaping him as emotional, puritanical, rigid, authoritarian and judgemental. He does not tolerate dissent and rewards those whose loyalty is unconditional – behaviour that has become much more pronounced in recent years. He is a 'man's man', comfortable in the company of men but not women. He is at his best and most charismatic in front of a crowd – a true performer. It may be that he needs a degree of distance, and that closeness or intimacy threatens him. Hardly known for a generous sense of humour, he once sued a political cartoonist who portrayed him as a cat tangled up in a ball of yarn and also prosecuted a doctor who presented him with the likeness of the Tolkien character Golum. In today's digital technology realm, one might say that that his personality's internal connectivity is not operating at optimum computing capacity and that he should be defragmented periodically. He has become more aggressive about avenging media critics, in particular.

A bundle of contradictions, Erdoğan is charismatic but not a deeply intellectual thinker; popular but arrogant; in favour of market freedom but also desiring religious community; populist yet authoritarian. Which Erdoğan is the true Erdoğan? Perhaps people tend to read their own political position back into his contradictory identities. And then there is the parallel many Turks as well as foreigners have drawn between Erdoğan and Abdulhamid II, the last de facto ruling sultan of the Ottoman Empire, which is discussed in the next section.

1.6 The Popular Construction of Erdoğan: Kabadayı, Köroğlu and Abdulhamid II

In 2017, in the middle of the debate about the merits of the presidential and parliamentary systems, a shop owner said:

> Erdoğan is constantly changing and the events have not left him alone so that he can be what he is. Either the events inside or outside Turkey have shaped his personality and decisions. I still do not know what he wants and what he represents. He is not a *kabadayı* but rather Köroğlu, who established his Camlibel in Beştepe [where the new office of Erdoğan is located] in Ankara.[61]

In another interview, a retired elementary school teacher said:

> Erdoğan is the reincarnation of Abdulhamid II. He uses Islam, he is in fear, and he wants to resist the international forces which seek to divide the country by utilising religion. He is also an autocrat just as Abdulhamid II was. Moreover, just like Abdulhamid II, he has surrounded himself with opportunists and has had to deal with a powerful Turkish opposition in the diaspora.[62]

A shop owner with a conservative perspective said that 'with the reopening of the Hagia Sophia, Erdoğan has restored our dignity and made us proud once again'. The teacher added, 'the next step should be the restoration of the caliphate'. By taking several symbolic steps such as moving the presidency from Cankaya (which was closely identified with Atatürk's legacy) to the Bestepe complex with a huge mosque and a palace of a thousand rooms, and converting the Hagia Sophia into a mosque, he has torn away decades of internalised worries about 'what would the West say', and replaced the void with the exuberant confidence of the conservative masses, who believe they now are in control of their nation's destiny. So, in order to understand Erdoğan, I will distil the contemporary references of *kabadayı*, Köroğlu and Abdulhamid II to shed light on how ordinary Turks understand Erdoğan. It has been widely acknowledged that

> on no subject is Turkish historiography more inflexible than the comparative merits of Abdulhamid II, the pre-eminent sultan of the empire's final half-century, and Mustafa Kemal Atatürk, the republic's founder. Some Turkish

historians like to describe Abdulhamid as a bloody dictator – murderous, paranoid, reactionary. It is true that he probably had the empire's most prominent early constitution done away with, and under his rule thousands of Anatolian Armenians died while rioting against Ottoman Muslims during the 1890s. Atatürk called Abdulhamid 'a hateful figure, addicted to pleasure and autocracy', and he rejoiced when the sultan was deposed and sent into exile in 1909.[63]

The Kemalist reforms, as recent books have noted, did not originate necessarily with Atatürk but had their precedents in the Ottoman Empire's last century, known as the Tanzimat (Reconstruction). Education was highly prized and Atatürk, whose own formative years were identified as Ottoman, benefited significantly from the Reconstruction efforts. As de Bellaguie explained:

> But the agreement of modern Turks with aspects of Atatürk's message has been accompanied by a growing distaste for its tone. Of the six 'fundamental and unchanging principles' that Atatürk incorporated into the constitution, just one – republicanism – remains unchanged. The other five – nationalism, populism, *étatisme*, secularism, and revolutionism (attachment to the process of change) – have been modified. The Islamic revival and the continuing strength of Kurdish ethnic consciousness have raised doubts about both secularism and nationalism, while the influence of the market economies of Europe and the US – not to mention the IMF, with which Turkey signed an agreement in 1999 – have made the rest seem outmoded. Most important of all, an increasing number of Turks resent being supervised by the generals and controlled by draconian laws and constitutional provisions.[64]

For the Kemalists, any comparisons to Abdulhamid II cannot be abided in any rational sense. Defending one of the last sultans of the empire, the Kemalists say, is equivalent to attacking Atatürk and the Republic's founding. When Kısakürek published *Ulu Hakan II: Abdülhamid Han*, his biography of Abdulhamid, he provoked polemical attacks from Kemalist journalists. An Islamist newspaper columnist (Abdurrahman Dilipak) – who was charged for anti-secular writings – claimed that 'Erdoğan would establish the "new ['ecumenical'] caliphate" once he wins the executive presidential powers'[65] and described Abdulhamid as 'one of the cleverest of sultans'.

When I travelled from the Istanbul suburbs of Pendik to Kartal in a visit to Turkey prior to the 2007 elections, I asked my taxi driver what he thought about Prime Minister Erdoğan. He said, '*Kasımpaşalı kabadayı olarak gitti, Etilerli olarak dönüyor*' (He went as a *kabadayı* of Kasımpaşa but returned as a man of Etiler). Kasımpaşa, as previously noted, is a rough neighbourhood with a machismo air, populated by a mix of day labourers, gypsies, new immigrants from rural Anatolia and fishmongers. Etiler, on the other hand, is populated by rich, secular White Turks who generally support the Kemalist establishment while looking down on people in neighbourhoods such Kasımpaşa. Etiler residents see them as being uneducated, religiously conservative and unrefined. Erdoğan's personal transformation has been shaped by the opinions of people in Turkish streets who either see him as *kabadayı* or as an evolving White Turk. In the 2007 elections, a poster proclaiming, 'Welcome *mağdur* and *mazlum* Gül!' was a common sight at many political rallies, indicating that many saw Erdoğan as the *mazlum* (the wronged one) of the 2002 elections. Gül became the *mağdur* (victimised one) of the 2007 elections. Popular perception regards Erdoğan as both *kabadayı* and *mazlum* because of his social background and political oppression by the establishment.

A *kabadayı* – normally a male and respected authority figure in his neighbourhood – represents an identity arising from well-earned reputation, authority and honour. A *kabadayı*'s authority is not derived from his knowledge, kinship lineage or state power but rather from an existing cultural code. *Kabadayı* is distinguished as a 'protector' of the weak, needy and oppressed against formal or informal power structures. He also deploys violence to impose informal settlement pacts among the conflicting parties. In addition, the *kabadayı* is defined by strong traits of courage, mercy towards the needy, strength and self-confidence. It is an acquired identity that one cultivates through neighbourhood interaction, and the *kabadayı* is the de facto neighbourhood disciplinarian who protects the area and serves as a catalysing force for restless youths who might be tempted into mischief and disorder. Every successful *kabadayı* embodies reputation, authority, and honour as the essence of his identity. The figures of *kabadayı* and *mağdur* allow us to glimpse the coalescing roles of symbols and social memory in Turkish society. These two role models exemplify the political culture of 'resistance' by stressing the role of heroic leaders who strive to resist all odds. They are self-sacrificing and powerful but also always cognisant of justice that is administered strictly – even harshly – while being fair. They lead the resistance to find order, fairness and justice. Erdoğan embodies this deeply entrenched political consciousness of Anatolian periphery in terms of his characteristic gestures, temperament and body language.[66]

The vindication of Turkey's marginalised conservative-religious periphery results in Erdoğan being framed as their Köroğlu – the heroic epic legend who drives the oral historical canon in many Turkic societies throughout Central Asia, including Azerbaijan.[67] Köroğlu is the hero who seeks to avenge a wrong and who struggles against and eventually punishes the ruler (or system) who was oppressive and unjust towards the common people. For many Turks, Köroğlu is akin to Robin Hood. In the Anatolian version of the epic story that exemplifies how justice is to be understood by ordinary Turks, Köroğlu is a murderous outlaw or bandit who robs the rich and distributes the spoils to the poor before rising to the status as a wise, just ruler. Köroğlu, along with his followers, eventually establishes his fortress hideout known as Çamlıbel.[68]

Erdoğan is closer to the imagery of Köroğlu than *kabadayı*. He is unquestionably viewed as a hero to oppressed Muslims and many Anatolians, as well as even many Muslims outside Turkey. They regard him as their legitimate avenger against oppression. When I asked a Turkish Muslim during my research what he means by comparing Erdoğan to Köroğlu, he responded, 'Köroğlu is a brave man who repays evil with evil and good with good.' The exclusion and marginalisation of Muslims and many Anatolians in Turkish societies have engendered deep resentment against the establishment of elites and Kemalist mainstreamers who have been in positions of power for many decades. For many, the resentment only can be satisfied through revenge and vindication – and Erdoğan is seen as the appropriate avenger of their resentment against the establishment.

As noted earlier, in their sharpest rebuke to Kemalist institutions, Turks enthusiastically compare Erdoğan to Abdulhamid II (1842–1918), the nineteenth-century Ottoman sultan, who ruled with absolute power and worked strenuously to protect the Ottoman territories from European imperialism by stressing pan-Islamic solidarity. Abdulhamid witnessed the loss of the Balkans along with the mass deportation and massacre of Muslims from the region. In the West, he was known as 'The Red Sultan' or the 'Abdul the Damned'. F. A. K. Yasamee, a leading scholar of Abdulhamid II, described him thus:

> He was a striking amalgam of determination and timidity, of insight and fantasy, held together by immense practical caution and an instinct for the fundamentals of power. He was frequently underestimated. Judged on his record, he was a formidable domestic politician and an effective diplomat.[69]

Abdulhamid II survived attempted assassinations and *coups d'état*, just as Erdoğan has done throughout his tenure. The AKP has encouraged the process of bringing Abdulhamid II back to frame Erdoğan as protecting and enhancing the sultan's legacy, which also has been reinforced in the national media along with many conferences, panels and publications about Abdulhamid II. The Turkish parliament, under the chairmanship of İsmail Kahraman, Erdoğan's closest friend and the former leader of the National Turkish Student Union (MTTB being the acronym for Milli Türk Talebe Birliği), hosted an 'International Symposium on Sultan Abdulhamid II and His Era', at the Dolmabahçe Palace in Istanbul. Kahraman praised the sultan as the leading 'compass to give us direction' in Turkey's dark days. The sultan's popular image among Turkey's conservative Muslims is undeniable, as he was regarded as the last great caliph-sultan who tried to save remnants of Muslim power in the international system and preserve the institutions and the practices of Islam. Kısakürek praised Abdulhamid II as 'the exalted sultan' whose piety and conviction could preserve the caliphate and protect Muslims all over the world against the encroachment of Western imperialism. In Kısakürek's writings, Abdulhamid II is presented as the Islamic alternative to Mustafa Kemal – the role model for the conservative Muslim leadership. The pious Abdulhamid II was an admirable diplomat who tried with limited means to protect the Muslim existence, but he was also an authoritarian ruler who oppressed intellectuals even as he carried out one of the most effective modernisation projects in education, transportation and institution building.

When I asked a former Turkish ambassador to explain why he compared Erdoğan to Abdulhamid II, he said:

> Abdulhamid came to power with high expectations among the people that he would proclaim the constitution and open the parliament. In fact, he proclaimed the first Ottoman constitution of 1876 and opened the first Ottoman parliament. He wanted to modernise the state and society at the same time. However, European imperialism provided neither time nor resources for him to carry out his reform agenda. They encouraged the Balkan ethnic groups to provoke an intervention by major powers so as to carve out the Balkans and end the Muslim presence in the Balkans. In fact, these all happened. The 1877–8 Ottoman–Russo War was the beginning of the end of the empire. It lost most of its territories in the Balkans. This resulted in the biggest human deportations and massacres that Muslims had suffered so Abdulhamid II had to suspend the constitution and close the parliament. The conditions mandated him to become what he did not want to become – an authoritarian leader.[70]

This wave of authoritarianism, however, turned secular and religious Muslim liberals against the state and to become allies with traditional Ottoman enemies against Abdulhamid II's autocracy. Erdoğan has referenced this history as well. In May 2015, he said, 'This newspaper [*The New York Times*] had been campaigning against Turkey's leaders going back to Ottoman Sultan Abdulhamid II. Now, they are spitting out the same hatred on me.'[71]

Erdoğan's supporters argue that just like Abdulhamid II, Erdoğan faces a similar existential threat against the homeland and the nation and it is 'understandable that he has become more authoritarian'.[72] Cemil Ertem, a senior adviser who explains the parallel mission against Western imperialism, said, 'Erdoğan is the follower of the mission of Abdulhamid II.'[73] Ebubekir Sofuoğlu, a professor of late Ottoman-era history, writing in an opinion piece for the *Daily Sabah* newspaper not only compared Erdoğan to Abdulhamid II but also argued that the sultan's fall resulted in the empire's disintegration. He identified the role of international governments, along with foreign ideas of nationalism, equality and the freedom of press, and liberal opposition as triggering disintegration. He contended that the opposition against Erdoğan is like the enemies of Abdulhamid II who sought to undermine the country's stability by calling Erdoğan a 'dictator'.[74]

The campaign to compare Erdoğan to Abdulhamid II is common throughout media and public discourse.[75] Mustafa Armağan, an editor of the pro-government *Derin Tarih* (Deep History) magazine, prepared a special issue by featuring Abdulhamid II and Erdoğan on its cover and trying to justify Erdoğan's policies against the opposition.[76] In the constitutional reform debate about the presidential system, the members of the Ottoman dynasty who live in Istanbul openly supported Erdoğan's position. For instance, Nilhan Osmanoğlu, an heir of the dynasty, announced his support for the new presidential system on Twitter, saying that 'in order to prevent our president from being isolated just as it was in the case of Abdulhamid II, and to support a more powerful Turkey, and a Turkey which makes its own decision, I support "Yes"'.[77]

Christopher de Bellaigue, an observer of Turkish politics and culture, aptly summarises the current reconstruction of Abdulhamid II as the new model for Turkish statesman. He argues that:

> In recent years, Abdulhamid has been the prime beneficiary of this revisionist current. He is spoken of with admiration by government ministers, who refer to him as the 'Great Emperor' and – again in reaction to Atatürk, whose campaign of language reform removed many Arabic words from the Turkish lexicon – couch his name with reverential, Arabic adjectives.[78]

The political debate in Turkey follows the historical fault lines and multiple readings of Ottoman history. One of the more intriguing wrinkles in this debate is offered by Abdulhamid Kırmızı, a leading historian of the Abdulhamid II period. Kırmızı argues that Erdoğan is more comparable to Mustafa Kemal Atatürk rather than Abdulhamid II. He contends that Erdoğan is more daring and bold in his decisions, while the sultan was timid and extremely cautious in decision-making and always tried to find a third way down the middle. Moreover, Erdoğan, like Atatürk, has constantly tested the boundaries of his power as he has expanded and fortified his governmental authority. Erdoğan, for Kırmızı, really wants to be Atatürk, as the father of the New Turkey – not as a status quo leader. Erdoğan, just like Atatürk, sees himself as 'the state-man' (*devlet adam*) – that is, he embodies the state. Erdoğan is a risk-taker and Abdulhamid was not. Moreover, Erdoğan, just like Atatürk, has pushed his closest friends out of politics as he has consolidated his position (notably, Abdullah Gül, Ahmet Davutoğlu, Ali Babacan and Abdullatif Şener).[79] But, Erdoğan is also focused on erasing Atatürk's unique legacy.

Leadership in modern Turkish politics is measured according to the benchmarks set by Atatürk. He gave people a sense of a grand and achievable destiny, whereas many politicians who succeeded him have often managed little more than platitudes that do not lead to concrete action or policy. Atatürk's mission required unquestioned commitment, while successive generations of politicians have been hampered, paralysed and crippled by trying to fashion fragile, tenuous compromises often dictated first by patron–client relations and then by overriding national interests. Turkey has always had a deep sense of the internalised image of Atatürk as the 'father' of Turks and every politician is measured in terms of this national cult. Atatürk led the War of Independence and implemented a great project of civilisational transformation of the country by suppressing collective memory and cutting off the Republic's Islamic and Ottoman roots. He is regarded as a hero and a successful victor against Western imperialism. Instead of keeping the feared Ottoman and Islamic past out, however, it ultimately fenced the Turks in, to their limitations. Atatürk built a cognitive wall that protected the Turks from their historical legacy. In that process, he sought to re-engineer a glorious past distinct and far removed from its authentic Seljuk and Ottoman heritage. Like many other national leaders, he deployed a *tabula rasa* which could not be challenged by scholars and politicians. The immediate Ottoman past was, by definition, inferior and a source of backwardness. The break with history – the illusion of a *tabula rasa* – offered an appealing youthful idealism. The goal was to create a new society free from the weight of religion and empire, forged by sheer human will.

During Atatürk's tenure (1922–38) and especially after his death, the guardians of his revolution believed they were modernising and civilising society. In fact, they were acting at Atatürk's will to create this new Turkey. The guardians of his legacy believed in his divine aspiration, often manifested by fear of imagined yet real enemies at home, and by the risky liberalising phenomena of freedom of thought and self-expression.[80] Atatürk promised prosperity and security without the messiness or diluted compromises of liberal democratic politics, which had a mass appeal in the early days of the Republic where the population had experienced widespread brutal massacres in the Balkans, Caucasus and in Anatolia.[81]

1.7 Conclusion

Throughout his life, Erdoğan has felt no other emotion except triumph and rage. In time he has lost the tempering feelings of respect, shame, altruism, compassion, loyalty and mercy. He became a leader inflaming the masses and instilling hatred in them towards certain targets. Erdoğan is an intelligent person who is cognisant of the inferiority complex of the Islamic masses and their demands from him. He always reacts to the demands of his grass-roots supporters. As Erdoğan does not allow anybody to come too close to him, very few people can observe the emotional background behind the veneer of a typical Muslim. A former friend of Erdoğan, who closely worked with him, says:

> During all this time I have worked with him, there were numerous times I met him one on one. I have come to realise that deep down this man has not felt any other emotions except rage mixed with fear and the will to win. One of the few feelings, he feels quite often, is the fear of death. But his feelings of rage are much stronger than death. He is a person who grew up without love. His feeling of hatred is much deeper and more active, and this always has worried me.[82]

Erdoğan's character was formed in his youth and one can identify the roots of his autocratic personality as they round out his sociocultural context. Erdoğan's vision capitalises on the republican legacy but he also has pointed towards a far more disturbing path that portends to be the most dangerous period ever in the history of the Republic. In the next chapter, Erdoğan's political ascendancy is chronicled, as his leadership underscores a dramatic dismantling of the legacy of Atatürk.

Notes

1. Erdoğan's speech in the parliament (11 June 2013), available at <https://www.youtube.com/watch?reload=9&v=RH-oOU5wgEw> (last accessed 6 November 2020); Özkök, 'Kardeşiniz Bir Zenci Türk'tür', 14 May 2003.
2. Interview with NA, Ankara, 12 July 2019.

3. Yılmaz, *Tayyip: Kasımpasa'dan Siyasetin*, pp. 34–45.
4. Interviews, Ankara, 9 July 2019.
5. Handy, 'Has Turkey had enough of Erdoğan?', 16 May 2018.
6. Interviews, Ankara, 10 July 2019.
7. Türk, *Muktedir*, pp. 211–94.
8. Smith, *Erdoğan Rising*, pp. 70–100.
9. For a detailed report about Erdoğan's biography and policies, see Baykal, 'Recep Tayyip Erdoğan', 22 December 2009.
10. Aksu, 'Kasımpaşa sokaklarından başkanlık koltuğuna'.
11. Kafka, *Kafka's "The Metamorphosis" and Other Writings*, p. 182.
12. Çakır and Çalmuk, *Recep Tayyip Erdoğan*, p. 16.
13. Aksu, 'Kasımpaşa sokaklarından başkanlık koltuğuna'.
14. Sontag, 'The Erdoğan experiment'.
15. Pamuk, *Yasaklı Umut*, p. 21.
16. Aksu, 'Kasımpaşa sokaklarından başkanlık koltuğuna'.
17. Aksu, 'Kasımpaşa sokaklarından başkanlık koltuğuna'.
18. Avcı, 'Erdoğan: Plaka Okusam da Suçlanırdım', 9 October 1998.
19. Aksu, 'Kasımpaşa sokaklarından başkanlık koltuğuna'.
20. Pamuk, *Yasaklı Umut*, p. 22; Çakır and Çalmuk, *Recep Tayyip Erdoğan*, p. 22.
21. Interview with Hüseyin Besli, Istanbul, 10 March 2014.
22. Dale, 'Implications of the rediscovery'.
23. Pamuk, *Yasaklı Umut*, p. 22.
24. The school in which Erdoğan was registered in 1973 was Aksaray Iktisadi ve Ticari Ilimler Yüksel Okulu (Aksaray Economics and Business Higher School). It was renamed and became part of the new established Marmara University while Erdoğan was a student; he graduated in 1981.
25. Scmitt, *The Concept of the Political*.
26. The key journals were: *Büyük Doğu* (1943–78); *Gölge Dergisi* (1976–8); *Akıncı Güç* (1978); *Akıncılar* (1979); *Selam* (1983–4); *Catı* (1975–8) of the magazine of MTTB; and *Cuma* (1990–2004). The common theme of these journals was anti-westernisation (specifically attacking the Tanzimat Reforms of 1839 and the westernising reforms of Mustafa Kemal). These journals advocated for Ottoman institutions and practices as Islamic. They also drew a sharp distinction between *dar al-harp* vs *dar al-Islam* (the territory of Islam vs territory of war), and called for the restoration of the Golden Age of Islam as achieved by the Ottomans.
27. Besli and Özbay, *Bir Liderin Doğuşu: Recep Tayyip Erdoğan*, p. 235.
28. Interview with Seyfi Say, Istanbul, 3 June 2017.

29. This translates to 'You are stranger in your own country, a pariah in your homeland!'
30. Çakır and Çalmuk, *Recep Tayyip Erdoğan*, pp. 21–2.
31. Özdenören, 'Necip Fazıl Kısakürek', p. 143; Mardin, 'Cultural change and the intellectual', pp. 243–59.
32. For more about his life, see Orhan, *Necip Fazıl Kısakürek*, pp.15–21. The authoritative source on Kısakürek's life is his autobiography, *O ve Ben*.
33. Duran, 'Transformation of Islamist political thought', p. 205.
34. Still in this period, he had good enough relations with the Kemalist establishment and intelligentsia to the extent that he wrote the poem of *Büyük Doğu* as the new national anthem in 1938, upon the request of Falih Rıfkı Atay to be presented to Atatürk, and he wrote a book on Namık Kemal for the Turkish Language Institution (Türk Dil Kurumu) in 1940.
35. Aybak, 'The Sultan is dead, long live "Başyüce" Erdoğan Sultan!', 31 May 2017.
36. Kısakürek, *İdeolocya Örgüsü*, p. 33.
37. Sevinç, 'Kılavuzu Necip Fazıl olanlar ve Başyücelik Devleti', 8 December 2015; Özbank, 'Erdoğan'ın hükümetten isteyip de alamadığı şey "Başyücelik" olabilir mi?', 11 April 2015.
38. Erdoğan, 'Necip Fazıl Kısakürek Awards will bring us the genuine voice, scent and soul of this land', 2 November 2014. At the beginning of his speech at the ceremony held at Haliç Congress Centre in Istanbul, Erdoğan expressed his gratitude to the *Star* newspaper members Ethem Sancak, Murat Sancak and Mustafa Karaalioğlu for organising this meaningful awards ceremony in the name of Necip Fazıl Kısakürek. Congratulating the award-winning poets, writers and philosophers and wishing them a long, and successful life, Erdoğan said: 'I congratulate the dervish of modern times, poet Hüseyin Atlansoy who cherishes great love and hope. I also congratulate the young writer Güray Süngü who opens a window into solitude, death and alienation and looks at hope, love and future through that window. I congratulate the distinguished academician Gülru Necipoğlu who reminded us of the peak of our civilisation, Sinan the architect. I congratulate the bibliophile academician İsmail Erünsal who vastly contributed to our culture, history of our civilisation and transferred his rich knowledge to young students.'
39. Erdoğan, 'Necip Fazıl Kısakürek Awards'.
40. Erdoğan, 'Our difference is conquest, not plunder', 24 December 2015.
41. Some aspects of Erdoğan's biography are derived from Gür, *Türk siyasetinde bir Kasımpaşalı Tayyip Erdoğan*. Muradoğlu, 'Hapisten başbakanlığa', 12 March 2003.

42. Okutan, *Bozkut'tan Kuran'a Milli Türk Talebe Birliği*, p. 205.
43. The play Erdoğan produced heavily borrows from Mustafa Bayburtlu's anti-Semitic play, known as *Kırmızı Pençe*, which was published in 1969. For more about the play, see Bayburtlu, *Kızıl Pençe*. I would like to thank Ahmet Kol for sharing his copy with me. For a summary of the play, see *Sol Haber Portalı*, 'Arşivden bulup çıkardık, Erdoğan'ın yıllar önce oynadığı piyesin metni', 23 May 2020.
44. For an excellent article about how MTTB tried to organise its alternative commemoration of the Gallipoli, see Özcan and Arzik, 'Haunting memories of the Great War', pp. 1240–57.
45. Erdoğan's speech at the award ceremony for Necip Fazıl Kısakürek, 2 November 2014, available at <https://tccb.gov.tr/en/news/542/3297/necip-fazil-Kısakürek-awards-will-bring-us-the-genuine-voice-scent-and-soul-of-this-land> (last accessed 8 November 2020).
46. Okutan, *Bozkurt'tan Kur'an'a Milli Türk Talebe Birliği*, pp. 133–204.
47. Erdoğan's interview in *Vatan*, 28 September 1994.
48. Duman, 'Mehmet Akif ve Bir Mecmuanın Anatomisi', pp. 78–95.
49. For more on Akif's writings and activities during the War, see Köroğlu, *Ottoman Propaganda*, pp. 130–41.
50. Ersoy, *Safahat*, p. 292: 'Biz almasak bile a'dâdan intikamınızı, / Huda ki defter-i ebrara yazdı namınızı, / Günün birinde şu dağlardan indirir elbet, / O intikamı alır kanlı canlı bir millet!'
51. Tansel, *Mehmet Akif Ersoy*, pp. 55; Ünsal, 'Mehmet Âkif Ersoy', pp. 76–7. The modern Islamist Ismet Özel rejected Akif's call to adopt Western technology. Özel argues that one cannot separate this technology from the Islamist experience. Özel, *Bir Akşam Gezintisi Değil*, pp. 207–8, 303.
52. Available at <http://umich.edu/~turkish/links/manuscripts/anthem/english.htm> (last accessed 2 December 2020).
53. Tarihi, 'The Prime Minister Erdoğan's perspective on Mehmet Akif', 27 December 2010.
54. Erdoğan's speech, see *Milliyet*, 23 January 2008.
55. For more on the MSP, see Toprak, *Islam and Political Development*, pp. 91–121.
56. In Turkey, not only Islamists but also some leftist groups are anti-Semitic. See Poyraz, *Musa'nın Cocukları*.
57. Besli and Özbay, *Bir Liderin Doğuşu: Recep Tayyip Erdoğan*, p. 28.
58. Aksu, 'Kasımpaşa sokaklarından başkanlık koltuğuna'.

59. Esra Erdoğan is married to Berat Albayrak, the current minister of finance and treasury in the government. Sumeyye Erdoğan is married to Selçuk Bayraktar. Both daughters were educated in the West, completing their baccalaureate studies at Indiana University. Esra earned a master's degree at the University of California (Berkeley), while Sumeyye completed her master's degree at the London School of Economists. Ahmet Burak Erdoğan co-founded a shipping company, MB Denizcilik, and questions arise periodically about his business dealings, especially in countries that have poor relations with Turkey. Necmettin Bilal Erdoğan, also a business executive, has been scrutinised extensively, including the 2013 corruption scandals and investigations for money laundering.
60. Maraniss, 'The woman who shaped the president', 7 February 1994.
61. Interview, Istanbul, 23 May 2017.
62. Interview, Istanbul, 22 May 2017.
63. Interview, Istanbul, 23 May 2017.
64. de Bellaigue, 'Turkey's hidden past', 8 March 2001.
65. For Dilipak's statement, see *Cumhuriyet*, 'Erdoğan halife olacak, Ak Saray'daki odalarda hilafet temsilcilikleri açılacak', 16 January 2017.
66. Yıldırım and Özler, 'A sociological representation', pp. 5–24; Vergin, 'Siyaset ile Sosyolojinin Buluşduğu Nokda', pp. 5–9.
67. Boratav, Köroğlu Destanı; Wilks, 'Aspects of the Köroğlu Destanı'; Barkey, Bandits and Bureaucrats, p. 182.
68. Bayat, *Köroğlu Destanı*, p. 9.
69. Yasamee, *Ottoman Diplomacy*, p. 20.
70. Interview, Ankara, 4 June 2018.
71. *Hürriyet Daily News*, 'Surrounded by Ottoman soldiers, Erdoğan toughens rhetoric against *New York Times*', 30 May 2015.
72. For more on pro-Erdoğan comparisons with Abdulhamid, see Kaplan, 'Abdülhamit ve Erdoğan', 3 June 2016; Tosun, 'Abdulhamid Erdoğan Benzerliği', 25 September 2016.
73. Ertem, 'Erdoğan, 2. Abdülhamit misyonunun takipçisidir', 20 December 2014.
74. Sofuoğlu, 'Abdulhamid'e yapılanlarla Erdoğan'a yapılanlar arasindaki benzerlikler', 25 June 2015.
75. Nuray Mert is critical of this comparison; see her op-ed, 'Abdulhamid Han ve Erdoğan', 23 September 2016.
76. *Derin Tarih*, September 2016 had a special issue. For a more sobering analysis, see Duran, 'Comparing Erdoğan with Mustafa Kemal and Sultan Abdulhamid', 6 October 2016.

77. *Diken*, 'Evet'çilere "hanedan" desteği: Erdoğan'ı 2. Abdülhamit Han'ın yalnızlığına bırakmamak için', 27 January 2017.
78. de Bellaigue, 'Turkey: the return of the sultan', 9 March 2017.
79. Kırmızı, 'Erdoğan Abdulhamid'e değil, Mustafa Kemal'e benziyor', 22 September 2016.
80. Atay, *Zetindağı*. Atay examines the sources of these historical fears among the first generation of republican elite.
81. McCarthy, *Death and Exile*.
82. Interview with Mir Dengir Fırat, Ankara, 6 March 2016.

2

ERDOĞAN'S WORLDVIEW

In the colonial context the settler only ends his work of breaking in the native when the latter admits loudly and intelligibly the supremacy of the white man's values.

Frantz Fanon, *The Wretched of the Earth*

Reis var; yeis yok (As long as there is Reis [Erdoğan]; there is no despair).

2.1 Introduction

One of the key fault lines of the Turkish Republic since its inception arises from the political and cultural divide between the ideological centre and its counterpart in the periphery. Tensions from the modernisation process have widened the gap between the two points: the republican/Kemalist centre is secular and nationalist, aided by statist policies that have made it more economically developed while the peripheral majority (in population numbers) remains conservative, religious and economically less developed. The motivating idea of the Western-friendly elite is that the country can only catch the West if the conservative Anatolian majority is forced to modernise – that is, to give up its religiously based practices and worldview and adopt and emulate instead the secularisation embodied in a generalised version of the West.[1]

The dynamics of marginalisation and exclusion form the centre of the current rebellion against the secular establishment in Turkey. This tension, indeed, has turned Islam into an oppositional identity for those who have been marginalised, beginning with the multiparty elections of 1950 in which the periphery (also the majority of the population) would cast votes for conservative, religious and economic development-oriented parties such as the Democrat Party of then Prime Minister Adnan Menderes. A second critical juncture occurred amidst the neo-liberal economic policies of Turgut Özal following the 1980 coup that opened the way for the periphery to enter in earnest the political, economic and cultural centres of the state and market. This process culminated in the emergence of the Anatolian Turkish Sunni majority as the dominant political and economic sector of Turkish society under the leadership of Erdoğan and the AKP in 2002.[2]

Erdoğan's version of religion (Islam), just like Özal, is not opposed to modernity or modernisation, but criticises a state-imposed lifestyle in the name of westernisation. While the traditional periphery emerged as the centre in Turkish state and society, it also failed to fill the institutional vacuum created by the displacement of the entrenched Kemalist regime. This fact is crucial to Turkey's current social and political crisis and Erdoğan's ambitions to strengthen his presidential powers.

Turkey's current crisis indicates that the Young Turk Revolution of 1908 has never been resolved, along with the standing issues of that time. Today, Turkish citizens continue to protest against autocratic power because the country is still ruled in an autocratic fashion. The democratic experiments of the last seventy years have not been able to break this tradition. Erdoğan is an autocrat no different to Abdulhamid II. The country today is held together by one man who rules it with his own hybrid mix of Islamism and nationalism infused into a majoritarian democratic system. The legacy of sultan-like autocracy looms larger than ever. Moreover, Turkey is haunted by its need to modernise and by its backwardness relative to the West. Today, Turkey is as politically and socially divided as it was during the last days of the Ottoman Empire. The country still struggles over national unity, between democracy and autocracy, and between Western and Islamic values. Although there were promising expectations that Erdoğan, once he came to power in 2002, would lead the reconciliation and bridge these divisions, since the Gezi Park protests he has increasingly played an imperious, divisive role. Erdoğan's motto in politics simply is *quibiscum viis* (by whatever means) in order to stay in power.

Erdoğan is a strong man with a vindictive personality. He prefers to be feared than loved. His policies helped the Ottoman past and especially nostalgia for the sultan to come back. He has supported movies, conferences, cultural activities to praise and exalt the Ottoman sultans. The ideal is a single, strong man that Turkey needs in order to restore its greatness.

Simultaneously loved, respected, feared and loathed, Erdoğan is now the most consequential leader of Turkey since Atatürk.[3] Erdoğan's worldview channels the culture and identity of Anatolian Sunni Turks, most of whom view the fount of their historic national identity as being not the relatively recent formation of the Kemalist Republic in 1923, but instead the entry of Turkic Muslim tribes and warriors into Anatolia following the battle of Manzikert in 1071 under the leadership of Alparslan and later Seljuk and Ottoman Turkic Muslim dynasties. As a result of the modern expansion of education, urbanisation and competitive mass media, this Anatolian majority has successfully reconstructed a counter-narrative of national identity and values to the Kemalist version.

This Islamic revival is not limited to shantytowns or provincial cities and villages. Today, it reaches far into the centre of elite cultures and the urban upper and middle classes. It is impossible to differentiate real intent from objectives in these waves of religious revival and Ottoman nostalgia in Turkey. Political Islam is linked to the simmering resentment of citizens being excluded and disparaged in their own country by a relatively small and enclosed republican elite. This counter-intellectual elite outside the militantly secular Kemalist sociopolitical environment not only has brought the concerns and terminology of the periphery to the centre but also has sharpened the political language and sense of grievance of the arriviste (newcomers) in expanding urban centres. For instance, one of the pioneering intellectuals of this restoration, Kısakürek, as well as other populist intellectuals who were inspired by him, highlighted this resentment that despite being the majority who had successfully repelled Western invaders as they rallied to the defence of their faith and homeland, Anatolian Turkish Sunnis after 1923 were devalued to the status of ignorant and unworthy custodians of the Islamic tradition or motherland. They responded for decades by refusing the Kemalist attempt to discard the nation's Seljuk and Ottoman Muslim heritage. Yet, alongside the Kemalists, they also shared the desire to create a modern and powerful Turkish nation state. A distinctly Ottoman Islam, for this conservative group of intellectuals, served as the lodestar to inspire an alternative path to society and state with the common purpose of restoring Turkey to its historic greatness.

In critically assessing the intellectual and ideological pathways which led to the (re-)emergence of this vision of Turkey that seeks to reconcile the imperatives of modernity with her glorious Seljuk and Ottoman Islamic past, several essential questions emerge. How did Erdoğan reflect and shape this great historic transformation? How does he really see himself today, and how does the world see him? Is he a democratic or an authoritarian leader? What is the role of his Islamic identity in shaping his domestic and foreign policy? Is there a well-established cultural and normative worldview of Erdoğan's? If there is, what constitutes this worldview?

One could argue that although his core identity and values are derived from his Muslim identity, his operational code which shapes his policy preferences is based on pragmatic and his anti-Western and anti-Kemalist resentment. This resentment was an 'intense mix of envy and sense of humiliation and powerlessness'.[4]

Erdoğan is not a puritanical Islamist politician, as commonly assumed in the West, but rather a pragmatic one who, none the less, draws upon certain core Islamic values and goals, not only because he believes in them but also because he realises that it is the essence for his popular appeal in much of the country and one that furthermore transcends the Turkish–Kurdish ethnic divide. Moreover, one would argue that Erdoğan is an astute transactional politician, always seeking to balance competing values in terms of their political benefits. Until 2013, Erdoğan's main strength was his ability to accommodate diverse and even competing demands across the secular versus religious, Turkish versus Kurdish, and centre versus periphery, ensuring that the majority of citizens saw him as *the* representative prime minister.

Until the Gezi Park events of 2013, the world had seen Turkey as the star of Islam – the one country in the region able to reconcile democracy and Islam, modernity and tradition; a country which had become a model for other Muslim countries experiencing and contending with the fallout from the Arab Spring. However, the Gezi Park disturbances tainted the respective positive images of Turkey and Erdoğan. His global image's favourability plunged to abysmal levels, which were not always justified and stemmed from his sharp critiques of Western exploitation of Muslim populations and resources. Erdoğan's intolerance of satire and his imperious manner also certainly contributed to this negative image.

Disturbingly, however, anti-Erdoğan animus in the West is now also entangled with historical and derogatory Western stereotypes of Islam and the Turks. This routinely includes depictions of Erdoğan as an 'oriental despot', and 'bloody sultan'. Populist neo-fascist leaders in Austria, Hungary, Slovakia and the Netherlands have invoked the 1683 Siege of Vienna as the reason to expel Muslim refugees. The German comedian Jan Boehnermann performed a ditty referring to Erdoğan as a 'goat f*****' and using other derogatory stereotypes common amongst European neo-fascists and the late Dutch anti-Muslim provocateur Theo Van Gogh as well.[5] In the controversy which followed, it was notable that Western commentators blithely ignored how inflammatory such discourse was to their fellow Muslim citizens. This topic is explored in more detail later in the book.

In this chapter, Erdoğan's understanding of religion and history is examined as the two fundamental sources of his *weltanschaung*. The fire of this worldview has always been his deep sense of resentment. After unpacking these two critical concepts, the analysis continues by focusing on his understanding of the state, nation, secularism, modernity, tradition, democracy and human rights. In addition to Islam, the second source of Erdoğan's worldview is history, especially his interpretation of two key Ottoman sultans – Fatih Mehmet and Abdulhamid II. His keen interest in these particular Ottoman personages is more political than scholarly. William Faulkner's words from *Requiem for a Nun* – 'The past is never dead. It's not even the past' – sums up Erdoğan's understanding of Ottoman history. History, for Erdoğan, is not merely appreciation of the past but the groundwork for framing present-day political identities and struggles.

His understanding of history constitutes the critical layer of Erdoğan's identity. It is a specific version of imagined Ottoman history as shaped by perceptions of victory, glory and defeats, which provides the raw material of his political identity. Unifying the AKP leadership is a powerful nostalgia for the Ottoman past as holding the key to Turkey's future greatness. Such nostalgic appreciations of the Ottoman and Seljuk eras run deep in many communities and media representations. This reconstruction of Ottoman identity has been ongoing for the last three decades, as it is articulated in art, literature, cuisine and politics. Turkey's Islamic movements always have emphasised the Ottoman legacy as offering an opposing national identity in contrast to Kemalism, which alternatively sought to construct modern Turkish identity from discordant European, Central Asian and even Hittite sources. This stress on Ottomanism also shapes for more traditional segments of society their understanding of Europe, over which much of the Ottoman Empire ruled for centuries. In today's Ottomanism, as with the AKP, Europe remains the Other and even the 'enemy'. Thus, at the grass-roots level, there is ambivalence among many common Turks towards accepting full EU membership even if this prospect didn't face long-held bad faith and dismissal on the part of many European powers.

Erdoğan's historic memories are contained, preserved and perpetuated within Islamic symbols and practices. His understanding of a ruler resembles Machiavelli's conception of *The Prince*. Machiavelli claims that a leader of the state ought to do good if it is possible, but also must be prepared to commit evil if he must for the greater good of the state.[6] As he approaches the end of his second decade in power, Erdoğan has tried to act within accepted moral boundaries of society, whenever it was necessary. However, he has not hesitated to use force to maintain the security of the state. The head of state is 'prepared to vary his conduct as the winds of fortune and changing circumstances constrain him and . . . not deviate from right conduct if possible, but be capable of entering upon the path of wrongdoing when this becomes necessary'.[7]

Erdoğan's strategic vision is rooted in an earlier Ottoman period, one in which Turks were the sword and shield of a glorious Islamic civilisation and the rulers of one of history's greatest empires. By contrast, he views Kemalists as having an emaciated vision of the nation which did not extend beyond the National Pact of 1920, known as the *Misak-ı Milli* that limited Turkey's boundaries and interests to Anatolia alone. Thus, Erdoğan's vision of progress is shaped by his understanding of former Ottoman Turkey grandeur. This also is manifested in his love of Istanbul over Ankara, as the Ottoman capital reminds him in its magnificent monuments and spectacular setting of the former empire's grandeur. For Erdoğan, Ankara is the drab Kemalist provincial city that stood in contrast to this golden past. Moreover, while hailing from a conservative family in the Black Sea, it was in Istanbul that he came of age and assumed leadership as the city's popular mayor. In 1994, the candidate Erdoğan told a rally: 'You and us, standing in front of sad Hagia Sophia, just opposite of the Sultan Ahmet Mosque, will accomplish the second conquest of Istanbul . . . 27 March will be a day for closing an era, and opening a new era.'[8] Following his election as mayor, he said, 'This city of goodness *belde-i Tayyibe* [a former name of Istanbul in the Ottoman times] will regain its spirit . . . After 541 years Istanbul was spiritually re-conquered.'[9] Years later, as prime minister, Erdoğan became obsessed with efforts to revive the Ottoman consciousness in twenty-first-century Turkish society.[10]

Among the numerous WikiLeaks documents from the 2010s, including those originating in the US embassy in Ankara, there are numerous observations by American diplomats about Erdoğan's personality and his decision-making style. By utilising these materials, with due caution, I will allude to certain character traits that emerge consistently alongside others and that offer a glimpse into Erdoğan's decision-making process. Erdoğan does not want to be seen as being pro-American, but he also is angered when people present him as anti-American. He prefers to be seen as a meticulously pragmatic politician who works to advance the interests of Turkey. For Erdoğan, the boundary between decision and belief can be tenuous. When he acts on policy and action, those decisions become beliefs that he defends resolutely with the well-known phrase, 'Tayyip does not back down'. As suggested in the WikiLeaks documents, again with advised caution, he has encircled himself with a small group of advisers but seldom has felt the need to heed their advice or that of the leaders of his own party. This is not particularly surprising and is a trait that could be just as easily applied to other heads of states, regardless of geography. Understandably, he asks his inner circle of followers to support resolutely his decisions. As one of his closest advisers explained to me, he listens most assuredly to those who agree with him while hardly listening to counter arguments. In the next several sections of this chapter, each of these factors is examined for its influence upon him.

2.2 The Ottoman Islamic Heritage as the Foundation of the Nation

The heritage of Seljuk and Ottoman Islamic civilisation for Erdoğan is not an unconditional set of values but rather a *logos* that orients the daily life of community and provides meaning to actions, decisions and relationships. Moreover, it is an emancipating force against oppression and foreign domination that determines a community's core values. It is religious tradition that gives coherence, unity and solidarity to social practices. Erdoğan's understanding of Islam is shaped by the aggregate of secular versus Islamic political rivalry, Islamic intellectual traditions and movements, and Turkey's economic and political development. The cultural as well as dogmatic aspects of Islam are critical in comprehending Erdoğan's worldview. By culture, this means a set of values, myths and beliefs that shape one's daily practices. The oppositional history of Turkish Islam in the Kemalist Republic also is a component of Erdoğan's intellectual personality. Atatürk and his colleagues worked strenuously to fence in the social and political manifestations of Islam in the public square with the idea of ultimately having it disappear.

In this secular context, one of the main questions that every Turkish politician, including Erdoğan, faces is: Where do you stand on religion? Turkish Sunni Islam and its high culture, for Erdoğan, always have been the deciding factor in what it means to be an honourable Turk. For him, the human being is a spiritual creature with the capacity to create moral order as well as the capacity to be pious, God-fearing and responsible, whose daily life and interactions are embedded in this transcendental moral framework.

Although the Islamic conception of God calls on Muslims to be merciful, love their community and work towards its advancement of humanity, Erdoğan's Islamist God is more an instrument of mobilising the masses and covering one's shortcomings. He rejects the idea of turning the other cheek but calls upon Muslims to defend their dignity and freedom from those who would seek to invade their region and exploit its resources. Erdoğan believes in the adage 'God helps those who help themselves'.[11] Thus, he is not fatalistic, always stressing the centrality of human agency in achieving success in this world and for improving the human condition. As a faithful believer, he believes that Islam could support the well-being of society and encourage economic development. Religion, for Erdoğan, is the wellspring of morality, so politics accordingly should protect and reflect this shared moral code of society. He believes that God should be sought not only through reason but through passion and feeling as well. Islamic faith, for him, should not be just professed but exhibited, if not lived. His understanding of God as an omnipotent force is incontrovertible in his mind. Erdoğan indicates that he puts faith and religious experience at the heart of his personal and public life, and he judges other people in terms of their religious practices. Thus, he never hesitates to use Islam as a weapon against his opponents or as a cover for his corrupt and authoritarian practices. He believes that the inner voice of Anatolia remains culturally and spiritually Muslim. The historical backdrop against which Erdoğan's personality and his understanding of politics were formed was the *Kulturkampf* between the Ottoman and Seljuk Islamic legacies and the militantly secular Kemalist ideology which sought to displace them.

Perhaps the clearest and most comprehensive example of Erdoğan's synthesis of his political ideology and his religious conscience came in his controversial Siirt speech (as discussed earlier) that led to his short imprisonment. Erdoğan later said that his speech was intended to show that state and religion need not be adversarial, adding that religious belief served principally for the individual's quest to become virtuous and that religion offered a linchpin for morality.

As discussed in the previous chapter, Erdoğan's religious beliefs and discourse took hold during his formative years in the Kasımpaşa neighbourhood of Istanbul. One prominent example of how deep those ideological roots had become arose in 2009 when Erdoğan abruptly ended a debate with Israeli President Shimon Peres at the World Economic Forum in Davos, Switzerland. At one point, Erdoğan chided Peres for raising his voice inappropriately, suggesting that the Israeli president was projecting a guilty conscience for Israeli's lack of hesitancy to exert state violence: 'I know well how you kill children on beaches, how you shoot them.' The moderator intervened, warning Erdoğan that his statement was out of bounds and that he should end his remarks. Erdoğan refused, concluding by reciting the Sixth Commandment: 'The Old Testament's sixth amendment says "Thou shalt not kill". There is murder here.'[12]

The exchange was widely reported in the international media with mixed responses, as some praised Erdoğan for his sincere bluntness while others were shocked by the lack of diplomatic tone. Some senior Turkish diplomats, including İlter Türkmen, a retired ambassador, and former foreign minister Mümtaz Soysal criticised Erdoğan during press interviews. Soysal said:

> It is wrong to expect a politician to be a diplomat; however, it was completely unpleasant of him (the PM) to speak with the language of the street and address the president of a country 'you' ['*sen*' – the informal second person pronoun]. Whoever you are, it is regarded as rudeness.[13]

Meanwhile, to many ordinary citizens in Turkey, Erdoğan's response was approved enthusiastically. There were many shades of the Kasımpaşa influences in the exchange, as well as an unforgettable demonstration of his honest commitment to Islamic values that also are held closely by the country's many devout Muslim Turks. Hasan Pulur, a popular columnist in Turkish media (2009), elucidated the Kasımpaşa comparison: 'This is an issue of style, an issue of perception. This style of the prime minister has not been constructed recently; on the contrary, he grew up in this way, he has lived in this way, and has made the people around accept it.'[14]

However, the most striking part was Erdoğan's use of one of the most famous parts of the Old Testament rather than the Qur'an. Likely, Erdoğan's reference highlighted that the Israeli government's military actions ran against its own religious beliefs and their moral conscience was riddled with grave guilt. It is a strong example of how effectively Erdoğan has inculcated and synthesised the language of the vernacular (Kasımpaşa), the language of his religious beliefs (Islam) and the language of his politics as a matter of both strategy and policy. Erdoğan successfully cashed in his confrontation with Peres in local 2009 elections. During the rallies, he said:

> Turkey today sides with the injured, the right and the exploited in the Middle East. Those who think big, with far-reaching horizons, with a wide vision, and with dreams would see and understand this Turkey, this Great Turkey. But some in Ankara could not understand it. In diplomacy, ex-mon chers, those diplomats with timid and westernised mentality who prefer to be led

rather than lead, could not understand this. Because they were always mon chers, and they will always remain so. In politics too, they have been mon chers, and they continue as mon chers.[15]

Modern Turkey is a country of refugees. As a country composed of many dispersed and persecuted Muslims from the Balkans and Caucasus, the unified amalgam of ethnic groups in Turkey has relied on Islam as its social glue. Islam, for these refugees, had been the shared and internalised sense of solidarity and the source of social morality. While during the reforms of Atatürk there were systemic and concerted efforts to replace Islam with a secular Turkish nationalism, these two identities became co-determinants. This was especially the case against the external threats of European powers or Russia, as the majority of the population would mobilise under the flag of Islam more than ethnic nationalism.

Yet, Islamism and Turkishness in the context of the country are not mutually exclusive ideologies and identities. Turkish citizenship is still a matter of allegiance to Islam. Erdoğan's decision to offer citizenship to Syrian Arab refugees, for example, aligns with this understanding that any Muslim could become a Turk. There is always the potential for a dormant nationalist rejuvenation within the Islamic revival, as Turkish nationalism is knitted within a Muslim framework. Thus, in the most critical times of his tenure, Erdoğan has always been supported by Turkish nationalists. Erdoğan's unbroken string of electoral victories could be seen as the revenge of a suppressed Islamic periphery against Turkey's secularised and Western-oriented elite. He seeks to redefine the sense of community in core Islamic values of who is in or out. Erdoğan has used his power to 'de-ethnicise' the population from its narrow ethnic nationalism (that is, Turkish/Kurdish) but also to 're-Islamicise' by stressing Islamic values as a unifying point. Erdoğan's educational and social policies are consciously designed to weaken secular identity and to strengthen subnational (for example, Albanian, Bosniak, Torbes, Kurd and Georgian) identities under an overarching Ottoman Turkish/Muslim formulation.

For Erdoğan, being a Georgian Muslim stems neither from blood ties nor of formal legal citizenship in the Western sense. Instead, it is a commitment to Islam and the Ottoman heritage to protect and perpetuate faith with the goal of maintaining social integration and restoring a moral order. Of course, what it means to be a Turk will never be a settled question. Turkishness, for Atatürk, was based on a 'we feeling', as Deutsch later developed in *Nationalism and Social Communication* (1953). This 'feeling', for Atatürk, is derived from language, territory, culture, or a real or imagined shared past. For Atatürk, a Turk is whoever feels himself to be a Turk and who is committed to the progressive ideals of Western civilisation. Unlike Japan and other East Asian countries modernising under the pressure of Western imperialism, the Kemalists enforced an unsophisticated understanding of what this modernisation process would entail, focusing instead on blindly imitating Western mores and customs rather than establishing their own brand of representative government and individual liberty.

Turkey, for Erdoğan, is the grateful inheritor of the Umayyad, Abbasid, Seljuk and Ottoman civilisations. A country with a significant role in the international community, Turkey sustains historical connections with these four Muslim empires and therefore is expected to advance and carry the torch of Islamic civilisation by opening its doors to oppressed Muslim communities. This sometimes is referred to as the neo-Ottoman myth of Erdoğan – a useful, necessary construction to explain who the Turks are, and how their lives are connected with their past. This imperial myth was not cultivated by Erdoğan but rather has been a part of Anatolian identity and politics since the end of the caliphate in the early twentieth century. This myth also has been at the core of the Gülen movement and the support it receives from Anatolian business communities throughout the world. The mission: protect and advance Islamic civilisation under the leadership of Turkey and create an economically powerful Turkey able to achieve this and deter ongoing Western imperialism and invasions of the Middle East.

Arnold Toynbee, one of the most prominent British historians of the past century, wrote about the pervasive sense of humiliation amongst global Muslim populations in the wake of brutal Western imperial invasions. In a 1948 essay, entitled 'Islam, the West, and the Future', he explained the Muslim world had been stuck in crisis mode since the nineteenth century because it had been defeated, left undeveloped and besieged by Western powers. The Muslims, rightly proud of their artistic, scientific and literary legacies, were 'facing the West with her back to the wall', causing stress, anger and humiliation among Muslims.[16] Erdoğan regards the restoration of Muslim identity as something like the decolonisation of the native mind, as famously expounded upon in the work of the Afro-Caribbean psychiatrist Frantz Fanon.[17] There is an entrenched sense of national humiliation – an unresolved sense of injustice among the Anatolian Muslims, as well as in Erdoğan. The humiliation of the vanquished Ottoman Empire haunts the conservative Muslim masses.[18]

Erdoğan's decision to convert the Hagia Sophia, a popular tourist attraction in Istanbul, from a church museum into a mosque has been welcomed by the conservative Muslim masses, who view it as a milestone in Turkey's rebirth as a powerful Muslim nation. Indeed, the decision to reconvert the Hagia Sophia to a mosque encapsulates his agenda of imperial delusions. Built in the middle of the sixth century as the Byzantine Empire's cathedral, the Hagia Sophia was converted into a mosque when the Ottomans conquered the city in 1453.

In an essay published in a Cambridge University Press volume about the Hagia Sophia from the Justinian age to the present, Gülru Necipoğlu, a Turkish-born scholar of Islamic art who is on the Harvard faculty, wrote that, 'the appropriation of Hagia Sophia as an imperial and religious symbol by the Ottoman sultans had involved an awareness of its former significance'.[19] She adds that the Ottoman conversion in 1453 is a 'striking example of cultural confrontation in a frontier zone where the conquerors chose to define their self-identity in terms of the conquered, while simultaneously remaining meaningful to their own past'. As Tugba Tanyeri-Erdemir of the Anti-Defamation League's task force on religious minorities noted on Twitter, the Christian imagery remained uncovered for more than three centuries, signalling that 'many Ottoman sultans did not have a problem praying under the image of the Virgin and the Baby in the apse'.

It was Mustafa Kemal Atatürk, at the founding of the Turkish Republic, who converted the mosque into a museum, which occurred in 1934 under the Ministry of Education's jurisdiction. This was a clear sign of Atatürk's commitment to the new Republic's humanistic, secular identity. As Necipoğlu concludes, the national museum proved its 'remarkable flexibility in adapting to a new context, a flexibility that ensured its continued life through the ages'.

Atatürk's decision triggered *ressentiment* in Turkey's conservative, religious groups that has festered since the 1930s. However, with the gradual emergence of Islamist political parties in recent generations, one could already see, beginning in 1991, the efforts to restore the Hagia Sophia to its former grandeur as an Ottoman mosque. In that year, a hall was reserved exclusively for Muslim prayers. In 2016, a full-time imam was appointed, who leads the Islamic call to prayer (known as *ezan* in Turkish).

If we return to the previous chapter, the Hagia Sophia decision is clarified in context. Erdoğan was raised and educated in an İmam Hatip school (religious seminary) with an Islamic-focused curriculum couched in deep resentment against secularised Turkey and Western influences they saw as forcing them to deny their true identities. The politics of resentment in Turkey has evoked similar movements elsewhere. It is nativist, nationalist and vengeful to the point of cruelty. Erdoğan's experiences as a youth were certainly filled with stories and hopes that at some point the Hagia Sophia would be restored as a grand mosque. Thus, he sees this as achieving a major act of political vengeance. He opened the museum to prayer on 24 July 2020, the anniversary of the signing of the Lausanne Treaty, which established the territory of the Turkish Republic. He sees it as the culmination of a vision of his sole intellectual muse who died more than 35 years ago – Necip Fazıl Kısakürek, a racist, anti-Semitic Islamist who tirelessly advocated for reversing Atatürk's secularising course. Kısakürek saw the restoration of the Hagia Sophia as essential. To wit: Albayrak, Erdoğan's son-in-law, sent a tweet reading, 'As master Necip Fazıl Kısakürek said 55 years ago: "Wait, youngsters. Either today or tomorrow, Hagia Sophia will be opened".'

Erdoğan's vision of Turkey is not secular or pro-European, but instead the Hagia Sophia is also integral to his campaign to make Istanbul the headquarters for the Muslim Brotherhood. In his speech to restore the Hagia Sophia into a mosque, he also renewed his call to end the occupation of Al-Aqsa mosque in Jerusalem. He said, 'The revival of Hagia Sophia is the harbinger of freedom of Al-Aqsa and the footsteps of Muslims emerging from the era of interregnum.' Erdoğan's Hagia Sophia decision is perhaps the clearest example to date of how he and his most loyal supporters espouse a political agenda predicated on nostalgia for the former Ottoman grandeur. They insist that the Kemalist reforms since the founding of the Republic had unfairly chained the people from realising fully their spiritual and cultural identities (that is, Islam).

One aspect of this humiliation is the concept of self-colonisation – becoming alien to one's own heritage. In Turkey, humiliation is not only the loss of the Ottoman Empire's core but also about how the national-self had been coercively reengineered by Kemalism. Erdoğan has become the tribune of Islamic nationalism that sought to vindicate this humiliation as first articulated by Kısakürek. He treats Islam as a counter ideology, a reservoir of shared perceptions that run against the impulses of 'self-colonisation'. By self-colonisation, these Islamist intellectuals see Kemalist-driven political culture as surrendering to Europe's cultural supremacy and imposing Western mores and customs wholesale on Muslim societies. By stressing Islamic symbols, concepts and narratives, he has managed to forge an emotional bond with large sectors of the Sunni population. The meaning of modern Turkish nationalism continues to evolve, shifting away from a near-total adoration of Atatürk and the state to a renewed love of homeland and the Seljuk and Ottoman heritage. However, Erdoğan has little regard for an ethnic sense of nationalism. His primary identity is Islam, and he sees the world from a religious perspective. For instance, in his widely criticised speech in Siirt he railed against divisions among Turkish citizens based on ethnicity and region, emphasising instead the existence of ties that bind all together in Turkey: 'When I was in the university, people used to say: "You are from Rize and are a Laz".' He continues to say that when he asked his father about his identity his father responded that he too had asked his grandfather the same question, and he had said:

> When it's time to die, God will only ask us: 'Who is your God? Who is your prophet? And what is your religion?' He will not ask: 'What is your ethnicity?' Thus, whenever someone inquires about your identity, you should simply reply: 'Thank God (*Elhamdulillah*) I am a Muslim!' That is adequate.[20]

For Erdoğan, an individual's ultimate identity is predicated on his faith and cultural enlightenment. He has little sympathy for other ideas of nation or nationalism. This should not be mistaken as a dismissal of patriotism as a legitimate dynamic, but it does signal that his worldview is shaped almost wholly by his religious upbringing, which supersedes his ethnic or regional origins.

During a recent visit to Moscow, Erdoğan had a revealing encounter with a Kurdish worker (Zulfikar Boran) who was a construction worker at the site of a new Turkish business centre. This was the first time Erdoğan had aired his views on the Kurdish problem in public. In these comments, Erdoğan's worldview on nationalism and the role of Islamic identity becomes clear. When Boran tells Erdoğan, 'The Kurdish problem must be addressed and the people should not suffer anymore', Erdoğan, after a short exchange, tells Boran that

> There is no Kurdish question in Turkey. If you believe there is a problem, only then the problem emerges; if you believe there isn't any problem, then the problem disappears. If we assert that there is a Kurdish question, we become part of a virtually created problem. No such problem exists for us.[21]

After this exchange, Erdoğan hugged Boran and said, 'I love you for the sake of Allah.' This conversation helps to decipher Erdoğan's lack of sympathy for nationalism and ethnicity as independent motivating factors for political mobilisation and social cohesion. From Erdoğan's perspective the nation is a religious community and the people of Turkey constitute a nation by sharing an Islamic heritage. This perspective not only prevents Erdoğan from pursuing an ethnic solution to the Kurdish question but also his lack of Turkish nationalism became a mobilising cry for many Turkish nationalists who worry the AKP government has been working to de-Turkify the nation.

Erdoğan's solution to ethnic nationalism, as a divisive force in the country, and to the problems caused by self-colonisation of the mind is to educate a pious generation of citizens. After the 2011 elections, there was a reluctant yet reassuring call from Erdoğan to raise a 'religious generation'.[22] He reiterated this proposition in February 2016.[23] Ackerman and Calisir aptly assert that:

> In Turkey, where there has been a rise in Islamic religiosity, President Recep Tayyip Erdoğan, founder of the pro-Islamist Development and Justice Party (AKP), is converting some public schools into seminaries called *Imam-Hatips* (or traditional training schools for Sunni Muslim clergy) in an effort to raise a generation of 'pious youth'.[24]

This call or objective assumes that moral problems and the perceived feelings of shame and inferiority in the public square can only be cured by giving the youth a mandatory religious education. Although the Republican People's Party (CHP), the main opposition party, criticised Erdoğan's proposal, stating it is not the secular state's duty to indoctrinate its youth by providing religious instruction, there is a shared assumption in the country that Islam is the antidote to corruption, crime and immorality. During the Cold War, conservative, as well as secular parties, regarded religious education as a necessary fortification against Communism and the radical leftist movements in the country. At the time of the coup of 1980, the military enacted a course on Islamic instruction as mandatory and regarded a 'Turkish-Islamic synthesis' as the essential cohesive element to enhance national integration.

2.3 Erdoğan and the Problematic of Secularism

> Those two cities are interwoven and intermixed in this era, and await separation at the last judgement.
>
> Augustine, *The City of God*

The secularising and nationalising reforms of the early Turkish Republic also politicised the extant four social cleavages around which political parties are organised. The major cleavages which remain are: Sunni vs Alevi; secular versus religious; and the Turkish versus Kurdish ethnic divide. As a result of these religious and ethnic cleavages, there is another political cleavage between those who demand and seek to impose a secular lifestyle against those who demand a more religious (Sunni) one. Thus, political parties in Turkey are organised around these cleavages. The AKP represents the Turkish Sunni majority, although it has also appealed to large segments of the religious Kurdish population.

For the AKP, Turkish secularism has been a maligned, oppressive social force because unlike the Anglo-American tradition of secularism, it was actively modelled on the anti-religious ideology of Jacobin France, which sought to drive all religious sentiment and influence from the public sphere and eventually the private one as well. For the AKP, secularism is defined as the freedom of religion from state intervention and the protection of both individual and communal religious rights. Secularism, for Erdoğan, is necessary for democracy but it should not at the same time infringe on the democratic rights of those who take their religious values and faith seriously.[25] Erdoğan's understanding of secularism is similar to that of previous Turkish leaders of centre-right parties, such as Süleyman Demirel who, in the face of the anti-religious Kemalist *Kulturkampf* led by the CHP's Ismet İnönü, contended that secularism should not be interpreted as hostility to religion: the state could and should be secular, but individuals had a right to choose to be or not to be religious. Erdoğan explains:

> Before anything else, I'm a Muslim. As a Muslim, I try to comply with the requirements of my religion. I have a responsibility to God, who created me, and I try to fulfil that responsibility. But now I try very much to keep this away from my political life, to keep it private. 'A political party cannot have a religion. Only individuals can. Otherwise, you'd be exploiting religion, and religion is so supreme that it cannot be exploited or be taken advantage of.'[26]

This understanding of secularism is also defended by the centre and religious-right parties in Turkey that treat secularisation as a process, not a project, demonstrating a flexible settlement between religion and politics that could be modified according to the needs of society through democratic negotiation. This version is based on four assumptions: (1) Islam is the source of Turkish identity and morality and it should have the primary role in society not in the state; (2) Islamic morality and networks are beneficial for social order and economic activity; (3) the state should provide religious (that is, Sunni-Hanafi) education in public schools and the DRA (Religious Affairs Directorate) should maintain its activities in accordance with the needs of the state; and (4) pan-Islamic solidarity should be utilised in foreign policy and Turkey should join the EU not to assimilate but rather to reinvigorate Islamic civilisation elsewhere. For Muslims, or those who support the AKP, Islam is the soul of the country and a crucial aspect of Turkish identity that should be respected and utilised.

Deeper than the normal struggles for political power is the conflict over values and identities superimposed on the conflict over secularism and what constitutes Turkish identity itself. The AKP's electoral successes from 2002 to 2013 were linked to the search for a new value system and the triumph of democracy over militaristic secularism and the restoration of the rule of law. This conflict over values should not lead to the tearing apart of Turkey's social fabric. Hopefully, it could compel Turkey to develop a social contract among contending political parties and institutions to deal with the diversity of values and to cultivate an expansive democratic understanding of secularism.

The Turkish-Muslim understanding of secularism is predicated on three major defining characteristics: the state should get involved in and promote religious education and impose religious morality. Islam, for Turkish-Islamic secularists, is an integral part of Turkish identity, and Islam should be integrated into the national identity and foreign policy as well. Turks historically served as the *seyfülislam* (the sword and shield of Islam) for defending the Muslim world from brutal invaders starting with the Frankish Crusaders, then the Mongols, and finally European imperialists commencing with the Portuguese, who even threatened to sack Mecca and Medina and desecrate the tomb of the Prophet until they were checked by the renowned Ottoman Admiral Piri Reis. The conflict between the first two understandings of secularism runs deeper than many anticipate. It is between the claims of a religiously rooted communal ethical life and that of the republican principles of a secular society in which a form of scientific materialism becomes the sole organising principle for both state and society.

Erdoğan's conceptualisation of religion and politics cannot be fully comprehended without understanding the master concept of *hizmet* (rendering social service and welfare in the name of Islam) as it is ensconced in the political language of Turks.[27] The ideal of *hizmet* weaves politics, community, historic mission and tradition together, which requires openness to change and the utilisation of technology to create better economic conditions for society's development. Erdoğan's politics is based on his understanding of community. Here, he emphasises shared religious language, symbols and values where the family serves as the building block of these communities. Thus, his social policies seek to encourage marriage and support families to have children. He also treats the educational system as the most effective tool to instil family values and to cultivate shared identities and values of the Turkish (Muslim) nation.

2.4 Erdoğan and Democratic Legitimacy

> Democracy is like a train; you get off once you have reached your [real] destination.
>
> Recep Tayyip Erdoğan[28]

Erdoğan's concept of politics and democracy must be understood within the general context of Turkish political culture. Machiavelli's *The Prince* offers some broad patterns of political legitimacy in Turkey. His comparison of the Turkish ruler with the King of France, for example, is instructive and relevant:

> The examples of these two governments in our time are the Turk and the King of France. The entire monarchy of the Turk is governed by one lord, the others are his servants; and, dividing his kingdom into *sanjaks*, he sends there different administrators, and shifts and changes them as he chooses. But the King of France is placed in the midst of an ancient body of lords, acknowledged by their own subjects, and beloved by them; they have their own prerogatives, nor can the king take these away except at his peril. Therefore, he who considers both of these states will recognize great difficulties in seizing the state of the Turk, but, once it is conquered, great ease in holding it. The causes of the difficulties in seizing the kingdom of the Turk are that the usurper cannot be called in by the princes of the kingdom, nor can he hope to be assisted in his designs by the revolt of those whom the lord has around him. This arises from the reasons given above; for his ministers, being all slaves and bondmen, can only be corrupted with great difficulty, and one can expect little advantage from them when they have been corrupted, as they cannot carry the people with them, for the reasons assigned.
>
> Hence, he who attacks the Turk must bear in mind that he will find him united, and he will have to rely more on his own strength than on the revolt of others; but, if once the Turk has been conquered, and routed in the field in such a way that he cannot replace his armies, there is nothing to fear but the family of the prince, and, this being exterminated, there remains no one to fear, the others having no credit with the people; and as the conqueror did not rely on them before his victory, so he ought not to fear them after it.[29]

This is an intriguing excerpt because what Machiavelli argues about the vertical power structure of the Ottoman sultan exemplifies the contemporary

Turkish political system, including the leaders of political parties who have a tradition of acting as sultans. Political parties are ruled by one charismatic leader and the members and parliamentarians are 'all slaves bound in loyalty to their master' – the party boss. Because these parliamentarians are nominated by the party leaders, they derive their positions from the party leader. Thus, they are more loyal to the party leader who is less likely to compromise with other parties on vital issues. Erdoğan asked Davutoğlu, then prime minister, to resign his post, a request that he followed. He was aware that the AKP is owned by Erdoğan. Rather than challenge Erdoğan on his own partisan turf, he established his own party and became its leader. However, when a new party leader takes over, it is not difficult to control the parliamentarians. In this regard, Erdoğan is no different from other party leaders in Turkey. He is the 'sultan' of the AKP, as Kılıçdaroğlu is of CHP, or Bahçeli of MHP.

Following his imprisonment in 1999, Erdoğan's political enemies in the Kemalist establishment were counting on public apathy as they removed him as a long-term popular and charismatic threat to their hold on power. Instead, the trumped-up charges and imprisonment over reciting lines from a famous poem led to a widespread backlash, greatly increasing his popularity. Both Muslim groups, especially the followers of the National Outlook Movement (Milli Görüş Hareketi (MGH), as well as many liberals impressed with his relatively clean and efficient tenure as Istanbul mayor did not forget Erdoğan while he was imprisoned. The masses saw him as a victim of a fundamentally corrupt and authoritarian political system bent upon subverting the popular will. Erdoğan's resurrection coincided with the growing popular faith in the electoral system and the sense that the newly emerging middle class was empowered to change the political landscape. In response to his increasing popularity and the intransigence of the establishment, Erdoğan cast himself as a moderate centrist open to appeals to liberal-minded Turks as well. It was at this time that he broke from the isolated Islamist outlook of his mentor Necmettin Erbakan and his National Outlook Movement.

In 2002 and on the heels of a financial crisis caused by the corruption and mismanagement of the ruling establishment, the AKP came to power in a sweeping electoral victory. Erdoğan was determined to focus on his main campaign issues of bringing about economic stability and growth and expanding and consolidating Turkish democracy. Privatisation and export-led growth were part of Erdoğan's magical solution for addressing Turkey's economic and social problems. One centrepiece of this strategy was pursuing diligently the Copenhagen Criteria set by the EU for attaining candidate status and eventually full membership. The irony here was that the Kemalist establishment since 1955 increasingly justified its authoritarian tutelage over Turkish society by arguing that it was necessary in order to achieve full membership in the community of European nations. However, as it became clear in the 2000s that this would entail sweeping political reforms and freedoms, the Kemalist establishment cooled on the European quest. Rather, it was the AKP which became the main champion of pursuing EU membership to secure Turkey's place in the leading Western bloc but also to complete the country's transition away from Kemalist authoritarianism. The Kemalist military-bureaucratic establishment found itself in an impossible situation. They had justified their authoritarianism and indulgence of 'corrective' *coups d'état* as necessary to safeguard the country's sacred march westwards and now could hardly disown their very *raison d'être*.

As Erdoğan distanced himself from his Islamist roots, even questioning them from a liberal-democratic perspective, he became more popular not only among the centre-right voters but also many liberals wary of Kemalist authoritarianism. In this period, he even rejected the label of 'Muslim democrat' to describe the AKP. *The Financial Times* quoted Erdoğan in 2004:

> Let me be quite open and clear in stating a fact – we don't find it appropriate to mix religion and politics . . . We are not Muslim democrats; we are conservative democrats. Some in the West portray us as [Muslim democrats] but our notion of conservative democracy is to attach ourselves to the customs and the traditions and the values of our society, which is based on family. This is a democratic issue, not a religious one.[30]

However, this did not overcome the scepticism of the Kemalist establishment regarding Erdoğan's actual intention to dismantle the Kemalist secular principles of the Republic. The military secularist media and intellectuals never believed in Erdoğan's self-declared conversion to liberalism, and they issued numerous warnings. After the Gezi Park protests, many liberals who had defended Erdoğan turned against him, accusing him of being an Islamist autocrat. A common narrative promoted by domestic and foreign critics is that Erdoğan was always disassembling regarding democracy and secularism, and once he consolidated power he showed his true face. However, such a teleological narrative lacks nuance and fails to account for how domestic and foreign crises reshaped Erdoğan's policies and worldviews. The backsliding on issues such as freedom of the press, democracy, the rule of law and toleration of political dissent did not occur in a vacuum after 2010. Turkey was buffeted by a series of crises which included last-ditch entrenched opposition efforts from the Kemalist 'deep state' and the attendant rise of a Gülenist 'parallel state', both of which sought to use subterfuge and extrajudicial and even violent means to overthrow the elected government. At the regional and international levels, the fallout of the Arab Spring triggered a huge crisis as the murderous Assad regime created millions of refugees and the PKK (Kurdish) militants saw an opportunity to resist disarmament and push for a separatist state in parts of Syria, Iraq and Turkey. One cannot take into account Erdoğan's harsh response to political opposition from actors linked to the Gülen movement as well as the Kurdish nationalist People's Democratic Party (HDP) without taking these factors into account.

In 2007, despite enjoying overwhelming popular support and a commanding parliamentary majority, Erdoğan felt besieged by the unelected Kemalist establishment in the judiciary, military and the media. Starting with the military's e-memorandum over the accession of Abdullah Gül as the Republic's president, ostensibly because his wife wore a headscarf, the Kemalist establishment sought to decertify the elections and declare the AKP illegal. It was then that Erdoğan consolidated a fateful alliance with the Gülen movement and through a series of controversial trials (Ergenekon and Balyoz) moved to neuter the entrenched Kemalist strongholds in the military, police and judiciary. He was able gradually to put these institutions under his control one by one. A prominent politician, who asked not to be named, said:

> In the case of Turkey, Islamic parties were always allowed to participate in political processes, but under close supervision of the secular establishment such as the military, judiciary and civil services. Thus, whenever Islamic parties tried to overstep their boundaries and bring religion back into the public sphere or undermine the secular nature of the state, they were either shut down by the Constitutional Courts or by forced out by the military in 1960, 1971, 1980 and 1997.[31]

The past four coups targeted the Islamic parties which enjoyed overwhelming popular support. Erdoğan was socialised in this context and with the stories of the traumatic execution of Prime Minister Adnan Menderes and when the future prime minister/president was freed from prison in 1998, he was fully cognisant that such a fate would threaten anyone seen as capable of displacing the Kemalist establishment. Erdoğan has always opened up more space for Islamic activism and rolled back opportunities for an unelected Kemalist establishment.

Since 2010, Erdoğan's dominance has eclipsed not only the political opposition but his colleagues and potential rivals in the AKP as well. Once a champion of democratisation and human rights, the irony is that this now occurs outside of the party and in opposition to Erdoğan himself. The attendant weakening of institutions can be seen in the AKP itself as Erdoğan has criticised his MPs for presenting amendments to bills drafted by bureaucrats.[32] He sees little merit in the sausage-making metaphor often associated with drafting and enacting legislation as a democratic norm. Stephen Kinzer, *The New York Times* reporter and author, concluded from a meeting with Erdoğan that he has a 'burning sense of his own authority. He sees himself personally, not his party or government, as the force driving Turkey today'.[33] He sees himself as a man of destiny with a God-ordained mission to lead the country, and he barely tolerates criticism. Moreover, there is a growing gap between AKP cabinet members and ordinary MPs. This behaviour has worsened at an accelerating pace, unfortunately.

Erdoğan embodies a tension between democracy and liberalism first highlighted by the philosophers of the Enlightenment such as Locke, Rousseau, Montesquieu and Constant. From Erdoğan's perspective, the primary meaning of democracy is the representation of the national will (*milli irade*), which is central to political legitimacy. By *milli irade*, he means winning the majority of votes in order to govern the country. He hardly realises that this conception of the general will could lead to the tyranny of the majority. Jacob Talmon, a leading political theorist on the origins of totalitarian democracy, explains that the idea of the general will as the only source of political authority leads to a 'totalitarian democracy'.[34] Indeed, major issue challenges we all face today (including the US) are the idea of the infallibility of the majority and attempts to subjugate the rest of the population to majority rule.

Erdoğan's understanding of democracy is a process of winning elections and ruling according to the needs and expectations of the electoral majority. It is a way of establishing legitimacy for the governance of the country. Democracy becomes a means rather than an end in itself. The end is to replace Kemalist system with his own Islamic hegemony, address the problems of his constituency, and offer the best possible social services to his supporters. This is what Erdoğan meant in his oft-cited controversial and yet honest statement that, 'Democracy is a train which takes you where you want to go, and allows you to get off at whatever stop you want.'[35] He always is hostile to criticism. We know from the testimony of Mehmet Metiner:

> Erdoğan does not like outright criticisms directed at him in public. He internalises all kinds of criticism and suggestions when relayed to him in person, but he would not shy away from guarding himself against highly oppositional criticism made in public. He also knows perfectly well to get back at those critiques when the time comes. It is known that he was relentless against those individuals and groups who were opposing him during his tenure as head of Istanbul Party Branch. He is extremely democratic when it comes to giving authority and opportunities to his advisers and teammates but has an authoritarian personality when it comes to ruling. While he wants to work with talented people, he demands unquestionable loyalty at all times. Oftentimes, he considers their criticisms and warnings as having been dictated by others; hence takes them head on while accusing them of disloyalty.[36]

Erdoğan's account of democracy flows from the belief that democracy provides the best possible source of legitimacy as well as offering the most efficient solution to meeting the demands of the majority of the population. The task of elected officials is to meet the expectations of those who elected them. This majoritarian view of democracy also is problematic, especially in a diverse and polarised polity like Turkey. It offers little in the way of reconciliation and the integration of the sizable electorate which voted against the AKP. This was not always the case in the early tenure of AKP rule when the much more conciliatory Abdullah Gül also played a prominent role. From 2002 to 2008, the AKP did make a genuine and quite successful effort to appeal to oppositional segments of society such as secular-liberals, Kurds and even Alevis. This changed as Erdoğan centralised decision making and faced increasing discontent following the 2010 elections.

Erdoğan discounts freedom of press as being an essential part of the definition of democracy. He has said the media in Europe unlike that in Turkey

> is not a hitman for criminal gangs, some journalists don't encourage coups, exploit the freedom of the press to execute psychological operations ... My esteemed friends, the allegations of establishing a terrorist organisation to disband democracy and constitutional order is an issue which cannot be overshadowed by debates of the freedom of the press.[37]

Although when he was in opposition, Erdoğan developed a powerful and effective criticism of the Turkish media and its use by the media bosses and politicians as a 'weapon' to delegitimise the opposition, Erdoğan in government fully controls the Turkish media (by owning some of them and controlling the almost every newspapers, TVs and radio stations) and he has 'zero tolerance' to any form of criticism. The Turkish media often does not operate according to a professional code of ethics. It has served to spread disinformation in the interest of powerful magnates. This has especially been the case since the transformation of the media ownership from Aydın Doğan, whose deep state ties have raised concerns along with his support of military coups like the one on 28 February 1997 when the government of Prime Minister Erbakan was forced from power, to the Erdoğan family or to his close associates. For instance, *Sabah* and its media outlet with magazines, TV and radio stations, are all controlled by Erdoğan and his son-in-law. Turkey's traditional newspapers, *Hürriyet* and *Milliyet*, used to be owned by Doğan, who was forced to sell to close Erdoğan associates, the Demirören family.[38]

In the past, as Erdoğan aptly puts it, the media was 'the representative of the authoritarian consensus that disempowers the National Will'.[39] He continued, 'we derive our political power from the nation only, not from the media'.[40] When he was not in control of the media, Erdoğan advocated that the media have a vital role in the functioning of democracy; now he complains that the media cannot be allowed to undermine the national will or the stability of the state. Many critics of Erdoğan accuse him of being an intolerant and ruthless despot who uses state power to enrich himself and keep his cronies in power. The main criticism of Erdoğan has been his kleptocratic practices to enrich himself and his family members. In fact, these charges have enough empirical evidence to open a case against him and his associates. However, since he has been controlling the judiciary, no prosecutor would dare to raise a question about these practices.

Erdoğan's views about democracy and religion are complex because he does not see the possibility of bracketing religious lives and belief in democratic society. Yet, he does not support a theocratic system and instead stresses the virtues of the republican system as long as the majority dictates the policies. He argues that religious citizens or faith-based organisations could enhance public life and enrich the political debate by bringing the perspectives of the religious sectors of the community into dialogue. Erdoğan, like some Republican communitarians in the US, is sceptical of the idea that the liberal state must be neutral in relation to public goods and cultural issues. He believes that in order for the state to have more solid legitimacy it must protect the lives, shared culture and memories of that society. Erdoğan's understanding of the state is not a neutral entity but one punctuated by the cultural ethos of that society. The state should have a task in soul craft or shaping the identity and moral character of its citizens as well. In his political life, he realises the role of Islam in socially integrating diverse communities and providing a shared language of political unity. He doesn't endorse a strict separation between religious and political views as necessary for a well-functioning democratic system, but he does accept that many people with alternative lifestyles and beliefs should not be coerced by those who are religious either.

Erdoğan's main concern has not been 'how could we all get along' within one political system regardless of our religious, ethnic and life-style differences. On the contrary, he believes that the state should represent Hanefi-Turkish concerns and defend their religio-political view. He belives that the religious minorities should be 'tolerated'. Erdoğan is a pragmatic populist, an authoritarian, who cares more about loyalty and obedience, as well as protecting and defending his Islamist lifestyle or his ideological position. Jan-Werner Muller's definition of populism is useful to understand Erdoğan's conception of politics.[41] He is a populist politician who speaks in the name of 'the people' and presents his policies and statements as the feeling and desires of the people. According to Erdoğan, a legitimate policy is what the majority of the people want. When the opposition questions the rule of law or the concerns of others who are also citizens of Turkey, Erdoğan as a populist politician frames them as adversaries who seek to flout the will of the majority. By 'the people', he means those who support his policies and identify with him. He ignores those who disagree or vote against his policies – framed as 'the other people' who seek to undermine the state. Muller also explains that populists operate in animosity to pluralism. Erdoğan appears to be agitated by liberal democracy's necessity of having a robust legal checks and balances system. The Kurdish politician Dengir Mir Mehmet Fırat, once one of Erdoğan's closest associates, said:

> He used the minorities in the early period of his government and then became the worst enemy of the Kurds. He, in fact, with his Kurdish reform programme, known as 'the Kurdish Opening', and his sharp attack on the Kemalist counterinsurgency policies in 1934 such as the Dersim campaign raised the expectations and appetites of the Kurds. The Kurds, including myself, rallied around him to humanise the exposed Turkish state. He first raised the Kurdish ethnic aspirations and then destroyed the Kurdish political movement at the same time.[42]

Reha Camuroğlu, a prominent Alevi intellectual, who also became a MP from the AKP, and then resigned from the party, explained that:

> His policy towards the Alevi community is horrible. He regularly insulted them and never promoted a single Alevi to any government position. For him, we Alevis are all *cünüb* [a pejorative term meaning a ritually impure condition if one does not wash himself after a discharge of semen]. He has polarised society and used this polarisation to keep his supporters always on the offence. He prefers divisions and tension in society so that he can use one side against the other.[43]

Likewise, my university colleague (also an Alevi), who is a government employee, said:

> I used to see this state as my state. Under the government of Erdoğan, I gradually came to realise that this state is a Sunni entity and there is no room

for us as Alevis. I do not see hope for my three children in this country. I told my son to move wherever he can. There is no single Alevi in any high position of the state. We have become the stepchildren of this state – and unwanted ones.[44]

On 23 November 2011, Erdoğan apologised on behalf of the state for the killings of Kurdish Alevi citizens in the province of Dersim [Tunceli] in 1937–8. He said:

> Is it me who should apologise or you [Kemal Kılıçdaroğlu] . . .? If there is an apology on behalf of the state and if there is such an opportunity, I can do it and I am apologising. But if there is someone who should apologise on behalf of the CHP, it is you, as you are from Dersim. You were saying you felt honoured to be from Dersim. Now, save your honour.[45]

The early Turkish Republic overreacted to the insurgency led by Alevi leaders against the state's authority. The insurgency was quashed by an overwhelming display of military power with aerial bombings that killed hundreds. Many Alevis interpreted this apology as a rhetorical manoeuvre against Kemal Kılıçdaroğlu, the leader of Atatürk's CHP party, whose family came from Dersim. Erdoğan said:

> Dersim is the most tragic event in our recent history. It is a disaster that should now be questioned with courage. If someone is to apologise for and face up to this tragedy, it is not the AKP and the AKP government but the CHP, the author of this bloody episode, as well as the CHP deputies and the CHP chairman who hails from Tunceli.[46]

The apology failed to win many Alevis over and today there is more fear and suspicion than ever among the Alevi community towards the AKP. Erdoğan's main goal was to expand the anti-CHP and anti-Kemalist front by politicising the sufferings of the Alevi community.[47]

When Erdoğan was in the political opposition, especially after his imprisonment in 1998, he regularly defended religious freedoms based on a Western model, along with Anglo-Saxon secularism. Erdoğan in government has hardly opened such spaces for Turkey's large Alevi community. This is especially true concerning the state's Directorate of Religious Affairs (DRA) which only recognises the Sunni form of Islam at the state level.

He is the most popular leader among the Sunni-Turkish majority population. Moreover, Erdoğan, as William Holt, a historian of the Ottoman Empire, explains, represents a larger phenomenon observed elsewhere in the world, even including the US. Holt writes of the political phenomenon:

> I have given it the name of 'the revenge of the countryside' and it is founded in an anti-elite, anti-intellectual, victim complex. It might be worth exploring more the anger of Anatolian periphery towards the elites and the wealthy. The question of course is when, if ever, will they start seeing the current government as a new set of elites disconnected from them?[48]

The cognitive dissonance intensified during the latter half of the 2010s, as Erdoğan fortified his executive powers and became more vengeful against his opponents.

2.5 Erdoğan's Political Language

Erdoğan's political language essentially resonates with the tone and discourse of the periphery. He talks frequently about the greatness of the Ottoman Empire, the catastrophic defeats and expulsion of the Muslims from the Balkans, Islamic civilisation, national sovereignty, independence and, especially, economic development. His political language returns to the basic challenge of how to restore Turkey's historic greatness. Erdoğan's experience as mayor of Istanbul in the 1990s shaped his strategic comprehension of politics, assuring him that citizens expect services (*hizmet*), not ideology or expansive ideas. His understanding of politics was transformed.

Politics, for Erdoğan, was to create better living conditions for the majority. His conception of politics as a function of constituent services was embodied in the AKP's name, highlighting justice and development. In his first parliamentary group meeting in Bilkent Hotel on 11 November 2002, after the elections, Erdoğan mentioned the term *hizmet* at least eight times to explain the mission of the Party as economic development and democratisation.[49] His conceptualisation of politics as offering service also shaped his comprehension of the state and bureaucracy. He states simply that 'the basic value is human being and the task of the state is to serve for this human being'.⁵⁰ Erdoğan sought to maintain the Özalian philosophy of public management in terms of shifting bureaucratic culture from its civilisation-building project to a platform dedicated primarily to the people for the purposes of improving their daily lives.⁵¹

Moreover, under Erdoğan, Turkey has adopted and implemented numerous democratisation projects which consolidated the rule of law and improved conditions for Kurdish political rights that included development projects in areas of the country with the strongest concentrations of Kurdish population. This was the first time in Turkish history that Kurdish civil and political rights were recognised and guaranteed. As a condition for joining the EU, Erdoğan amended the constitution several times and put the military and the judiciary under civilian government control. For the first time in Turkey's history, elective Kurdish courses were introduced in middle schools (2012) and legislation was passed in 2013 to allow establishing private Kurdish language schools. Furthermore, the AKP abolished the mandatory national security course that was proctored by military officers in high schools. As part of the democratisation package, Erdoğan announced, on 30 September 2013, that the national oath-taking ceremony in primary schools would be abolished.

As he has controlled the different layers of power, his conception of politics has also changed. Politics for him means a bundle of activities: the process to disestablish Kemalist secularism; bringing Islamic values into the public sphere and defending and imposing Islamic conservative values on the society; removing the hegemonic position of the military from the decision-making processes; and as he controlled almost every branch of the state since 2013, politics became a business to amass wealth and enrich his family and destroy his opponents. Thus, after 2013, Erdoğan's political ideology changed in several ways: (1) how to control the power and consolidate his grip on society; (2) how to deploy state institutions, especially the judiciary, to undercut the opposition; and (3) how to use patronage to create a class of loyal crony capitalists around him. The shift from politics as offering services to perpetuating a self-serving elite unconcerned about checks and balances has become the story of modern Turkey.

When I asked Hüseyin Besli, a close confidant and speech writer of Erdoğan, 'How do you explain the shift from pro-EU, pro-democracy, and pro-human rights defender Erdoğan to oppressive Erdoğan who does not allow any form of criticism?', he agreed that there has been a 'major change' in the vision and practices of Erdoğan. Not only Besli but a number of his close associates who used to work with him before 2013 agree that there are two Erdoğans: democrat Erdoğan before 2013, and autocrat Erdoğan after 2013. They usually explain this shift as a result of the three seismic events of 2013. A group of past and present advisors of Erdoğan, just like Besli, summed up these 2013 events in the following way: the Gezi Park incident which was funded and organised by the West; the coup against the democratically elected Morsi [Mohamed] in Egypt, which was also defended by the US; and the Gülenist judiciary coup against the government of Erdoğan. An advisor who served as his minister argues that

> these three events convinced *Reis* [an honorific term bestowed upon Erdoğan by his supporters] to realise that they [the West] is after him and he had to protect himself with all means. What do you expect him to do? He had to become more authoritarian and suspicious of the people around him.[52]

There are several reasons for the AKP's unbroken string of electoral successes. They include the party's socio-economic connections with the conservative networks of society; the efficient and effective performance in local and national governance; Erdoğan's charismatic personality as the leader of the conservative political platform; and improvements through healthcare, transportation and mega-construction projects. When the AKP came to power in 2002, Turkey faced a major economic crisis which resulted in the collapse of the coalition government led by the popular prime minister Bülent Ecevit. Erdoğan closely pursued the economic policies introduced by Kemal Derviş after the 2001 crisis and curbed inflation and brought stability to the chaotic markets. Turkey adopted a new currency and eliminated the papers of Turkish lira that had been inflated to seven figures. Under his government, Turkey has enjoyed long-term economic stability and phenomenal growth on its way to becoming the seventeenth largest economy in the world, at the time of this book's publication. Erdoğan's economic and foreign policies were instrumental in bringing huge foreign investments from the Gulf countries as well as from European countries. Thus, Turkey's infrastructure has been transformed as a result of economic growth.

After 2013, Erdoğan stressed the 2023 vision as the benchmarking goal of Turkey becoming a major economic and geopolitical power by the centennial of the establishment of the Turkish Republic. Considering the AKP's opposition to the founding symbols of the Republic, the goal and the vision of 2023 is to produce a new identity for the state and nation. Erdoğan's 2023 vision promises an economically powerful Turkey but not necessarily a vibrant civil society that champions the rule of law and pluralism. Erdoğan has supervised mega projects worth more than US$200 billion, easily representing one-quarter of Turkey's annual GDP. This includes the expansive mosque project on Çamlıca Hill overlooking the Bosporus that is larger than the mosques built by the Ottoman sultans. At $45 million, it will have a capacity for 37,500 people and the structure will be seen from nearly every point in Istanbul.

With this mosque, Erdoğan wants to put his signature on Istanbul as major Ottoman sultans did – projecting his vision, grandeur, a sense of national self-confidence. Although many Turks appreciate these projects, some also question the need for such extravagant spending. For instance, he led the construction of the third airport in Istanbul which will be the biggest air transit facility in the world. The price tag is $24 billion. Major road construction from Izmir to Istanbul reached $7.5 billion in costs. In 2017, Erdoğan opened the third bridge to span the Bosporus, which was named after Yavuz Sultan Selim and carried a $3 billion price tag.

One of his most publicised dreams is to build a canal that will effectively operate like a second Bosporus, running parallel to the original body of water and linking the Black Sea with the Sea of Marmara. At the opening ceremony of the third bridge, Erdoğan told the assembled crowds, 'Be proud of your power, Turkey.' These projects are being built by pro-Erdoğan consortiums, which are guaranteed profits thanks to government allocations. For instance, the government guaranteed the passage of 40,000 vehicles daily on the bridge and on days when traffic fails to match that target, the government has agreed to match the shortfall in revenue with payments to these consortiums. These projects have increased the national budget deficit and have raised questions about their utility along with significant environmental costs.

Erdoğan's shift in vision and policies, in part, follows a familiar path: a leader usually reconfigures his policies and language on the basis of the expectations of his followers. As the AKP and Erdoğan free themselves from the precedents of constitutional and societal constraints, they openly bring their Islamic vision into the public sphere to shape the state and society together. For instance, Abdurrahman Dilipak, considered a vulgar Islamist and an ardent supporter of Erdoğan, has openly called for establishing a Sunni caliphate and wants Erdoğan to take on the title. Kadir Mısıroğlu, a popular historian who is on record for despising the westernisation programme of Atatürk, used to lead a movement to resurrect the caliphate. However, Erdoğan has ignored these calls, reiterating his belief in sustaining the secular nature of the Turkish Republic.

Erdoğan has switched back and forth in being sceptical or sensitive to Atatürk's legacy, as he has attempted to redefine Kemalism within the framework of democracy and Turkish-Islamic nationalism.[53] Erdoğan's speech on 10 November 2004 at the Atatürk Language and History Higher Council was aimed at detaching Atatürkism from its rigid and authoritarian aspects by reinterpreting the principles of Atatürkism not as fixed and universal truths but rather as conjectural precepts to modernise society:

> As you all know, Atatürk did not deliver or promise an ideology; neither had he imposed any ideology on the people. Rationality is the basis of his worldview. His goal was to create a modern civilisation through reason, rationality and the realities of daily life. We know the fact that Mustafa Atatürk never cared or took rigid and fixed ideas seriously. Atatürk shared a worldview that was open to development and advancement and he trusted the guide of reason in the process of development . . . The founding principles of the Republic of Turkey are republicanism, national sovereignty, nation state and secularism.[54]

Before 2013, Erdoğan disavowed the hardline Islamic views of many followers of his mentor Erbakan and tried to recast himself as a pro-European conservative. Earlier, he worked to balance liberalism and the founding principles of the Republic. On 25 April 2006, he outlined his vision to the AKP group:

The AKP government has undertaken very important projects and taken very important decisions which in the future will be seen as a silent revolution. But the most important of them was to protect both the *republican principles* and *democracy* together through maintaining the necessary conditions for the economic and spiritual development of the people and through removing the political, economic and social obstacles that restrict basic rights and freedoms which are stipulated as the task and purpose of the state in our constitution, in ways that aren't compatible with the social state, the rule of law and principles of fairness.[55]

One of the major changes in the republican grammar of politics is to protect republican principles of secularism and nationalism through the democratic process. Erdoğan contends the AKP is 'aware that republican principles can't be protected through limiting democracy but through protecting republican principles and democracy together'.[56] There was an incrementally progressive democratisation process taking place until 2013 only to be reversed after the coup in Egypt and the Gezi Park protests. These two events shook his perspectives about the Western commitment to democracy and the rule of law in the Muslim world. They also amplified his suspicions about the good faith of Western-oriented secular and liberal groups in Turkey. It was not lost on many in the AKP leadership that many so-called liberal democrats in the West as well as liberals in the Middle East applauded General Sisi's bloody coup against Egypt's first democratically elected government.

After 2013, Erdoğan was frequently proclaimed *Reis* (in Arabic, the term is *rais*: it means chief or leader of a kinship-based group) by his followers who previously had referred to him as *Beyefendi*, loosely translated as 'gentleman'. This shift in reference summarised his new image in Turkey. Today, when people say *Reis* they no longer need to attach a name because everyone knows it refers to Erdoğan. Meanwhile, the opposition prefer to call him *baş hırsız* (the head of the thieves).

Those seeking the favour of the state, and especially bureaucrats, are bound to implement his wishes. For instance, when he detested a statue in Kars, calling it monstrous, the next day the provincial governor removed it. When he complained about the al fresco dining tables on the sidewalks of Beyoğlu, the municipality banned sidewalk dinner tables. Journalists and media personalities have been fired by their bosses when Erdoğan did not like what they wrote and published. To be clear, Erdoğan neither ordered the destruction of the statue nor banned sidewalk dinner tables, nor asked any media boss to fire an employee. However, given his domineering personality, many who seek power or wealth seek to appease him, even when not asked to do so.

2.6 Conclusion

Erdoğan's greatest strength and weakness arise from an amorphous party identity and platform. Each election has resulted in greater consolidation of his power and this, in turn, has led to more authoritarian practices and his intolerance towards other AKP leaders within the party and outside. As Fırat explains, 'As he consolidated the power, his suppressed Islamic and authoritarian identity stroked back with vengeance.'[57] In fact, especially after the June 2015 national election in which he lost the parliamentary majority, he sought to consolidate his power by surrounding himself with a 'less educated, parochial group of "yes-men"'. The AKP's parliamentary groups and cabinets formerly were more heterogeneous with powerful personalities among its membership. However, starting in 2017, 'the cabinet is nothing but the secretaries of Erdoğan, who cannot think but just follow his orders'. Thus, neither the cabinet nor the AKP developed its own sociopolitical brand.

Now the only bond that keeps the party together and provides its identity is the force and fear of Erdoğan's personality, a dangerous development that also has been seen in the US and elsewhere where politicians have remade their respective parties to serve their interests and narcissistic demands exclusively. Erdoğan's political career started on a different path, however. In the next chapter, we chronicle the first phase of Erdoğan's political career, first as the youth leader of the National Salvation Party of Erbakan and then as Istanbul's mayor.

Notes

1. Berkes, *The Development of Secularism in Turkey*, pp. 5–8.
2. Yavuz, *Islamic Political Identity*, pp. 81–102.
3. Cagaptay, *The New Sultan*, pp. 4–8.
4. Mishra, *Age of Anger*, p. 14.

5. *Deutsche Welle*, 'Böhmermann: How a German satirist sparked a freedom of speech debate', 5 October 2016.
6. Machiavelli, *The Chief Works and Others*, p. 58.
7. Machiavelli, *The Chief Works and Others*, p. 62.
8. *Millyet*, 26 March 1994.
9. *Milli Gazete*, 29–30 May 1994.
10. Tavernise, 'Turkish leader Erdogan making new enemies and frustrating old friends'.
11. Although this phrase is originated in the writings of ancient Greek philosophers, it is commonly used by the Muslims of Anatolia.
12. For the entire exchange, see *Radikal*, 'Davos'da Kasımpaşa Havası', 30 January 2009.
13. *Hürriyet*, 'Mümtaz Soysal: Erdoğan Batı'da ikinci kez çizildi', 30 January 2009.
14. Pulur, 'Davos'ta siz olsanız ne yapardınız?' 30 January 2009.
15. Erdoğan's speech at a meeting in Sivas on 5 March 2009, available at <http://web.akparti.org.tr/ak-parti-genelbaskani-ve-basbakan-Erdoğanin-sivas-mitingin_5969.html> (last accessed 12 June 2017).
16. Toynbee, *Civilization on Trial*.
17. Fanon, *The Wretched of the Earth*, pp. 167–89.
18. For more on the impacts of humiliation, see Barkan, *The Guilt of Nations*.
19. Necipoğlu, 'The life of an imperial monument', p. 225.
20. Sarıoğlu, 'Kimlik Değişimi', 13 December 2005.
21. Özgül, 'Erdoğan ile Kürt İşçisi Boran'ın tartışması', 27 December 2002.
22. Alpan, 'AKP's "conservative democracy"'; Duran, 'Understanding the AK Party's identity politics', p. 104.
23. Gürsel, 'Erdoğan Islamizes education system to raise "devout youth"', 9 December 2014.
24. Ackerman and Calisir, 'Erdoğan's assault on education: the closure of secular schools', 23 December 2015.
25. Erdoğan, 'Atatürk'ün dünya görüşünün temeli akılcılıktır', 10 November 2004.
26. Sontag, 'The Erdoğan experiment'.
27. The Seljuk and the Ottoman Turkish Empires were definitively more pragmatic than ideological with the goal of maintaining order, justice and peace. This pragmatism still remains part of the Turkish political culture.
28. For Erdoğan's comments and democracy and his desire to change the constitution, see *Milliyet*, 14 July 1996. Gunter, 'Erdoğan's Train to Authoritarianism', pp. 127–49.

29. Machiavelli, *The Chief Works and Others*, p. 16.
30. Quoted by Gözaydın, 'Religion, politics', p. 173.
31. Interview, Ankara, 12 August 2019.
32. Akçalı, 'Başbakan Erdoğan'ın bir itirafı, Türkiye'de kanunları kim yapıyor?', 27 July 2004.
33. Kinzer, 'Will Turkey make it?', 15 July 2004.
34. Talmon, *The Origins of Totalitarian Democracy*.
35. Nilgün Cerrahoğlu's interview with Erdoğan, *Milliyet*, 14 July 1996; *The Economist*, 'Getting off the train', 4 February 2016.
36. Metiner, 'Dünden bugüne Tayyip Erdoğan', 6 July 2003. Metiner changed his views of Erdoğan; he became the poppy of Erdoğan as he wrote 'Biatsa, biat, itaatsa itaaat', 6 January 2014.
37. *Hürriyet*, 'Başbakan gazetecilerin neden tutuklandığını açıkladı', 8 March 2011.
38. For more on the corruption of the Turkish press, see Hansen, 'What remains of the Turkish press'.
39. *Hürriyet*, 8 March 2011.
40. *Hürriyet*, 8 March 2011.
41. Müller, *What Is Populism?* See also Mounk, 'Pitchfork Politics', pp. 27–36.
42. Interview with Dengir Mir Mehmet Fırat, Ankara, 6 March 2016.
43. Interview with Reha Camuroğlu, Ankara, 8 June 2019.
44. Interview with SK, Ankara, 7 June 2018.
45. Dogan, 'PM Erdoğan apologises for Dersim massacre on behalf of Turkish state', 23 November 2011.
46. *Hürriyet*, 23 November 2011.
47. Erdoğan's advisor Yalçın Akdoğan calls Alevis to join Islamist and Kurds since they are all victims of the Kemalist nation-building, see Akdoğan, 'Dersim 2011', 28 November 2011.
48. Interview with William Holt, Salt Lake City, 8 July 2018.
49. Regarding a closer content analysis of Erdoğan's first published speeches, one sees the constant use of *hizmet*, people (*halk*), nation (*millet*, but not the Kemalist version of nation), country (*memleket*), state (never the republican state), Turkey (*Turkiye*) and civilisation. Erdoğan's speeches indicate that he delivers his remarks in declarative form without much foreshadowing analysis or explanation. He is not a man of nuances or complex thinking but rather relies on a charismatic personality with good recitation skills. Erdoğan emphasises that EU membership is a civilisational project. See Erdoğan, *Konuşmaları*. This book includes Erdoğan speeches in the parliament delivered between 10 November 2002 and 28 July 2003.

50. Erdoğan, *Konuşmaları*, p. 194. Erdoğan, speech at the Grand National Assembly (TBMM), 6 May 2003.
51. He argues that the bureaucracy should be the 'civil servant' as the service provider to people. Speech at the Grand National Assembly (TBMM), 6 May 2003, in Erdoğan, *Konuşmaları*, p. 194.
52. Interview with YA, Ankara, 9 July 2018.
53. Erdoğan, 'Atatürk'ün dünya görüşünün temeli akılcılıktır', 10 November 2004.
54. Erdoğan, 'Atatürk'ün dünya görüşünün temeli akılcılıktır', 10 November 2004.
55. Erdoğan speech, see *The New Anatolian*, 26 April 2006.
56. Erdoğan speech, see *The New Anatolian*, 26 April 2006.
57. Interview with Mir Dengir Fırat, Ankara, 6 March 2016.

3

ERDOĞAN'S AS A MAYOR AND THE 2002 ELECTIONS

This chapter will examine Erdoğan's engagement in party politics after the 1980 military coup. After recounting Erdoğan's rise within the Welfare Party machine, I will explore how he mastered working with the grass-roots levels of Islamic networks to translate their activism into voting blocs in the municipal elections of 1994, when he became the first Islamic-focused mayor of Istanbul. As mayor of Turkey's largest city, Erdoğan gradually rose in the ranks to become the national Islamic leader. The third section will detail the soft military coup of 28 February 1997 and its implications, such as the imprisonment of Erdoğan, which advanced his cause for becoming the leader of Turkey. The fourth section will explore the split within Turkey's leader-based Islamist movement and the establishment of the AKP. The final sections examine the 2002 elections as the first tsunami to transform the old Turkey and the beginning of a 'new Turkey' in his worldview.

3.1 Erdoğan as local politician (1984–2002)

During the violent student protests before the 1980 coup, a group of National Salvation Party (MSP) youths went to Küçükçekmece, a district of Istanbul, to bury two of their friends who had been killed. It was a large gathering where anti-government protestors chanted slogans. Due to the widespread violence in Istanbul at the time, a state of emergency was in force for the entire province. The police intervened and took many protestors, including Erdoğan, to jail. He served initially in the Metris Military Prison and then was moved to the Selimiye Military Prison. In the first court session, the judge released Erdoğan and his friends because there was no evidence of wrongdoing, except for violating the state of emergency rules. This was Erdoğan's first jail sentence; he would be imprisoned twice more. He always risked confrontation with law enforcement due to his volatile personality, often aggravated by a deep personal sense of being marginalised as an outsider. For instance, when his football manager asked him to shave off his beard, he refused to do so on the basis of his religious convictions. After the military coup on 12 September 1980, Erdoğan gave up football and went to work in the private sector, before fulfilling his mandatory military service in 1982 as a commissioned officer.

After the 1980 coup, which led to the banning of the MSP, Erbakan founded the Welfare (Refah) Party (RP). Nearly every MSP politician joined the RP.[1] Because of the ban, Erbakan and the people around him became more careful and sensitive to the needs of the secular constitutional system as they focused more on delivering social services than ideology. Erdoğan joined the RP in 1984 and became the chairman for the Beyoğlu district organisation.[2] In 1985, he was elected as the chairman for the Istanbul provincial organisation as well as to the party's central decision committee. In 1986, at the age of thirty-two, Erdoğan ran as a deputy candidate for the RP in the by-election, but failed. The following year, he ran again in the general election for a party post and won.

In the 1989 local elections, Erdoğan was the party's mayoral candidate in the cosmopolitan Beyoğlu district of Istanbul. Erdoğan's first campaign for major political office was focused on all social classes and demographics, which mirrored the district's composition, and while he narrowly lost the election, he was noticed by RP officials as well as the national political community. Erdoğan's candour, his egalitarianism in campaigning, and the strategically important loyalty to Erbakan served his rising political portfolio well, as he became chairman of the party's Istanbul branch. With the 1989 municipal elections, Erdoğan became the voice of the peripheral community segments in Istanbul, representing the under-represented, underprivileged and largely ignored individuals in the dense metropolis of Istanbul and the

Beyoğlu district. This served to prime Erdoğan's ability to connect with ordinary Muslims.[3]

Although Erdoğan was expected to win the mayoral elections in Beyoğlu, his friends, along with him, were convinced that the election was stolen. Erdoğan and his friends stormed the election commission and when Erdoğan lost his temper, he yelled at the head of the election commission, Nazmi Özcan, a district judge, accusing the official of being drunk and incompetent. The judge sentenced him to one week in jail for being disrespectful in an official judicial setting. Regarding the complaint forwarded to the judge, the court proceeding was initiated. Realising that he could face imprisonment, Erdoğan attempted to avoid the court but was arrested on charges of disrespect in an official judicial proceeding on 27 April 1989, when he finally showed up in court. He spent a week in the Bayramoğlu prison until his next court appearance on 4 May 1989. The judge sentenced Erdoğan to six months in jail and a fine of 20,000 Turkish lira. In lieu of his jail sentence, he was forced to pay a greater fine of 920,000 Turkish lira.[4] This was the second time Erdoğan had been in jail. He recounted his experience as such:

> When I was in jail, the month of Ramadan was already started. After they showed me the room where I was supposed to stay, I moved to a corner and began reading the 'meal' (interpretation of the Qur'an). Other prisoners also came to me and asked me about the book I was reading. I told them this was the Turkish translation of the Qur'an. They were impressed by my religiosity and showed their respect. There were two bosses of the prison: one of them was an Abaza from Düzce, and the second was from Sinop. I had developed close ties with the boss from Düzce.[5]

This recollection shows that Erdoğan was fully aware of the power of religion and how religious knowledge commands respect in Turkish society. Moreover, he understood how the informal networks of power and hierarchy are maintained in every corner of the country, along with legal and illegal power in all sectors of Turkish society.

The 1991 general elections saw Erdoğan stand once again as a candidate for parliament and this time he was declared to have lost as a result of a recalculation of votes, even if he had been considered victorious in the first instance. Cumulatively, these electoral losses whetted his desire to win the ensuing election. Erdoğan wanted to win public office because he was aware that 'in order to overcome one's economic problems and make money, one has to be either a mayor or in the parliament. Politics was the quick way to wealth'.[6] In addition, the elections did not only teach him how to survive within the party machine but also connect with the people.

Although Erdoğan was influenced by Erbakan's National Outlook Movement, he diverged from its ideology in his vision, strategies and goals. Erdoğan became popular with the youth of the party by giving more weight on the revanchist aspect of the politics and stressing the value of Islamic and Ottoman history. He not only strived to provide a clear road map of what Turkey should become on the basis of his understanding of Kısakürek's polemical writings, but also supported the activism of Islamist resentment and advocated direct confrontation against the Kemalist system. In this confrontation, he sought to instrumentalise Islamic tradition for mobilising the marginalised conservative sector of the Turkish population. He never defended the Islamo-Ottoman tradition purely for the sake of it but saw it instead as a spring of past wisdom to dip into for quenching the need of sustaining an identity as the nation assimilated and absorbed its ongoing experiences as a Republic.

Erdoğan treated religious and national values, symbols and memories as transactional as long as they served his goal of getting elected and enriching himself. For instance, as the RP chair of the Beyoğlu district, despite sharp criticism from party elders, he defended the role of women in politics and political activism. When he ran for mayor of Beyoğlu in 1989, he established a women's branch of the party, engaging them to participate in the political process. This move, however, was not to empower women but rather use them for his own political victory. Moreover, he informed his campaign workers not to bring religion into any political debate or discussion, but rather to focus on issues pertaining to the city's neighbourhoods. Women working on behalf of the campaign chose on their own whether or not to wear headscarves or the hijab or niqab. Along with Bahri Zengin, Erdoğan revolutionised the political campaign of the RP.[7] Zengin argued that 'in those days, Erdoğan regarded politics as *dava* (religious mission) and political activism as a religious duty. When you act with that conviction, ends would always justify the means'.[8] For instance, in the Beyoğlu district, Erdoğan carried his campaign to coffee shops, restaurants and pubs. He strived to reach every citizen, regardless of their lifestyle and social and religious identities. He told his campaign workers, essentially: 'You must absolutely build relations with people outside your community. Salute even the customers in places where alcohol is served.'[9]

Erdoğan's skills of oration were evident even then, with his speeches taking on poetic rhythms that resonated with crowds at campaign events. Likewise, his body language amplified the resonance of his spoken text. Erdoğan's arrest for polarising and insulting speech in Siirt was a shock to him and his supporters. This experience consolidated his view that many of his fellow citizens and political peers saw him as an outsider and as a threat. My interviews in the early 2000s with Islamist intellectuals and members of the sociopolitical elite indicate there always has been an underlying inferiority complex among them as with Erdoğan.[10] Conservative Muslims are enslaved by their perceived feelings of inferiority; while secularist/westernised Turks are enslaved by these sentiments as well, but instead they are attributed to the constant struggle to prove to Europe that they are Europeans. For many Islamists, including Erdoğan, rather than seek to develop a Muslim ethical and moral system with distinctive artistic and philosophical dimensions, they have instead taken refuge in consumerism and accumulation of wealth – most consequentially in their roles as public servants and governing authorities. Politics, for Erdoğan, was thus 'a short cut to enrichment and also for taking his revenge from the Kemalist establishment'.[11]

3.2 Mayor of Istanbul and Rise of National Profile (1994–2001)

When Erdoğan was elected as the mayor of Istanbul in 1994, he stepped away from the lessons he mastered under Erbakan's influence. As mayor, one of Erdoğan's first acts was to ban the sale of alcohol in all municipally operated restaurants and facilities – he always despised alcohol and tobacco products. However, he proved to be an effectively pragmatic mayor in dealing with Istanbul's chronic urban problems of congested traffic, shortages of potable water and the persistent blight of ghetto neighbourhoods and shanty towns.

As mayor of Istanbul, at the age of forty, Erdoğan began the earnest work of recovering and restoring the heritage of Ottoman grandeur. He not only refurbished important and long-neglected Ottoman monuments, but also turned the anniversary of the 1453 conquest of Istanbul into a major national celebration, sending a powerful message that the Turkish nation was not really born in 1923 and that its illustrious 'fathers' extended from Alparslan (r. 1063–73) to Fatih Mehmet (r. 1451–81) and Kanuni Sultan Süleyman (1520–66). Erdoğan was also a capable technocrat, resolving problems which gave Istanbul residents safe, clean water and efficient public transportation. There was no doubt that Erdoğan's aspirations for higher office were evident, as he regularly visited Anatolia, where he delivered highly emotional speeches recalling the glories of the Ottoman past.

Istanbul was ideal for testing Erdoğan's model of governance. Istanbul's operating budget and population matched or exceeded any state in the Balkans. Erdoğan rejuvenated the infrastructure and learned how to connect with diverse sectors of the population. He learned about both local and national politics and the role of local networks in the political life of Turkey. He realised the power of hometown (*hemşerilik*) networks and cultivated a down-to-earth communication style. He preferred to solve problems directly rather than refer them to a committee or wait for responses from other state institutions. Erdoğan's popularity grew as he solved the city's major problems. Although he was elected by the greatest plurality of votes (25 per cent), his popularity rose above 40 per cent in the first year of his term.

The main factor in Erdoğan's success in Istanbul, however, was his reach to middle- and low-income classes as his broadest target audience. He went door to door, speaking with voters and listening to their demands and grievances while informing them of proposed urban improvements. This approach elevated Erdoğan above his political competitors. He achieved success through his dialogue with not only marginalised communities but also reached out beyond to other regions to garner as many votes as possible. His efficient style of governance quickly became a successful showcase for the RP, which would leverage it in the 1995 national elections. When Ahmet Taşgetiren, a prominent Nakşibendi journalist, asked him: 'How does the Mayor bear all the wrath he faces, can he sleep comfortably at night?', Erdoğan responded:

> Some nights I cry. Aren't we also people of this country? I was born and raised in Istanbul. My parents had come from Rize and settled down here. I don't have any other goals than seeing my country in a better position at the contest for civilisation ... Let everybody live as he thinks and believes it fit.[12]

The party gained the greatest plurality of votes to form the coalition government with Erbakan as the prime minister. As mayor in 1995, Erdoğan used the office to make a reputation as a competent, enterprising politician with an immediate familiarity of people's everyday problems. He always compared his administration with the previous social democrat mayor (Nurettin Sözen), whose administration symbolised huge piles of uncollected garbage, potable water shortages, nepotism and a major corruption scandal. Erdoğan presented himself as the underdog representing the historically excluded segments of the Turkish population. He called himself as among the Black Turks to distinguish himself from the opposition which he labelled as the White Turks. His narrative has always been divisive, exclusionary and vengeful. However, the political stability under Erbakan's stewardship was short lived.

Before and during Erdoğan's tenure as mayor, the citizens living in Istanbul's marginalised sectors embraced him as one of their own, given his own experience with poverty and his success in moving out of Kasımpaşa to make his own social destiny. To them, Erdoğan was 'our Tayyip' (*bizim Tayyip*) and they were impressed by his willingness to ignore and defy the rules, institutions and bureaucracy that had perpetuated the Kemalists in political power. In a Turkish context, Erdoğan endured and eventually succeeded against a stacked deck in a system designed to keep those of his social background and religious beliefs from the corridors of wealth and power. In many ways, he resembled everyone's favourite irascible, down-to-earth uncle, who cuts through the socially acceptable (or politically correct) nonsense and speaks the plain truth.

3.3 The February 28 Process and Erdoğan's Imprisonment

After winning control of major municipalities such as Istanbul and Ankara in the 1994 local elections, the RP received the highest national vote in the 1995 national elections by capturing 21.4 per cent of the total and became the senior coalition partner in 1996–7. Having the first openly Islamic prime minister angered the Kemalist establishment and they used all means to end the government.

Because of the Islamisation project of Erbakan and the intolerance of the Kemalist military toward diversity, on 28 February 1997 a soft coup – also known as the February 28 process – occurred.[13] The military mobilised major business associations, media cartels, university rectors and the judiciary, long subservient to its commands, to engineer an anti-Refah drive to force the Erbakan government to resign. The military, the self-appointed custodians of Kemalism, decided to ban virtually all independent sources of Islamic social and cultural expression to prevent a 'fundamentalist' Islamic takeover. They banned the RP, restricted İmam Hatip schools, severely curtailed the building of new mosques, implemented a dress code outlawing the wearing of headscarves in institutions of higher education, and suspended and imprisoned elected mayors by the order of the Ministry of Interior.[14] This was followed by measures to curtail all activities that sought to Islamicise the state and society. By pointing out the shortcomings of the Refah Party-led government, the Gülen movement avoided becoming a target of the military. However, the Gülen movement and its leader, Fethullah Gülen, could not avoid the assaults of the February 28 process, and Gülen had to leave Turkey and take refuge in the US.

Behind this public campaign was the unmistakable message that Erbakan would voluntarily resign or be forced out by the generals. The coup framed Islamic identity as a national threat, along with numerous directives to cleanse the Islamic presence in public spaces where it had been present even in the most reactionary period of Kemalist zeal. The coup is known as the February 28 'process' because it was not only limited to the removal of the Erbakan government but also became a process of monitoring, controlling and criminalising all Islamic activism as a security threat. Furthermore, it was about institutionalising a permanent legal framework for ostracising devout and/or active Turkish Muslims from the market, educational and political spheres.

The military achieved its objectives and Erbakan was out. Erdoğan was removed from his elected mayoral office and imprisoned because he delivered a divisive speech which the authorities characterised as insulting to the Turkish state and its citizens. On 12 December 1997, Erdoğan had delivered his emotional speech in Siirt, which would derail his political career temporarily. In that speech, Erdoğan divided the Turkish society as 'two fundamentally different camps' – 'those who follow Atatürk's reforms and those who follow sharia and the Islamic way of life'. In his speech, there was a concerted effort to 'otherise' secular Turks as 'aliens' and 'strangers' in their own country.

Erdoğan, in fact, told *Milliyet* daily that 'praise be to God, we are for sharia (*Elhamdulillah seriatçıyız*)'.[15] In the same speech, he also recited the lines:

> The Minarets are our bayonets
> The Domes are our helmets
> The Mosques are our barracks
> The Believers are our soldiers.

Many Kemalists saw Erdoğan's speech as his campaign to bring sharia to Turkey and to divide the nation into 'believers' (*dindar*) and 'non-believers' (*dindar olmayanlar*), and inciting 'believers' against 'non-believers'. Later, he clarified that the religious references were of his own personal character and that he remained committed to the integrity of the Republic's constitution and secular and democratic principles. The Siirt incident exemplifies the need to be more meticulous and contextualised when trying to distil Erdoğan's proclamations, which are as much rooted in the symbolic discourse formed by his foundational influences stretching back to his childhood as they are in political rhetoric. The challenge is to analyse Erdoğan in the unique indigenous frame that constituted his life, education and his entry into politics. Likewise, the public prosecutor of the Diyarbakır State Security Court also argued that in the Siirt speech, Erdoğan contextualised Islam in his assessment of his personal morality. Despite the argument of the prosecutor, the State Security Court convicted Erdoğan and ordered a ten-month prison term. As a result of this criminal conviction, Erdoğan was removed from the office of mayor of Istanbul and barred from running for public office. However, he only served four months of his sentence before being released in July 1999.

3.4 The Impacts of Prison on Erdoğan

The February 28 process ended the Erbakan-led government, but, as previously mentioned, it also curtailed Islamic activism, especially the İmam Hatip schools; closed two Islamic parties (in 1998 and 2001); and forced a new generation of Islamists to distance themselves from direct confrontations with the secular establishment. Yet, the coup also forced all Islamic groups to form an alliance against the Kemalist establishment. The process engendered numerous long-term impacts on state–society relations as well as compelling Islamic movements to become, even if reluctantly, advocates of democracy and full membership of Turkey in the EU. Thus, the post-1997 history cannot be understood without understanding the February 28 process and its intended and unintended consequences. By disbanding two Islamist parties, the February 28 process created fresh opportunities for the reformist members of political Islamic movements and encouraged adopting liberal versions of democracy. As stated by Öniş regarding the post-February 28 process:

> It became increasingly clear that a party that failed to respect the principles of secularism would have no chance of sustained and effective participation in the Turkish political system given its constitutional boundaries. Hence, this learning process was extremely important in pushing Islamists in Turkey toward a moderate, centrist direction. There was a learning process in the sense that hard-line Islamist politics would appeal only to a small segment of the Turkish population. Moderation was therefore a key toward the construction of a mass party of broad electoral support.[16]

Some reformists, such as Bülent Arınç, have argued that as a result of the February 28 process they concluded that an Islamist ideology is *not* an option.[17] The newly established AKP leadership declared that they gave up Islamism to become a conservative democratic party. This change in policies and the emphasis on EU membership has led many scholars of Turkish politics to dismiss the Islamic label and argue that the AKP is a centre-right party.[18]

The policies of the February 1997 coup aimed to cleanse political Islam from the public sphere. Erdoğan reacted to these decisions, especially his imprisonment, by differentiating justice from legality or the court of law from the court of the public opinion. He cited the 'court of hearts (*mahşer-i vicdan*) of the people' as the ultimate reference for deciding on justice and being more important than the court of the law.[19] This emphasis on the court of public opinion being more important than the legal process would shape Erdoğan's thinking. He lost faith in the law and would use every opportunity to overcome it by populist alternative.

Prior to beginning his ten-month prison sentence (which eventually would be commuted to time served), Erdoğan said:

> I wanted to carry to the public space your wishes and aspirations. Those wishes and aspirations are locked up in the secluded rooms of your modest homes. They are conveyed to others only by the hopeless expressions on the

faces of your children who have no jobs and are silently kept in the wounded hearts of your mothers and fathers. I love your voices, because I am one of you. I do not regret what I have done, because we have done it together.[20]

The February 28 process and the imprisonment of the Islamist politicians had several impacts. It forced Islamists, especially Erdoğan and Bülent Arınç, to become 'reluctant' or 'forced' democrats in their respective political discourse. However, later when the secular constraints were removed with the help of the Gülen movement, Erdoğan lapsed back into his earlier Islamist position to become an Islamist autocrat without any respect for the basic rules of democracy. The irony is that a similar set of circumstances that brought about his rise in national politics has become the foundation for his single-handed dismantling of the Turkish Republic's historic democratic state institutions.

Moreover, the way in which Erdoğan was removed from his post as the mayor of Istanbul and then banned from politics, on the basis of 'provoking public conflict' with divisive speech, angered the conservative Islamic sector of the population and bolstered his popularity. With Kısakürek as his ideological muse, Erdoğan has always been a revanchist looking for an opportune time to take revenge against the Kemalist establishment. His speech in Siirt illustrates this deep-down anger and rage against the Republic and its secular values. Erdoğan's removal from office and his imprisonment deepened his rage against the establishment. However, he changed his tactics and avoided direct confrontation by pretending to be tolerant, pro-EU and a democrat.

The February 1997 coup brought the Erbakan's government down, put the Constitutional Court under the thumb of the military, disbanded the RP and barred Erbakan from entering politics for five years. Because this was the third ban of an Erbakan-led party, he knew how to reconfigure the party and reactivate the political networks. With his latest political effort banned, Erbakan supported the establishment of the new Virtue Party (Fazilet Partisi, FP). Although Erbakan was not legally in charge, he was the de facto leader of the party and was running its policies behind the scene. The FP included the same political elites, adopted a nearly identical political platform, and followed the same networks of influence. As a result, the Kemalist establishment closely followed the FP's activities. When Merve Kavakçı, who was elected to Parliament as an FP candidate in the April 1999 elections, wore a headscarf to the swearing-in ceremony, she was prevented from doing so and scores of secularist parliamentarians demanded her expulsion. President Demirel accused Kavakçı of being an 'agent provocateur working for radical Islamic states'. As a result, Turkey's chief prosecutor opened a case against the FP at the Constitutional Court on 7 May 1999.

This crisis helped to polarise intra-party politics.[21] The younger political generation accused its elders of being too aggressive for not accommodating the sensitivities of the establishment. Moreover, they defended shedding old concepts of Islamism and adopting pro-EU and democratic ideals. As the court case proceeded, the newly incarnated FP became not an agent of change but rather a subject of change. The fear of being banned drove the main context of the FP's politics, forcing it not to engage in politics but rather to become, ironically, in a sense an apolitical party. This discursive shift from the West as *the* foe of political Islamic identity to a friend is an outcome of several factors. The banning of the RP, systematic oppression of Islamic presence in the public sphere and the establishment of the FP created an opportunity for the Islamic movement to redefine itself in terms of global discourses of human rights and democracy.

With the RP's ban, a group of young politicians, such as Erdoğan, Abdullah Gül, Abdullatif Şener and Bülent Arınç, criticised Erbakan's authoritarian tactics and his old-style governance. The faction between the reformists (*yenilikçiler*) and the traditionalists within the party was exposed. The reformists led by Erdoğan advocated a new style of politics, defending intra-party democracy, and stressing de-Islamisation of the party in order to become more legitimate in the eyes of the establishment both inside and outside the country. The first time the reformists organised, they nominated Gül as a party leader against Recai Kutan, a close friend of Erbakan. On 14 May 2000, two candidates ran against each other at the first FP party congress and Gül received 521 votes while Erbakan-backed Kutan garnered 633. This contested congress deepened the factionalism within the party and Erbakan sent the ringleaders of the reformists to the disciplinary board to be purged from the party. While intra-party quarrels continued, on 22 June 2001, the Constitutional Court disbanded the FP for anti-secular activities. The traditionalists, under the control of Erbakan, established the Saadet Partisi (Felicity Party, SP) and Kutan became its leader in July 2001. The reformists welcomed the banning of the FP, as they organised their own political party, the Adalet ve Kalkınma Partisi (AKP) on 14 August 2001.[22]

While in prison, Erdoğan had reconsidered his political circumstances and recast himself as a moderate conservative who was pro-European. He broke or loosened his ties from the Islamic movement and its ideological networks and formed his own political team that consisted of younger politicians who sprang from the same Islamist origins. In 2001, Erdoğan delivered the opening speech for the new party, the AKP, at the Bilkent Hotel in Ankara. Although he was the leader of the movement, there were three other prominent members of his team: Abdullah Gül, Bülent Arınç, and Abdullatif Şener. It was a cadre-based arrangement in which Erdoğan became the most popular of the AKP's political leaders. The AKP had well-established Islamic networks in the countryside to be activated. The nascent AKP coalesced as a bottom-up movement, which had clear goals of democratisation and economic development. The party, however, would go through a major transformation and move from a team- and network-based party to a one-man-based 'machine' to control all state resources and intimidate all groups of opposition.

In the early 1990s, Özal had initiated economic, social and political liberalisation; focused on the boundary separating the state and society; and used opportunities to empower the society vis-à-vis the state. Özal carried out a peaceful revolution of opening opportunity spaces for the excluded (*dışlanmış*) sectors of Turkey's population. Since his untimely death in 1993, the process of liberalisation was not only interrupted but was also reversed by the February 28 process. Moreover, the military establishment expanded its power at the expense of the elected government. The military, along with the judiciary, used all available means to criminalise the opposition. Because of these developments, many Muslims witnessed the erosion of their rights and freedoms and the shrinking of opportunity spaces by the establishment – the coalition of corrupt politicians, the media, business leaders and several power-hungry generals.

In August 2001, Mesut Yılmaz, then a deputy prime minister, boldly stated that the military orchestrated a so-called 'national security syndrome' that was responsible for the slow progress of democratisation and integration with the EU. The military responded to Yılmaz's 'unfortunate speech' by issuing a sharp retort, noting that it was not the 'national security concept' but 'those [that is, politicians] who did not fulfil their responsibilities or those who gave priority to personal gains rather than political stability in the face of such pressing issues as economic bankruptcy and widespread corrupt activities who were to blame'.[23] The Ecevit government of the time, in turn, was ineffective and, consequently, the political spaces gradually shrunk so that all major decisions were made by the state bureaucracy in the name of the state and much of society was excluded from the political process. Nearly twenty years later, the same could be said of Erdoğan's regime.

3.5 The Tsunami in Turkish Politics: the 2002 Elections

The 2002 Turkish national elections represented an unprecedented moment in the history of the Republic in allowing an overtly Islamic party the opportunity to reach the commanding heights of the political landscape and expand the public sphere. Of the eighteen parties that competed for seats in the parliament, only two actually won seats, due to the required 10 per cent nationwide vote threshold required to obtain seats. The AKP came in first by winning 34.3 per cent of the popular vote and two-thirds (363 of 550) of the seats in parliament. The establishment Republican People's Party (CHP), mustered almost one-fifth or 19.4 per cent of the votes and won one-third or 178 of the 550 seats. Independent candidates won another nine seats. These election results were decisive and represented a popular repudiation of the February 28 process and Kemalist political establishment.

This was more a protest vote against the establishment than a vote for the AKP. Among the public grievances that influenced the vote was the great earthquake of 1999, which, combined with the 2001 economic crisis and various corruption cases, made daily life more difficult and, more importantly, undermined the public's faith in state institutions. Many people considered the 1990s as the last decade of a unified Turkey. During this pessimistic political environment, Erdoğan, and the team of politicians around him, namely Gül, Şener and Babacan, emerged as the most trusted leaders to address the problems of the country.

A large plurality of voters believed in the leadership of the AKP, or at least were willing to take a risk for broader political change. The elections swept away a generation of established politicians, giving the AKP a majority of seats and the right to form a government on its own, even though Erdoğan, the head of the party, was barred from holding a formal post because of his conviction for his provocative speech in Siirt that the military contended was an attack on secularism. One may also see this election as a restoration of a broad-based Islamic movement that was forced out of power in 1997.

Thus, for the first time, the elections significantly transformed the political establishment, bringing to power the AKP with a clear mandate to redefine the political centre in terms of a restoration of traditional religious identity and values. However, this was only part of the reason for the AKP's success. A majority of the electorate across social, ethnic, ideological and regional lines was searching for a new social contract based on the global discourses of democracy, human rights and social justice, which the AKP successfully championed. The 2002 election victory was not a call to establish an Islamic state or institute Islamic law but rather about redrawing the boundary between the state and society, in favour of increased pluralism and consolidating civil society in a more liberal and democratic direction. The excluded and marginalised sectors of society, along with those who hoped to expand opportunity spaces, wanted their leaders to make decisions that inherently shared their moral language of the meaning of a good, productive life in Turkish society.

In the transformation of the Islamic movement in general, and the electoral victory of the AKP in particular, a new urban class, consisting of horizontally connected solidarity-based groups with rural origins and a shared Islamic ethos, played an important role. This newly constituted urban class had been excluded culturally, politically and economically by the Kemalist elite. Thus, Islamic networks facilitated both their integration into modern opportunity spaces and offered hope for social mobility.

Sociologically, the AKP appeared to engage people of many diverse backgrounds, from teachers, police officers, vendors, traders and new Muslim intellectuals, to humble shopkeepers and business executives. The AKP, however, was only formed in August 2001. Thus, it was not so much the AKP that utilised traditional solidarity networks in neighbourhoods to mobilise voters but rather these religiously inspired networks mobilising themselves to redefine the political centre of Turkish politics in terms of their values. In short, this was a rapid bottom-up political transformation in which the more traditional segment of society wanted to expand the boundaries of the public sphere and political participation, especially in the Anatolian heartland.

The AKP utilised these culturally rooted grass-roots networks, personalities and cultural frames to project itself as the party of a nominally 99 per cent Muslim electorate in a country where many civil society groupings are inspired by religion but are also infused with the discourse of secular modernisation that had developed as a result of eighty years of Turkish secular republicanism. Furthermore, many Islamic groups offer some form of community service, making such activities more common than prayer meetings. These religious groups act as the social base of Islamic identity and have strong commitments to social justice and direct participation in communal outreach programmes. The AKP became the favoured political organisation for these networks, and this translated into electoral support and victory.

The most pertinent electoral cleavage in modern Turkish politics was determined by the normative value conflict between the Kemalist establishment and the Muslim-oriented majority. In Turkey, the political centre and the societal centre do not necessarily overlap and have often been in conflict. Elections have often been attempts by society to penetrate and socialise the political centre in terms of its own values and norms and identity claims. Society can use electoral processes to create new political compasses in accordance with its values and to redraw the boundary between the state and society. This is what happened in the November 2002 elections and continued until the 2011 elections. The 2002 elections created a new political actor with the mandate to restructure the state–society boundary which had prevailed in an ever-diminishing sense since the formation of modern Turkey in 1923. The emergence of a vibrant Turkish middle class inevitably meant that much of the population insisted that the state should become the servant of society rather than vice versa. The cognitive shift ending the Kemalist military-bureaucratic tutelage was started, in actual practice, during the Özal era, nearly a decade earlier.

Why and whom among so much of the Turkish electorate decided to vote for the AKP in 2002? To understand what they had voted 'for' we need to start with what they had voted 'against'. They voted against the 'centre-right' parties of ANAP, DYP, and the two nationalist parties (MHP and DSP).[24] The AKP received votes from former supporters of the FP, MHP and ANAP.

Thus, secular national (Turkish), conservative (Muslim) and economically liberal voters cast ballots for the AKP. The major flow of votes in comparison with the 1999 elections came from the following parties: RP (69 per cent), MHP (29 per cent) and ANAP (29 per cent). Moreover, 29 per cent of new voters also voted for the AKP.

The centre-right parties had been based on the tenuous balance between state and society. Since the February 1997 soft coup, however, this accommodation had been lost at the expense of society. By attacking not only the RP party of former Prime Minister Erbakan, but also the typically apolitical Sufi orders and Anatolian Muslim social networks, the 1997 Kemalist coup authorities had thus seriously miscalculated their move, eroding the social bases of the establishment centre-right parties. This, in turn, delegitimised the centre-right parties, which came to be viewed simply as agents of an oppressive and alien state. The voters sought to reorient the political centre according to its social needs rather than those of the state. They voted for the AKP for political, economic and social reasons. The traditional Anatolian social classes who had been reliable supporters of establishment centre-right candidates, such as Süleyman Demirel, Tansu Ciller and Mesut Yılmaz, defected after the oppressive 1997 coup process. They were mobilised in the hope that the AKP would halt the ongoing humiliation of their willing embrace of an Ottoman/Islamic identity and lifestyle by restoring Özal's public policy of reconciling with this historic Turkish Muslim identity and culture. The net result was a political earthquake of great magnitude. The carefully managed consensus between the tutelage of the Kemalist military-bureaucratic establishment and domesticated centre-right parties, which dated to Turkey's first competitive multiparty elections in 1950, was dramatically overthrown with the decisive AKP victory in the 2002 elections.

In accounting for this 2002 electoral victory, one needs to appreciate Erdoğan's successful identification with and constant appeal to Özal's policies and legacy in mobilising the Anatolian heartland and its many recently arrived offspring in the booming urban megalopolises of Istanbul, Ankara and Izmir. Erdoğan was also the only leader who identified himself with the spirit of Adnan Menderes in the 1950s and Özal in the 1980s. Invoking Özal's legacy had a particularly powerful resonance since Özal had been successful in creating opportunity spaces for the emergence of a dynamic urban and modern Muslim bourgeoisie. In this way, the 2002 election was intended as an act of restoration that rather turned into a wholesale upset of the carefully managed official post-1950 consensus, which had survived precariously for half a century.

3.6 The Post-election Impact

The AKP came to power in 2002 with the support of millions among the Turkish public from a variety of secular, Islamic and ethnic backgrounds, most of whom had been marginalised by a previously oppressive Turkish state. There are several sociological factors that help explain how Erdoğan became Turkey's unchallenged leader.[25] The first is Erdoğan's experience as mayor of Istanbul. In that position, he had shown his ability to govern effectively and tackle the city's urgent problems. He was tested regularly by Istanbul's voters, succeeding in each instance by delivering above and beyond voters' expectations. He is the model of a self-made politician who brought incredible local experience and the ability to connect with ordinary Turkish citizens.

The second most important factor in the AKP's 2002 electoral victory was the country's 2001 economic crisis which had resulted in near collapse.[26] Almost all parties, with the exception of the AKP, were continually tainted by corruption charges. But the AKP presented itself as the '*ak*' (pure) party and voters decided overwhelmingly to vote for it due to Erdoğan's success as Istanbul mayor and an assumption of the party's integrity and honesty. Most importantly, Erdoğan adeptly built a coalition that embraced all of the historically marginalised and excluded sectors of Turkish society. He has always been an effective speaker and engaging networker.[27]

The third factor influencing the AKP's 2002 electoral victory was its then commitment to the EU process of full membership. In order to establish his reputation as a moderately liberal Muslim leader, Erdoğan embraced the idea of Turkey joining the EU. He believed that Turkey's membership in the EU would help grow the economy and build a genuinely democratic society reconciled with her Ottoman Muslim heritage. In this endeavour, one of Erdoğan's crucial strategies was to ally with the highly successful and well-placed Gülen movement, the country's most powerful modern Islamic entity of its kind.[28] This movement included highly trained, educated and competent bureaucrats who eventually took control of critical state institutions and worked together with Erdoğan to transform the state organs. Pro-Gülen bureaucrats were appointed to nearly all key government positions, including the police, judiciary, and departments of education and health.

Because of the February 28 process and the rigid Kemalist institutional constraints, Erdoğan spent more time distancing himself from the Islamist roots in the National Outlook Movement of Erbakan. Erdoğan and his team did not have time or opportunity to develop an identity for the AKP. Yet, its major distinctive features were the fact that it was a party of resentment against the existing corrupt political establishment, it stressed providing best social services over ideology, and Erdoğan proved to be a successful leader in solving the problems of society. Its identity more or less developed while it was in government after the first election in 2002. Yet, the party presented itself as a 'party of service' (*hizmet partisi*), that is, serving the economic, social and cultural needs of the nation by developing infrastructure, economic growth, healthcare and effective education systems with the power of the state. It gradually presented itself as a conservative democracy to remove the charges of Islamism and also claim the legacies of two popular centre-right statesmen: Adnan Menderes and Turgut Özal. The AKP organised a major academic symposium in 2004 on 'Conservative Democracy' with the opening speech given by Erdoğan,[29] in which he explained that the AKP 'is neither a "political community" (*siyasi cemaat*) nor a "political company" (*siyasi sirket*) but rather a "conservative mass party" by recognising the bridge role of Turkey "between East and the West; between Islam and Christianity; between Asia and Europe"'. Erdoğan insisted that the AKP is committed to democracy and the rule of law, and seeks to reconcile tradition and modernity; local with global; spiritual values with rationality.[30]

The immediate problem of the AKP in government was its need for internal and external legitimacy. It decided to overcome the Kemalist suspicion and resistance by expanding its external legitimacy, (that is, getting support from the EU and the US). In the 1990s, overwhelming popular support for EU membership, even among traditional Muslim society segments who were critical of the Kemalist legacy, was a direct result of the popular perception that the carrot-and-stick approach of potential EU membership was the most persuasive mechanism for pressuring the Kemalist military-bureaucratic establishment towards reform. The AKP thus capitalised on EU pressure to curtail the dual-track government of military tutelage over elected civilian government after the 2002 elections. Voters outside of the official establishment legitimated their claims of rights and recognition of identity by framing their demand in terms of the broader European discourse of democracy, freedom of thought and expression, and human rights. During this period, Erdoğan's political language was not one of exclusion but rather inclusion, blending the local and the global. In addition to its leader and a group of recognised Islamic-oriented politicians in the AKP, the hybrid identity of the party also played an important role in its electoral success. The AKP's identity and ideology resemble one of those fabrics or creatures that changes colour depending on the light and circumstances. The eclectic aspect of the party was the reason for its broad appeal, having branded itself as simultaneously Turkish, Muslim and Western. This pluralist aspect also served a political necessity, given the presence of diverse lifestyles in the country.

In the 2002 electoral success of the AKP, Turkism and Islamism were conflated. For instance, in the heartland of Turkish Islam, such cities as Erzurum, Kayseri and Konya, the public voted overwhelmingly for the AKP. Thus, the normative base of the AKP consists of a Turkish-Islamic synthesis within new global discourses of human rights and democracy. The 2002 elections represent the nationalisation (Turkification) and westernisation of Islamism in Turkey. The AKP's understanding of Europe and its stress on Turkey's membership in the EU were outcomes of its Western layer of identity. It was Western in terms of stressing human rights, rule of law, economic liberalism and respect for the popular will. Its Western formulation differed from the Kemalist version by stressing bottom-up modernisation and respect for the popular will and societal autonomy from the state. Erdoğan's desire to join the EU did not seek assimilation but rather something like 'cream, rather than sugar, being added to the coffee', a metaphor for changing the make-up of the EU. Until 2010, Erdoğan advocated a type of secularism that was based on freedom of religion from state intervention. He and the people around him attempted to rearticulate the Ottoman Islamic ethos as the spirit of tolerance, accommodation and co-existence of faiths, cultures and ideas. This formulation of modernist and Western-influenced Islam also appealed to many secularised, urban and well-to-do Turks who believed the AKP could provide a highly desired corrective to what had by then become a corrupt and authoritarian prevailing secularist Kemalist political structure.

3.7 Conclusion

Erdoğan was a critical leader from a group of Islamist politicians who were bruised, marginalised and pushed aside by the February 1997 military intervention. Moreover, the political establishment was bogged down in corruption and the government, then led by Bülent Ecevit, was unable to address the growing problems of the country. The public was ready for a radical cleansing of the old political guard. In the eyes of the public, Erdoğan was a popular politician who happened to be a successful mayor of Istanbul. By jailing him, the establishment inadvertently helped his popularity.

Although Erdoğan's political personality and identity were shaped within Erbakan's National Outlook Movement (MGH), for many years, he consciously did not bring the Islamist ideology of the MGH into the government. Until 2013, Erdoğan defined the AKP as the *conservative* democrat party with a commitment to secularism, democracy and the rule of law. He consistently refused the charges of representing an Islamic party and, instead, presented his party as a conservative centre-right party that seeks Turkey's full membership in the EU. Erdoğan thus acted as a pragmatic politician who was not much interested in Islamic ideology but rather was shaped by a mission of providing the best social services and of meeting the practical needs of society. One indeed wonders whether or not Erdoğan's pragmatism and commitment to democracy were tactical moves or if he initially had genuinely given up his Islamist identity and only later structural conditions forced him back to his old Islamist mould.

While the AKP came to power in 2002, until the 2007 elections, the secularist Kemalist establishment still enjoyed the full support of the military and judiciary as it guided public policy from the background. During this period, the Kemalist establishment closely followed the policies of Erdoğan and this active monitoring, in turn, angered Erdoğan, forcing him to look for an opportunity to undermine the hegemonic position of the Kemalist establishment, especially the military, in order to build his own envisioned system of *başyücelik* (which can be translated as a sultan-like presidency without checks and balances).

In this trajectory, Erdoğan was not alone as he was initially surrounded by a team of ethical, educated politicians who enhanced the perception of Erdoğan as a reliable leader in the public's eyes. The public gave its faith that this team of politicians would address the social, political and economic challenges of Turkey. His early successes were thus not only his own but also credited to a well-coordinated effective team. This team and the conservative Anatolian bourgeoisie were instrumental in Erdoğan's 2002 electoral victory. However, as Erdoğan consolidated power, by more and more resembling an anachronistic sultan and a populist autocrat, he would purge members of his team one by one while turning the party into a family business to enrich himself and his most loyal business associates. The next chapter will explore how Erdoğan became the unchallenged new autocrat of Turkey.

Notes

1. Yıldız, 'Politico-religious discourse', pp. 187–210.
2. Erdoğan, *Bu Sarkı Burada Bitmez*, p. 47.
3. Turgut, 'AKP Beyaz Türk İktidarını Yıktı', 3 June 2004; Özkök, 'Beyaz Türklerin Tasfiyesi mi', 21 April 2006. 'Are we experiencing a revolution of the first generation rural-origin "strangers" in the cities? Did this revolution start the exclusion of the "white Turks" from predominating political power structures?' As a result of Ataturkist reforms and urbanisation, the Turkish society experienced a major social mobility movement affecting students from mainly rural regions who came to college in the country's urban centres and eventually made their way to important roles in governing their country. A prominent example was Durmuş Yılmaz, who came from a traditional family background and was appointed by the AKP-led government, and this, in turn, triggered a major debate over the exclusion of the 'white Turks' by the 'black Turks'.
4. Terkoğlu, 'Erdoğan'ın "Saddamlaştırılması"nın başlangıcı', 9 May 2019.
5. Besli and Özbay, *Bir Liderin Doğuşu: Recep Tayyip Erdoğan*, p. 50.
6. Interview with Mir Dengir Fırat, Ankara, 6 March 2016.
7. Bahri Zengin (1942–2011) said, 'Politics for me has always remained an intellectual engagement to bring our civilisational outlook to the forefront. Erdoğan sees politics as a way of enrichment. He never cared for the power of ideas and used them instrumentally to have economic power. Politics, for Erdoğan, is the best path to economic wealth. He became a very wealthy person when he was the mayor of Istanbul.' My interview with Bahri Zengin, Istanbul, 4 July 2009.
8. Interview with Bahri Zengin, Istanbul, 3 July 2009.
9. Besli and Özbay, *Bir Liderin Doğuşu: Recep Tayyip Erdoğan*, p. 16.
10. Yavuz, *Islamic Political Identity*, pp. 103–30.
11. Interview with Bahri Zengin, Istanbul, 3 July 2009.

12. Interview with Recep Tayyip Erdoğan, quoted in Taşgetiren, 'Boğulma Hissi', 18 January 1995.
13. Birand and Yıldız, *Son Darbe: 28 Şubat*, pp. 20–36.
14. For more on the West Working Group, see Salt, 'Turkey's military "democracy"', pp. 72–8.
15. *Milliyet*, 21 November 1994.
16. Öniş, 'The political economy of Turkey's Justice and Development Party', pp. 211–12.
17. Yetkin, 'Beni 28 Subat AB'ci yaptı', 5 June 2005.
18. Hale and Özbudun, *Islamism, Democracy, and Liberalism in Turkey*, p. 20.
19. 'Erdoğan Anlatıyor', interview by Göksel Özköylü, *Radikal*, 18 November 2002.
20. *Milli Gazete*, 26 March 1999.
21. Güngör, *Yenilikci Hareket*, pp. 57–72.
22. Birand and Yildiz, *Son Darbe: 28 Subat*, pp. 340–4.
23. *Yeni Safak*, 8 August 2001.
24. FP – Fazilet Partisi or Virtue Party; ANAP – Anavatan Partisi or Motherland Party; DYP – Doğru Yol Partisi or True Path Party; MHP – Milliyetçi Hareket Partisi or Nationalist Movement Party.
25. Yavuz, *Secularism and Muslim Democracy*, pp. 45–78.
26. Many years of corruption and inefficient governments ruined the fundamentals of the Turkish economy and the conflict between the president and the prime minister led to a major economic meltdown in 2001. The Turkish stock market plummeted and interest rates reached 3,000 per cent. The central bank lost $5 billion in reserves and the US dollar rose to 1,500,000 Turkish lira. The immediate effects of the meltdown were higher unemployment and an increase in income inequality.
27. Yavuz and Özcan, 'Political crisis in Turkey', pp. 118–36.
28. Hendrik, *Gülen: The Ambiguous Politics of Market Islam*; Yavuz, *Toward an Islamic Enlightenment*.
29. I was invited to the international symposium and presented a paper on the AKP and its problems. I met with Dengir Mir Mehmet Fırat at the meeting and have kept close ties with him. He was the deputy chairman of the AKP and the most respected politician. Yet, he never felt that he fitted into the AKP as Erdoğan relapsed into its Islamist identity.
30. Erdoğan, 'Keynote Speech', *Uluslarasi Muhafazakarlik ve Demokrasi Sempozyumu*, pp. 7–17.

4

ERDOĞAN AND THE SECULAR RESISTANCE (2007–12)

This chapter will examine the events that sharpened sociocultural cleavages leading to an increasingly polarised Turkish society. The events such as the 2007 presidential crisis, the EU's reluctance to accept the Turkish membership, the closure decision of the Constitutional Court in 2008 and the 2010 constitutional referendum played a critical role in the gradual radicalisation of Erdoğan.

Although the AKP won the 2002 elections, the Kemalist establishment remained sceptical of Erdoğan. To counter these uncertainties, Erdoğan worked hard to assure the public that he had 'cast off his Islamist shirt' as he reassured the public and political colleagues about his commitment to the republican values of secularism, human rights and democracy. This was the era of the 'politics of patience' in which Erdoğan avoided any confrontation with the secular establishment at any cost. Between 2002 and 2007, Erdoğan modulated his political language as he expanded his domestic and external legitimacy as the country's leader. For instance, he refrained from addressing cultural or religious issues, such as a headscarf ban or religious education. This politics of avoidance helped him a great deal to consolidate his power. In a speech, Erdoğan said the 'headscarf issue is a matter of patience. It took twenty-three years for even the Qur'an to be revealed. Alcoholic beverages were even prohibited gradually at that time'. Erdoğan believes that one needs to create the 'physical situation' and then prepare the 'legal situation' to 'normalise it'. He always stresses that one's duty is to prepare society for change and do it gradually. He said, 'It takes nine months for a baby to be born.' Erdoğan followed this with, 'A baby may be disabled in case of a premature birth. The important thing is the health of the baby. The headscarf is a right; an innate right.'[1] Erdoğan is known for his patient, calculating personality. He acts when he feels powerful enough to determine the outcome. Therefore, his first term as prime minister differed dramatically from his second, and later when he became a president with expanded powers.

In addition to the politics of patience, Erdoğan's other advantage was building a coalition of groups to expand his legitimacy and consolidate his power. He allied himself with the Europhile liberals, moderate Islamists and the Kurdish nationalists to present himself as a 'new' leader of the coalition of forces. However, the military, the major businessmen and a large sector of secularist elite stayed at a distance from Erdoğan's tactics, always questioning his intentions. Pro-Western business groups were unsure of Erdoğan and hardly trusted him.[2] In government, because of public scepticism about Erdoğan's Islamist intentions and the deep suspicions of the Kemalist establishment about the role and power of political Islam, the Kemalist institutions, especially the military and the court, closely watched Erdoğan's policies. Realising this, Erdoğan committed to Turkey's Western orientation, especially EU membership, avoided cultural issues and focused on the country's economic issues. During the early period, Ali Babacan, then the minister of finance, carried out the IMF programme and ended chronic hyperinflation. Turkey's average GDP annual growth rate between 2002 and 2007 was 6.8 per cent. In tandem, Erdoğan's government passed a series of harmonisation packages to fulfil EU membership requirement. The EU process shaped Turkey's domestic and foreign policies because virtually everyone anticipated achieving full membership. Moreover, Erdoğan took the initiative on the Cyprus conflict to push towards the UN-led reunification process in 2004. When the new European political elite, such as France's Nicolas Sarkozy and Germany's Angela Merkel, came to power and rejected Turkey's membership, the Turkish government lost its EU orientation and its faith in the spirit of continental unity. Thus, the domestic and external events between 2007 and 2013 are critical to understand the return of Erdoğan's autocratic and narcissistic personality to his governing approach.

4.1 The Presidential Crisis of 2007 and Polarisation

> The army shall protect the glory and honour of Turkey and the Turkish community against all kinds of internal and external dangers.
>
> Mustafa Kemal Atatürk[3]

The Turkish military has always been suspicious of Erdoğan's intentions. The fears and concerns of the Kemalist establishment concerning the AKP's victory were rooted in their perceptions of secularism and nationalism as the cardinal principles of the Turkish Republic. In April 2007, a political crisis emerged at the end of the seven-year term of the secular president Ahmet Necdet Sezer, who had never been involved in a corruption scandal. To the Kemalists, Sezer was a crucial bulwark against the Islamisation of the state, while, at the same time, the AKP leadership regarded Sezer as the main obstacle to the appointment of key bureaucrats, the decentralisation of power, and further democratisation and liberalisation of the system.

Many Kemalists feared that the nomination of Abdullah Gül, who behaved like Erdoğan's lapdog, to the presidency would lead to the Islamisation of the state through the recruitment of Islamic-oriented bureaucrats into the higher echelons of the state. As the president had considerable power in blocking laws and appointing high officials, he enjoyed the authority to appoint judges to the Constitutional Court and members of the Council of Higher Education, as well as university rectors, high level judges and the general directorate of Turkish Radio and Television (TRT). The president is also commander-in-chief of the armed forces, presides over the national security council, and has authority to impose a state of emergency and even declare war if parliament is not in session. As commander-in-chief, the president plays an important role in the promotion of generals and can drive out officers who challenge the ideological unity (that is, Kemalism) and homogeneity of the military.

In addition to the fear over the Islamisation of the state, the second most important concern was Kurdish politics. The Turkish military feared potential developments in Iraq, such as an eventual independent Kurdish state (Kurdistan), which could encompass Iraq's oil-rich region of Kirkuk. This possible development, the Turkish military feared, would undermine national unity and the territorial integrity of the country. The military believed that the AKP government either was not aware of such a long-term threat or wanted to solve the Kurdish issue to steer the regime in Turkey away from Kemalist principles. The military also feared losing its autonomy over recruitment, promotion and budget, in addition to being penetrated by ideological divisions through the Copenhagen criteria, which are required for EU membership. With the appointment of General Yaşar Büyükanıt as chief of general staff in 2006, the military became more assertive in protecting its privileges and political role. Finally, the independence and assertiveness of some Islamic groups, especially the Fethullah Gülen community, within the bureaucracy and business was another source of fear among secularists.[4]

With little consultation inside or outside his party, in the spring of 2007, Erdoğan single-handedly nominated Gül, then the foreign minister, to become the next president – this having occurred twenty-four hours before voting was to take place in parliament. Secularists and their supporters in the media, courts, universities and military mobilised to stop the process. When the centre-right parties (DYP of Mehmet Ağar and ANAP of Erkan Mumcu) and the secular leftist main opposition (CHP of Deniz Baykal) boycotted the poll for president on 26 April, the generals published a statement on the official website of the Turkish Armed Forces the following day that threatened to overthrow the government, if necessary, to protect the secular nature of the Republic:

> The problem that [has] emerged in the presidential election process is focused on arguments over secularism. The Turkish Armed Forces maintain their sound determination to carry out their duties stemming from laws to protect the unchangeable characteristics of the Republic of Turkey. It has been observed that some circles have been carrying out endless efforts to disturb fundamental values of the Republic of Turkey, especially secularism, and have increased their efforts recently. Those activities include requests for redefinition of fundamental values of the Republic and attempts to organise alternative celebrations instead of our national festivals symbolising the unity and solidarity of our nation. Those who carry out the mentioned activities, which turned into an open challenge against the state, do not refrain from exploiting the holy religious feelings of our people, and they try to hide their real goals under the guise of religion . . . Those who are opposed to the Great Leader

Mustafa Kemal Atatürk's understanding of 'how happy is the one who says I am a Turk', are enemies of the Republic of Turkey and will remain so. The Turkish Armed Forces maintain their sound determination to carry out their duties stemming from laws to protect the unchangeable characteristics of the Republic of Turkey. Their loyalty to this determination is absolute.[5]

This statement created a political stand-off, one which polarised Turkish society between the military and the AKP sympathisers. The main opposition party, the CHP, took the first poll to the Constitutional Court on 28 April. The Constitutional Court, under the influence of the 27 April military e-memorandum and mass rallies in Ankara and Istanbul, annulled the parliament's vote for Gül on technical grounds that it lacked a two-thirds majority for a quorum. There was no real precedent that a majority of three-quarters of MPs had to be in Parliament. Erdoğan called the Court's decision 'a bullet fired at the heart of democracy'.

In the face of such opposition, Gül withdrew his candidacy. Erdoğan called for early elections and proposed a number of constitutional changes intended to prepare the ground for electing the president through direct popular vote.[6] These changes threatened a constitutional crisis after the 22 July 2007 national elections. For example, future presidents would be elected for a five-year term, renewable for an additional five years, a change from the existing single seven-year term. The proposal also reduced the parliamentary term to four years and the quorum from 367 to 184. Parliament passed the constitutional changes, but President Sezer vetoed the package on 25 May 2007. When parliament voted for the package the second time, Sezer sent it out for a referendum on a proposed amendment to elect the president by popular vote and requested the Constitutional Court to annul the legislation. Meanwhile, on 3 June 2007, the CHP petitioned the Constitutional Court to cancel the reform package on the grounds that parliament had violated its bylaws. The Court ruled against the CHP and Sezer and opened the way for a referendum, which took place in October 2007.

This referendum would sow the seeds of the current political crisis in the country over a strong presidential system. The referendum took place on 21 October 2007 and a majority voted for it. Electing the president by popular vote, however, was controversial, as it ultimately bypassed the parliament, which theoretically enjoyed a check on the executive branch. Turkey, unlike the US or France, was a parliamentary system of government and the prime minister was the head of the elected government, while the president was the head of state and guardian of the constitution. The election of the president by popular vote strengthened the office's political weight, as the president could claim more democratic legitimacy than the other governing branches. By 2007, Erdoğan was confident enough in his broad popular support to refuse to back down to the military and the Kemalist establishment. He had foreshadowed this in an earlier statement:

> My story is the story of this nation. Either this nation is going to win and come to power or the arrogant and oppressive minority group, who look at Anatolia with contempt and are alien to Anatolian realities, will continue to remain in power. The nation has the authority to decide, and enough – sovereignty belongs to the nation.[7]

The main impetus behind the 2007 crisis was the Kemalist establishment's animus towards the AKP and Erdoğan's style of managing the presidential election. They accused Erdoğan of confusing the AKP parliamentary group and the synergetic nature of Turkish society. They believed that the AKP had not tried to create new bridges to diverse sectors in society. Instead, it stressed the 'bonding' nature of communitarian politics, with a tight circle of advisors. The assertive secular groups, especially the Alevi minority, were threatened by the unfolding social and political processes. The government ignored the public policy of creating a sense of belonging and coexisting among diverse groups in the country. And the presidential election became an avenue of mass mobilisation both at elite and popular levels.

The military did not want someone like Gül, who criticised Kemalism, never developed a principled position, and identified as a deeply pious Muslim with a wife who always wore a headscarf. Thus, an attempt by Erdoğan to control the presidency was seen as upsetting the checks and balances of the state and an attempt to change its secular character. In fact, it was Gül who promoted the Gülenists and some other Islamists in the security establishment along with the judiciary, because of their piety rather than meritocracy.[8] In response, numerous anti-AKP civil-society organisations joined forces and organised mass rallies, known as '*cumhuriyet mitingleri*' (republican meetings) in Ankara, Istanbul, Manisa, Canakkale, Izmir and Samsun. These rallies, which gathered more than a million people, unsettled the delicate equilibrium among the Kemalist military, the AKP government and diverse sectors of society.

4.1.1 Republican rallies: Kemalist establishment opposition to the AKP

Anti-AKP protesters were mobilised in opposition to specific concerns: (1) there was an Islamic threat to their secular lifestyle; (2) the AKP government was too pro-Kurdish and sought to change the founding principles of the Republic to accommodate Kurdish political demands; and (3) the government was too willing to accommodate Western powers in pushing for democratic reforms. The mass rallies reflected the lack of societal consensus on the basis of coexistence with new actors and voices in the public sphere. The pragmatic constellation of Özal's neo-liberal economic policies coupled with the Anatolian Islamic movements had undermined the old sociopolitical landscape and class dynamics by creating new opportunity spaces for marginalised groups. In the 1990s, the Anatolian bourgeoisie leveraged its interests against the dominant class alliances between the metropolitan bourgeoisie (TÜSİAD) and the secular military establishment. After the 2002 elections, TÜSİAD saw the advantages of joining the AKP's political as well as economic liberalisation programme. They drifted from their allegiance to the hardline Kemalist establishment and instead stressed the need for good governance and transparency over militant secularism.

The four major anti-AKP mass rallies of early 2007 played an important role in the sociopolitical mobilisation. Although these rallies were organised by retired military officers, Kemalist associations and secular women's groups, the majority of protesters were from the urban middle classes, who responded to perceived threats to their lifestyle. This more recent Kemalist urban middle class differed from the traditional merchant class, which was more conservative and usually voted for centre-right parties.[9] The Kemalist urban middle class emerged out of the service economy, comprising self-employed lawyers, engineers, doctors, and professionals in the computer technology, banking and insurance sectors of the economy. They stressed individualism and self-actualisation. They also emphasised formality and the rule of law rather than the rule of ethnic, tribal or religion-based solidarity networks. Many in the Kemalist middle class were insecure about the orientation of the country under an Islamist party – albeit a moderate one like the AKP.[10] The common opposition slogans at the time were: 'Turkey is secular and will remain secular!' 'No pass to the headscarf in the Cankaya Palace.' 'We are all Turks!' 'Neither *seriat* (Islamic Law) nor military coup.' 'Look at us! Count! How many are we here?'

The demonstrators included many from the most modern, secular and pro-Western sectors of the country. However, there were contradictions reflected in these demonstrations. There was a sense that the AKP was using the EU to counter the Kemalist establishment. These secular nationalists (primarily ethnic) Turks also believed that the EU, along with the US, only cared about their national interests and not secularism or modernity in Turkey. While claiming to favour secularism and liberalism, they often were intolerant about the rights of religious citizens and failed to appreciate the contradiction in defending Western-style freedoms while championing the right of unelected military officers to intervene in civilian politics and dictate to citizens how to dress and behave. This cognitive dissonance prevails to this day among pro-Kemalist groups. Many believe the US desires the evolution of 'moderate' Islamic movements by using Turkey as an experiment. Also, many have seen the European and American governments believing it would be much easier to work with the AKP rather than with secular sectors of society because the AKP leadership depends on Washington and other Western powers for insurance against another soft coup that could be launched by the Kemalist establishment.

4.2 The Turkish Military's Fears: Kurdish Secessionism and Islamism

During the April 2007 crisis, the military acted as an opposition party. To understand the defiant reaction of the military to the presidential election, one must examine the critical intersection of internal and external forces. The military worried about Kurdish secessionism and the challenges of the Islamic movements, especially the Gülen community. Moreover, both Kurdish and Islamist activists invoked the EU-centric human rights discourse and the US occupation of Iraq to redefine the founding principles of the Republic. The analysis of this cognitive framework which drove the Turkish military's erstwhile intervention was important for understanding its policies and strategies against the Kurdish and Islamic challenges they sought to pursue.

The military played a decisive role in the Republic's founding and the formation of modern Turkish identity.[11] The military was extremely sensitive about secularism – the cardinal principle of the Republic's ethos of modern nation-building. In light of the sectarian and ethnic violence in Iraq, the military was sensitised ever more so to the principles of national identity and secularism. Moreover, with the collapse of the Ottoman Empire, the military believed that consociational multiethnic and multireligious polities could not survive and that they would always lead to constant outside interference in domestic affairs, eventually leading to the destruction of the state.[12] To avoid the potential breakup of the state, the military stressed unitary national integration and the maintenance of a homogeneous nation through secularism and Turkish nationalism.

General İlker Başbuğ, chief of staff, argued that

> the gist of the reforms of Atatürk is to create a nation state and Turkish nation . . . Atatürk's understanding of nation state does not have an ethnic or religious base. His reforms represent a shift from a religion-based political community to a secular nation state. Thus, secularism is the cornerstone of the founding principles of the Republic.[13]

Any challenge to this ethos has been regarded as a threat to the state. There have been two major challenges to the project of secular nation-building: Islamic and Kurdish activism, both identified as enemies of the Republic. Atatürk enunciated the military as the guardian of secularism and nation-building. The military appropriated this core mission during the military coup in 1961. It legally assigned the task of preserving secularism and nationalism to itself with Article 35 of the Internal Service Law of 1961: 'Turkish Armed Forces are responsible for guarding and defending the Turkish Republic as defined by the constitution.'

Since then, the military has functioned as a quasi-political party against civilian governments with its own vision of politics and grass-roots supporters. However, there is a tacit consensus in society that when the country is under threat, it is the task of the military to intervene and save it – that is, stage a *coup d'état*, as warranted. Yet, the same public has never voted for a pro-military party after the coups – carried out in almost every remaining decade of the twentieth century (1960, 1971, 1980 and 1997), either to eliminate or contain political challenges. It has been largely successful in containing them, though its often-brutal methods (especially at the expense of the Kurdish minority) have led to a self-fulfilling prophecy, strengthening Kurdish nationalist and separatist demands.[14] The relations between the military and the Islamic National Outlook Movement were always confrontational. The military was involved in two coups (in 1980 and 1997) against Erbakan's pro-Islamic parties. Since the AKP evolved out of the National Outlook Movement, the military has always been suspicious about the intentions of the Party and its leadership – Erdoğan, Gül and Arınç, who also were active members of prior Islamic movements.

There was a deleterious contradiction built into the educational system of the Turkish officer corps. While they were indoctrinated into staying away from daily politics with a negative view of politicians, they also were asked to safeguard and, if necessary, sacrifice themselves for the founding principles of the Republic. In the education of the military officers, two events were constantly stressed to the young cadets. One event referenced the group of ideologically oriented military officers who took control of the government between 1908 and 1918 as part of the 'Young Turk' revolution, where they set in motion domestic and foreign policies leading to the Ottoman Empire's collapse. The military's humiliating and shattering breakdown was observed during the first Balkan War in 1912–13. Due to the ideological polarisation and politicisation of military commanders in the field, the Ottoman military was not capable of undertaking coordinated defensive operations, leading to disastrous defeat at the hands of the Balkan Holy League. The Ottoman presence in the Balkans, which had lasted more than five centuries, was extinguished as millions of Ottoman Muslims fled genocidal ethnic cleansing at the hands of Balkan states. These traumatic events left a permanent mark on the institutional ideology of the Turkish military, which only could overcome the trauma and humiliation through Atatürk's military victories during the Turkish War of Independence from 1919 to 1923.

The second decisive institution-shaping event comprised a series of small military mutinies after 1950 against the newly elected Democrat Party of

Prime Minister Adnan Menderes. The 1960 coup against Menderes was carried out by thirty-seven lower-ranking colonels who called themselves the Committee of National Unity. The violent coup resulted in the hanging of Menderes and two cabinet ministers. This coup also forced higher ranking officers into early retirement and purged much of the senior staff of the Turkish Armed Forces. This was the first and only time when the military chain of command was totally violated in a *coup d'état* – that is, until the 15 July 2016 coup attempt. After the 1960 coup, the military centralised command around a four-star general with the chief of staff becoming the unchallenged head of the Turkish Armed Forces. The politicians agreed to the centralisation to avoid the risk of another breakdown in the chain of command.

When the AKP came to power in 2002, the new chief of staff was General Hilmi Özkök, a moderate and a democrat who aspired to defend European standards of civilian–military relations. Yet most of the commanders, who did not go along with General Özkök, viewed the AKP's intentions suspiciously. The AKP government failed to utilise General Özkök to develop healthier ties with the military and allay their suspicions. The first negative interaction between the military and the government took place over the US desire to open a second front through Turkey during the 2003 Iraq War. The AKP blamed the military for parliament's decision not to allow American troops into Turkey or to send Turkish troops to Iraq.[15] This criticism engendered increased hostility on the part of the military, with many mid-level officers questioning Özkök's soft line towards the government.[16] In the perception of high-ranking officers, the AKP government shifted the blame for deteriorating relations between the Turkish military and the Pentagon by constantly complaining about the military's positions on Iraq, the Kurdish question, and the Islamic Republic of Iran. In short, internal divisions in Turkish society led the AKP government, like its Kemalist opponents in the past, to appeal to the US as an ally against its domestic foes and search for legitimacy in Washington by opposing the military's role in the Turkish political system.[17]

One of Turkey's deepest domestic problems has been the lack of shared understanding of the sources and nature of the Kurdish question. The AKP leadership has treated the Kurdish challenge as stemming from past Kemalist authoritarianism and even regarded the Kurds as an ideological ally against rigid Kemalist ideology. Erdoğan, for example, has been accused by nationalist circles of having too many advisers of Kurdish background. The military, in turn, has defined the separatist Kurdish challenge in terms of territorial integrity, national unity and the homogenous Kemalist nation state model. Thus, strategies for containing the Kurdish challenge have varied. In response to the military's aggressive posture, the AKP government tried to use the EU institutions and norms to rein in the armed forces.[18] Some close to the government voiced the opinion that 'the military wants to maintain its power and budget by exaggerating [the threat] and constantly engaging in military operations against the PKK'. The Kurdish question became the most significant weapon with which the military and the AKP government delegitimised each other.

The worst crisis concerned the recruitment of followers for moderate Islamist religious leader Fethullah Gülen into the national police and the ministry of education. In a series of interviews, a high-ranking military officer had this to say:

> The Islamisation of society was completed by different Islamic groups and Sufi orders. Now we are seeing the Islamisation of state institutions and bureaucracy. It is very similar to the Islamisation of the bureaucracy in Pakistan, especially the education and the police force. They have not been able to penetrate the military. The group which leads this Islamisation of the state is the Fethullah Gülen community. They use almost every means, even those which are un-Islamic, to achieve their goal of controlling the state. The AKP government, which lacks its own educated cadre, is very much dependent on Gülen's followers. Moreover, the university exams are now dominated by the graduates of these Gülen schools. They will dominate the bureaucracy.[19]

Kemalist bureaucrats criticised the attempts of the Gülen community to use police force against the military.[20] During my interviews in Ankara, several high-ranking military officers raised questions about the degree to which promotion in some ministries took place on the basis of religious-network-based solidarity. This alleged penetration by the Gülen community of the bureaucracy concerned the military, and they did not want a similar process to take place within the military as well.[21]

In addition to policy differences between the AKP government and the military, General Yaşar Büyükanıt, new chief of general staff, who succeeded

Hilmi Özkök, defended the traditional activist role of the military within the political system and did not hesitate to resist government policies. Before Büyükanıt was appointed, there was a vicious – one could claim racist – campaign against him. He was first accused of not being a 'Turk' but rather of Sabbatean/Jewish ancestry.[22] 'When these accusations were spreading around websites,' a military officer explains, 'Büyükanıt became the target of the Gülen community via the Semdinli incident', in which Turkish special security forces were accused of bombing a bookstore owned by a former Kurdish activist in Semdinli (in Van) in 2005, among other events. Ferhat Sarıkaya, a prosecutor in the city of Van and with known close ties to the Gülen community, was called to investigate General Büyükanıt, along with three other generals, over allegations of abusing their positions and setting up an illegal group to foment unrest in the mainly Kurdish cities in order to prevent Turkey's bid to join the EU. A paramilitary group, which was claimed to have been set up by General Büyükanıt, was indicted for the bombing of a bookstore in Semdinli which resulted in one death and several injuries.[23] Some AKP deputies suspected the military hardliners' involvement in the incident and supported the Van prosecutor's indictment of Büyükanıt. For instance, Faruk Ünsal, the AKP deputy from Adiyaman, said, 'The indictment prepared by the office of the Van prosecutor has done what we were unable to do.' Another AKP deputy, Hasan Taşcı from Manisa, said, 'What we left unfinished is now completed by the Van prosecutor. He did his job.'[24]

The military believes that the Gülen community launched a campaign through its media outlets and pro-Gülen police force against General Büyükanıt to halt his appointment. Indeed, the Gülen community did not want Büyükanıt to be the next chief of the general staff because when he was commander of Kuleli Military High School and the War College in Ankara, he purged many students who had ties with the Gülen community. The anti-Büyükanıt campaign and negative reporting on the military created an anti-Gülen mood within the military and some high-ranking generals blamed the AKP government for having allowed Gülenist infiltration in the first place. General Büyükanıt regarded the campaign against him as the work of the Gülen community within the police and the government. This, in turn, made him more confrontational, and he watched suspiciously the Gülen community's alliance with the AKP government. The leading daily newspaper *Zaman*, which is owned by the Gülen community, and the weekly magazine *Nokta*, sought to associate him with underground organisations of the 'deep state', accusing him of fomenting instability in the country. The government did not defend the military or challenge journalists who voiced such suspicions.

The Kemalist mobilisation against Gül's candidacy, along with the April 2007 military ultimatum, sparked many consequences for Turkey's political landscape. Gül withdrew his candidacy and became a '*mazlum*'[25] – one who has been wronged in the eyes of the public. Early national elections were called; fragmentation among political parties ended through one successful and one failed merger. Erdoğan changed the list of newly nominated deputies by purging almost all critical voices,[26] along with many liberal voices from the Party such as Ertuğrul Yalçınbayır, known to be the 'moral conscience of the AKP'.[27] In an unsuccessful attempt to appease Kemalist/secularist critics, Erdoğan nominated former leftists, a few intellectuals from the Alevi community and some women to overcome charges that the AKP was a obscurantist movement.[28] Erdoğan excluded a significant number of AKP deputies from the National Outlook Movement in an effort to alter perceptions that the Party was too Islamist and to position it in the centre of the political spectrum.

4.3 The 2007 Elections as a Historic Breakthrough

The configuration of forces in the republican meetings, the statement by the military, the decisions of the Constitutional Court and the merging of the leftist parties failed to prevent the takeover of the presidency by the AKP. Furthermore, the AKP used the crisis to finally break the Kemalist establishment's control over the political system – a political breakthrough for the country. The AKP emerged as the dominant political force in the 22 July 2007 elections.[29] After receiving 34.4 per cent of the vote in the November 2002 elections, the AKP increased its total to 46.5 per cent in the July 2007 elections. For its second term, the AKP gained 12 percentage points in its parliamentary apportionment, as the AKP claimed 341 of 550 seats in parliament. The secularist CHP and the nationalist MHP won 112 and seventy-one seats, respectively. Up to twenty-five seats went to independent candidates, including twenty Kurdish representatives who merged under the pro-Kurdish Demokratik Toplum Partisi (Democratic Society Party, DTP).

That Erdoğan and the AKP emerged once again as the leading party following the 2007 elections was no surprise. However, very few, including the AKP itself, expected such a landslide victory. The AKP was able to unite many disparate voters in its bid to retain control of the Turkish parliament. Some voted for democracy, others voted against the military's e-memorandum, yet others voted with the expectation of a new constitution, and yet still others voted in favour of EU membership. With interests and demographics ranging from business groups to shantytown dwellers, from devout Muslims to Armenians,[30] liberals and conservatives came together to vote for the same party. The AKP electorate was not unified by a single identity but rather a coalition of identities that attracted nearly half (46.5 per cent) of the total votes.

The AKP campaign was based on Gül's candidacy as being, in the Party's own words, the 'election of a pious president representing the will of the majority'. By framing the reaction to Gül as an attack against traditional Turkish Muslim values and identity, the AKP mobilised the Islamic networks throughout Anatolia, along with Muslim-owned media, to stir the masses against the opposition parties. As the state machine was in AKP hands, along with municipal governments, the AKP had an advantage over the military in reaching the people. The military e-memorandum rescued the AKP from hard questions regarding its own platform in the debates and the election turned instead into a referendum over Kemalism versus democracy and respect for Turkey's Seljuk and Ottoman Muslim heritage.

Another critical factor in the AKP's success was Erdoğan's charisma as the supreme leader of the newly mobilised conservative masses. He was always viewed as one of them in terms of his body language, idiomatic language and lifestyle. The impact of the presidential election worked in favour of the AKP. The Party's election platform was based on *mazlum* (feeling of being wronged) and *mağdur* (feeling of being victimised) and the exclusion of pious individuals (AKP supporters characterised as Black Turks) from the public sphere by White Turks of the Kemalist establishment. With the support of Islamic networks, the AKP organised more meetings and carried its message to every corner of the country.[31] For instance, the AKP organizsd mass rallies in fifty-eight provinces during the 2007 election campaign, whereas the CHP sponsored them in just twenty provinces.

4.3.1 The post-election struggle over drafting a new constitution

The AKP's electoral victories (parliamentary and presidential) heightened concerns in the more secular sections of society in western Turkey, while the military continued its vain attempt to hold back the tide of popular mobilisation.[32] With the poor showing of the traditional Kemalist party (CHP), however, the military had less public ground to make its opposition tenable. With the battle to ban the AKP and bar Gül from the presidency lost, the main concern of secular groups focused on dealing with the AKP's initiative to craft a new post-1980 coup civilian constitution. Through this constitutional debate the AKP sought to recast the founding Kemalist principles of the Republic. Although Islamist groups wanted to undo the authoritarian basis of the Kemalist system, the secular Kemalists wanted to protect the secular nature of the constitution, along with the military-cum-judiciary 'insurance' against the majoritarian Islamo-communitarian temptations.

The AKP wanted to redefine the founding principles of the Republic with the support of the liberals in order not to be accused of seeking to establish an Iranian style theocracy. Some liberal intellectuals ardently supported Erdoğan's proposal of a new constitution. Some of these intellectuals, who argued for the establishment of the Second Republic, encompassed a rather controversial historical understanding of the evolution of the political system.[33] By the Second Republic they meant a completely de-Kemalised Turkey, with a new definition of secularism to open more spaces for religiously based political arguments. They supported an arrangement in which much of the Turkish states' centralised power was devolved to the provinces (as a way of meeting the political demands of the Kurdish minority), and a polity without any officially enforced ideology. By championing this new liberal direction, they believe that the Republic should not side with any national or ideological position but rather maintain equal distance to all preferences, opinions and religions in the true Western democratic fashion, something which the ostensibly westernising Kemalist was challenged to argue in the opposition. Many of these intellectuals were jailed by Erdoğan since their utility for building an autocratic system had expired.

4.3.2 Fear of Islamic majoritarianism

This shift in political language and public spaces in terms of Islamisation goes to the heart of fear and the mass mobilisation in April and May 2007. Many people worried about the long-term implications of this Islamisation at societal and state levels. However, it would be a mistake to read this process as anti-modern or anti-democratic. Islamic groups have played an important role in economic development and, as a result, many Muslims have become more moderate. Yet, for secular Turks, these moderating influences represent the first stage of inevitable Islamisation of the state in an authoritarian direction. A jewellery shop owner tells a *New York Times* reporter that: 'In a very quiet, deep way, you can sense an Islamization ... They're not after rapid change. They're investing for 50 years ahead.'[34] The growing fear among the traditionally secular segments of society was real and the AKP used all its power to Islamise the state by appointing appropriate followers. When former President Sezer tried to stop the appointments of pro-Islamic staff to key government positions, the government appointed them as substitutes (*vekil*) to override the presidential veto. With the election of Gül as president, most high positions in the bureaucracy were staffed by Islamic-oriented officials.

This more subtle form of Islamisation was not forced but rather it was unconsciously internalised and acted upon as new sociopolitical actors entered the public sphere. It is Islamisation by moral pressure which creates an aura of a new normative system. People imitated Islamic forms of behaviour through adopting greetings and dress codes as well as praying to reflect a sense of belonging to a broader Sunni Muslim community even if many individuals were not religiously observant themselves. Şerif Mardin, a Turkish sociologist, termed this as *mahalle baskısı*, or neighbourhood pressure, which evolved out of this institutional process and was seen by critics as potentially restricting personal freedoms.[35] The debate during the presidential election crisis and the 2007 national election rallies exacerbated societal polarisation. Many secularists directly felt neighbourhood pressure from Islamic-oriented groups to modify their dress code and lifestyle routines. This neighbourhood pressure was evident to civilise and homogenise the neighbourhood's life rhythms and practices by shaming the dwellers into feeling like they have to obey, dress and live just like the rest of them. *Mahalle baskısı*, even in the period of high Kemalism, persisted in Turkey and permeated throughout high schools, neighbourhoods and state institutions.

Erdoğan's conception of a plebiscite democracy, which was not only majoritarian but also communal, was the main source of fear in more secular sectors. His example of communalised democracy comprised two parts: those who share the same religion ostensibly had common political and economic interests regardless of their ethnic origins or social class. It followed that the interests of believing Muslims were different from the interests of followers of ethnic or ideological identity groups. By stressing Islamic solidarity and Muslim nationalism above ethnic nationalism, Erdoğan sought to provide sanction (or licence) for government action. The polarisation and deepening fears of the secularist sector of the population put the pressure on the judiciary and the military to act against the AKP's newfound confidence and attempt to Islamise the rhythms of daily life.

4.4 The Kemalist Establishment's Last Gasp: the Closure Case against the AKP

In February 2008, the AKP, with the parliamentary support of the MHP, amended the constitution to lift a ban on the wearing of headscarves at universities.[36] While the constitutionality of the headscarf law was being debated, the chief prosecutor of the Court of Appeals asked the Constitutional Court to close the AKP on 14 March 2008. The chief prosecutor argued that the ruling AKP should be banned on the grounds that it had become a centre of anti-secular activities. After a judicial review, on 31 May 2008, the Constitutional Court announced that the case had merit and the Court agreed to accept the indictment from the chief prosecutor. The key evidence cited in the indictment was a constitutional amendment lifting the headscarf ban that was initiated by the AKP and the Nationalist Movement Party, which was approved by 411 out of 550 members of parliament. The indictment cited the speeches of Erdoğan, Arınç and Gül in favour of religious and personal liberties as being 'anti-secular and against the founding principles of the Republic'. The eleven judges unanimously decided to take up the case for disbanding the AKP and banning the prime minister, along with dozens of other Muslim politicians.

The case was decided on 28 July 2008, as six judges voted for closure, while five were against it. The Party would have been disbanded if the vote had been seven–four for closure. However, ten out of eleven judges voted to cut the public funding for the Party, citing that it became a focal point of anti-secular activities and Islamic parties, which were predecessors of the AKP that had been previously closed by such judicial coups for violating the separation of religion and state, including the Welfare Party (1998) and Virtue Party (2001).

The AKP narrowly missed being banned in a court case which relieved months of pressure in the country and handed a victory to the Party's leader, with concerns about the AKP's future. The court case did not moderate Erdoğan but instead made him more confrontational. A ban would have brought down the government and would have resulted in the exclusion of AKP members from politics. However, after the decision, Erdoğan said: 'A great uncertainty blocking Turkey's future has been lifted', reiterating that this was the beginning of the AKP becoming more aggressive in insisting on civilian control over state institutions with the help of the Gülen movement. The 'coup' e-memorandum of General Büyükanıt and the Constitutional Court closure case made Erdoğan even more dependent on the Gülenists, with fateful consequences for the future. Interviews with two members of the Constitutional Court who adjudicated the case indicated that the Court was under intense pressure from the military to ban the AKP, as well as some high-ranking civilian bureaucrats, and major media outlets. One of the judges said:

> The case turned into a battleground to save the Republic against Islamic fanaticism. The major pressure came from the most prominent media owners. They wanted Erdoğan to be banned from the political domain. I voted against the petition for closure of the party because of concern for the stability of the country. The evidence was overwhelming to conclude that the AKP was systematically Islamising the country. Look where we are today in 2017. The country has been Islamised and there is no more rule of law.[37]

The Court's serious warning that the AKP was steering the country in a direction that could be characterised as heavily Islamic was a major concern for the AKP. Many analysts read the decision as probation for the Party. Erdoğan became even more determined to restructure the Constitutional Court and, with the help of the Gülen movement, cleanse the army from the hardline secularists. With recent revelations coming out regarding the clash between the AKP and the Gülenists, many learned that the Gülen movement tightly controlled the police intelligence apparatus and shared select information with the government.[38] These revelations also indicated that with the support of Erdoğan, the movement unleashed a well-crafted attack on the military to undermine its popularity and penetrate its respective institutions. During the campaign to depoliticise the military, both the AKP and some pro-AKP media outlets argued that they were engaged in a process of restoring civilian democratic control over the military.[39]

4.5 Chastising the Military: the Cases of Ergenekon and Balyoz

During the closure case in 2008, Erdoğan was fully aware that the military, especially General İlker Başbuğ, who succeeded Büyükanıt, was pressuring the court to ban the AKP. Erdoğan, a patient individual waiting for the most opportune time to strike back and with the help of the Gülen community and its networks in the police, army and the intelligence networks, unleashed a systematic attack on the military to cripple it and remove the entire high echelons from the army. The assault started with numerous high-profile arrests of retired and active-duty military officers, journalists and media figures, and civil society leaders within the context of what is known as the Ergenekon trial. The prosecutor alleged that the Ergenekon, the name given to a clandestine web of ultra-nationalist organisations with alleged deep state ties, engaged in plots to overthrow Erdoğan's civilian government and destabilise the democratic regime. The Gülen movement, which owned the daily *Zaman* and TV station Samanyolu, engaged a full public campaign to mobilise AKP supporters against the military to 'end military tutelage' and 'consolidate democracy'.[40] The secularists and Kemalists claimed that Erdoğan was using the case to intimidate and suppress opposition both within and outside the state.

Although the military was deeply involved in the 2008 closure court case of the AKP and the top echelons concentrated on how to overthrow the Erdoğan government, the Court, rather than going after specific cases, politicised the case and it became a tactic of intimidation against the opposition. These court cases were effective in destroying the morale of the military by intimidating judges, businessmen and journalists with cooked evidence either invented after the arrest or manufactured during the arrest. Beginning in 2008, in the 'Ergenekon' case, Erdoğan, relying on Gülenist judges and police, arrested more than 1,350 people, who were affected by life-altering consequences. One of those detained and imprisoned was Başbuğ on 6 January 2012 with the judgement of 'being the director of an armed terrorist organisation and attempting to abolish the Republic of Turkey government or partially or completely prohibiting it from performing its duties by use of coercion and violence'.[41] These Erdoğan critics were detained and humiliated before the public with daily early morning operations carried out by the Gülenist police and the judges but also with Erdoğan's solid support. They were accused of 'being a member of an armed terrorist organisation', 'attempting to destroy the Republic of Turkey or preventing it from performing its duties by use of force and violence', and 'provoking an armed rebellion against the Republic of Turkey's government'.[42]

On 5 August 2013, Istanbul's High Criminal Court sentenced 275 of the accused, including the former chief of the general staff (Başbuğ), to life or long prison terms. Another controversial court case against the military was known as the Balyoz Plan, which involved 365 suspects. The court sentenced former naval and air force commanders and the First Army commander to twenty years' imprisonment on the basis that 'they sought to destabilise the elected government and remove the elected government by force'. The EU and many liberals supported these court cases as a way of pushing the military out of the policy arenas. These court cases became a learning ground for the Gülen–Erdoğan coalition about how to use state institutions to criminalise the opponent. And, what they had learned about the military and the Kemalist civilian networks would be used against each other. These cases polarised society along secular/Kemalist and Islamist lines, which included the Erdoğan-led AKP and the Gülen movement. The secular sectors of society grew to despise the Gülen movement and its unethical use of the court and the policies against anti-AKP opposition. *Ergenekoncu*, signifying a supporter of the Ergenekon terror organisation, became a handy label to otherise or criminalise one's opponent. These accusations against the Turkish military ruined its domestic and international legitimacy and many European countries, including the US, distanced themselves from any engagement with the Turkish military. After the 15 July 2016 coup, Erdoğan needed the secularists and the military against the Gülen movement so he persuaded the High Court of Appeals to overturn the convictions of the military officials on the grounds of procedural flaws and lack of merit in the cases.

4.6 The Trojan Horse: 2010 Constitutional Amendments

In August 2009, the government, without any consultation with the parliament or within civil society, announced its desire to amend the constitution and hold a referendum over the amended articles. The referendum took place on 12 September 2010. Both the CHP and the MHP were against the referendum and the constitutional amendments. However, the proposed amendments were approved by 58 per cent of the electorate. The main debate focused on the proposed reform of the judicial system. While these amendments were welcomed by some as measures that would weaken the Kemalist guardianship role of the judiciary and thus make it more responsive to the demands of society, others pointed to the dangers that they posed for judicial independence in Turkey.

The 2010 constitutional reform was a Trojan Horse to control the judiciary and end the secularist hegemony within the judicial system. It transformed the structure of offices like the Supreme Council of Judges and Prosecutors, and the Supreme Court. It set the conditions for active government interference in this body.[43] The total number of judges on the Supreme Court bench would be increased by six, each to serve twelve-year terms, thereby weakening the powers of the constitutional courts to ban political parties. Although these changes were defended on the basis of consolidating democracy, they were instead set to destroy the rule of law and build an autocratic system. Erdoğan steadily gained control of the executive, legislative and judiciary branches of his government, with the help of the Gülen movement.

These changes were pushed by Gülenists and it created opportunities for Gülenist judges to control the judiciary with the help of the AKP government. Gülenists promoted a mass mobilisation for passing the referendum and Gülen himself called on his followers to vote for the changes. Moreover, it also allowed all citizens to file a petition with the Constitutional Court if they believed they did not receive a fair trial. With this decision, Turkey attempted to reduce the number of petitions being sent to the European Court of Human Rights (ECHR). These amendments also removed the constitutional protections and amnesty granted to the military officers of the 1980 coup. General Kenan Evren, the leader of the 1980 coup, and then president of Turkey, was forced to stand trial at ninety-three years of age. This served as a humiliating lesson for the military when it came to issuing orders to elected civilian leaders.

Any criticism of these constitutional changes brought the accusation of being a member of the Ergenekon terror organisation. Rather than seeking to build a consensus, the alliance between Erdoğan and the Gülen movement pushed their own preferences and the Gülen movement expanded its power within the judiciary. The chasm between conceptions of secular versus Islamo-communitarian understandings of society widened. Controversially, as Erdoğan became more powerful, constraints to majoritarian democracy were removed. After the referendum, Erdoğan revealed his goal of cultivating a 'pious generation' (*dindar nesil*) and subsequently used the Ministry of Education to open more İmam Hatip schools and appoint state employees who shared the Islamic way of life and followed Islamic rituals.[44] Erdoğan argued that:

> Those parts, of course now cannot understand our concept of 'pious generation'. Because they do not know our sufferings; they do not hear our painful voices. They have never seen what bureaucrats, media, intellectuals and the wealthy elites have done to us, and they do not want to see. From now on, those elites do not take this offence but we have in this country. We are the owners of this country and we are the sons of this country.[45]

Erdoğan, along with some AKP members, formulated their vision for the youth in terms of an Islamo-Turkish (as opposed to a Turkish-Islamic) civilisational perspective (*medeniyet tassavvuru*) by establishing new foundations, education systems and cultural policies. There were limits, as the AKP did not fully appreciate the role of women in the public domain, especially in politics. The only female minister in the cabinet so far under AKP rule has been the minister of women and family affairs. Erdoğan's political Islamic identity brings politics, piety and morality together to offer a unified civilisational vision. For Islamists, piety is the basis of morality and politics. If a person is pious, that individual is assumed to be moral and, therefore, would be expected to support Islamic causes in politics. In that sense, Erdoğan always claims that his goal is to 'raise a pious generation' because he assumes that this pious generation will constitute his grass-roots base. In fact, the 2020 Pew Global survey report indicates that the overwhelming majority of Turks (75 per cent) believe that religion is necessary for morality. That is, to be a moral person, one also is expected to be a pious person.[46]

Fırat, who served as the AKP's deputy leader and then resigned from his administrative position within the party in 2008, summed up the post-referendum environment as follows:

> I decided not to become a candidate for the 2011 national election. I saw what was going on because it's clear that Erdoğan had decided by 2010 he was going to take complete control over the AKP. Why 2010? After winning the constitutional referendum in 2010, Erdoğan realised that he had gained the power to play with the judiciary. The referendum was the final step to beat the system, to beat the traditional order. However, at the time, we thought Turkey was continuing its path of democratisation with these constitutional amendments. The judiciary was now going to be taken away from the old state elites that had been static and authoritarian. Yet, Erdoğan ultimately had something else in mind and this was complemented by the way he structured the party in 2011.[47]

4.7 The Deepening Polarisation: the 2011 Elections

The major event in 2011 was the unfolding Arab Spring which helped Erdoğan to present himself as a regional leader and as a 'model' for those Arab-Muslims who were seeking to reconcile democracy with Islam and achieve economic growth. The Arab Spring was a series of rebellions, demonstrations and protest movements against the government to demand democracy, better living conditions and the restoration of the rule of law. As most of the protests were led by the Muslim Brotherhood, Erdoğan presented himself as the leader of the *umma* and tried to orchestrate the governmental change in some Arab countries by supporting the Muslim Brotherhood. During the 2011 elections, Erdoğan had strong positive ratings both inside and outside the country. Yet, he never hesitated to invoke his old tactics by reigniting the sociopolitical cleavages in the Turkish society to win the election. Erdoğan never missed the opportunity to otherise his opponents. He said:

> Those people who have exploited our country's benefits for decades speak with authority to our people from there. Those people have looked down to our nation from their glasshouse. These are the elites. They do not know anything about poverty. They are unaware of village without a path, a field without water. They do not know the sufferings of our nation. They do not trust even the will of nation; they do not believe in democracy. We gave the game away! Here we put an end to this elite sultanate. Here with your authorisation we have stopped them. From now on, the word is yours (nation), from now on, you will take decisions, and from now on, the authority and the seal are in your hands.[48]
>
> They are supposed to humiliate us. They also today look the same way to us as yesterday, yesterday they call us drumheads and the man who scratches his belly, and today they say we are brainless and stupid. In their newspaper, they write 'he could not manage even a village' about me, but today, thanks to God, the nation has taken power in his hands, and the nation has done what he has to do.[49]

Erdoğan has realised the fact that social polarisation is vital to his electoral success. Thus, in every election, he has a perceived enemy. He mobilises his Islamist grass roots by providing them with a target to hate and fight. In that sense, he has been the most divisive politician in the history of Turkey. In the 2011 election, his targeted enemy was Kemal Kılıçdaroğlu. He tried to stigmatise Kılıçdaroğlu by reminding the crowd that he is an Alevi, as if being an Alevi is a shame.[50] In his rallies in 2011, Erdoğan reminded the crowd about the Alevi background of the new CHP leader (Kılıçdaroğlu) to discredit him in the eyes of pious Sunni voters. He used the term 'Alevi,' as if it were inhuman or as an alien enemy. By doing this, he was exploiting the existing prejudice among conservative Sunni voters and portraying the CHP as a party of Alevis and devoid of Islamic values. For example, between 29 April and 13 May of that year, he brought this issue up in seven separate election speeches. No national politician has ever used the term Alevi as an insult as much as Erdoğan has done. He created neighbourhood pressure (*mahalle baskısı*) to control the Sunni voters and persuade them to endorse his dehumanisation of the Alevis and the stigmatisation of anything secularised. This social pressure has led to feelings of insecurity and shame among secular Turkish peoples as if they are living immorally and are wrong in their ideas and societal interactions.

To heighten this division, he offered a weak-hearted apology for the 'the massacres carried out by the CHP-led Kemalist state against the Alevi Kurds of Dersim'.[51] The truth was that when there was a rebellion against the reforms of the state which was governed by the CHP at that time, the state took harsh measures to suppress the rebellion and many local people were killed. However, the Alevi community knew the tactics of Erdoğan, who exploits every form of suffering for political ends. Erdoğan's apology failed to ease the worries of Alevis, who saw this gesture as a superficial attempt to belittle the CHP whose leader, Kılıçdaroğlu, is, in fact, Alevi. For Erdoğan, his entire value system is based on winning an election by defeating his opponents regardless of the cost or disregard of a widely accepted moral principle

His polarisation tactics, along with strong economic results, in 2011, won him a third consecutive round of parliamentary elections with an impressive 49.9 per cent of the vote.[52] The main opposition of the Republic People's Party (CHP), under Kılıçdaroğlu, won an increase in seats from 112 to 135 in the parliament, on 26 per cent of the vote. The biggest loser of the 2011 elections was the nationalist party, the Nationalist Movement Party (MHP). With 13 per cent of the vote, it won just fifty-three seats, down from seventy-one in 2007. Due to the 10 per cent national threshold requirement to secure any representation at parliament, the pro-Kurdish Peace and Democracy Party (Barış ve Demokrasi Partisi, BDP) decided to run with numerous independent candidates. The Party won thirty-five seats (up from twenty-seven) in parliament.[53] During the election, several Kurdish independent candidates were arrested on suspicion of being loyal to the PKK. This, in turn, angered many Kurdish voters.

The biggest winner in the 2011 elections was Erdoğan, who stressed the economic achievements of his government and cemented societal divisions along the lines of secular versus Islamic, and Alevi versus Sunni. The main political platform of this election focused for the first time almost exclusively on internal Turkish issues – the EU membership question remained in the background. On the 2011 election platform, the AKP criticised the EU over the Cyprus issue and voiced its disappointment against resistance to Turkey's full membership.[54] The people voted for Erdoğan because of successful economic development and a stronger democratic commitment. The GNP increased in the last quarter of 2010 by 9.2 per cent from a year earlier. This, in turn, translated into lower unemployment and higher confidence in the economy. Economic satisfaction was the key reason for Erdoğan's electoral successes.

The objective during the election was achieving a two-thirds parliamentary majority in order to draw up a new constitution. The AKP promised a new constitution without laying out the content of the document. However, Erdoğan emphasised that the new constitution would be civilian, since the 1982 constitution had been written under the direction of the military coup authorities. Moreover, Erdoğan wanted to increase the powers of the presidency. In the 2011 elections, he did not get the mandate he sought to craft a new constitution. The AKP had hoped to win the 367 seats in parliament (two-fifths of the total) so that it could amend the constitution without the support of other parties. By gaining only 327 seats, it fell three votes short of the threshold needed.[55]

4.8 Conclusion

It took some time to realise that Erdoğan's goal with the constitutional change was to remove the headscarf ban and to permanently neuter the military's political power. Erdoğan's understanding of human rights was centred on the freedom of Sunni/Hanefi religious practices, but his conceptualisation of democracy veered towards majoritarian rule.

The 2008 court cases against the military, the 2010 constitutional referendum and the AKP's 2011 election victory radically transformed the political landscape in favour of Erdoğan becoming a more autocratic ruler. Between 2002 and 2007, Erdoğan sought to cultivate an inclusive political language to reposition Turkey for a future he preferred, highlighted by a relationship between the state and society moving in a more liberal, democratic direction. The military, however, wanted to maintain the power structure of old Turkey (that is, what it knew best), whereas the AKP government sought to dictate its own version of a new Turkey in which

Islamic identity and Ottoman heritage would cement a new national bond. Although Erdoğan had genuinely sought at the beginning to discontinue the authoritarian nation-building project of Kemalism and instead recognise the pluralistic composition of the country – though with Islamic undertones – and including cultural (not political) rights for the Kurdish minority, this project would eventually be derailed by 2013.

In Turkey, one of the critical obstacles in realising full democracy has always been the domineering role of the party leaders. They preside over a highly centralised decision-making process in which they determine the list of candidates and set the policies of their parties. They act like old Ottoman sultans of their parties. Erdoğan's domineering role is more powerful than any other leader because he 'owns' the party and it functions like his self-owned business corporation. Especially after Abdullah Gül became president of the country, Erdoğan fully controlled the entire hierarchy and echelons of his party. Yet, Turkish political culture, especially with the conservative sector of the population, enjoys his confrontational style, straight talk and charismatic leadership. A certain significant sector of the public support his sultanesque style and admire his political machismo style of governance, and are envious, not critical, of his kleptocratic practices. It has been set as a dangerous risk for Turkey's political health as a functioning democracy.

Notes

1. *Hürriyet*, 'Erdoğan'ın anket tepkisi: Fecaat', 22 February 2013.
2. For instance, Rahmi Koç, owner of a major corporation in Turkey, publicly accused Erdoğan of 'having over $1 billion' while he was the Istanbul mayor. He alleges that Erdoğan always received a certain percentage from major bids for municipal projects. See Gür, *Esaretten Zirveye*, pp. 62–4. For Rahmi Koç's accusations, see *Milliyet*, 3 August 2002.
3. Koçak, *Türkiye'de Milli Şef Dönemi*, p. 113.
4. The Gülen community was pursuing a policy of cooptation of scholars and politicians through promotional 'academic' conferences in different countries and also organised regular 'tours' to different countries to 'buy' these scholars or politicians. The last two such conferences at that time to promote the Gülen community took place in Arizona and London.
5. *Hürriyet*, 'Genelkurmay'dan çok sert açıklama', 29 April 2007.

6. Before the presidential system was adopted, there were two legal ways to amend the constitution: (1) through a two-thirds majority in parliament (that is, 367 out of the 550 MPs voting in favour), or (2) a three-fifths majority (330 votes) plus passing a popular referendum. As Erdoğan lacked the necessary two-thirds majority, it compelled him to court the nationalist MHP to support his cause.
7. *Yeni Safak*, 25 October 2002.
8. The actions of Gül as president affirmed the fears of the secular establishment. Gül made two appointments (Alpaslan Altan and Erdal Tercan) to the Constitutional Court and they ended up being sentenced because of their Gülenist connection. Moreover, Gül's long-time advisor and confidant, Ambassador Gürcan Balık (b. 1973), who was promoted and appointed to key posts in rapid succession, was sentenced to six years and three months in prison for 'membership of an armed terrorist organisation (the Gülen movement)'. Balık was once one of the most promising diplomats in the foreign ministry. His quick path of promotion angered many diplomats who targeted him. Gül never defended any of these bureaucrats, especially Balık.
9. Ayata, 'Meydanlardakiler 'yeni orta sınıf'tır', 21–2 May 2007.
10. *Reuters*, 'One million Turks rally against government', 29 April 2007.
11. When Büyükanıt was the commander of War College in Ankara (Kara Harp Okulu), he organised a conference to examine, as titled, 'The Lessons of the Balkan Wars and Their Contemporary Impacts', on 26 April 1995. The proceedings of this panel were published by the War College. For more on the impacts of the Balkan Wars on the Turkish military, see Selek *Anadolu İhtilali*, pp. 105–17. For more on the impacts of the military coups on military discipline, see Akyaz, *Askeri Müdahalelerin Orduya Etkisi*.
12. İlker Başbuğ, then the ground forces commander, speaking at the beginning of the 2007–8 academic year at the Turkish Military Academy in Ankara, warned the cadets about the new threats to the founding principles of the Turkish Republic. He identified the nation state, unitary political structure and secularism as the founding principles of the Republic and asked the cadets to be vigilant in the protection of these principles. He said, 'It is interesting to see that the country's nation state structure is being targeted by both anti-secularists and ethnic nationalists.' He went on to say that the Turkish Armed Forces would always stand with those who want to protect the nation state and would thus defend secularism. Başbuğ said that some groups are trying to change the 'political structure' established by the Turkish Republic founder, Atatürk, into one based on religion or ethnic nationalism. In the same speech, in response to an

ongoing debate by the AKP over the draft constitution, Başbuğ argued that the principle of 'secularism should not become a topic of discussion' (*Milliyet*, 24 September 2007).
13. *Milliyet*, 24 September 2007.
14. Yavuz and Özcan, 'The Kurdish question and the AKP', pp. 102–19. Yavuz and Gunter, 'The Kurdish nation', pp. 33–9.
15. Kardaş, 'Turkey and the Iraqi crisis', pp. 306–30. Bila, *Sivil Darbe Girişimi*, pp. 42, 43.
16. For the dissent against the soft policies of Özkök, see Balbay, 'Genç subaylar tedirgin', 23 May 2003.
17. One of the key reasons many Islamist deputies, along with pro-Barzani deputies of the AKP, voted against the 1 March motion has to do with the possibility of the enhanced role of the military and the declaration of emergency law around the Turkish–Iraqi border. For instance, Ahmet Davutoğlu told CNN-Turk TV: 'If we were to allow in US troops, we had to declare an emergency situation in south-east Turkey. This could have created a problem in our relations with the EU', 16 February 2004.
18. Uzgel, 'Dış politikada AKP', pp. 69–84.
19. Interview in Ankara on 12 April 2007. Nihat Ali Özcan and I had interviewed a total of twelve high-ranking security and civilian bureaucrats in April 2007. Some of the findings were published in 'Political crisis in Turkey', pp. 118–35. The interviews were conducted face-to-face in Ankara. All interviewees agreed to be quoted, subject to anonymity.
20. İnsel, 'Neofeodal devlette ilerlerken', 4 March 2007. For more on the military vs Turkish police force, see, <http://www.tsk.mil.tr/10_ARSIV/10_1_Basin_Yayin_Faaliyetleri/10_1_7_Konusmalar/2006/harpakademilerikonusmasi_02102006.html> (last accessed 11 August 2010).
21. Cemil Cicek, the minister of justice, became one of the main targets of the Gülen community because of his support for the anti-terror law. For more on the reaction of the military, see *Cumhuriyet*, 9 April 2007; Hakan, 'Cemaat, ey cemaat', 2 April 2007; Hakan, 'Cemaat diyor ki: O bakan bize düsman', 4 April 2007.
22. These accusations spread around the websites. See critical responses to these rumours: Yılmaz, 'Amaç Orgeneral Büyükanıt'ı yıpratmak!', 6 March 2006; Coşkun, 'Yol ne yana', 7 March 2006.
23. See the full indictment at *Hürriyet*, 'Semdinli iddianamesi', 7 March 2006.
24. Mehmet Yılmaz, *Hürriyet*, 6 March 2006.

25. The etymological definition of *mazlum* means 'oppressed', 'tormented' or 'wronged'. *Mazlum* is someone who has been subjected to a grave injustice. In Islam, the Prophet Muhammed's grandson Imam Hussein, the son of Ali, was the archetypal epitome of a *mazlum*.
26. Many ex-parliamentarians such as the AKP's Adana MP Abdullah Çalışkan claimed their vote was due to the 27 April memorandum of the military and the meeting between Erdoğan and Büyükanıt on 5 May 2007, at the Dolmabahçe Palace. Former MP Ersönmez Yarbay of Ankara, who had always been in favour of democratic processes within the AKP, explained the major transformation of the list as a reflection of a region-based solidarity network (*Milliyet*, 7 June 2007).
27. Ertuğrul Yalçınbayır said, 'The AK Party won the 2002 election with a platform that stressed three 'Ys': Yoksulluk (Poverty), Yasaklar (Restrictions), and Yolsuzluk (Corruption). Now we need to add five more 'Ys' to describe the Party: Yozlaşma, Yandaşlık (clientelism), Yağcılık, Yiyicilik (bribery), and Yobazlık (religious fanaticism)' (*Radikal*, 8 June 2007). According to Kenan Camurcu, a leading analyst of Islamic politics, 'Erdoğan cannot allow some "native" politicians to criticise his policies, and he preferred to bring "guests" such as Ertuğrul Günay into the Party to give the impression that the Party is inclusive. But he does not want to lose his authoritarian control.' Interview with Camurcu, in Istanbul, 8 June 2007.
28. The AKP included a number of prominent leftist politicians such as Ertuğrul Günay, Zafer Üskül, Haluk Özdalga, Erdal Kalkan and Ayşenur Bahçekapılı; and two prominent Alevi intellectuals Reha Çamuroğlu and Hüseyin Tuğcu; some singers and businessmen (Zafer Çağlayan, Osman Yağmurdereli and wrestler Hamza Yerlikaya) as a way of becoming a party of the centre.
29. Bacık, 'The parliamentary elections in Turkey', pp. 377–81.
30. The Armenian Patriarch Mesrob II Mutafyan told *Der Spiegel* that the 'Armenians will vote for the AKP', quoted in *Yeni Safak*, 4 June 2007.
31. On the mobilisation of the Gülen networks in Kurdish provinces, see Altan Tan's interview in 'Kürtler AKP'ye sadece kredi açtı', 30 July 2007.
32. General Hilmi Özkök, a retired chief of general staff, shared his concerns over numerous issues with Fikret Bila, *Milliyet*, 1–5 October 2007.
33. Mehmet Altan, one of the proponents of the Second Republic debate, defines the term as 'The Republic which was founded in 1923 has no democratic and pluralist qualities; sovereignty belongs not to the people but to the bureaucracy and the military; and its understanding of a statist economic system turned into

a "robbery system". Therefore, the Republic should be democratised and the political structure should go into a period of radical re-structuring. This was the core of the ideology behind the Second Republic. What did this suggest? It sought to transform the bureaucratic polity into a democratic system. In concrete terms this meant reducing the role of the state in the economy, developing a transparent political and economic system, and giving more control to local levels of governance.' *Hürriyet Daily News*, 28 September 2007.
34. *The New York Times*, 1 June 2007.
35. Şerif Mardin's interview in *Vatan*, 'Mahalle havası diye bir şey var ki AKP'yi bile döver', 15 May 2007.
36. The Court ruled on the law and characterised the law as 'an attempt to change non-amendable articles of the Turkish constitution'. *Hürriyet Daily News*, 20 November 2012.
37. Interview with a judge, who did not want to be named, Ankara, 20 March 2017.
38. According to recent police reports, the Gülen movement recruited police officials who had a long-term relationship with the movement into police intelligence. In an interview, an ex-police intelligence chief said, 'We were all removed from our jobs for various reasons to open space for the Gülenist police force.' In fact, police intelligence would eventually be used against the military itself. For details of the Gülen movement's recruitment and promotion policies within the police force, see a detailed examination by the head of the Intelligence Department of the National Police, Sabri Uzun, *İn-Baykal Kaseti, Dink Cinayeti ve Diğer Komplolar*. On the confrontation between the head of the Istanbul Police and Prime Minister Erdoğan, see the interview with Fuat Yılmazer, the former chief of Istanbul Police Intelligence, *Zaman*, 19 March 2014.
39. The Turkish military has always regarded itself as the founder and guardian of the secular nation state and remained resolute not to allow any ethnic or religiously motivated clique to infiltrate the military. The last major purge of suspected non-Kemalist officers took place against those who were suspected followers of the Gülen movement during the 28 February 1997 soft-coup. The AKP government either reversed the discharge of these officers who were accused of Islamist tendencies or paid their retirement dues so that they could retire as military officials. *Milliyet*, 'Askerden atılan personel geri döndü', 23 January 2013.
40. In fact, in 2010, when I was visiting Istanbul, I met with Sahin Alpay, ex-Maoist and newly liberal journalist who was a columnist for the Gülen-owned daily *Zaman*, at a bookstore in Beyoğlu. He was elated by news of the arrest of the

generals and journalists, claiming that 'the system is cleaning its intestines!' Ironically, after the coup, Alpay was one of those journalists who was arrested by the Erdoğan government for supporting the FETO terrorist organisation and spent almost a year in jail.

41. In my interviews with a prosecutor in Germany who handled some aspects of Ergenekon, including the Başbuğ case, he said, 'It was a direct order from Erdoğan to go after İlker Başbuğ because he directly pressured the Constitutional Court in 2008 to close the party. Erdoğan hated him.' In fact, Erdoğan, undoubtedly a vengeful person, never gave up his hatred of Başbuğ and, even in 2020, he called upon the prosecutors to go after Başbuğ.
42. *The Economist*, 'Justice or revenge?', 10 August 2013. This essay examines the verdict of the Ergenekon case.
43. Küçükkoşum, 'European Commission wary on restructured HSYK', 17 September 2010.
44. *Hürriyet*, 'Dindar gençlikyetiştireceğiz', 2 February 2012. The minister of education increased the number of İmam Hatip schools from 440 to 1017 by 2015. *Hürriyet*, 28 January 2015; Ismail Çağlar, *From Symbolic Exile to Physical Exile*, pp. 27–54.
45. Erdoğan, 'The 3rd Ordinary Congress of AKP's Youth Branch, 29 April 2012', Ankara.
46. Tamir, et al., 'The global God divide', 20 July 2020.
47. Interview with Mir Dengir Fırat, Ankara, 6 March 2016.
48. Erdoğan, AKP Kayseri Providence Meeting, 21 August 2010, Kayseri (unpublished raw data from TBMM).
49. Erdoğan, AKP Sakarya Province Meeting, 5 June 2011 (unpublished raw data from TBMM).
50. Ergin, 'Erdoğan ve CHP liderinin Aleviliği', 18 May 2011.
51. *Yeni Safak*, 'Basbakan, Dersim katliamı için devlet adına özür diledi', 23 November 2011.
52. Peet, 'Turkey after the 2011 election: challenges for the AK government', 5 July 2011.
53. Jenkins, 'Turkey's election, and democracy's shadow', 21 June 2011.
54. Ülgen, 'Is Brussels the loser in Turkey's elections?', 15 June 2011.
55. Gottschlich, 'Erdoğan falls short of goal in Turkish elections', 13 June 2011.

5

THE *ANNUS HORRIBILIS* (2013)

The year 2013 was Erdoğan's *annus horribilis*. It also marked the beginning of the most serious domestic and foreign challenges to his and the AKP's rule. Erdoğan's government was rocked by three distinct, though interlaced, crises:

1. Demonstrations in Istanbul's Gezi Park in June 2013, which were sparked by a campaign to save green spaces and quickly morphed into a broader anti-government social movement.
2. The coup in Egypt on 3 July 2013, backed by Saudi Arabia, the United Arab Emirates and Israel, which removed President Morsi and derailed the Arab Spring, and directly targeted Turkey and her ally Qatar.
3. The corruption probes against Erdoğan and his key ministers in December 2013. The probe was the declaration of war between Erdoğan and Gülen's *Hizmet* movement, which occurred when Erdoğan sought to shut down the movement's educational and indoctrination centres. Gülenists retaliated by calling upon its loyalists in the police investigation agencies and judiciary to launch a series of corruption investigations targeting Erdoğan and his inner circle.

None of these seismic events had been predicted by either the AKP or its domestic and foreign critics. Just a year earlier, Erdoğan and his government appeared to move seamlessly from success to success in domestic and foreign policy arenas. These three events proved all the more traumatic for being completely unexpected. Their fallout has scarred the Turkish state and society while undermining the country's democratic consolidation which many had by then taken for granted. It also presented Erdoğan with the greatest crisis of his personal and political life, and his response fuelled by fear, anger and determination has dramatically affected the country, often appearing worse than better.

5.1 Taksim Square and Gezi Park as the Public Square of Modern Turkish Politics

Gezi Park is a small patch of green space located in the heart of Taksim Square, which signifies not only Istanbul's quintessential public square but also that of Turkey. Literally and figuratively, it also represents Turkish society's fulcrum and fault line par excellence. In sociopolitical terms, this means an area where different ideological groups and lifestyles meet, coexist and contest each other. It usually is filled with artists, writers, actors and others who pursue bohemian lifestyles and subscribe to unorthodox ideas. The many neighbouring bars, theatres and cafes of Beyoğlu and İstiklal Caddesi, and the people they attract, mark Taksim as the epicentre of anti-establishment gatherings. However, the square is also ringed by four- and five-star hotels for the local bourgeoisie and international tourists. In more recent years, the square also has attracted more traditional members of Turkish society who tend to vote for the AKP. At its centre is an iconic republican monument of Atatürk almost single-handedly leading the nation to victory in the National War of Liberation and onwards to a modern secular Western future.[1] To underscore this point, the monument is flanked by the large modernist Atatürk Kültür Merkezi (Atatürk Cultural Centre), dedicated to the performance of classical Western music, theatre and dance, though in later years Turkish folk art and dance have been included.

Before we can make sense of the Gezi Park demonstrations and social movement which broke out between 27 May and 12 June 2013, we must understand how Taksim Square came to signify the modern fulcrum of Turkish politics. The centrality of Taksim in contemporary Turkish politics goes back to the Young Turk Revolution of 1908 when Sultan Hamid II was forced to accept constitutional restraints by a group of young officers known as the Committee for Union and Progress (Ittihat ve Terraki Cemiyati, CUP). The CUP reforms, impinging upon both the traditional prerogatives of the sultan as well as the *ulema*, engendered a backlash. A group of religiously conservative officers of an artillery regiment based at the Topcu Kışlası (artillery barracks) in Taksim Square launched a counter-coup on 31 March 1909 (as fixed in the old Rumi calendar), to restore the *ancien régime*. The CUP brought in reliable troops from Salonika under the command of Mahmut Sevket Pasha, including Atatürk, then a young officer, to put down the uprising. Amidst heavy fighting and casualties, the barracks and a neighbouring mosque were destroyed. Since that event, Taksim Square has been the literal and figurative fulcrum over which fundamental questions of Turkish identity and politics have been contested. During Kemalist rule, republican leaders insisted that the square would symbolise Atatürk's vision of banishing religious symbols and influence from the public square. Erdoğan sought to symbolically turn the page on this Kemalist vision by restoring the old order with the reconstruction of the barracks and mosque. The fact that the proposed construction would incorporate a shopping mall and hotel and be built by AKP-connected construction firms inflamed critics.[2]

Initially, the Gezi Park protest movement was sparked by local citizens trying to save what little green space remained in the core of the city. While Istanbul is a world-class city in an unparalleled historic and natural setting, haphazard development during the republican period has left it with a dearth of green space in comparison to New York, London or Paris. The fact that what in many countries is a local urban planning decision morphed into a national crisis was in significant ways an outcome produced by structural/institutional variables stemming from fateful path dependent choices made at critical historic junctures.

Indeed, many of the baleful conflicts in modern Turkish history stem from the Ottoman Empire consciously adopting features of republican France rather than those of the US or Great Britain as a model to emulate in the contentious nineteenth-century process of modernisation. The most obvious is adopting the Jacobin French model of *laïcité* (in Turkish, *laiklik*), or secularism, rather than the Anglo-American formulation.[3] While the Anglo-American tradition of secularism has sought to safeguard religious beliefs and practices from state interference and control, it also has tried to protect multiconfessional states and societies from being captured by a particular religious sect or doctrine imposing its will on the rest of society. The French Jacobin tradition was hostile to religious belief.

The second baleful influence was a *dirigiste* Turkish Republic which sought to micromanage governmental decision-making and foster uniform policies for the whole nation from high levels of government. This notion of the state as a stern but benevolent father was of course pioneered and embodied by Atatürk, but it also was a pose adopted by Erdoğan, beginning in 2010 to the chagrin of many supporters. Furthermore, like the great potentates of the past, he was interested in leaving an indelible legacy for Turkey and especially in his beloved imperial capital of Istanbul.

The construction activity and transformation of the physical infrastructure of the country proved both a boon and an Achilles heel for the AKP. Mammoth state-sponsored construction programmes were central to the AKP's electoral successes and to Turkey's political-economy. These included new bridges, airports, metrolines and even a submarine subway traversing the fabled Bosporus. The Turkish Housing Development Authority (TOKI) also built hundreds of 'cookie-cutter' but comfortable apartment blocks in the major cities to ease the country's chronic urban housing shortage. These projects cemented the loyalty of newly arrived migrants to Erdoğan and his party. Alış-Veriş Merkezi (AVM), or glittering shopping malls, sprouted like mushrooms across the urban landscape, encouraging a crass debt-driven consumerism among the public.

Furthermore, many of the projects were not environmentally or aesthetically sound, such as Erdoğan's self-professed 'crazy scheme' of carving a second Bosporus shipping channel through Istanbul. Çamlıca is a scenic hilltop and park overlooking the city from its Asian shorelines. Just as Ottoman sultans competed with their Byzantine forebears to endow the hills of the European side of the city with monumental edifices, Erdoğan decided to leave his mark on Çamlıca by erecting an outsized and ersatz Ottoman mosque on the hill. The construction epitomised all that was flawed in the AKP's emphatic interpretation of imperial rule and disregard for constructive criticism from the country's intellectual and cultural elite. Instead of adopting an innovative and proportional design for the site as urged by architectural experts, the AKP decided to erect a monstrous facsimile of the Ottoman mosques across the Bosporus while ruining the vista of the hill and reducing the project to kitsch quality. Similar philistinism was shown in the construction of the new presidential palace complex in Ankara, mischievously labelled the AK Saray, or White Palace, by critics. Costing a reported $670 million, the mega palace sits largely empty and gives the impression of an Orientalist Versailles. As in the case of Çamlıca, the AKP spurned the advice and criticism of professional planners and architects as well as many common citizens. The AKP's failure to include local communities in decision-making and delegate authority to regional and urban party leaders became a serious source of public alienation.

Massive construction projects also played a vital role in not only the party's political fortunes but also in the nation's political economy, such as TOKI's housing projects that primarily the urban lower classes and their newly arrived migrant cousins from the rural provinces. These cookie-cutter apartment blocks were not architecturally inspiring but were spacious, clean and efficient. Their presence eased the severe housing shortages in major urban centres. However, along with this positive side of massive infrastructural spending came serious issues of governmental corruption and accountability. The AKP attracted support in 2002 because it was seen as being strikingly clean and efficient in contrast to the establishment parties of the left and right. However, by 2010, there was widespread public discontent over the rising perception of corruption in ruling party circles, tied to these massive infrastructure projects. These perceptions were born out by *Transparency International's Corruption Perception Index* which noted a marked fall in Turkey's standing. Modern Turkey has always been plagued by the massive use of patronage politics by those in power. The AKP seemed committed in its first term in power in breaking with this tradition. However, given the absence of institutional checks and balances, the party clearly started awarding these massive state contracts to conglomerates and families tied to ruling circles.

By 2010, Erdoğan's personal leadership style had changed. After the September 2010 constitutional referendum, Erdoğan started to believe that he could do whatever he wanted, even eliminate his onetime allies. Confident in his successes and genuine domestic and international popularity, he took on the role of the nation's *in loco parentis*, a role pioneered by Atatürk.

This included admonitions against indulging in smoking, drinking or public displays of affection as well as more eyebrow-raising suggestions such as encouraging women to bear at least three children. The prime minister stirred controversy by intervening in such matters as the design of uniforms for Turkish Airlines' flight attendants and the plot of the internationally wildly popular serial drama *Muhteşsem Yuzyıl* (Magnificent Century), set around the reign of Suleyman the Magnificent. Erdoğan found the plot focus on palace intrigues and romances to be insulting and insisted instead to emphasise Suleyman's martial conquests as opposed to his bedroom activities. This presidential invective apparently led to Turkish Airlines curtailing the broadcast of the drama on its flights. Such interventions, however, didn't seem remarkable to many in the AKP's Anatolian base. However, they were grating for younger well-off urban citizens, who believed that the party's social conservatism was encroaching on their lifestyles.

5.1.1 The seeds of discontent leading to the Gezi Park demonstrations

The Gezi Park demonstrations arose from deep historic societal divisions, which can be traced to the late Ottoman period and the Young Turk Revolution. However, the immediate catalyst, in addition to the preservation of green space in Istanbul, were laws passed by the Turkish National Assembly on 24 May 2015 restricting the sale and consumption of alcohol. On the surface, the laws were unremarkable by Western standards – restricting the sale of alcohol within 100 metres of schools or houses of worship and after 10 p.m. at kiosks known as *tekels*. There is a perverse irony that in Turkey and many surrounding Eastern Bloc countries during the period leading up to the fall of the Berlin Wall, unrestricted access to alcohol, tobacco and pornography were seen as symbols of liberation and modernity. A Western visitor to Istanbul in the 1980s, for example, might be shocked to see the unrestricted display of degrading pornographic images at news-stands in full view of families with children. Similar displays prevailed in much of the Balkans. The AKP reasonably argued that its restrictions in these matters were hardly unusual by even Western standards, and indeed they seemed to find support across a broad spectrum of society.

However, the controversy over the restrictions on public consumption of alcohol, like much else in Turkey, also reflected a deeper ongoing *Kulturkampf* between secular and religious segments of society centred on competing sociopolitical identity claims in the public square, as mediated and demarcated via public displays of dress, decorum and consumption. While the consumption of alcohol and being in a state of intoxication are proscribed for observant Muslims, historically, such prohibitions were flouted in the royal courts of high Islamic civilisation from the time of the Ummayads to the Ottomans. This is, of course, avidly illustrated in the Sufi-inspired poetry of such masters as Hafiz, Saadi, Rumi and Khayyam, where wine-drinking and intoxication were celebrated metaphorically as well as literally. For commoners, drinking various village homebrews was common, but public consumption and intoxication were considered serious social and even civil offences.

This long-prevailing tacit acceptance of the tension between religious dictates and private practices existed until the symbolic politics of ostentatious alcohol consumption was inaugurated by Atatürk. His passion for alcoholic indulgence exceeded even his prodigious appetite for the opposite sex, leading to his death from cirrhosis of the liver in 1938. The public and ceremonial consumption of alcohol for the Kemalist establishment was a *de rigueur* display of loyalty and belonging alongside Western dress. Erdoğan alluded to this, citing Atatürk and his successor İsmet İnönü in 2013, when he stated, 'How come a law that was made by two drunks, has been recognized while one that follows the values of faith is unacceptable and must be rejected?'[4]

This unstated but widely acknowledged requirement for validation was a litmus test often used, until recently, to determine entry into Turkish establishment circles. Abstaining from alcoholic consumption by Turkish officers, for example, was seen as a sign of 'religious fundamentalism' and routinely led to dismissal. Dexter Filkins in *The New Yorker* recounts how Gülenist officers evaded this litmus test by leaving out empty alcohol bottles in the trash for Turkish military inspectors to find.

A friend who was raised in the US learned about this in a surprising and personal way. His father was a professor of computer science in Chicago and was invited by a Turkish friend and ally of Özal (then prime minister) to come to Turkey in 1985 and advise the Turkish Council for Scientific and Technological Research (TUBITAK) on the introduction of personal computers in Turkish higher education. At an introductory dinner in his honour, his father casually refused the wine being served by the waiter. This immediately caught the attention of a Kemalist bureaucrat of equal rank to his father's friend at the dinner. He remarked, 'Well Mr Khan, you are an American but don't drink; it seems you are a different kind of Muslim than we are.' The author's father was taken aback and explained that drinking was a personal choice and should not offend anyone. This, of course, is perfectly understood in Western countries, but in Turkey it was a choice laden with a profound ideological valence. The dinner escalated into a bitter row between Özal's bureaucrat and an individual from the Kemalist old guard.

This dinner debacle is reflective of Turkish state and society's failure since 1923 to come to a secular-liberal understanding of modernity, which allows individual freedom of conscience and expression without the imposition of one's beliefs on others or vice-versa. While the Kemalists were guilty of past discrimination for imposing their values, social identities and lifestyles on Turkish society, the AKP had a golden opportunity to break from this mould but largely failed to do so, to the bitter disappointment of many of its liberal democratic supporters.

This would directly lead to the dramatic standoff in Gezi Park. The new alcohol regulations were unremarkable and could hardly have been expected to set off a social explosion in Taksim Square. However, they came on the heels of governmental policies seeking to restrict the city's nightlife and regulate the social behaviour of students on campus. When confronted by a public outcry, Erdoğan responded that people could drink in the privacy of their homes, an inversion of the Kemalist campaign pledge to restrict religious expression to the private sphere. This was a serious miscalculation as the government's heedless response to the needs of accommodating diverse lifestyles deeply alienated many urban liberal-democratic voters and the youth who had in previous elections supported the AKP's promise of moving away from Kemalist authoritarianism and intolerance of diversity. It was these urban youths from Istanbul's campuses who would join with green activists to launch the Gezi Park demonstrations and social movement.

5.1.2 The Gezi Park movement mushrooms

On 27 May, the protest started as a sit-in by a group of green activists opposing the proposed development project. The activists were not interested in wading into the religious versus secular conflict but merely sought to preserve what little green space remained in central Istanbul. The next day, the police used pepper spray to disperse the protestors. More militant demonstrators, who identified as anarchists and leftists, reacted by vandalising property in the area, such as shop windows and cars. On 29 May, a larger, more organised crowd established a camp in the park. As the media covered the protestors, more young people and students disaffected by the AKP's social policies joined them. Taksim Square soon took on the atmosphere of Paris 1968 or Woodstock 1969. On the positive side, it represented a genuine grass-roots social movement, which sought to bring people of diverse beliefs and lifestyles together. Along with many artists and musicians, the protestors brought together leftists, green activists and Kurdish political activists, as well as groups identifying as anti-capitalist Muslims.

The Gezi Park movement, at its best, was truly revolutionary and inspiring in the sense that it allowed Turkish citizens of diverse sectarian, ideological and ethnic backgrounds to rub shoulders and undertake critical engagement. Leftist and Kurdish activists created and protected areas where observant Muslim demonstrators could conduct prayers. These scenes and the police's harsh tactics initially fostered a groundswell of sympathy for the protestors, even amongst religious AKP supporters.

It is important to first identify who the protestors were, and then analyse their demands. They were usually between eighteen and twenty-five years old, educated and well-connected to the expanding global social media. They were raised during the recent economic growth spurt of Turkey, and hardly remember the economic and political problems of the previous decades. This new generation, caring more about personal freedom and lifestyle choices, showed little awareness of the historical and ideological background of the Gezi Park movement or the institutional shortcomings that still threatened Turkey's democratic consolidation. Ironically, it was Erdoğan's successful economic and political stewardship that nurtured and created opportunity spaces for this confident, at times self-indulgent, and globally connected youth.

Those who participated in the protests, confronted the police force and were 'washed by the water of the anti-riot TOMA vehicles (Intervention Vehicle for Social Events)', were changed people by the time they returned to their homes.[5] Their participation heightened their political consciousness and distanced them further from the government and the state authorities. During my interviews in Istanbul with protestors who initiated the sit-ins, and then the demonstrators who joined the protests after 31 May, it was clear that there was a distinction between the two kinds of protestors, in terms of their aims and their modus operandi. The original protest campers usually stressed the importance of the environment and how some urban projects are destructive for the cultural fabric of Istanbul. Others were upset about the recent conservative social legislation relating to the sale and consumption of alcohol.

By the end, one could glean four main complaints coming from the protestors: some resented 'the authoritarian style of the prime minister'; for some, the grievance was the 'widespread corruption in municipalities', specifically regarding urban planning in Istanbul and how it was designed to have loopholes that allowed for kickbacks for the supporters of the party and bureaucrats; some argued that 'there are no more checks and balances in the political system and that Turkey is becoming a sultanistic regime'; and most of them expressed general concerns that their 'lifestyle is threatened'.

The typical complaints that were vocalised during the Gezi protests, did not just travel in many directions, but in certain instances even contradicted one another. For instance, on the one hand, some of the protestors opposing the government were cautious and prudent concerning Turkey's identity, namely that it is not and should not become 'an Arab country', because Turkey's place is in Europe, not in the Middle East. On the other hand, a group of militant youths, who were members of the right-wing anti-imperialist Doğu Perinçek-led group, were violently anti-American and anti-EU. Thus, there were several competing political discourses that failed to produce a unified positive political platform.

The only unifying bond for most people was their anger at Erdoğan and his style of governance. By the time the civil disobedience reached its peak, the protestors comprised leftists, nationalists, feminists, anarchists, socialist-oriented Islamic groups, Alevis, environmentalists, LGBT activists and leftist pro-PKK Kurds. This diversity and lack of integrating values and goals weakened the movement's bonds. Thus, the Gezi movement would not serve as functional opposition or party to challenge the ruling establishment. Yet, the Gezi movement offered for the first time a glimpse of what was possible in the public sphere in terms of bringing Turkish citizens of diverse backgrounds together to share their fears, hopes and aspirations. For many from the non-violent factions of demonstrators, for the first time it allowed the development of cross-cutting linkages between Sunnis and Alevis, Turks and Kurds, and even the secular and religious. It also forced introspection, self-criticism and intra-party polarisation within the AKP by those who opposed Erdoğan's harsh response.[6]

Initially, the police were unable to dislodge the camped demonstrators, and as their numbers grew, the police, under Erdoğan's orders, cracked down to disperse the protest. Prior to this, the government had met several times with the demonstrators, promising to wait for a court decision before continuing with the plans for the park. On 30 May, when the protestors refused to empty the park, the police intervened and forcefully dispersed the demonstrators and campers. The protestors used social media to share images of police brutality provoking anger among other anti-AKP sections of the population. The anti-government channels, such as Ulusal TV and Halk TV, provided live coverage.

On 1 June, the government decided to pull the police forces from the site. The next day, all opposition groups poured into Taksim Square with a single slogan: 'Erdoğan resign!' The protests in other locations were much smaller and they were concentrated in major squares in Ankara, Izmir, Eskişehir, Adana and in other parts of Istanbul. With the exception of Izmir, a heavily CHP municipality, they failed to replicate the popular support generated in Gezi Park and had limited interruption on daily life. As the protests had swelled, Erdoğan unwittingly inflamed the greatest political crisis he would face, until his break with the Gülen movement, by exposing his Achilles heel, his *amour propre* or pride. At the beginning of the crisis, the AKP, under the leadership of Gül and Arınç, appeared initially to defuse it through a conciliatory approach, acknowledging the legitimate concerns of many protestors and assuring them that the government would respect impartial judicial rulings on the park controversy. Arınç condemned the excessive use of police force against peaceful demonstrators and Gül, in particular, issued thoughtful messages stressing that democracy was about more than winning elections and that peaceful protestors had a right to express their views.

However, this approach was undermined when more radical and ideologically implacable demonstrators were able to bait Erdoğan by personally insulting him and his family members. Hard-line Kemalists in the crowds held up signs and led chants calling for a military coup against the democratically elected government. His pride wounded, Erdoğan responded as he unfailingly did in showdowns with local toughs in his gritty Kasımpaşa neighbourhood, 'Tayyip does not back down!'

Erdoğan overruled the tactful approach of Gül and Arınç and denounced the protestors as *capulcu* (marauders). The protestors actually embraced the name and *capulcu* became a household term. There is now a *capulcu* teahouse, a *capulcu* library and *capulcu* summer camps to coordinate anti-establishment protests. To show solidarity, even prominent opposition leaders like Cem Boyner, a leading industrialist, and Ergun Özen, the CEO of Garanti Bank, claimed that they are also *capulcu*.[7] Erdoğan vowed that the Gezi Park project would proceed regardless of what the opposition thought. He also warned correctly that his support base in the country still remained larger than theirs and that he could turn out more people in the streets than they could.

Ultimately, the police gained control, with seven people including a policeman dying in the demonstrations. The protests and the government's harsh response were the first events to tarnish the Erdoğan administration's democratic credentials at home and abroad. Critics of the AKP tried to portray the Gezi Park demonstrations in the same light as those against tyrannical regimes in the Arab Spring. However, there were notable differences not only in the numbers killed and injured but also in the Gezi Park movement's ability to bring the majority of society together to displace the ruling establishment. Instead, the Gezi Park demonstrations mainly reified the existing divisions in Turkish society, and, except for the urban elites, there were few defections from Erdoğan's majoritarian electoral base. The main reason for this was that when anarchists, football hooligans from the Beşiktaş club, and leftist radicals gained prominence, their widespread vandalism and looting turned the majority of the Turkish population away from them and garnered much more sympathy for Erdoğan and the police forces.[8] Much like conservatives in Nixon's or Reagan's America, Erdoğan was able to appeal to the silent majority by casting the demonstrators as disloyal radicals who viewed the traditional Anatolian hinterland with contempt. His remarks:

> According to them we don't understand politics. According to them we don't understand art, theatre, cinema, poetry. According to them we don't

understand aesthetics, architecture. According to them we are uneducated, ignorant, the lower class, who has to be content with what is being given, needy; meaning, we are a group of dark Turks.[9]

Ultimately, the Gezi Park protest movement had a longer lasting negative impact upon foreign public opinion regarding the Turkish government in New York, Paris and Berlin than it did in Ankara, Konya or Edirne.[10] The movement's concerns and sensibilities focused on protecting secular lifestyles that identified with the West. Like many other notable commentators, the prominent sociologist Nilüfer Göle praised the Gezi movement, stating that it 'marked a new threshold for democracy'.[11] The demonstrations started as a small coherent group with a clear positive sociopolitical agenda. However, as it morphed into a much larger anti-government social movement, it was not able to integrate the more radical and violent factions into a coherent democratic movement that would appeal to a broad-based Turkish electorate.[12]

5.1.3 Implications of Gezi Park

From a domestic political perspective, the initial goal of the Gezi Park protest was confined to environmental concerns about the park. However, with the media's help, it morphed into urban civil disobedience over Erdoğan's governing style. The protests were not organised by any single ideological body. Thus, the outburst was short lived and unable to sustain a movement. Yet, its impact is profound both on society and the government. Due to this spontaneous outburst the government worried about the unpredictability of these protests and the power of using social media. The 'spirit of Gezi', like a haunting ghost, roams in the public sphere, casting a persistent shadow over government policies.

Before the Gezi Park protests Erdoğan's divisive, insulting language and the manner in which he had driven the amendments to the constitution had already polarised Turkish society. The sense of popular discontent, especially among the urban middle and upper-middle class, was widespread, against his Islamisation policies and more pronounced kleptocratic and autocratic practices. Erdoğan framed the spontaneous outburst against his corrupt practices as an international plot to overthrow his government. As time passed, he worked harder to rewrite the history of the Gezi Park protest as the beginning of an orchestrated assault by foreign enemies against his administration. Erdoğan orchestrated counter rallies against the 'spirit of Gezi protests' all over the country. These rallies, called 'the Respect for the National Will' (RN; Milli İradeye Saygı Mitingleri), set the new discourse of Erdoğan. These enemies, depending upon the time and circumstances of his remarks, could be Gülenists, the EU, the US, Israel, or the 'interest-rate lobby'.[13] He said:

> The interest lobby should better behave itself. This lobby exploited my people for years. We have shown patience for a long time. I am not saying this only for one bank or two but for all whoever making this lobby. Those who have started this fight against us, you will pay the price heavily.[14]

Under Erdoğan's order, the prosecutor of Istanbul indicted numerous individuals on charges of financing, plotting and working as agents of foreign governments to overthrow Erdoğan and end political stability and democracy in Turkey. Because Erdoğan named him in his political rallies, the leading alleged financier of the Gezi Park protest was Osman Kavala, a philanthropist and businessman.[15] Erdoğan even described him as 'George Soros of Turkey' or 'the representative of Soros', paralleling the claims of extreme right-wing activists in the US. Erdoğan's prosecutor, however, failed to come up with a coherent narrative against Kavala. He was guilty because Erdoğan said so, which was the best that prosecutors could determine.

The Gezi Park demonstrations, according to Babacan, signalled the end of an era in Turkish politics, especially in the favoured political life of Erdoğan. As Erdoğan was the target for the coalition of diverse demonstrators, he became more ruthless and reckless against any form of dissent, particularly within his party. More paranoid, he questioned the loyalty of the people around him and he lost his democratic credentials. Many prominent politicians distanced themselves from him as well as the AKP. During the Gezi protests, Erdoğan invited Reha Çamuroğlu to his office with the hopes of cooling the tensions with the Alevis.[16] In a RN meeting in Kayseri, Erdoğan directly attacked the main opposition party, the CHP. He accused the CHP of manipulating the Alevi community against him. He said: 'They [CHP] have been playing dangerous games on our Alevi brothers and sisters. The CHP is part of the conspiracy organised by international dark forces.'[17] In his mind the Gezi Park protests represented an Alevi rebellion, supported by the major powers to overthrow him – not that different from President Trump's claim about Antifa agitators, who could never be identified as a cohesive or coherent movement. Erdoğan's language and policies served to fragment society and he appealed to hardline Islamists to counter the demonstrators. According to a former minister of interior, Erdoğan 'lost touch with reality during Gezi. I do not know any event as transformative as Gezi was in terms of changing his thinking. Muammer Güler, who was the minister of the interior, totally failed to manage the situation'. According to this former minister of interior, he happens to be a critic of Erdoğan now:

> Erdoğan's reaction to Gezi was well calculated. His goal was to polarise the public and mobilise conservative Muslim groups. He gave up all previous pretensions and donned his 'Islamist shirt' to prepare for a bigger, more difficult struggle against the Gülen movement. By invoking Islamic symbols and pointing out the West as the enemy of Turkey, Erdoğan was also trying to bring the grass roots of the Gülen movement into his fold.[18]

While the Gezi Park protests continued, Erdoğan said:

> They have entered the Dolmabahçe Mosque with their beer bottles and their shoes on. They have insulted my headscarf-wearing daughters and sisters. And they haven't stopped at that.[19]

In fact, during the Gezi Park protests, he was preparing his strategy for coping with his potential and deadly 'enemy': the Gülen movement. When I asked Dengir Mir Mehmet Fırat about Erdoğan's reaction to Gezi, he said:

> As you know, in 2012, the Gülenist prosecutor called Hakan Fidan, the head of the MIT, whom Erdoğan calls 'my secret box', for questioning on charges about PKK activities. Erdoğan realised that the Gülenists are targeting him now. He strongly reacted and became extremely suspicious of everyone. The Gezi demonstrations further scared him as he worried about a potential coalition of the left and the Gülen movement. Thus, he ignited the Islamist language and symbols to prevent an open alliance from forming between the Gülen movement and the demonstrators.

The Gezi Park protests were expected to break the wall of fear and facilitate the questioning and criticism of the policies of Erdoğan. As a result of the police force, 8,000 people were injured and eleven protestors were killed by the police.[20] However, Erdoğan marshalled all his rhetorical and ideological power to delegitimise the protesters and distance the conservative Islamic grass roots by portraying them as 'foreign dark forces that envied Turkey's rise to greatness' and he also pointed out that the Gezi protesters were funded by the 'interest-rate lobby'. Erdoğan asked the protesters to end their activities: 'I am having difficulty in keeping 50 per cent [those who support Erdoğan] in their homes.'[21] Not only at the rhetorical level, but especially at the operational level he ordered his prosecutors to go after the leaders of these amorphous social movements in order to intimidate them from planning for future protests.

The post-Gezi climate was much worse, since Erdoğan became paranoid of the people around him. This climate forced the business community to shy away from any form of political statement; Turkey's urban middle-class youth, who respect meritocracy and human rights, sought opportunities outside the country and the brain drain became the pattern; and by ordering police to shoot the protesters, Erdoğan made any street protest against the government costly and somewhat impossible. The violence Erdoğan unleashed upon the Gezi protesters accomplished his objective so that no ordinary Turks would risk injury or death to take part in an anti-government protest. The Gezi Park protests left their mark on the images of Erdoğan and Turkey. President Obama and many Western powers had regarded Turkey as a successful case in reconciling modernity and Islam as well as Islam and democracy and they advocated for the AKP experience as a model for post-Arab Spring protestors. This image of Erdoğan as a model for other Muslim countries would morph into an autocrat and dictator. As a result of Erdoğan's heavy-handed response and conspiratorial rhetoric, Obama stopped calling Erdoğan. The relations once praised on the basis of shared values of democracy, the rule of law and individual freedoms were reduced to regional security issues. His authoritarian policies not only isolated him but also helped to create more opposition to Erdoğan's rule.

After the Gezi Park protests, Erdoğan forced the Doğan media conglomerate to sell its media outlets and created the most controlled media in the region.²² Finally, Erdoğan's policies combined with the corruption probes forced a new form of opposition within the party itself; Erdoğan would use all means to get rid of them as well. He tried to mobilise his grass-roots supporters through his 'Respect for the National Will' rallies.²³ At the rally in Istanbul, Kazlıçeşme, he stated:

> They carried out the 27 May coup and the late Menderes' execution against this nation. But this nation replied to them at the ballot box. They carried out the 28 February coup against the late Erbakan, and this nation again replied at the ballotbox . . . This nation always protected democracy and the national will . . . I am asking you again: will we protect the national will?²⁴

Erdoğan went on to personally associate himself with Menderes, with a clear intent to represent Gezi as an illegitimate attempt to overthrow a democratically elected government:

> They say, 'This prime minister is too tough, too conflictive, a dictator'. Mr Menderes was too kind and you executed such a nice and kind person . . . Now you are plotting the same for me.

One of the key posters of these public rallies was an effort to equate Menderes, Özal and Erdoğan with the following words under each photo: 'The Men of the Nation: You killed him? [Menderes] You poisoned him? [Özal] We won't let you have him [Erdoğan]'.²⁵ These photos and words appeared on billboards all over Turkey and became the key banner during the 'Respect for the National Will' meetings. In these meetings, Erdoğan start to use '*bunlar*' (you or them) who seek to destroy the national will through the Gezi protests versus the 'real' people who support Erdoğan and represent the national will. Erdoğan, just like Menderes, justified his authoritarian practices by believing that he and his party directly represent the national will since he controls the majority of seats in the parliament. This (mis)use and sacralisation of majoritarianism as the direct representation of the national will started with the Democrat Party of Adnan Menderes. On 23 June 2013, during one of the public rallies in Erzurum, Erdoğan stated: 'I don't recognise any will higher than my nation's will. They [protestors] will first learn how to respect the national will.' Erdoğan also called on the people of Erzurum to hang Ottoman flags next to Turkish flags.[26] After the Gezi Park protests, Erdoğan eulogised about Ottoman history, comparing his policies to those of the Ottoman era and proclaiming that he would make Turkey great again. He said:

> Turkey is the successor of the Ottomans, who united the whole Middle East under one banner. No conspiracy would work against us ... Turkey is not a country which they could redesign through the international media. BBC and CNN: I challenge you to show this crowd too ... Shamelessly, they are saying that it is time to have a 'Turkish Spring'. You miserable people, the Turkish Spring happened on 3 November 2002 [the date of AKP's first national election victory] ... There was torture in prisons and police stations. We said we would show zero tolerance to torture. We provided a shift from the rule of the superior to the superiority of the law. Freedom of expression was limited; we removed the limitations.[27]

Abdullah Gül, then the president, was not subject to the same type of pressure, and was able to leverage public anger to present a moderate, level-headed alternative to Erdoğan. As a result, the Gezi outbursts deepened the split between supporters of Gül and Erdoğan. Moreover, the Gezi experience gave an opportunity for the Gülen movement to distance itself from the AKP and Erdoğan. From this point, the news outlets of the movement criticised Erdoğan and the people around him. This coverage led to increased tensions between the followers of Gülen and the pro-AKP media. Among the circle of Erdoğan, the protests were viewed as a sinister plot by certain Western powers. This stems from the perception that the EU and some circles in the US have never felt comfortable with an overly stable and economically powerful Turkey.[28]

One of the main outcomes of the Gezi Park demonstrations was a more pronounced climate of paranoia that rattled political leaders who watched warily for Erdoğan's reaction. The paranoia spread quickly throughout the AKP political ranks and it drove the main motive behind Erdoğan's increasingly autocratic policies. Moreover, according to Osman Can, a professor of constitutional law and former member of the AKP, this rapidly spreading paranoia morphed into an existential fear that bedeviled Erdoğan.[29] This paranoia is based on the ceaseless feeling of being under siege by real and imagined enemies (opponents or those loyalists who were reconsidering their connections), fortified by Erdoğan's sense of moral justification to act pre-emptively against those he considered his enemies. Erdoğan's election rallies in 2014, 2015 and 2019 sprung from this existential sense of his paranoia. His sense of being a Black Turk (that is, one who is marginalised and not accepted), explains, in part, the contextual roots of how his paranoia developed and became entrenched in his political mindset.

After the Gezi Park protests in 2013, Erdoğan's understanding of Ottomanism was deeply informed by the personality of Abdulhamid II.[30] In this re-reading of neo-Ottomanism through the personality and policies of Abdulhamid II, Erdoğan tried to justify the concentration of absolute power to protect the interest of *umma*, oppression of independent media, and treating all critical voices both in and outside the country as the enemy of the nation, and especially Islam. In fact, this new neo-Ottomanism was more Islamist less Ottomanist and deeply suspicious of European powers. They reduced the Ottoman state into an Islamic state and explained its collapse as a result of European external powers' intervention in the name of minority rights.

5.2 The Egyptian Coup: Erdoğan's Fears

If there were critical events that led to the transformation of Erdoğan to become more authoritarian with an instinct to destroy democratic institutions of Turkey, one of them was the bloody Egyptian coup that overthrew President Mohamed Morsi. The coup was supported by major EU countries, the US, Saudi Arabia and the United Arab Emirates and this, in turn, had a major impact on Erdoğan, in that he could also be overthrown by the 'local arms of Western powers', especially in light of the Gezi Park demonstrations.[31] After the demonstrations, Erdoğan gradually searched for an alternative to Turkey's Western ties by developing closer ties with Russia and using every opportunity to consolidate his power at the expense of democratic institutions.

The coup in Egypt hardened Erdoğan's views regarding the bad faith of his domestic and international critics, coming on the heels of the Gezi Park demonstrations. Turkey had supported the Muslim Brotherhood after Morsi assumed the presidency on 30 June 2012. However, the military coup on 3 July 2013 saw the arrest of Morsi as the military suspended the constitution and installed an interim government under Adli Mansour, the chief justice of Egypt's supreme Constitutional Court, prior to organising new parliamentary and presidential elections. The coup and Morsi's arrest shocked Erdoğan, who recognised the three sectors responsible for the coup: the military establishment, the judicial elite and the secular media. Morsi had never gained control of these three elements. Erdoğan, sensing his own vulnerability, moved to consolidate his control over the corresponding institutions in Turkey. Morsi, like Erdoğan, understood democracy as a majoritarian rule and refused to listen to opposition voices. The biggest mistake was the exclusion of a large sector of the Egyptian population from the process of establishing a new constitution that sought to legalise the Islamisation of the state.

Erdoğan described the Egyptian coup as 'state terrorism' and referred to General El-Sisi as a 'tyrant'. Erdoğan not only welcomed the Muslim Brotherhood to Turkey but also provided necessary means to keep the Egyptian opposition effective by allowing them to establish one of the most sophisticated Arabic media outlets in Istanbul. The Egyptian government reacted by asking the Turkish ambassador to leave the country and severed relations with Ankara. Moreover, El-Sisi allied Egypt with Greece and the Greek Cypriots to draw a maritime economic zone in the Mediterranean in order to exclude Turkey from the region. As Erdoğan attacked El-Sisi and questioned his legitimacy, Egypt became more adamant in pursuing an anti-Turkey foreign policy by supporting the PKK terrorists in Syria and actively engaging to overthrow the pro-Turkish Libyan government.

Turkey, more so than Egypt, has paid dearly because of Erdoğan's ideological commitment to the Muslim Brotherhood. Moreover, Erdoğan's government invested nearly $2 billion in business deals and loans to open up Egyptian markets for Turkish business. The coup destroyed these investments. Turkey became isolated from the Middle East and new authoritarian governments in the region turned against the AKP. Turkey shifted from being a 'regional playmaker' to 'precious loneliness', the price paid for Turkey's support of the region's pro-Islamist democratic movements.[32] When Morsi died in the court room during the trial, Erdoğan said, 'Morsi did not die, he was murdered by the Egyptian authorities', and called on the UN and the Organisation of Islamic Cooperation to investigate the circumstances of his death.[33] After the coup in Egypt, Istanbul became the regional hub for the diverse Muslim Brotherhood organisations and media outlets. There are more than 15,000 people, mostly from Egypt, settled in Turkey and most of them have received Turkish passports. Although their 'patience strategy' has been funded and supported by Turkey and Qatar, the presence of the Muslim Brotherhood has a deep negative effect on Sufi-oriented and sharia-free Turkish Islam. Since 2014, we are witnessing a gradual process of the Salafisation of Turkish Islam by the new ideological alliance between Erdoğan and the Muslim Brotherhood.

There are several consequences of the coup in Egypt. The first is that Erdoğan lost his faith, trust and confidence in the international community and, as a result, he stopped listening to criticism about democracy or human rights, as many of the Western powers supported the coup, which resulted in the massacre of 3,000 people. Second, Erdoğan was convinced that the US and Israel used the Egyptian military to end the emerging democratic process in Egypt and he feared something similar could happen in Turkey by using Gülenist officers in the army. An adviser of Erdoğan said, 'Erdoğan's concerns about the Gülenist networks in the army became his nightmare. After the coup, he came to the conclusion that the Gülen community is tightly controlled by the Western powers and they could carry out a similar coup against him.' Third, Erdoğan's approach to Saudi Arabia radically changed. He compared the country's rulers to the 'brothers of Prophet Joseph who threw him into the well'.[34]

5.3 Corruption Probes: Erdoğan versus Gülenists

In 2013, Erdoğan turned on his erstwhile Islamist allies, the Gülenists, after they accused him of corruption. On 17 December 2013, the Istanbul Police Department's Financial and Anti-Corruption Unit detained forty-seven people, including the sons of three ministers: Barış Güler (the son of the minister of interior), Kaan Çağlayan (the son of the minister of economy), and Oğuz Bayraktar (the son of the minister of environment and urban development). Also detained were Mustafa Demir, the mayor of the Fatih district of Istanbul, and high-ranking officials of the Housing Development Administration of Turkey, known as TOKİ; Süleyman Aslan, the general director of the state-owned Halk Bank; and Iranian businessman Rezza Zarraf. In addition, Egemen Bağış, the minister of European Union affairs, was suspected of bribery in association with Zarraf as well as Babak Zanjani, an Iranian multibillionaire.

As the investigation became a major media spectacle, the police confiscated $17.4 million believed to be connected to bribery charges. Also, $4.5 million was found at Aslan's home, and $750,000 at Güler's residence. The Istanbul prosecutor charged fourteen people, including the sons of ministers and Egemen Bağış with bribery, corruption and fraud. Because of these charges and evidence, the court ordered the arrest of all fourteen on 21 December. The prosecutor also ordered search warrants for the homes of numerous individuals, including Necmettin Bilal Erdoğan, the prime minister's son. Istanbul's newly appointed police chief at the time, Selami Altınok, refused to carry out the prosecutor's orders and the head of the Deputy Director of Public Prosecutions office also did not endorse the operation. The following day, prosecutor Muammer Akkaş, the man behind the operation, and believed to have close ties with the Gülen movement, was dismissed from his job.

The entire operation was carried out on live television. News outlets associated with the Gülen movement were the first to have information about where the police would carry out the next operation. Thus, the war between the Gülen movement and the AKP was carried out visibly through police investigation and the court system. Police officers and court officials connected with the Gülen movement played an important role in these anti-corruption probes. The Gülen movement's motive was not morality, or a desire to clean up the democratic institutions, or the restoration of the rule of law. Rather it was to undermine the government's position because it refused to share power with the movement. Corruption has been the main problem since the 2007 elections when the AKP established its position with the help of the Gülen movement, which had been the main supporter of the government until 2012.

The AKP-led government vehemently denied the corruption charges and Erdoğan claimed that the arrests were an attempt by the prosecutors, police and judges connected with the Gülen movement to overthrow the government. The leaks of secretly taped conversations between Erdoğan and his son, and between the ministers and their sons exacerbated the problem.

Meanwhile, Erdoğan responded quickly, marshalling all of his resources against the accusers, and targeting, in particular, the Gülen movement as the principal agent of outside forces.

Erdoğan's swift response helped the government to gain control of the political narrative. However, the corruption charges and the vicious struggle between the AKP and the Gülen movement, who were once committed allies, had a negative effect on Turkey's political life that will likely persist for a long time. The probes and the government's reactions to them tarnished the once clean image of Erdoğan and his party. Moreover, it poisoned the political climate and caused a shift among the country's political groups, thus facilitating the formation of an anti-corruption – or, more practically, an anti-AKP front. The ripples in Turkey's political landscape continue to reverberate years after these events.

The government undertook draconian measures by reassigning thousands of officials to marginal bureaucratic positions, especially in the police and judiciary. It also modified the laws and regulation's regarding judiciary appointments, the Internet, homeland security and intelligence gathering in order to cleanse pro-Gülen officials from the state structure. Any criticism of the government is now labelled Gülenist, while any criticism of the Gülen movement is labelled Erdoğanist. However, a majority of voters are not convinced by the argument of the Gülen movement or the AKP's contention, and most appear to welcome the current clash between the two former allies.[35]

The AKP government also removed 350 police officers from their positions and reconfigured prosecutorial powers to cover up ongoing investigations of the corruption allegations. Erdoğan described these two related corruption investigations as a judicial coup undertaken by the Gülen movement. In response, the AKP-dominated parliamentary commission voted against the trial of the four ministers. According to the Turkish constitution, the ministers and high government officials must go to trial in Higher Council, a constitutional court reserved for the state's most serious crimes and irregularities. The parliamentary committee, which carried out the first investigation, voted nine–five to end the investigations of the most widespread corruption scandal in the Turkish Republic in modern times. The AKP-dominated parliament also voted along party lines. The four ministers were acquitted and did not face further prosecution. However, in due time, the effects of corruption have penetrated the public discourse and the AKP appears to have lost the upper hand, as evidenced by the results of recent elections.

During our interviews, one of Ahmet Davutoğlu's advisers, who asked not to be named, said unequivocally that 'it was a big mistake not to send these ministers to trial'.[36] When asked 'why the AKP did not do it previously but could do so now', his response was that 'the major concern is that these probes could include the son of Erdoğan and even himself. No one in the party wants to discuss this and Erdoğan is still the boss of the AKP'. None of the AKP parliamentarians or advisers interviewed for the book denied the charges. One said:

> Everybody knows that those charges are mostly true. Egemen Bağış and some other ministers are involved in a series of corrupt activities. However, as a party we invested too much capital and time denying them and now it is almost impossible to reverse the course.[37]

In private conversations, many AKP politicians asserted that the four ministers must face trial in order to free the party from accusations. The parliamentary investigation committee, which had examined the details surrounding the wealth acquired by the four ministers, concluded that the personal wealth of the four officials, especially Bağış, went beyond what would be the reasonable expectations of earnings, given their respective positions.

Although the AKP managed to use its power to end the investigation, the political effects still resonate. The majority of AKP voters believes that the corruption charges are true and that those ministers must be tried before court. In order to end the investigation and fight back against corruption charges, Erdoğan and the AKP have fought against the Gülen movement as a national security issue, leveraging all means to delegitimise the movement and undermine its presence in the state's political and governing institutions. The confrontation between the AKP and the Gülen movement has brought many secret dealings and the symbiotic relations to the public eye, including the AKP's strategy to use the Gülen movement to undermine the Turkish military through a series of kangaroo courts in which the integrity of legal and judicial principles has been disregarded.[38] In addition, the Gülen movement's followers working in the police force, the judiciary, forensic laboratories and the media have played an important yet incriminating role in these mock courts.

The conflict has revealed the true nature of both sides and their narrow interests at the expense of the public good. Cemil Çiçek, then speaker of parliament, called for the ministers to face trial for the sake of the party and their families. However, the four ministers used all available tactics to stop the investigations. In the court of public opinion, because the court of law failed to adjudicate and resolve these issues, these four ministers were perceived to be corrupt and this undeniably played a fundamental role in the 2015 elections. The unfinished investigation did not only demoralise the AKP electorate, but, more importantly, botched the AKP's image as a clean and moral force to shape the country's future. Finally, the investigation aggravated fears about the AKP government, which, in turn, became more authoritarian and more prone to paranoia towards any form of political opposition. In conclusion, the conflict between the AKP and the Gülen movement has been as devastating as the December corruption investigations themselves. Unfortunately, this conflict eclipsed the most productive and revolutionary changes the AKP brought about during its time in political power. The corruption probes shaped Erdoğan's understanding of politics that power should not be shared with any group and it must be asserted boldly against his opponents.

5.4 The 2014 and 2015 Elections

5.4.1 The 2014 presidential election

Turkey entered a new era in August 2014 when it organised the first popular vote to elect the president. Erdoğan won the popular vote with 51.79 per cent against the other two candidates: Ekmeleddin İhsanoğlu, a retired professor and the former secretary general of the Organisation of Islamic Cooperation, who was the joint candidate of the two opposition parties (CHP and MHP), and Selahattin Demirtaş of the People's Democratic Party (HDP). Erdoğan had two reasons why he wanted to run for the presidency: according to AKP rules he was not eligible to apply for a fourth term as prime minister, and he wanted to change the political system from a parliamentary to presidential system. During the campaign, Erdoğan aired his vision for an executive presidential system that would be free from checks and balances. He justified this system as the best way of delivering services, economic growth and making Turkey great again. The two other candidates insisted on the parliamentary system as the best way to maintain democratic order in the country.

Erdoğan aimed to make Turkey the tenth largest economy and a regional power by 2023. Since 2002, his pro-business policies had helped to improve the economic situation of the Anatolian economically and culturally marginalised sector of the population. Economic development in Anatolia played an important role in the consolidation of civil society and this, in turn, gave a political voice for the country's conservative population to air a system as they envisioned. The Anatolian bourgeoisie supported Erdoğan, along with some nationalist Turks who also voted for him due to his new harsh policies against Kurdish nationalism.

5.4.2 The 2015 national elections: Erdoğan's nationalism

Although the 2015 elections results represented the end of the era of Erdoğan-dominated Turkey, they also produced the most representative parliament in recent memory, at least for a short period. In addition to an ethnic Kurdish party, a large number of Alevis within the CHP and HDP, and members of religious minorities – Armenians, Assyrians and Yazidis, along with Romas – were also elected to the parliament. In short, the 2015 elections represented the end of old-era politics. However, hopes for a new Turkey were also dashed, as the later chapters demonstrate.

The 2015 campaign focused on three issues: the establishment of a presidential system, corruption allegations surrounding the AKP leadership, and the Kurdish question. In this election, the AKP shed its transformative identity, fully becoming a party of the status quo, while charges of corruption from the top down in the AKP's structure undermined its long-standing pure (*ak*) image. Erdoğan's demagogic language irritated many people, including those who admired his economic achievements. The electorate voted against the presidential system, concerned that the government would not abide by the rule of law, and the AKP-led Kurdish initiative (*Kürt açılımı*), which was limited in scope. As the elections were not about any sort of clear plan to grow the economy or democratise the political system, they turned into a referendum on Erdoğan's attempt to control all branches of the state and to halt any further investigation of corruption charges against the four former

AKP ministers, namely Bağış, Güler, Cağlayan and Bayraktar.[39] Erdoğan's construction of a giant new 1,150-room palace in the Beştepe district of Ankara further convinced the public, and even many AKP voters, that the corruption charges might have been true. The cost of the palace, approximately $620 million, was the major subject of an embarrassing debate in the run-up to the elections.[40] In an interview I conducted in Ankara, a former politician of the AKP said, 'After November 2015, the AKP government is for and by one person: Erdoğan.'

After the June 2015 elections, Erdoğan sought to restructure the political landscape with a series of new tactics. Astute about the urgent need to rejuvenate a formerly solid political brand that now is flailing, Erdoğan deepened his involvement in the AKP's routine political decision making. He relied on two parallel strategies that are meant to move together. In order to dampen any public criticism that he avoided forming a coalition government despite its being in the nation's best interest, Erdoğan instructed Davutoğlu to demonstrate a showcase coalition that convenes regularly with other parties, especially with the CHP. Simply put, Erdoğan did not want a coalition government that would jeopardise or restrain his executive powers and, even worse, focus on corruption charges involving his closest political associates.

Erdoğan and the AKP ran down the clock on the forty-five days required by the Turkish constitution to try to establish a coalition government. Then, as soon as the deadline passed, he dissolved the parliament and called for the November snap elections, a fourth visit to the ballot box by Turkish voters in barely a year and a half. During this period, marked by several signs of economic weakness, including the country's faltering currency and a slowdown in construction, Erdoğan took full control of AKP governance to ensure the political infrastructure was stocked with his loyalists. It is evident that the AKP's candidate list for the November elections was shaped according to Erdoğan's preferences, whereas Davutoğlu's involvement in crafting the new AKP list seems to have been minimal at best.

Erdoğan's snap elections strategy comprised several key points. He was disappointed that the Kurdish electoral decision left the AKP to support the HDP, which for the first time gained enough representation to enter parliament formally and garnered more than six million votes in the process. Once eager to court pro-Kurdish groups, Erdoğan focused heavily on

Turkish-nationalist groups. He declared the end of the 'Kurdish Opening', accusing the HDP, along with the PKK, of acting in bad faith. The PKK, in turn, gradually intensified its attacks on security officials and state institutions since June, killing 145 security officials, including policemen and high-ranking military personnel. Likewise, HDP-dominated municipalities proclaimed their governmental autonomy, thereby rejecting the tenets of the Turkish Republic's rule of law. The PKK militias, with HDP support, were more aggressive and assertive, suggesting that soon the spectre of Turkish state sovereignty could be reduced to the status of a paper tiger. In responding to these attacks, Erdoğan hoped to garner a solid bloc of nationalist votes in the November elections. As a second dimension to this strategy, Erdoğan successfully recruited Tuğrul Türkeş, the son of the nationalist Alpaslan Türkeş and the deputy chair of the nationalist MHP, to run in AKP's list of candidates.

The results of the November elections defied the predictions of most political polls and analysts. It was an overwhelming victory for Erdoğan. The AKP saw an increase of more than 4.5 million votes, while the Kurdish HDP, along with the Turkish Nationalist Movement Party (MHP), suffered major losses. What political and social factors can explain this decisive reversal within a six-month period? Erdoğan managed to convince more than 4.5 million voters to support its political platform, despite the climate of ethnic and ideological polarisation and the negative international image of Erdoğan as a new 'autocrat'. The electorate, especially many conservative Kurds and Turks who had voted for the HDP and the MHP in June, decided to vote for the AKP in November.

There are four reasons for this electoral shift: (1) fear, stemming from the wave of PKK and ISIS terrorist attacks against civilian and government targets, bringing to mind images from Syria and Iraq and making many voters worry whether Turkey was going to become a failed state; (2) the worsening economic situation of the previous six months, in contrast with the economic success of Erdoğan in last decade; (3) public perception of irresponsibility and incompetence aroused by the conduct of the opposition parties, especially the refusal of the MHP to adopt a constructive approach to a coalition government, and the failure of the HDP to repudiate PKK terrorism (the failure to condemn PKK militants in the Kandil Mountains was seen as

Table 5.1 Election Results 2015

	June 2015			November 2015		
			Seats			Seats
AKP	18,867,411	40.9%	258	23,673,541	49.49%	317
CHP	11,518,139	25.0%	132	12,109,985	25.31%	134
MHP	7,520,006	16.3%	80	5,691,737	11.90%	40
HDP	6,058,489	13.1%	80	5,145,688	10.75%	59
Others	2,199,198	4.7%	0	1,322,429	2.55%	0

doublespeak by many liberal and leftist Turks, who decided not to vote for the HDP this time); and (4) the failure of many intellectuals to offer convincing alternatives to the AKP. The politics of fear became the major force in the snap elections and this fear, in fact, was deliberately engineered by Erdoğan. It was Erdoğan who prevented the formation of a coalition government and, again, his policies very much provoked the PKK to use violence which, in turn, helped Erdoğan. Erdoğan cannot win an election without enemies. For him, politics without enemies is meaningless. He has always engineered some degree of paranoia as a source of unifying his grass roots. In the 2015 elections, when the masses were scared, they looked for an autocratic leader. In fact, stability and security became the main concerns of the electorate. The vote of the AKP increased from 40.9 per cent to 49.4 per cent.

5.5 Conclusion

The year 2013 became the *annus horribilis* for Erdoğan. He had to face the major urban rebellion in Taksim, his closest ally President Mohamed Morsi was overthrown in Egypt by an internationally supported coup which shattered his foreign policy agenda, and there was civil war in Syria. Aggravating the circumstances were the corruption probes which erased public perceptions of him being a clean public official. He was now viewed as the most corrupt leader in the history of Turkish politics. When President Gül and Ali Babacan, among other AKP politicians, called for a full investigation of these corruption charges, Erdoğan regarded their position as 'treacherous' (his word) attempts to remove him from power. His attitude was akin to Caesar's classic line: 'Even you, Gül?'

The major by-products of the events of 2013 were the politics of fear and the paranoia that drove most of Erdoğan's policies, which sharpened the gaps in Turkish society. Political polarisation in Turkey can be described as follows: secular versus Islamic; and sharing of sovereign power through federalism (Kurds) versus a unified nation state arrangement predicated on historical Turkish identity. Then, there are the tensions between the Sunni majority and Alevi minority. The events of 2013 compelled Erdoğan to don his Islamist bearings and pursue a heavy-handed top-down Islamisation policy. He redefined himself as a Turko-Islamist nationalist by identifying Abdulhamid II as his role model.

The coup in Egypt and the civil wars in several Arab countries represented either the end or transformation of the Islamic political movement. The verdict is still up for question. The prevailing regional sociopolitical context has deeply transformed Islamism in almost every country. Islamic actors have been effective in ending existing authoritarian systems by establishing an oppositional movement to bring diverse groups together in the name of justice, but they also have failed miserably at forming a functioning democracy. In the case of Turkey, pro-Islamic forces came to power with high moral expectations to purify society and restore the rule of law. After more than nineteen years of the AKP political experiment, none of the moral goals or political aims have been realised. Turkey is more corrupt than in 2002, less stable, and the gap between the rich and poor has widened considerably. The main questions are: What is left from political Islamism today? Did it end for good or has it been transformed into something far more chaotic and destabilising?

The Islamic political movement has become the most powerful societal force in many Muslim countries to criticise respective governments in the name of justice and by ignoring a shared moral code in governance. In many countries, distinct variations of the Islamic movement have come to power on the premise of being effective representatives of historically oppressed and persecuted groups. In Turkey, the variant of this movement has spent its moral and political capital either involving the process of corruption in order to become rich or it has ignored ongoing examples of injustice. In summary, political Islamism in Turkey shed its moral language and became a naked search for power. The evidence is glaring in 2020. It has degenerated into an oppressive, corrupt force that seeks to empower itself through illegitimate means. By consuming what had been a long tradition of a more humanistic and liberal Islam, Turkish society is now intellectually disarmed against more radical and nihilistic Islamic movements. Never has the Republic faced such a political crisis.

The worst development under Erdoğan's rule was that Islam and Islamic groups were all closely tied to the state through subsidies. The domain of Islamic civil activism has been restricted and the entire education system and civil society associations are controlled by the state more than ever. Under the Erdoğan government, civil domain was restricted through politicisation and cooptation by the state while the religious domain has been further regulated and tightly controlled by the AKP government. In short, Islamism, as we know it, has come to an end and what has emerged is a more nihilist Salafi version of Islam. The future is tenuous at best and incessantly volatile at worst, as the AKP's legacy of consuming and exploiting moderate Islamic movements in Turkey has instead opened up space for Islamist cells with more radicalised nihilist political visions.

Notes

1. The monument was built by Italian sculptor Pietro Canonica and it was opened in 1928. It was built to commemorate the formation of the Republic. The monument has two sides, one incorporating the military and civilian aspects of Atatürk, and the other honouring two Russian generals (Mihail Vasilyevic Frunze and Marshal Kliment Yefremovic Vorosilove), in recognition of the Russian military and financial aid to the Turkish War of Independence.
2. Bardakcı, 'O kışla neler gördü', 9 June 2013.
3. Berkes, *The Development of Secularism in Turkey*, pp. 431–78.
4. Kenyon, 'Not everyone cheers Turkey's move to tighten alcohol rules', 7 June 2013.
5. TOMA is an armoured vehicle that is designed to control urban social unrest by use of its powerful water cannon. These vehicles are produced in Turkey, and effectively serve their purpose. It was because of this very effectiveness that they became part of the narrative concerning the Gezi Park events.
6. Bal, 'AK Party parliamentarian, issued a report criticizing government policies', 13 August 2013. He claimed that a small-scale local issue unnecessarily turned into a major crisis, with negative implications on the democratic credentials of

the AKP government, all because of Erdoğan's 'misguided strategies'. Bal blamed Erdoğan's advisors for misinforming and misguiding the prime pinister. Bal also argued that democracy is not only about the ballot box but also about the protection of minority rights and different lifestyles.

7. *Milliyet*, 'Yeni buluşma noktası: Gezi Parkı', 9 June 2013. Boyner said, 'I am neither a leftist nor rightist but rather a *capulcu*.' In *Taraf*, 5 June 2013, Özen said, 'I support the Gezi resistance. I am also a *capulcu*.'
8. The Beşiktaş stadium and neighbourhood are located in nearby Taksim in what is traditionally a Kemalist stronghold. The football club fans are known as the *Çarşı* and, like their Egyptian Al-Ahlawy counterparts played a central role in the street fighting with police. In Turkey, like much else, even football clubs carry a strong political valence, with Beşiktaş being a traditional favourite of Kemalists and the Fenerbahçe team, located on the Asian side of the city, enjoying the support of more religious people. The clubs initially suspended their bitter rivalry and cooperated during the initial stages of the demonstrations, but later parted ways again.
9. Erdoğan's speech at the AKP Group, 11 June 2013.
10. For such a facile and typical Western comparison between Tahrir and Taksim, see Fukuyama, 'The middle-class revolution', 28 June 2013.
11. Göle, 'Gezi – anatomy of a public square movement', p. 7.
12. Coşkun Taştan discusses the 'carnivalesque' aspect of the outburst in his excellent paper, 'The Gezi Park protests in Turkey', pp. 27–38.
13. Zalewski, 'Protocols of the interest rate lobby', 27 June 2013.
14. *Hürriyet Daily News*, '"Patience has its limits", Turkish PM Erdoğan tells Taksim Gezi Park demonstrators', 9 June 2013.
15. When Kavala was acquitted in February 2020 because there was 'not enough concrete evidence' against him, Erdoğan denounced the acquittal in his weekly parliamentary speech. He said, 'Gezi is not an innocent protesting event. There are Soros-like figures behind the curtains who seriously seek to stir up things by provoking revolt in some countries. His [Soros] Turkish leg [Kavala] was in jail. They tried to acquit him yesterday by a manoeuvre'. After this speech, the prosecutor rearrested Kavala, this time accusing of him supporting and organising the 2016 coup against the government. *Bianet*, 'Erdoğan calls Osman Kavala "domestic Soros"', 24 October 2017.
16. Interview with Çamuroğlu, Ankara, 8 June 2019.
17. *Milliyet*, 21 June 2013.
18. Interview, Ankara, 6 June 2018.

19. *Hürriyet Daily News*, '"Patience has its limits", Turkish PM Erdoğan tells Taksim Gezi Park demonstrators', 9 June 2013.
20. Berkin Elvan became the symbol of the Gezi Park protests. He died on 11 March 2014, at the age of fifteen, after having been in a coma for 269 days. Elvan was shot by the police. Erdoğan had ordered the police to shoot and clear the area of protestors. Erdoğan also accused him being a terrorist. BBC, 'Berkin Elvan: Turkish PM accuses dead boy of terror links', 15 March 2014.
21. *Hürriyet*, 'Başbakan: Yüzde 50'yi evinde zor tutuyorum', 4 June 2013.
22. Orucoglu, 'How President Erdoğan mastered the media', 12 August 2015.
23. Bilgiç, 'Reclaiming the national will', pp. 259–80.
24. *Star*, 'Başbakan Erdoğan Milli İradeye Saygı mitinginde halka seslendi', 16 June 2013.
25. Adnan Menderes was hanged by the military coup in 1960; Turgut Özal had heart problems and he was overweight; he died in the presidential palace. However, Erdoğan and his conspiratorial circle believe that Özal had been poisoned by the enemies of Turkey who were jealous of Turkey's economic development.
26. *Milliyet*, 'Erdoğan, Erzurum'da halka seslendi', 23 June 2013.
27. *Star*, 'Başbakan Erdoğan Milli İradeye Saygı mitinginde halka seslendi', 16 June 2013.
28. On 31 July 2013, the US Senate discussed the Gezi protests in a panel at the Committee on Foreign Relations. Those who spoke stressed Turkey's strategic importance for the US and called on Turkey and the Erdoğan government not to drift away from democratic and Western values. 'Where is Turkey headed? Gezi Park, Taksim Square, and the future of the Turkish model', <https://www.foreign.senate.gov/imo/media/doc/073113_Transcript_Where%20is%20Turkey%20Headed%20Gezi%20Park%20Taksim%20Square%20and%20the%20Future%20of%20the%20Turkish%20Model.pdf> (last accessed 16 November 2020).
29. For Osman Can's statements, see Taşgetiren, 'Dökülme', 26 June 2020.
30. Armstrong, 'The sultan and the sultan', 8 November 2017.
31. Tharoor, 'Turkey's Erdoğan always feared a coup. He was proved right', 15 July 2016.
32. *Hürriyet Daily News*, 'İbrahim Kalın told that 'Turkey not "lonely" but dares to do so for its values and principles, says PM advisor', 26 August 2013.
33. *The Independent*, 'Mohamed Morsi death: former Egyptian leader was murdered, says Turkish president Erdogan', 19 June 2019.
34. For more on his speech, see, *Sabah*, 21 August 2013.

35. Gültekin, 'Ak Parti-Cemaat Kavgası', pp. 68–71.
36. Interview, Ankara, 11 June 2015.
37. Interview, Ankara, 11 June 2015.
38. Cakırözer, 'Tek sorumlu cemaat değil', 26 June 2014. Those military officials who spent several years in prisons wrote about their ordeals and how the rule of law was violated. See Erenoğlu, *Aldattılar Siz Duymadınız Sesimizi*; Önsel, *Silivri'de Firavun Töreni*.
39. Dombey, 'Turkish commission votes against the corruption case', 5 January 2015; Idiz, 'Is the AKP shielding former ministers from the corruption charges', 6 January 2015.
40. On the coverage of the new palace, see Arango, 'Turkish leader, using conflicts, cementing power', 31 October 2014; for a more critical review, see Mishra, 'The Western model is broken', 14 October 2014.

6

THE EXISTENTIAL CLASH: ERDOĞAN VERSUS GÜLEN

This chapter examines the evolution of the Gülen movement, a transnational religious movement from pietistic to educational aims, which increasingly became consumed by a desire to amass political power.[1] Inside the Gülen movement, a key assumption has been that there was never a wholly unified or fixed movement but rather something much more organic which was in a continual state of evolution. Its members adapted their political and religious language and practices to different sociopolitical settings. However, the movement's flexible pragmatism ended when it allied itself firmly with the AKP. As a result of prioritising its ambition for short-term power over its core moral concepts, it planted a seed of self-annihilation. No longer a purely religious-social movement, it had abandoned its former self with major political consequences affecting all aspects of Turkish society.[2]

Turkey's two most powerful religious-political groups, the AKP and the Gülen movement, have choreographed a political tango to interact, socialise and share power in ways that have led both entities to unexpected and unprecedented political success for religiously oriented organisations in the history of the modern Republic of Turkey. They have reaped the rotten harvest of their 'belligerent complicity', pushing each other into an escalating political game that has destroyed the country's institutions and respect for the rule of law. They shared the same social base and a decade-long alliance against the Kemalist state, but once the kitchen had been cleared of other potential sources of resistance, they decided that there was not enough room for two chefs. Both movements turned on each other in a fiercely acrimonious way.[3]

Erdoğan sought to shift the blame for the current political crisis onto the Gülen movement, or what it imagines as Turkey's external enemies – mainly, the US and Israel. However, the AKP's contention here suggests that it also was willing to exchange the pragmatic fact of Turkey's NATO membership and its long-term relationship with the US for political rhetoric robbed of any nuance or tactful purpose. However, this power play has taken an apocalyptic turn because of the AKP's venality and unwillingness to share control with the Gülenists. On the other hand, the Gülenist transnational networks leveraged a worsening trend of human rights violations to carve a new political space for their activities, as they positioned themselves as a democratic, liberal, if not secular, civil society movement against Erdoğan's increasing authoritarianism.[4]

This chapter demonstrates how the conflict between the Gülen movement and the AKP, which eventually became the repository of Erdoğan's political base, has devastated the institutions of the state and squashed, at least momentarily, the mutual objective of civil stability and order. How did Turkey's democratic process derail so badly and why? These questions have elicited a major debate among scholars of Turkish politics. One group has argued that what has taken place in Turkey is proof that Islam and Islamic movements are inherently anti-democratic and illiberal because Islam relies on Islamic law, which is incompatible with modern sensibilities and democracy.[5] Thus, the AKP and the Gülen movement have always been anti-democratic, but both movements simply pretended to espouse values of democracy in order to obtain international support (especially in their battle to remove the Turkish Armed Forces from politics) and fortify their claims of legitimacy against Kemalist hegemony.[6] Meanwhile, other scholars reject the assumption of incompatibility between Islam and democracy, arguing that in the beginning both the AKP and the Gülen movement genuinely believed in democracy and promoted liberal values of tolerance, the rule of law and individual freedoms.[7] Changing domestic and international circumstances persuaded them to become anti-democratic and authoritarian.

The author's fieldwork on political Islamic movements in Turkey has supported the latter scholarly view that both movements, even though they always harboured some illiberal characteristics, initially supported a democratic system and desired to see Turkey become a fully fledged member of the EU. Even though illiberal aspects are noted in the two movements, one could have reasonably anticipated that religious movements would become more moderate once they were allowed to participate in political processes. However, the Islamist experience in Turkey indicates that political participation without the institutional structures, such as rigorous checks and balances, and a democratic culture allowed Erdoğan, along with the Gülen movement, to backslide to authoritarianism, corrupted by power.

The power struggle and changing circumstances domestically and globally forced Erdoğan and Gülen, respectively, to reveal their suppressed authoritarian tendencies. Both leaders came out of the closet, so to speak, and displayed their hidden illiberal positions.[8] Therefore, one must explain the metamorphosis of these two powerful Islamic movements: Why, how and when were both Islamic movements transformed from relatively liberal-religious orientations into an authoritarian political machine?

To establish a baseline understanding of identities and ideologies representing the AKP and the Gülen movement, the discussion explores their respective socioreligious contexts by outlining the structure of solidarity (that is, social cement that bonds people together as a religious or secular community (*cemaat*). To understand both political culture and political struggles in Turkey, one needs to understand the meaning, function and structure of the communal (*cemaatci*) mentality.

Communalism in the context of Turkish history means amalgamation of human groupings built on religious identities and loyalties. Although each community suppresses distinctions within the community to preserve unity, it also highlights simple differences between communities to insist on its discrete identity. Thus, communalism has always nurtured a politics of dislike between religious communities. These religiously sanctified communities function to protect the interests of the group against other competing local communities. In this segmented-Muslim amalgamation, there are no unifying core values but rather the expectation for 'the charismatic authority of a leader to fill the cracks of a compromised, unrealized system of justice, a feature that in Europe was minimized by the rationalization of legal practice and the self-referential aspect of law'.[9]

Instead of a civil entity, Ottoman society was an amalgamation of segmented communities engaged in a constant struggle between High Islam versus Folk (vernacular) Islam as well as among diverse Sufi and localised Islamic groups. Communalism, under a charismatic leader, then becomes the essential building block of the Turkish sociopolitical structure. The AKP, under Erdoğan, acts as a *cemaat* (a religion-based political and business community (*siyasi ve ticari cemaat*)) more than as a democratic political party. Thus, Turkish society comprises an amalgamation of secular and Islamic *cemaats*, living together by living apart. This sets up the context for exploring the social and political origins of the alliance joining the Gülen movement and the AKP (2002–12), and the political causes of the tension that arose between the groups (2013–15). The questions that emerge include the following: Did the Gülen movement take such drastic steps to shed the blood of its adherents as well as fellow Turkish citizens, which included an attempt to kill Erdoğan? Did the Gülen movement invoke violent measures, as opposed to working through the political system, as it had previously done? Why did Erdoğan, in turn, rush to turn the seduced *coup d'état* into an opportunity to eliminate all forms of opposition? How did this opportunism thus revise the understanding of the coup as a 'controlled coup'? Notably, Erdoğan's declaration of a state of emergency and decisive use of this legal power have transformed the debate regarding the government's human rights violations and Erdoğan's increasing authoritarianism.

6.1 The Transformation of the Gülen Movement

The Gülen movement, a former ally of Erdoğan, officially referred to as the Fethullah Gülen Terror Organisation (FETO), started as a faith group that evolved from a piety-focused education movement to a network of business organisations. It was eventually transformed into a secretive religio-political configuration, defined by an arrangement bonded by religious ideas and material interests.[10] The most effective way of understanding each transformation of the Gülenist movement is to differentiate its new goals and strategies at each stage of development. Each stage of the movement represented a response to changes on the basis of Gülenists' local conditions and concerns.

To understand the Gülen networks in the security structures, it is useful to discuss them in the context of a secret society. George Simmel's conceptualisation deciphers the inner working of these networks both within the police force and within the military. Simmel defines the secret society either as 'a group whose existence is concealed from the public', or 'a group whose existence may be open, but whose goals, rituals, and structure are concealed from the public'.[11] Simmel's sociological study on secret societies indicates that movements like Gülen either hide their presence or conceal their goals and strategies. The defining characteristics of secret societies are their internal hierarchical ranking, vigilant recruitment from an early age, full control of lives of its members such as whom they should marry, and the movement's ability to project more power than it actually has.

The Gülen movement had a well-established chain of networks and always took care of the promotions and needs of its members while controlling and telling with whom they could socialise, and where to serve. This trust and unquestioned loyalty would shape the interactions of the Gülen followers in the army as well. Moreover, the Gülenist secret networks in the military had similar characteristics of secret societies in terms of secret communications by learning to live a double life in public as secular officers and private spaces as Gülenists, maintaining rigid hierarchical divisions between members, and sacrificing for the greater good of the movement.

The Gülenists comprised circles of peaceful idealistic followers as well as an inner circle willing to use diverse means to attain power. Following a period of official hostility and persecution it became a movement with a tradition of secrecy and a desire to control the security establishment such as the police force, military and intelligence service. The movement often masked its activities and denied its connections with schools and associations to avoid police monitoring. The Gülenists in the police and the military carefully concealed their intentions and goals in order to control the key power positions. Although many Turks tended to explain this shift to secrecy in terms of its real or imagined ties with the CIA, this conspiratorial narrative became an attempt to cover up the mistakes of the Erdoğan government as they pertain to the Gülenists' evolution. The movement has not always been secretive, at least not in most of its public activities. Due to the oppression following the 1997 'post-modern' coup in Turkey, many cells of the movement became more secretive and focused on the control of the police force. After gaining control of the police academy and two-year police training schools with the help of the AKP government, the movement turned its focus on the military.

The movement's most recent evolution coincided with developments in Turkish politics that have been defined variously by corruption, nepotism and a vulgar understanding of Islam. In 2007, the Gülen movement became the government's partner, controlling the Ministries of Interior, Education and Justice as well as the respective department of personnel for every ministry, including Foreign Affairs. The movement's success within the last decade is not the product of claimed cooperation with the CIA but rather failing state institutions and widening sociological fault lines in Turkish society, a polarised party system, weak political leadership in ministries, and especially misuse of police and judiciary by the movement. The arming of the Gülen movement in terms of ideas and networks is the outcome of Turkey's weakened social, political and legal circumstances.

The movement has succeeded in controlling many spaces of power with the help of the AKP-led government. More so than the conviction of ideology, this success has fostered the movement's growth as Gülenists have flexed their moral charter enough to bend on every occasion in order to secure and fortify its control. Although some scholars who worked on the movement have questioned its hidden, dark side, after the seduced coup in 2016, more scholars began questioning the movement's lack of transparency. A speech Gülen gave to his followers in a 1997 broadcast on Turkish television has been cited regularly to prove the movement's secretive nature:

> You must move in the arteries of the system without anyone noticing your existence until you reach all the power centres . . . until the conditions are ripe, they [the followers] must continue like this. If they do something prematurely, the world will crush our heads, and Muslims will suffer everywhere, like in the tragedies in Algeria, like in 1982 [in] Syria . . . like in the yearly disasters and tragedies in Egypt. The time is not yet right. You must wait for the time when you are complete and conditions are ripe, until we can shoulder the entire world and carry it . . . You must wait until such time as you have gotten all the state power, until you have brought to your side all the power of the constitutional institutions in Turkey . . . Until that time, any step taken would be too early – like breaking an egg without waiting the full forty days for it to hatch. It would be like killing the chick inside. The work

to be done is [in] confronting the world. Now, I have expressed my feelings and thoughts to you all – in confidence . . . trusting your loyalty and secrecy. I know that when you leave here – [just] as you discard your empty juice boxes, you must discard the thoughts and the feelings that I expressed here.[12]

Following this and other video broadcasts, a Turkish court charged Gülen with anti-secular and destructive political activities in 1998, and he fled to the US, where he settled in the rural Pennsylvania town of Saylorsburg. Erdoğan's electoral victory in 2002 elections did not only clear the way for Gülen's rehabilitation; with the help of the AKP his followers took control of the judiciary, and he was acquitted in 2006. However, he has never returned to Turkey and continues to coordinate global political and educational activities from his Pennsylvania headquarters.

During the military intervention on 28 February 1997, the Gülen movement, by pointing out the shortcomings of the RP-led government, avoided becoming an National Security Council target. However, the court case against the leader pushed the Gülen movement into the shadows and the group focused on underground intelligence gathering. When the AKP came to power in 2002, the Gülenists stepped forward to improve their public image as a moderate Muslim group. As mentioned earlier, the Gülenists were appointed to major government positions, determined to protect against Kemalist coup attempts against the democratically elected government. The movement's secret networks launched a campaign against its opponents accused of real or imagined coup plotting in the military, media and the bureaucracy through a number of court cases. With the help of the Erdoğan government, it successfully used police intelligence and the judiciary to criminalise its opponents.

The defining example came with the Ergenekon trials, which represented a convoluted investigation carried out with hundreds of early-morning house raids, and with many scholars, journalists and generals being detained.[13] Zekeriya Öz, the chief prosecutor leading the Ergenekon trials, and some key heads of police who were sympathisers of the Gülen movement, investigated the matter.[14] It produced an indictment running to nearly 6,000 pages but the case collapsed as the Gülenists tried to reach key AKP ministers in the 2013 corruption investigations. Some of those who were arrested during the

Ergenekon trials, which were exclusively carried out by the Gülenists police and the judiciary, died in jail without ever seeing the indicting documents.

6.2 An Alliance of Necessity: Gülenists and the AKP

When the AKP came to power in 2002, it encountered major resistance from state institutions, especially the secularist military, due to its Islamist roots and anti-secular rhetoric. Erdoğan's priority was to counter the military and control state institutions by appointing Gülen's followers to key government positions. It was the Gülen movement which provided the necessary administrative support for the AKP to govern the country and monitor the military with the help of the police force. In order to consolidate his reputation as a moderately liberal Muslim leader, Erdoğan endorsed Turkey joining the EU, while becoming an ally with the highly successful and well-informed Gülen movement, then the most powerful Islamic faction.[15]

This movement included highly trained, educated and competent bureaucrats who would control key state institutions while working with Erdoğan to transform them. Moreover, the movement helped AKP officials to establish international connections and it functioned as parallel embassies for the government. Pro-Gülen bureaucrats were appointed to nearly all prominent government positions, including the police, judiciary and departments of education and health. Before the failed 15 July coup, Turkish citizens were all aware that the Gülen movement had a significant presence in the police and judiciary while sharing select information with the government regarding key security policies.[16] However, the coup revealed the powerful presence of the Gülenists in the military and this stunned the public because the military was known as the most anti-Gülenist institution.

As the marginalised conservative Islamic sector of the population, the Gülenists and followers of Erdoğan sprang from similar socio-economic origins. The leaders and followers of both movements identify with the same Sunni-Hanefi background, and share historical memories, along with the goal of Turkey as an EU member. The AKP's ideology and identity early in its development also shared many aspects with the Gülenist agenda. Party members favoured the EU, tempered versions of secularism, supported Kurdish cultural rights, and advocated for the consolidation of democracy and the empowerment of civil society at the expense of the Kemalist state's political power. They viewed the Kemalist-cum-secularist state as the enemy and were determined to restructure sociopolitical relations between the state and its citizens. The founders of the AKP belonged to Turkey's Islamist National View movement of Necmettin Erbakan, the domineering leader of political Islam, who was anti-Western, anti-US, anti-Israel, and who called for a movement of Islamic solidarity with all Muslim countries.[17] But, the AKP's nascent leaders also explicitly rejected this Islamist legacy, suggesting that they give up the old identities and now fully supported democracy, Anglo-Saxon secularism and the EU.

Meanwhile, the Gülenists evolved from the larger and more powerful faith movement of Said Nursi (1878–1960).[18] Nursi's main goal was to rejuvenate faith to rebuild an ethical society where justice prevailed. Thus, Nursi's followers stayed away from Islamic politics, usually voting for the centre-right parties that tried to open more spaces for societal groups and limit the excessive power of the secularist state.[19] The Gülen followers evolved through three major stages: a communitarian network of piety (*cemaat*); education-cum-media global movement (*hareket*), and a secret religiopolitical configuration commonly referred to as a 'parallel structure of the state' (*parallel yapı*), with the goal of controlling the mechanisms of the state.[20] The Gülenists gradually shed their faith-oriented activities, involving themselves in conquering secular spaces by articulating a new Islamic discourse, which stressed 'service' (*hizmet*) to humanity, rigorous educational standards for a new generation who eventually would rule the country, and involvement in strategic economic sectors to leverage new financial and market power.

As the Gülenists penetrated and controlled these secular domains of education, market and media, these secular spaces also penetrated the Gülen movement's networks. In this mutual sociopolitical osmosis, the logic of the market and search for power prevailed in redefining the Gülen movement. With the Gülen movement's expanding political powers in secular spaces, Gülen fashioned a brand of Islam to suit everyone's social tastes, not far removed from the style or tone of non-denominational Christian and Protestant ministers that are popular in US television programming and in megachurches across the American landscape. Gülen presented a liberalised Islam by whitewashing Qur'an verses and hadith that could be seen as offending Western modern sensibilities. Through this path, the movement's evolution was enacted through hubs of power-seeking, leader-based networks of activities that were sanctioned by an overseeing entity – essentially the central clearing house as administered by Gülen and his most trusted adherents.

These complex networks in the movement operated less upon generally accepted standards of ethical communication and advocacy than on a winner-takes-all political objective. The Gülenist attempt to control the state bureaucracy also was supported by a large segment of conservative Turkish society, which regularly complained about the heavy-handed policies of the state bureaucracy. The Gülen movement penetrated state institutions, gaining control only by the support of Erdoğan. Both entities feared another event such as the postmodern coup in 1997 led by the military and the secular establishment and this concern, in turn, united the partners in their campaign against the Kemalist elite. They understood success was only possible by working in tandem. The Gülen movement needed political support to protect its networks and economic gains as well as place its own educated elite in governmental positions. Meanwhile, Erdoğan needed the Gülenist networks as a buffer against a hostile secular bureaucracy along with Gülenist media channels to transmit their message to the largest politically friendly audiences possible.

6.2.1 National police force and encroachment of government bureaucracy

The Gülenists first targeted the national police force and they eventually controlled the entire recruitment and promotion process. By 2002, when the AKP came to power, the Gülenists had full control of the police academy in Ankara. A high-ranking guide in the Gülenist movement became the police chief of the academy – the key development in the movement's adoption of an authoritative, law enforcement character. This, however, went beyond the traditional roles of policing normally associated with the aim of preserving public safety, welfare and peace. For the Gülenists, police were encouraged to use intelligence and blackmail against Gülen's opponents. Police officials habitually fabricated facts to scare, control and manipulate the entire bureaucracy. It 'served and protected' not the public interest but rather that of the Gülen movement against other groups. The Gülenist police became ever more involved in collecting intelligence about politicians, business leaders, high ranking military personnel and journalists. In sum, 'police work' became the main function of Gülenist networks' intelligence gathering for specific self-interests. For instance, a police officer who worked for the department of police intelligence, said in an interview with the author:

> The decision taken to collect intelligence was not aimed at preventing criminal activities but rather it became the criminal activity itself by listening in on the conversations of politicians; secretly taping encounters involving intimate relations between some politicians and their mistresses; and bugging almost all critical high-level government meetings. This entire enterprise was carried out with the support of the AKP ministers of the interior because they shared this collected intelligence with Erdoğan to go after the opposition. It was the Gülenist police force which carried out these illegal activities. I want to reiterate again that the AKP government fully supported these illegal police activities as long as they helped its own purpose.[21]

A retired police chief, who also became the director of the police high school academy in 2006, said in an interview with the author:

> The Gülenist networks would prepare the students for the police high schools and they controlled the exam system, and this resulted in the Gülenist-dominated police force. They even had the teachers of these schools from the movement. Those who were not Gülenists in the police force realised the power of the Gülenists in the system and thus wanted to be viewed as Gülenists to protect their jobs.[22]

Likewise, an ex-minister who was once among Erdoğan's closest associates and who scheduled secret meetings with Kurdish groups but was then later pushed aside, said the following in an interview with the author, which took place in his office in parliament:

> We made too many mistakes and the biggest one was to rely totally on Gülenist intelligence. Some of the ministers did not run their departments but allowed the Gülenist bureaucracy to run it for themselves and they just sought to accumulate wealth. Yes, unfortunately, the Gülenists were a state within the state. In other words, a 'parallel state'. It was the Gülenists who also thought about how to take and give bribes. The coalition with the Gülenists destroyed the morality of the party and I am sorry to say it now but the AKP is neither *ak* (pure) anymore nor is it moral. I cannot even recognise the party myself.[23]

After the 2002 national elections, the Gülen community and the AKP gradually merged, with the Gülenists working more than as mere functionaries of the AKP branches in provinces across the country. By 2010, the Gülenists became the dominant group within AKP municipal strongholds, especially in Istanbul and Ankara. Some AKP politicians openly questioned the growing power of Gülenists within the party, especially in municipalities. One interview subject who preferred to be identified by the initials of his name (HY), an AKP deputy, said:

> The 2010 referendum was key for many reasons. This referendum showed the extent to which the Gülenists had become the most powerful force. The AKP totally relied on the Gülenists for the referendum campaign and used the Gülenist media to disseminate its position. This was a major concern for many AKP leaders who did not want the expanding power of the Gülenists. Erdoğan, then prime minister, was not very happy either.[24]

IG, the former minister of urbanisation and construction (2013–15), described the extent of the Gülenist role in municipalities, relative to its presence in national government. He said:

> The Gülenists were most powerful within the municipalities and succeeded in transferring huge swathes of public land to their foundations, associations and schools. In other words, the main source of income for the Gülenist activities more or less came from their hegemonic position at the municipal level. The main source of Gülenist power after 2007 became the municipalities.[25]

Gülenists also dictated the tone and direction of the AKP discourse in and out of the country. As the movement became the main force in controlling Ankara's state bureaucracy, it also controlled the bidding process regarding its operating budgets. When I asked another member of parliament whether or not the AKP was aware of the increasing power of the Gülenists in the bureaucracy, he said:

> It was no secret that the Gülenists were the preferred group to be recruited into the Ministry of Justice or the Ministry of Interior. Moreover, we all knew that there was no chance to get any bid from the state, if you don't work with a Gülenist-owned company.[26]

Gülenist enterprises would win almost every bidding process in every ministry with the help of their adherents in the respective bureaucracy. This, in turn, generated a major source of income for Gülenists upon which they built their financial empire with revenues from government contracts. Significant consequences were the destruction of free market rules, the spread of corruption and the higher costs inevitably passed on to the public.

When governmental ministers visited foreign countries in formal state visits, their programmes were always organised by the respective Gülenist networks in those countries and they would report to the Turkish embassies about the visit of government officials.[27] The Gülenist networks in many foreign countries were more active than the staff in embassies. A retired ambassador said:

> The foreign ministry lost its ability and capacity to organise the foreign policy of Turkey. The AKP has always been hostile to the diplomats because they were much better educated, pro-Western and secular. As you know, Erdoğan calls us 'monsieur' to indicate that we are 'alien' and disconnected with his Islamic sector of the population. The goal was to weaken the power of the foreign ministry. The Gülenists helped the AKP by turning their networks outside the country as alternative 'embassies' with more resources and access to the government in Ankara. I would become aware of the visit of ministers only after their programme was prepared by the Gülenists.[28]

The coalition with the Gülen movement served to assist, at least initially, Erdoğan's larger aims. The Gülenists provided him with manpower for bureaucracy, and media outlets such as *Daily Zaman* and Samanyolu TV became the AKP's outlets. The stability and the current state of the republic were now in question. When Erdoğan came to power, the Kemalist establishment, along with its support of Doğan Media outlets, exercised various legal, political and economic means to get rid of the AKP, which fought back by aligning itself with the Gülen movement. The Gülenists pushed the army back into barracks through fabricated court cases and placed their strongest sympathisers in various departments of bureaucracy to control state institutions.

The struggle between the Kemalists and the AKP culminated in the 2010 constitutional referendum, which empowered the government to restructure state institutions, especially the Constitutional Court.[29] Thus, the 2011 national elections represented a new era in which the Kemalist bureaucracy was subordinated and the Gülenists, not the AKP, became the domineering force within the state system. The Gülenists, with firm control of the state bureaucracy in hand, targeted the AKP in the parliament and asked Erdoğan to allocate more than 100 elected positions for Gülen movement followers. However, the Gülenists in Ankara wanted more power than they really represented. Erdoğan and his closest circle of advisers and aides were never comfortable with the expanding mass of unchecked Gülenist power in the bureaucracy and they worried about the consequences of Gülenist cooperation with the US, Israel and European powers. A local politician in Maltepe, Istanbul said, 'The local branches, media outlets and municipalities, in particular, are controlled by Gülenist networks. This also served well for Erdoğan to consolidate his power and become our sultan.'[30]

In the 2020s, those who were pushed aside by Erdoğan because of their close association with the Gülen movement or those who were involved in corruption probes are now even more vocal in criticising the Gülen movement. There were no politicians or parliamentarians before 2013 who refused to visit or carry out an act of loyalty to Gülen. Thus, it is almost impossible to eradicate Gülenist influence, as long as Erdoğan refuses to deal with the Gülenists in his own party. In an interview with the former minister of education, who observed and permitted the efforts of Gülenists to control the ministry, he said:

> As you know I have read and always shared the ideas of Said Nursi and I am a follower of the Risale-i Nur. The Gülen movement also evolved out of the Nur movement. When I became minister, we did not have any supporters in the bureaucracy except the Gülenists. So they helped us to get to know the ministries and run them because the secularists and nationalists were using every means to show us as incompetent. The only group we had to rely on was the Gülenists. Thanks to them we survived the siege of the Kemalists and secured the constitutional referendum.[31]

Although ÖÇ was candid about the alliance between the AKP and the Gülenists, the news of cooptation with the Gülenists devastated the national education system by allowing one religious group to dominate the enterprise. This alliance was not only limited to the Ministry of Education, but the damage was more visible in the grass roots of the institutional framework of education. The quality of education declined, standards of meritocracy in the bureaucracy were abolished, and there were gradual yet persistent signs of Islamisation in the education system and curricula. This would be repeated elsewhere, as the AKP was besieged and challenged by all major sectors of the secular bureaucracy – especially the military, the judiciary and university system. Under these conditions, the AKP relied on the Gülenists in the bureaucracy to save them and unintentionally aided their desire for empowerment.

The goal of the Gülen movement was to empower Turkey's marginalised conservative Muslim population through education, media outlets to bring their voices into the public sphere, and support to strengthen the economic infrastructure in the regions. However, as the movement expanded to work with local and national governments, it underwent a transformation that saw it move far from its original humanistic intentions. By allying itself with the AKP, the Gülen movement became a religious-political entity with its target moving to control the state.

Why did Gülenists focus on controlling the state? There are several factors that explain why the movement systematically built networks of their adherents within the various spheres of decision-making positions in the state. The Gülenists wanted to control any potentially problematic or unruly sector of civil society through the power of the state while using state means to police their own community. Their purpose was to create a unified, homogenised society under their tight control. With the power of the state, they sought to make themselves a formidable force for others, especially the US and the EU, to be taken seriously. This became evident in the de facto access by which the state empowered the Gülenists in foreign capitals.

By controlling the police force and intelligence system in the state, the Gülenists used these agencies to collect personal information about a sizable number of individuals, which would be held for possible future uses, including, most prominently, blackmail. The Gülenist police forces amassed a vast collection of personal information about every public official and private citizen they have disliked or suspected would turn against them. Never before in the history of the Turkish Republic has the police force seemed to cede control as extensively as it has during the AKP's political tenure. The Gülenists became the main enemy of Turkish civil society, principally because of their unconstitutional and illegal collection of private information. This likely explains why popular opinion throughout various segments of Turkish society did not react, at least publicly, to the persecution of Gülenists by Erdoğan's government. The Gülenists have been accused, for example, of stealing the national entry exam questions to universities and government jobs (and evidence has been collected to corroborate these allegations). This is seen as an action dismantling the government-hiring precedents that were seen as non-discriminatory and meritocratic in order to ensure that Gülenist adherents could pass the grade for civil and governmental positions.

6.3 The Clash between the AKP and Gülen Movement

The attempted coup of 15 July 2016 occurred as a breaking point in the political confrontations that had percolated between the AKP and the Gülenists for three years. Their symbiotic relations deteriorated rapidly as a result of ongoing conflicts over the control of the key government positions and the allocation of resources. The first event that exposed the differences between the Gülenists and the AKP was Turkish foreign policy. Gülen opposed Erdoğan's foreign policy stances which were anti-Israeli, pro-Iran and Muslim Brotherhood-focused. The disagreement arose in the case of the Mavi Marmara in May 2010. Gülen opposed sending a flotilla (named Mavi Marmara) to Gaza to break international sanctions and show solidarity with Palestinians. Gülen criticised this illegal act as a violation of Israeli sovereignty. The Gülenist media criticised Erdoğan's pro-Muslim Brotherhood foreign policy, insisting that Turkey should not drift from the cause of EU membership and should attend to its relations with the US.

The second conflict arose with the wiretapping of Erdoğan's office and home in 2011. Police officers assigned to Erdoğan, including his former chief bodyguard, were convicted of placing bugs in various locations inside his office.[32] This wiretapping scandal destroyed Erdoğan's faith in the movement and forced the AKP government to curb the movement by going after the recruitment and financial sources of the Gülenists. The government's decision to close private university preparatory classes in 2012, the main source of funding for the movement and a prime recruiting ground, aggravated the conflict. A deputy chair of the AKP said:

> I was in Ankara when they discovered the listening devices in Erdoğan's house. Erdoğan was terrified. He knew everything – all his legal and illegal dealings were now in the hands of the Gülen movement. This was a major shock and since then he has never been able to sleep comfortably as he is obsessed with how to eliminate the Gülen movement.[33]

I asked him how he knew that those who wired his home were Gülenists, and he said:

> He was sure because the Gülenists had always fed him information they used to collect through wiretapping and illegal ways, including some compromising tapes of his opponents engaged in sexual acts. He never thought they would do the same against him.

I followed up by asking him what he did to resolve the situation: 'He collected all of the names of the Gülenists who were slated to be promoted. He even asked for more lists from the Gülenists to know where the Gülenists were.'

The clash also intensified with Istanbul prosecutor Sadrettin Sarıkaya's decision to summon Hakan Fidan, the director-general of the National Intelligence Organisation (MIT), and Fidan's predecessor Emre Taner to answer questions relating to a probe into the Kurdistan Communities Union (KCK). It was revealed that the MIT recruited agents from within the KCK who had carried out acts of violence against Turkish state officials and civilians. According to the AKP leadership, the prosecutor was a Gülenist who sought to arrest Fidan, an Erdoğan confidant. Some AKP supporters claimed the target was actually Erdoğan, not Fidan.[34] Erdoğan was convinced the Gülen movement was about to destroy him and his family.[35] Consequently, the AKP government removed Sarıkaya from the probe and the law was amended to shield the MIT officials from political prosecution.

The Gülenists struck back against Erdoğan and his supporters by exposing corruption within the government extending all the way to the prime minister himself on 17 and 25 December 2013 (see Chapter 5). This became the most extensively investigated corruption case in Turkish history. The Gülenists were determined to inform the public and to weaken Erdoğan's legitimacy. The AKP-led government vehemently denied the corruption charges, as Erdoğan claimed the arrests were an attempt by the prosecutors, police and judges connected with the Gülen movement to overthrow the government via a judicial coup. Leaks of taped conversations between Erdoğan and his son along with those between the ministers and their sons seemed to reinforce public perception about the legitimacy of the corruption allegations. Meanwhile, Erdoğan responded quickly, marshalling all of his resources against the accusers and targeting, in particular, the Gülen movement as the principal agent representing foreign forces. The probe was framed as a global operation orchestrated by the Gülenists and foreign allies to topple the government. Erdoğan's swift response helped the government gain control of the political narrative. Following the 2013 corruption investigation, Erdoğan claimed he had been 'conned and deceived' by the Gülen movement and subsequently asked for forgiveness from the nation.

The Gülenist psyche, driven by its own political ambitions and threats, became more emboldened in the aftermath of the 2013 corruption probes and Erdoğan's daily threats against them, which may have hastened and amplified feelings and expression of radicalisation. Part of any ongoing discussion should be focused on how negative emotions – fear, anxiety, suspicion, rage and panic – have constituted the psychological background regarding incidents of Gülenist violence. A sense of grave panic seems to have prevailed throughout the Gülen movement's security establishment, immediately prior to the scheduled military council meeting of August 2016, a potentially critical event at which governmental officials would decide who among the military's senior-level officers would be promoted, demoted, forced to retire or resign, or subjected to criminal investigation.

The fear of forthcoming arrests, torture and purges swept every Gülen network by word of mouth, as the movement's followers were convinced that Erdoğan was about to destroy them. The fear crystalised into a mindset that put forth the moral justification essential to exercise coercive – even violent – measures. The upshot was the use of all means available to remove Erdoğan from power.

After the 2013 corruption probe, any criticism of the government had been labelled Gülenist, while any criticism of the Gülen movement was labelled Erdoğanist. Thus, the Gülenists and the Erdoğanists were unprecedentedly polarised. A majority of Turks were not convinced by either the Gülen movement or the AKP, and most appeared to welcome the current clash between the two former allies up until the 2016 coup attempt.[36]

Erdoğan described the corruption investigations against his government and his family as a police and judiciary coup by Gülenists.[37] The government reacted to this investigation by purging, suspending and retiring almost 70 per cent of the police force and halting education programmes in all police academies by expelling the students. The Gülenists have had few options to fight against the government. In order to end the investigation and fight against corruption charges, Erdoğan and the AKP rebuffed the investigations as an issue compromising national security, subsequently leveraging all means of the state to delegitimise the movement and undermine its presence in the state's political and governing institutions. Erdoğan used state power to eliminate his political opponents.

The confrontation between the AKP and the Gülen movement has brought forward many secret dealings and the symbiotic relations to the public eye, including the AKP's strategy to use the Gülen movement to undermine the Turkish military through a series of mock court proceedings in which the integrity of legal and judicial principles has been disregarded.[38] Yet, these same fears also intensified among the AKP elite, especially the members of Erdoğan's innermost circle of advisers. They also deployed unethical means to cleanse, persecute and force the Gülenists into complete silence. Erdoğan's fear of the Gülenists became obsessive, yet it also has arisen from a strong basis in reality – the Gülenists knew almost every deal and corruption practice of Erdoğan. Fear and anxiety have driven Erdoğan and his inner circle into believing they cannot survive as a political opposition and therefore must keep their hold on power, regardless of the cost. Erdoğan's immediate target was the Ankara-based nest of the Gülenists networks within the bureaucracy.

The coup was carried out with the support of Ankara-based Gülenist networks. In Ankara, there are several characteristics of the Gülen movement that must be clarified and understood. As the movement became a major coalition partner for the AKP government, it also became an enemy of civil society, in effect revoking the principles of equality, diversity and a free, entrepreneurial market that also valued non-discrimination. The movement's lack of transparency and its secretive organisational structure have persistently thwarted scholarly efforts to make sense of the movement's peculiar dual-nature dynamics: religious but political; statist yet civil society oriented; vertical yet horizontal; local yet global. But the movement's duality and its forward- and backward-looking faces were fully exposed during the 15 July 2016 coup attempt.

6.4 Conclusion

If one analyses the cultural and social transformation of Turkey since 2002 when the AKP came to power, one could easily conclude that Turkey is going through a process of Islamisation. Unfortunately, this process, which was carried out by the Gülenists and AKP in competing realms, is free from any moral and ecumenical concerns or from full public engagement. This process of Islamisation has plainly been an instrumentalisation of Islam to exploit current historical conjectures – preferably referenced as 'Islamless Islam'. The main goal of the Gülenists and Erdoğan has been to reconstruct the Turkish state and to redefine the Republic's founding philosophy. They have both worked to replace the secular and pro-Western elite with one that is more conservative and oriented to Islamic. The tensions and crises have been orchestrated to restructure the state as an *àlla Turca* (Turkish style) presidential system, one dangerously vulnerable to abuses that will reverberate for a generation or longer in Turkey, which had only found a modicum of political stability after the 1997 postmodern coup.

The Gülen movement wilfully pushed its way into the highest levels of political engagement while carrying no shame about sacrificing its non-partisan character of moral conscience on the pathway towards becoming an entity that now appears more tyrannical than collaborative. The December 2013 corruption probes and the 15 July 2016 coup against the Erdoğan government were comprehensible responses to the clash of power between the two Islamic movements that had paralleled each other, both in demographics and in perspectives of remembering their political history. After the split between the groups, Erdoğan's decision to persecute and eventually eliminate the Gülen movement, which came after the 2013 corruption probes, cornered the movement into a most desperate survival strategy – carrying out a coup attempt.

This was the first time in the Republic's history that a pro-Islamic government sought to destroy another Islamic movement. This clash will have a lasting impact not only on the state but also upon state–society relations, as well as the legitimate role of religion in politics. Erdoğan characterised the Gülen movement first as a 'parallel structure', and then as a 'terror group' and, later, after the failed coup, he referred to the Gülen movement as a 'virus' that ruined the institutions of military, police, education and the entire state infrastructure. Ironically, it was Erdoğan who encouraged and allowed the Gülen movement to penetrate and ruin these institutions because he envisioned a path for dismantling the Kemalist secular structure. Again, it is the same Erdoğan who once fully supported the Gülen networks and their 'poisonous' practices, as long as their purposes served him to consolidate his power. When they disagreed over the boundaries of power control, and the Gülen movement sought to strengthen its own leverage, Erdoğan turned against the movement.

Notes

1. Yavuz and Balci, *Turkey's July 14th Coup*, pp. 1–19.
2. Yavuz and Esposito, *Turkish Islam and the Secular State*; Yavuz, *Toward an Islamic Enlightenment*.
3. Yavuz, interviews with the followers of the Gülen movement in Washington DC, New York and Boston, August 2016, January 2017.
4. Esen and Gümüşcü, 'Rising competitive authoritarianism', pp. 1581–606.
5. Azeri, 'The July 15 coup attempt in Turkey', pp. 465–78.
6. Tibi, 'Europeanizing Islam, or the Islamization of Europe', pp. 204–24.
7. In 2004, the AKP and the Liberal Thinkers Associations organised a wide-ranging international conference to discuss the AKP's identity and ideology, and the proceedings of this conference is published: *Uluslarası Muhafazakarlık ve Demokrasi Sempozyumu, 10–12 Oçak 2004* (Ankara: AK Parti, 2004). Erdoğan delivered the opening speech, discussing the AKP's identity. He differentiated the party from others by arguing that 'previous political parties before the AKP exemplified two group characteristics. The first group of parties perceive politics on the basis of ideology, functioning as a "political community" (*siyasi cemaat*) rather than as a party'. As a result, Erdoğan contends these parties would further

radicalise national politics and polarise society. He identifies the second group of parties as a 'political company' (*siyasi sirket*) in terms of distributing favours and contracts while making key supporters wealthy. Erdoğan concludes that, 'The AKP is against these two forms of parties as a "political community" or a "political company".' In 2018, the AKP has achieved a hybrid in becoming the most rigid 'communitarian political party' on the basis of Islamist political ideology of Kısakürek and the 'company' that leverages assets of wealth from the Anatolian tigers of commerce and distributes public bids for infrastructure projects to party supporters.

8. Baser and Öztürk, *Authoritarian Politics in Turkey*; Cagaptay, *The New Sultan*; Akyol, 'Turkey's authoritarian drift', 10 November 2015; Onar, 'The populism/realism gap: managing uncertainty in Turkey's politics and foreign policy', 4 February 2016; Kadercan, 'Erdoğan's last off-ramp: authoritarianism, democracy, and the future of Turkey', 28 July 2016.
9. Mardin, 'Civil society and Islam', p. 287.
10. I have published two books and several articles on the Gülen movement. In these works, I have examined the visible part of the movement, while remaining sceptical that there is another side of the movement. However, I had a sympathetic yet critical view of the movement until the July 2016 coup.
11. Simmel, 'The sociology of secrecy and of secret societies', pp. 441–98.
12. Baran, *Torn Country*, p. 43.
13. Sarızeybek, *Ergenekon Gölgesinde*, pp. 13–52.
14. In an e-mail interview with Zekeriya Öz, he said, 'Whatever I did during the Ergenekon trials was directed by Erdoğan, then the Prime Minister. He, in return, supported all our demands and allowed us to go after the key generals, including İlker Başbuğ. When Erdoğan learned that my life might be in danger, he sent his owned armed officials' car to be used by my office as a prosecutor. Now, I realized that he used all of us and in that process our legal system was totally destroyed.' Başbuğ, *Suçlamalara Karşı Gerçekler*, pp. 73–84.
15. Hendrik, *Gülen: The Ambiguous Politics of Market Islam*.
16. According to recent police reports, the Gülen movement recruited police officials, who had a long-term relationship with the movement, into police intelligence. In an interview, an ex-police intelligence chief said, 'We were all removed from our jobs for various reasons to open space for the Gülenist police force.' In fact, police intelligence would eventually be used against the military. For details of the Gülen movement's recruitment and promotion policies within the police force, see a detailed examination by the head of the Intelligence Department of the

National Police, Uzun, *İn-Baykal Kaseti*. Regarding the details of the confrontation between the head of Istanbul Police Chief and Erdoğan, see the interview with Fuat Yılmazer, former the Chief of Istanbul Police Intelligence, *Zaman*, 19 March 2014.
17. Kalın, 'AK Party in Turkey', pp. 423–30.
18. Mardin, *Religion and Social Change in Modern Turkey*.
19. More on the similarities and differences between Said Nursi and Gülen, see Yavuz, *Toward an Islamic Enlightenment*, pp. 30–4.
20. There are several different approaches to outlining the periods of development within the Gülen movement. This particular period structure is based on the movement's evolving relationship with politics and development of its political objectives. For a different perspective on periodisation, see Tittensor, *The House of Service*, p. 71. Tittensor introduces three distinct stages, arguing: '(1) the 1960 and 1970s were years of religious community building; (2) the 1980s witnessed domestic community expansion, and lastly (3) in the 1990s a global vision was born that instigated rapid expansion'.
21. Interview with IB, Ankara, 2 July 2017.
22. Interview with KA, Ankara, 2 July 2017.
23. Interview with YA, Ankara, 6 May 2017.
24. Interview with HY, Ankara, 2 July 2017.
25. Interview with IG, Ankara, 2 July 2017.
26. Interview with ÖÇ, Ankara, 3 July 2017.
27. When Abdullah Gül was foreign minister, he sent regulations to all embassies on 16 April 2003 and called upon embassies to work closely with the Gülenists and visit their schools and provide necessary support. These regulations of the Foreign Ministry were removed on 18 May 2014. See *Cumhuriyet*, 'Abdullah Gul'un 16 Nisan 2003 tarihli cemaat genelgesi', 18 May 2014. Although Gül totally rejected any ties with the Gülen movement in his letter to the Turkish Grand National Assembly Commission of Inquiry convened to investigate the 2016 coup, he had maintained close ties with the Gülen movement.
28. Interview with Ambassador EA, Ankara, 12 July 2017.
29. Kalaycıoğlu, '*Kulturkampf* in Turkey', pp. 1–22.
30. Interview with KB, Istanbul, 21 June 2017.
31. Interview with ÖÇ, Ankara, 6 May 2017.
32. More on the wiretapping is available at *Hürriyet*, 'MİT'ten böcek harekâtı', 25 December 2012.
33. Interview with ES, Istanbul, 20 July 2017.

34. For more on the AKP's interpretations of the events, see Özhan, '17 Aralık Süreci', pp. 53–66; Ete, 'Gülen'in Dünü, Bugünü, Yarını', pp. 72–84.
35. The conflict between Hakan Fidan and the Gülen movement has not been fully studied. Moreover, there are too many questions about the reasons that the Gülen movement disliked Fidan, as well as Fidan's resolve to end the hegemonic position of the Gülen movement in key state institutions. The Gülen movement has accused Fidan of being pro-Iranian, an Islamist and a Kurd who does not care about the security of the state and society. In recent months, the Gülen movement has argued that the failure of the Turkish state in foreign policy as much as on the Kurdish issue has been a deliberate act of the MIT, which is controlled by Fidan.
36. Gültekin, 'Ak Parti-Cemaat Kavgası', pp. 68–71.
37. In response, the AKP-dominated parliamentary commission voted against the trial of the four ministers. According to the Turkish constitution, the ministers and high government officials must go to trial in Higher Council, a constitutional court reserved for the state's most serious crimes and irregularities. The parliamentary committee, which carried out the first investigation, voted nine–five to end the investigations of the most widespread corruption scandal in the Turkish Republic in modern times. The AKP-dominated parliament also voted along party lines. The four ministers were acquitted and did not face further prosecution.
38. Çakırözer, 'Tek sorumlu cemaat değil', 26 June 2014. These military officials who had spent several years in prisons wrote about their ordeals and how the rule of law was violated. See Erenoğlu, *Aldattılar Siz Duymadınız Sesimizi*; Önsel, *Silivri'de Firavun Töreni*.

7

ERDOĞAN'S 'SEDUCED COUP' AND THE PRESIDENTIAL SYSTEM

This chapter will examine five competing coup scenarios, and then briefly summarise how the coup unfolded, to conclude that it was 'seduced' by and mainly organised by Erdoğan and Hulusi Akar. Finally, it will analyse the short- and long-term social and political consequences of the conflict on state–society relations as well as the role of Islam within Turkish politics. The seduced coup resulted in the authoritarian shift to 'one-man rule', bereft of any checks or balances. The coup offered a much-longed-for opportunity for Erdoğan to unleash his revenge against the Gülen followers and to discontinue even the façade of norms surrounding the rule of law. However, it also should be noted that the 'circumstances' and the mutual fear of elimination have justified unforgivable acts on both sides. As Erdoğan gradually tightened his grip on state institutions by destroying the institutional checks and balances of secular organs such as the Constitutional Court and the military, he gradually rediscovered Turkey's suppressed Islamist identity and initiated an aggressive agenda for the Islamisation of education after the failed 15 July 2016 coup attempt.

7.1 Five Competing Scenarios

On the basis of a critical reading of the comprehensive reports, articles, interviews and newspaper essays, along with police testimonies and the court documents that have been filed to date, one can disaggregate the existing narratives into five competing scenarios about the 15 July coup attempt:[1]

1. Fethullah Gülen and his Hizmet movement masterminded the coup, and it was carried out by secretive Gülenist networks embedded in the military, and especially the air force.[2]
2. A coalition of factions within the military launched the coup. There are two contending articulations of this thesis: (1) the coup was organised by a coalition of factions relatively equal in weight within the military which included the Gülenists, Kemalists, nationalists and some opportunists who are not firmly aligned with the other groups;[3] and (2) the coup was carried out by a coalition of military officers and factions in which the Gülenists were the prime organisers and the main force that led the coup. Although other factions such as the Kemalists, nationalists and political opportunists were also involved, the coup could not have been planned and initiated without the secretive Gülenist networks coordinating the events.
3. The coup, reminiscent of Germany's Reichstag event, was staged by Erdoğan as a strategy to justify a sweeping purge of all opponents and to consolidate his power. As noted, Gülen had stated in interviews after the coup attempt that it 'could have been staged by Erdoğan'.[4]
4. It was a 'controlled' coup. Kılıçdaroğlu has argued that Erdoğan learned of the coup prior to it taking place, and he allowed it to go ahead so that he could harvest the windfall of the seduced coup.
5. The court cases and my interviews have helped me to conclude that it was a 'seduced coup'. By 'seduced coup', I mean the Gülenists were forced to contemplate it and Erdoğan, who was suspicious – if not paranoid – about the potential for a military coup, recruited Adil Öksüz as well as vulnerable and pliable Gülenists to push for a coup. Then, Erdoğan would be able to eradicate the Gülenist presence in state institutions and use the post-coup conditions to impose his political project on Turkey. Erdoğan nudged the Gülenists to carry out the coup and he and Akar skilfully set the trap for the Gülenists along with some anti-Erdoğan forces within the military.

7.1.1 Scenario 1: the Gülenists coup

Since these competing narratives are still being debated in discussions about the events of 15 July 2016, it is worth assessing each perspective on the basis of existing evidence. As far as the first scenario is concerned, Erdoğan and those who benefit from one-man rule insist that Gülen and his close associates organised the coup.

There are three major arguments in favour of the proposition that the coup was organised and implemented by the Gülenists. These arguments are as follows: first, a major war between Erdoğan and Gülen was already underway before the coup, and the Gülenists were under fierce attack by the state. Thus, they were left with one option, namely a *coup d'état* to oust Erdoğan. Second, the coup was in many regards the continuation of the corruption probe to bring Erdoğan down. Finally, a few Gülenists (Adil Öksüz and Kemal Batmaz), along with a dozen other military officers known as Gülen sympathisers were either directly or indirectly involved in the coup. The Gülenists and the AKP had been on a collision course since 2012 and once the Gülenists instigated corruption probes against Erdoğan and his circle, de facto an all-out war against Erdoğan and the AKP was proclaimed. The only organised group with which Erdoğan was in hot conflict before the coup was the Gülenist movement and by extension its networks in the bureaucracy. Not coincidentally, a month before a crucial meeting of the Supreme Military Council (Yüksek Askeri Şura (YAŞ)), which is responsible for promotion and retirement, the media explicitly stated that the YAŞ intended to 'clean out the Gülenist generals' from the armed forces. In his testimony to the prosecutor, Hulusi Akar, a four-star general, said:

> I believe those coup-plotters are members of [Gülen's] organisation . . . I think they thought their organisation would take a huge blow after our Supreme Military Council meeting in August – for which we studiously prepared. This terrorist organisation most likely foresaw the outcome of the upcoming meeting and put into action a coup by bombing the parliament building and security offices, killing civilians, attacking their own brothers-in-arms and units with a ferocity and dishonour never seen before.[5]

Thus, the Gülenist officers were aware they would likely be purged from the army at the next meeting of the YAŞ. It is reasonable to think that the

Gülenists wanted to use their prized strategic bullet against Erdoğan and the AKP to thwart the pending purge from critical nodes of power in the military. In fact, the Turkish media, which was tightly controlled by Erdoğan even before the coup, reported the 'confessions' of some generals who admitted they were members of the Gülen movement. The confessions that implicate the direct involvement of Gülen in the coup attempt were extracted through torture and duress, a fact which has been highly referenced by international human rights activists and organisations. These 'confessions' were all later withdrawn as the detainees complained of widespread torture and violence.

Was it a Gülenist coup? Gülen himself, in the immediate aftermath claimed innocence and even contended that he had always opposed coups in Turkey, even though he is on record supporting and seeking to curry favour with the leaders of the 1980 coup and the 28 February 1997 'soft coup'. Gülen later went on to contend that the coup seemed to be 'staged' by Erdoğan himself with his supporters comparing it to the alleged Nazi orchestration of the Reichstag Fire of 1933. Gülen himself denounced the coup the very night it happened, and there was almost no mass involvement of the Gülen movement in the coup process. If it was a Gülenist coup, one would have expected a mass participation and an organisation designed to support the coup. Many Gülenists were surprised by the coup and stayed away. There are four reasons why it was not a Gülenist coup:

1. The government has failed to produce any evidence to show that Gülen or his entire movement was involved in the coup. Erdoğan, who tightly controls every branch of the state, used the post-seduced coup legal processes to cover up the events rather than expose them, their participants and their motives.
2. Except for a few people, such as Adil Öksüz and Kemal Batmaz, there is no evidence to show that the Gülenist leadership was involved either in the planning or in the implementation of the coup.
3. Those who gave incriminating testimonies were compelled to do so through inhumane torture and all have since denied their police testimonies in court.
4. Nearly all respected intelligence agencies have refused to accept the government's narrative. Moreover, the outcome of the coup may shed some light about the key organisers of this 'seduced coup'.

Although Erdoğan and the state institutions he controls all insist that it was a pure Gülenist coup and no other group was involved, this argument has melted faster than snow at the equator in light of an inundation of evidence to the contrary. Given the fact that the government controlled all means of telecommunication and has a highly sophisticated surveillance system (as proven during the Khashoggi case), it has failed to produce a convincing case against Gülen or the Gülen movement. In fact, neither EU nor US courts have deemed Turkey's shady file of evidence against Gülen convincing. The files that the Turkish Ministry of Justice handed to the US Department of Justice for the extradition of Gülen consists of statements of those under police custody (tortured), anti-Gülen books, articles and YouTube videos. (They weigh more than 20 kilograms and each minister has added more to the file.) They have all refused to cooperate with Turkish officials to extradite members of the Gülen movement. It is possible that some of the coup plotters themselves might be affiliated with the Gülen movement. This does not mean that the entire movement or Gülen himself supported or was involved in the conception or implementation of the seduced coup. Moreover, even moral support for the coup would not prove that the movement was behind it.

Had the Gülenists considered this initiative as a final resort and life-or-death kind of move, then would they not have done more to ensure its success? There are a few Gülenists who were involved in the coup or who were, at least, visible during the night of the coup attempt and were arrested near the headquarters of the coup. Although the Gülenist movement was most powerful within the police force, there was, oddly, no police involvement in this coup attempt. If it was a Gülenist coup, one would have expected some police involvement as well. Several police officers killed in the special operations bombing were later alleged to be members of the Gülenist movement.

As time has passed, Erdoğan has made the Gülen movement into an ineffective and unconvincing bogeyman. Gülen was blamed for all Turkey's past and present sins and crimes. Even the pilot who shot down the Russian jet over Syria in 2015 was accused of being a member of the Gülenist network; the Erdoğan regime even claimed that the Gülen movement poisoned Turgut Özal, the late president of Turkey. The ongoing joke in Turkey is that it was, in fact, the Gülenists who crucified Jesus in Jerusalem and sank the Titanic.

As the court cases were concluded, first-hand testimonies provided a murkier picture about the seduced coup, and the fingerprints of Erdoğan, Akar and Fidan have become visible regarding the preparation and implementation of the coup. These three individuals have refused to testify both at the parliamentary investigation committee tasked to examine the coup as well as in any court proceedings.[6] The parliamentary commission worked diligently to cover up what really took place and who executed the orders for the coup. Although some generals who were accused by Akar confronted him at the court, Akar refused to be questioned by the lawyers of these generals. This does not mean the Gülenists had no involvement in the coup because they were the first to think about and discuss the coup among themselves. Embarrassingly, the government failed to provide any direct proof that it was a Gülenist coup. However, there is more evidence to show that the coup was prepared with the lists of generals and other military officers intended to be dismissed before the coup attempts.

Although the AKP government recruited some prominent Gülenists such as Hüseyin Gülerce and Latif Erdoğan to speak out against the Gülen movement, it failed to produce a convincing narrative about the coup. For instance, Gülerce and Latif Erdoğan were recruited by Erdoğan to mobilise the conservative Islamist sector against the Gülen movement. Neither of these men had much credibility within or outside the movement. Their credentials as opportunists were never called into question. Latif Erdoğan (no relation to the Turkish president) was once one of the closest Gülen aides and was believed to be the movement's second in command before he quit. Gülerce is someone who disassociated himself from the movement after the 2013 corruption probe. He eventually became a government witness to several cases seeking to prove that these people or institutions were Gülenist. For instance, he shamelessly took the witness stand in court to tell the judge that Emin Cölaşan, a fierce Erdoğan critic and long-time opponent of the Gülen movement, was a 'hidden Gülenist'. Erdoğan's court convicted Cölaşan of being a member of the Gülen movement. Overall, the Gülen followers kept their loyalty and there have been few cases involving people who acted as informants.

Many Western media accounts have also attempted to cast suspicion on the official coup narrative stemming from contradictory narratives of Erdoğan and his exploitation of the seduced coup to establish an authoritarian system. *The*

New York Times in the immediate aftermath aptly referred to it as a 'countercoup' while also questioning those AKP supporters who had poured into the street and risked their life as Erdoğan's blind followers. Another revealing example is from *Der Spiegel*, whose correspondent Maximilian Popp claims that Erdoğan, omnipotent as he was, surely must have known about the coup in advance and let it go ahead:

> The Turkish president governs his country like a despot, but he says he only learned of the coup attempt from his brother-in-law that evening? Erdoğan's account supports the suspicions that he knew of the coup earlier than he claims, but allowed it to go ahead to reap the political benefits.[7]

Erdoğan's version of the coup was rejected by numerous intelligence agencies, experts of Turkish politics and scholars. For instance, Bruno Kahl, the head of the German foreign intelligence BND, claimed that Ankara had failed to convince them that Gülen was the mastermind of the coup attempt. He also argues that on the basis of Germany's own intelligence, Gülen himself was not part of the coup process.[8] Moreover, the EU's intelligence-sharing unit, Intcen, concluded that Gülen must not have ordered the coup and the Turkish government's narrative is either incoherent or not backed by evidence.[9]

7.1.2 Scenario 2: a coup conducted by a coalition of officers

The second perspective – that the coup was carried out by a coalition of factions within the military – was first aired by Metin Gürcan, a retired officer who presently works as an analyst of military affairs. Gürcan insists that the coup was orchestrated by a coalition of factions in which the Gülenists were also centrally involved. Moreover, İlker Başbuğ, a former chief of staff, has contended that the coup was organised and implemented under the leadership of the Gülenist faction, but that other groups were also involved in its implementation.[10]

This scenario does not address the important question of why the coup took place. Nevertheless, Erdoğan has used the coup to get rid of almost all those officers whose loyalty he questioned. Notably, more high-ranking officers were purged than those actually involved in the coup process. A retired general said the following:

The post-coup practices of cleansing the army of any suspected Kemalist, leftist and nationalist indicate that the lists of the purges were prepared before the coup. The goal was to destroy the Gülen movement, create an army that is totally submissive to Erdoğan, and create a new political system such as a sultanistic presidency. I prefer to read and make sense of the coup on the basis of its outcomes.[11]

Many officials who were against the coup yet critical of Erdoğan's grab of power were also purged. Even those officials who distinguished themselves in the fight against the PKK were purged. Erdoğan wanted to create an army in his own image and totally subordinate to his adventurist policies. An officer, with sympathies to the Gülen movement, said:

> If there was a genuine Gülenist coup, the first target would have been Erdoğan. He should have been killed in order for the coup to succeed. The pilot who brought him to Istanbul was later arrested on the charges of being a member of the GM. This was not a Gülenist coup, rather it is an Erdoğan–Akar coup against the military and the parliamentary system.[12]

On the basis of my own work on the ideology and praxis of the Gülen movement, I reject the second argument as being implausible. The Gülenists would never trust any external group or cooperate with a coalition of factions, especially if it might include Kemalist officers – a group to whom they feel special enmity, to organise such a consequential event that risked the gravest of sanctions and criminal punishment if word were to leak out prematurely. Moreover, concealment and secrecy have always been essential to the operations of the Gülenist networks. The Gülen movement has also been suspicious of other Islamic groups, and there are few cases outside of the Ergenekon and Balyoz trials in which they would be willing to join other groups in politically sensitive projects or missions or which could lead to the collapse of their own movement. Since the beginning of their purges and campaigns of intimidation from the late 1990s, the Gülenist prosecutors targeted highly ranked and respected generals (secularists) as well as lower-ranking officers and cadets to open the way for their own cohorts to rise through the military ranks. The Gülenist-owned media have also played a prominent role in these court cases. Because of this, there has always been the deepest antipathy between the Kemalist officers and the Gülen movement. When the Gülenists realised that there would never be any chance of working with the Kemalist officers in the military, they used their adherents in the police force, medical establishment and judiciary to purge these Kemalist officers in numerous high-profile court cases that also targeted cadets in the air force academy. Likewise, given this history of the subversive Gülenists' activities in the army, there was no chance that the Kemalist officers ever would cooperate with them. This division would fully be exploited by Erdoğan to pacify the military, the guardian of the Kemalism, and eventually build his own pious army firmly under his control.

To understand who organised and carried out the coup, it is helpful to look back to December 2013 when the Gülenists attacked the AKP government and Erdoğan in a pair of corruption probes designed to arrest and remove Erdoğan and his cabinet from power. However, this plan backfired after Erdoğan won both the local and presidential elections.[13] A prominent military analyst and a strategist, explains that

> before the coup, the Gülenists were losing the war [for political dominance] and the government not only closed their schools but also their news outlets, along with the Asya Finance Bank. However, the government was in fear of what would be the Gülenists' next move. So, they had to take pre-emptive action to liquidate the Gülenists from the system. Normally, such a risky step is not what Gülenists would do, but Erdoğan was able to coax the Gülenists into taking this final and fatal step.[14]

A navy official, who retired as an intelligence officer, said:

> Three years have passed since the coup attempt but no plan for the coup detailing the steps, contingency plans, etc., has been discovered. Nearly all the previous coups have left a paper trail and records of some meetings. In this case, Erdoğan and Akar have thus far failed to provide any evidence. How can you plan a coup without any meetings? Whose coup was this?[15]

Experts who have studied previous coups in Turkey, as well as the inner workings of the country's military, emphasise that no coup ever simply arose through a coalition within the army. If the coup was not within the chain of command, a single faction often coordinated coups because secrecy is among the most critical factors, if not the single most important factor in carrying out a successful coup. As regards the 2016 coup, the plotters rarely met to coordinate and interact with each other for such a consequential event. Contrary to the government's claims, there is little evidence to indicate cooperation among the generals, who had been involved in previous coups or similar events.

7.1.3 Scenario 3: Erdoğan's staged coup

Gülen and some his followers claim that this was a staged coup (that is, Erdoğan planned and implemented it in order to control the country and decimate his critics, especially the Gülenist movement and anti-Erdoğan Kurdish parties). This scenario rejects any Gülenist role and fails to explain the participation of some Gülenists, such as Adil Öksüz or Kemal Batmaz. Erdoğan planned the coup in terms of putting the idea into the minds of some Gülenists, and he and Akar succeeded in getting some Gülenists to act on their idea. Some who reject this scenario claim that it was impossible to think that Erdoğan was somewhat involved or gave the green light for the coup, given that 250 people were killed.[16] Knowing Erdoğan and his philosophy of ends justifying the means, this is not the first time he has regarded human life as an expendable means for his broader goal. So, he seduced a small group of officers, which included some Gülenists, to carry out a highly destructive fake coup to consolidate his power, given that his current status and position suggested that he already had maintained, if not strengthened, his control of the government and that inside observers believed that he already had gained the upper hand in an ultimate contest of political power against the Gülen movement.

7.1.4 Scenario 4: the controlled coup

The fourth perspective, which has been put forth by Kılıçdaroğlu, is more an outcome of the opposition's attempt to blame both Erdoğan and Gülen for the traumatic events, rather than being a sincere attempt to understand what took place during the coup.[17] Kılıçdaroğlu's argument does not make sense since it was not a Gülenist coup but rather a coup of Erdoğan to decimate the Gülenist movement and silence his opponents. By labelling it as a 'controlled coup', the CHP provides the half-truth and given its animosity against the Gülen movement wilfully ignores the entire picture. As of 2019, after dozens of court verdicts against high military officials, more evidence supports the 'seduced coup' scenario.

7.1.5 Scenario 5: the seduced coup of Erdoğan

The seduced coup scenario is presented in four layers for consideration. First, the Gülenist movement knew of the Turkish government corruption and the illegal practices of the Erdoğan government through the probes they launched in 2013. The Gülenist movement feared that Erdoğan was committed to annihilating the movement at all costs to quash any dissemination of information that the Gülenists could have used to expose and embarrass the Turkish leader. With the probes, Erdoğan, as expected, declared political war against the Gülenist movement and officially framed the Gülenist movement (FETO) as part of a terrorist organisation. Erdoğan saw the Gülenists as a fifth column operating in the service of American interests and was thus compelled to remove Gülenists from the state's institutions, most notably, the military. This set up the confrontation that would lead to the coup, in the hopes of halting Erdoğan's oppression of the Gülenists and other political opponents.

The second layer to bear in mind is that the notion of a coup was disseminated among high-ranking military officials suspected of Gülenist sympathies. General Hulusi Akar played a key role in the dissemination process. He was then the chief of the general staff who later would become Erdoğan's minister of defence and has been suspected of orchestrating the coup. It was not uncommon for Turkey's top military leaders to criticise the foreign policy platforms of the country's civilian leaders. However, Akar was more of an Erdoğan loyalist than perhaps many of his military colleagues and peers might have anticipated. In fact, two months before the coup attempt took place, Akar attended the wedding of Erdoğan's younger daughter to a defence industry business executive, a gesture that was ultimately defended by the Turkish military as part of state protocol after a storm of criticism erupted on social media. Incidentally, other guests included the outgoing prime pinister Ahmet Davutoğlu and former president Abdullah Gül, both of whom had been rumoured as having their own disagreements with Erdoğan.

The incidental appearances served Erdoğan's purposes effectively. The belief that Akar might have been involved in plotting the coup was set up as a strategic bluff for Erdoğan's intricate plot to orchestrate a deliberate coup attempt that would certainly fail. As Akar was pressuring the Gülenists and other opposition groups within the Turkish Armed Forces (Türk Silahı Kuvvetleri, TSK), he was also creating the perception that the Supreme Military Council (YAŞ) had purged every Gülenist from the military. So, leading up to August 2016, the YAŞ had entered the stage. During my own interviews, several military officers told me that Akar himself was openly cursing and criticising Erdoğan and the AKP, implying that he would support any attempt to get rid of the AKP government. In a way, he was the dupe in the process.

In addition to Akar, Erdoğan recruited Adil Öksüz, a former theology professor at Sakarya University, to persuade Gülen to support the military coup. From an interview with a high-ranking Gülenist who stayed at Gülen's residence, he indicated that Öksüz visited Gülen, informing him that Akar was planning a coup and was seeking advice about how to handle sympathisers in the military. Öksüz assured Gülen that Akar had always been considerate of Gülenists in the military and Gülen gave his support for the coup. Thus, the bluff was being fleshed out according to Erdoğan's desire that Akar would lead the coup. However, all the evidence indicates that Erdoğan and Akar closely worked together to create an atmosphere of the likelihood of a coup.

There is no evidence of a single preparatory meeting of the coup by the supposed plotters. Adil Öksüz, the Gülenist's 'air force Imam' recruited by Erdoğan, was observed, along with some civilians, giving orders at the Akıncı air force base on the night of the coup.[18] Öksüz was a double agent; he was working simultaneously for the government and the Gülen movement. Gülen was unaware of this, but Turkish Intelligence was aware that Öksüz was a confidant of Gülen. Öksüz had counselled subordinates to continue working on the government's behalf even as they maintained their ties to Gülen. Öksüz travelled to the US 109 times between 2002 and 2016 and always met with Gülen. He was one of his closest confidants and had access to him without any intermediaries. Thus, Erdoğan and his intelligence chief Fidan used Öksüz to persuade the Gülenists to organise the coup. However, the treatment of Öksüz and his disappearance during the coup prove that he had been working for the Turkish Intelligence since 2013.

The third layer involved tactics to put pressure on the Gülenists and their sympathisers in the military to expect a coup and endure the inevitable anxieties that would accompany it. Erdoğan intensified his oppression against the Gülenists by taking over the *Zaman* newspaper, closing the Asya Finance Bank, and purging Gülenist adherents in the police and judiciary. Moreover, pro-Erdoğan newspapers reported on massive purges of Gülen sympathisers in the military. These pressures were calculated with timely impact by Erdoğan to push the Gülenists to the extreme position of becoming involved in this artificially orchestrated coup of the president's own doing.

The fourth layer for consideration is that Erdoğan, Akar and Fidan collaborated so closely on every intricate detail to ensure that the contrived plot would have no chance of success. A retired Turkish general informed the author that

> the one thing this army knows best is how to instigate a successful coup. This was a coup which was planned to fail. So you need to examine the outcome of the coup, in order to understand the intent of those who set up this failed coup.

Furthermore, the retired general's remarks reiterate that if one examines the lists of Gülenists compiled by Erdoğan and Akar in the civilian and military bureaucracy, one can easily conclude that there was extensive planning about how to leverage the seduced coup for political power. The complicated steps leading up to this unsuccessful coup assured that Erdoğan's ulterior motive would be realised to construct a new constitutional framework centralising his powers in a republic that did not resemble what Turkey's founders had intended. Returning to the retired general's remarks:

> Erdoğan is just like the Hindu deity of Shiva, both destroyer and creator. He is more successful in the former than the latter. He destroyed the Republic we all knew and created a new system that has been redefined by authoritarianism, kleptocracy and a severely compromised version of Islam.

In the seduced coup scenario the pre-coup political atmosphere is key to understanding the coup itself. This poisoned atmosphere was created by

Erdoğan and Akar. They both worked closely in and outside the Gülen movement to prepare the coup. There is enough evidence on the basis of my interviews with the former military officers. A high ranking general, who lives in the US, told me, 'Akar was known as a staunch supporter of the Gülenist generals in the military. He encouraged us to organise the coup and he sold us out! We all had the impression that Akar was the head of planning the coup.' In 2015, Akar hinted at his disagreements with Erdoğan's government and gave the impression to some generals that he was thinking of doing something. Erdoğan and Akar were aware about the discontent concerning Erdoğan's policies within the military and they were aware of the Gülenist presence in the armed forces as well.

Erdoğan deployed any available means to cleanse the bureaucracy of Gülen sympathisers and frame them as members of a terrorist organisation. These oppressive policies forced the Gülenists to search for a radical solution to stop Erdoğan's policies. Their last bullet was a potential military coup. During these dark hours, some important members of the Gülenist movement contemplated a coup as an option to end their oppression. Erdoğan created this atmosphere and seduced some Gülenists to be involve in his coup plot. Although Gülenists thought they were planning and carrying out a coup, in fact, it was plotted and imposed on them by Erdoğan. The coup was a 'gift of God', as Erdoğan indicated, to get rid of his opponents in the state institutions, restructure the state and consolidate a sultanistic position, above and beyond the law. Erdoğan had prepared the list of whom should be purged well before the coup. He most likely planned the coup, focusing on how to take advantage of it for his own personal interest.

To conclude, on the basis of evidence exposed at court, I believe that, going forward, Erdoğan's claims are very problematic to defend. Although there are overlapping areas covering the five scenarios I have summarised, the overwhelming evidence indicates that Erdoğan, Akar and Fidan were directly involved in this coup attempt. It was designed to fail, and, more or less, it advanced as they had planned, especially in the creation of an authoritarian regime following the coup. As time goes on, additional evidence implicates Erdoğan in preparing the coup. At the same time, we also recognise that high-ranking military officers such as General Adem Huduti of the Third Army based in Malatya and a few others did not know which side to support during the onset of the coup and so they sat on the fence, although they did not have any connections with the Gülenists. However, it remains uncertain as to why General Akar has remained silent on the arrests of General Huduti and other likely innocent military officers.

While evidence of Erdoğan, Akar and Fidan orchestrating of the coup has become more apparent with time, one agrees with the earlier Western intelligence reports about the coup in Turkey, as well media accounts which continue to portray it as 'amateurish' and 'indeterminate', as well as Erdoğan's coup.[19] Although Erdoğan insisted that *Bylock*, an encrypted communications application developed by software engineers in Lithuania, was being used by Gülenists to communicate leading up to and including the coup attempt, it has become clear that the application was not used for these events. The MIT officials claimed that they had 'discovered a hidden network compromising more than 165,000 end users before the Gülenists switched to another encrypted application code named *Eagle*, just prior to the coup launch'. These statements, however, are problematic in that they don't clear up discrepancies in the accounts of events leading up to the coup attempt.

7.2 What Happened and the Contradictory Evidence

On the afternoon of 15 July 2016, Turkish Army helicopter pilot Lt Osman Karaca made his way furtively to the headquarters of the National Intelligence Organisation (MIT) in Ankara. He had an urgent warning to deliver to MIT officers about a pending coup plot.[20] Although the government newspapers insisted that Karaca was a Gülenist, since 2019 Karaca has been working for MIT. As MIT officers listened wide-eyed to Karaca's testimony, their sense of alarm was at a fever pitch because Gülenist circles some months earlier, having discovered the *Bylock* decrypt, had gone 'dark' by switching to another encrypted application known as *Eagle* which had yet to be cracked by MIT cryptologists. At the same time as Karaca's tip-off, MIT headquarters was receiving reports of irregular military movements. Convinced that something ominous was on the horizon, MIT chief Fidan went directly to see the chief of general staff, General Akar, at the military headquarters at 6 p.m. to ascertain whether a coup within the chain of command was being prepared.

In addition to Karaca, another central figure and the point man for this plot was a seemingly mild-mannered theology professor at Sakarya University:

Adil Öksüz. Öksüz had long served as a devoted student of Gülen, making more than 100 trips since 2003 to meet with him in Saylorsburg, Pennsylvania. Öksüz was unknown to anyone outside the core leadership of the Gülenist movement. Although there is no evidence, the prosecutors allege, based upon prisoner interrogations and captured evidence, that Öksüz assembled the coup leaders and gave the go-ahead for the operation on 9 July at a safehouse in Ankara. Two days later, Öksüz along with Kemal Batmaz, a Gülenist, would fly to the US to meet with Gülen, returning to Turkey together only two days prior to the coup. There is evidence of these two entering the country, passing through the Istanbul airport passport control together. The coup plot was moving forward with urgency because the YAŞ, in its planning meeting for August 2016, was preparing to purge hundreds of suspected Gülenist military officers from their ranks.

Some people rightly questioned why Fidan did not inform Erdoğan earlier and took several hours to mobilise against the pending plot. This indicates that Erdoğan knew what was going on and there was no need to inform him. So then, there was coordination between Erdoğan, Akar and Fidan about the coup and there was no reason for Fidan to inform Erdoğan. Although Erdoğan claims that he learned of the coup from his wife's sister's husband, this is not very convincing in light of later developments. The sequence of the coup indicates otherwise. According to the government version of the story, Fidan's information caught General Akar off guard; he expressed genuine surprise at Fidan's queries and assured him that he and his subordinates had authorised no such move, making a coup quite impossible outside the chain of command. Again, the government version of the story is that in order to make certain that no subterfuge was underway, General Akar supposedly ordered a suspension of all military flights and further investigations. Akar's assurances worked to assuage Fidan's acute sense of alarm. Again, according to the government version, both men (Akar and Fidan) were ignorant of the fact that General Akar's own aide-de-camp Lt Colonel Levant Turkkan, was sitting outside his very office, and was supposedly a long-standing Gülenist plant tasked with bugging the chief of staff's office and regularly delivering electronic recordings to Gülenist movement leaders abroad. However, the government failed to prove this in court.

According to the government narrative, shortly after Fidan left General Staff Headquarters, around 8 p.m., soldiers led by Brigadier General Mehmet Dişli, the brother of Saban Dişli, a key member of the AKP, took over and barged into General Akar's office to try and convince him to join the plot. A shocked Akar refused and told them they were mad, demanding to know who was leading them. Akar claimed that Dişli offered to put him in contact with 'their respected leader Fethullah Gülen'. However, Dişli vehemently denied Akar's claims. General Dişli told the court that he had always worked according to Akar's orders. Akar claimed when he refused to sign the document they tried to strangle him into submission but eventually transported him to their coup headquarters at the Akıncılar airbase. What is surprising is that Akar flew to Cankaya together with Dişli in the same helicopter. Upon arrival, Akar asked the police to arrest General Dişli.[21]

Marmaris, 9 p.m.: Erdoğan's escape and the moment of truth

The government version of the coup claims that Erdoğan was the major target of the coup. During the evening of 15 July 2016, Erdoğan and his family were relaxing at the lavish Marmaris Grand Yazici Club Turban on the Aegean coast. The sprawling resort complex held private villas, and the exact location of the presidential family was a closely guarded secret. Again, the government version claims that the coup plotters planned to launch a heliborne assault on the complex in the early morning hours timed to coincide with troops securing key locations in Ankara and Istanbul. They planned on capturing Erdoğan, if possible, and taking him to a ship off the coast to be held incommunicado. However, they were also prepared to assassinate the president if this was not feasible. They claim that the assault was planned and carried out by Brigadier General Gökhan Sönmeztaş and a select group of trusted commandos, many of whom were members of the SAT or Underwater Assault Teams, the Turkish equivalent of the US Navy Seals. Yet, Erdoğan claimed that he was informed of the coup at least by 9 p.m., according to various accounts. The government also claims that the military did not know where Erdoğan was, and his personal aide-de-camp Colonel Ali Yazıcı demanded to know the exact location of the presidential party within the sprawling resort complex. All these claims raise more questions than answers. How did Erdoğan manage to leave the hotel and fly from Antalya to Istanbul? He claimed that there were several planes waiting in and around Antalya. If it was not organised, why were these planes on stand-by? It strongly suggests that the coup was prepared and coordinated. Later on, the government declared that Colonel Yazıcı was handpicked by the Gülenists to infiltrate Erdoğan's inner circle, but the prosecutor could not produce any corroborating evidence.

At 10 p.m. on that Friday evening, the time when Istanbul's nightlife begins, another poorly timed incident occurred. Residents heading out to enjoy the city's fabled nightlife were startled to see military personnel taking up positions in key locations, including the Bosporus Bridge. Rumours soon spread that a military coup was taking place and the president had been captured or killed. Spontaneously, Istanbul residents started massing in the streets.

At 11 p.m., the Turkish citizenry first learned that the government had not yet fallen. Prime Minister Binali Yıldırım phoned the broadcaster NTV from a construction tunnel where his convoy had taken cover on the Black Sea to announce that the coup had been launched by a small illegal faction in the military and was not supported by the chain of command. Shortly after midnight, Erdoğan appeared on CNN Turk, using WhatsApp, declaring that the democratically elected government was still in charge as he denounced the coup, calling upon the people to take to the streets and 'send a fitting response to the coup plotters'. Erdoğan called upon his followers to organise against the coup, and anti-coup demonstrations rapidly assembled. It was Erdoğan who mobilised the masses in favour of his government and also against the Gülen movement as the agent of foreign governments, especially the US. No serious scholar, policy analyst or intelligence service professional believes the narrative of the government. The US House Intelligence Committee chairman has said it is 'hard to believe' that the US-based Turkish cleric was behind the military coup attempt while also questioning Turkey as a reliable ally. The same applies to Germany's spy chief, Bruno Kahl, who claimed in a 2017 interview that the government of Turkey failed to convince them that Gülen was the mastermind of the attempted coup.

Although Erdoğan won six general and three municipal elections, three referendums and two presidential races, he portrayed the coup as a 'gift from God'. He welcomed this coup and used it to destroy the parlimentary system and prop himself up in power. Erdoğan transformed the political system by moving from a parliamentary to a super-presidential system. The establishment of the presidential system was an outcome of the close alliance between Erdoğan and the Nationalist Movement Party. Erdoğan and many centre-right politicians criticised the 1982 constitution as a 'military-made' constitution which sought to protect the position of the Kemalist ideology and the position of unelected institutions, such as the military and the judiciary. The constitution that Erdoğan crafted is more oppressive and anti-democratic than any previous constitution in Turkey's history.

7.3 The Destructive Consequences of the Seduced Coup

After the events of 2013, Erdoğan first purged those who dared challenge his authoritarian tendencies and gradually regressed to an Islamist ideology in the mould of the Muslim Brotherhood. Over time, he shed his liberal and democratic skin and reverted to his old Islamic identity that was intellectualised by Kısakürek. He used Islamism-cum-Turkish nationalism to appeal to the electorate and consolidate his power. Four days after the seduced coup, on 20 July 2016, Erdoğan used the constitution to initiate a state of emergency. As a constitutional provision, the state of emergency normally functions to protect the integrity of the rule of law and to deal with those challenges that threaten the constitution's earnest provisions facilitating a democratically governed republic. However, in Turkey, Erdoğan used the state of emergency to suspend the constitution and consolidate his power at the expense of the institutions and rules that had placed Turkey among the world's democratic nations. He has become the de facto authoritarian ruler of Turkey as a result of exploiting the state of emergency provisions.

Rather than using the state of emergency to remove the threat against the constitutional system, as developments have indicated since the summer of 2016, the government has used the power of the state of emergency to restructure the state and its functions, along with closing schools, newspapers and radio stations without any legal recourse or relief. To date, the government has dismissed more than 150,000 civil and governmental employees and imprisoned more than 50,000 people. According to Amnesty International, torture has become a common practice in Turkish jails.[22]

The most concerning development after the attempted coup was the new alliance between the MHP and the AKP against the Kurdish nationalist insurgency. Erdoğan, increasingly insecure, has become more nationalist in the tone of his statements and speeches, and has relied on the MHP's support in parliament. The MHP has supported Erdoğan's efforts to transform the governing system from a parliamentary to an *àlla Turca* executive presidential system.[23] Both parties agreed to submit the constitutional changes to a referendum on 16 April 2017, which were approved in a national vote: 51 per cent voting for, and 49 per cent against. The referendum took place in a non-democratic environment: lack of press freedoms, intimidation (in the form of jailing critics of Erdoğan under a statute of insulting the president) and the state of emergency. In addition, reported irregularities were widespread, including the rigging of votes in some regions. According to the Organization for Security and Co-operation in Europe (OSCE), the referendum was not conducted under the normal constitutional provisions for a national election and it was evident that the government had used the state of emergency to silence any opposition against the constitutional change.[24]

The constitutional changes have led to a super-presidential system, in which Erdoğan has become an all-powerful, omnipresent *başyüçe* (supreme leader). Thus, not only did Erdoğan use the coup to enhance his power but also to redefine the state and its identity. The manipulation of the media and the deepening corruption within the state system have destroyed public trust in the government. Erdoğan's response to the coup by manipulating the constitutionally designated state of emergency powers to enhance his grip on political power seems counter-intuitive. If his intention was to unify the fractured population and convince the public to defend democracy, the firing of more than 150,000 government officials and employees and abusing his constitutionally mandated powers to silence the opposition while restructuring the governing system contradict such purposes.[25] There is no sense of political unity, as Erdoğan has sought to divide the populace against itself by framing any political opponent as an enemy or as a hostile force in the country. He has put his own personal and family interests ahead of Turkey's democracy and stability. To summarise, there are five major ongoing consequences of the seduced coup.

7.3.1 Islamist authoritarianism

Although the AKP with its record of winning elections made it a successful case study for the possibilities of Muslim democracy, its authoritarian shift has already undermined its most enlightened contributions to international politics. The AKP leadership now leverages a complex of religious, historic and social factors to justify its titular head's turn to authoritarianism. Erdoğan has not only polarised the national community but has also poisoned his country's political environment, a fact which may take several generations to rehabilitate. He has deployed Islam and Islamic history to justify intellectually the need for autocratic rule in the current crisis. Erdoğan is a man of many large-scale contradictions. Despite his humble beginnings and his formative experiences of living in a disadvantaged environment, he now seems more consumed by a self-absorbed sense of grandeur and wealth accumulation without concern for the public or for those who have experienced precisely similar circumstances in their own upbringing. Erdoğan's recent actions would disturb any individual concerned with the normal functioning of a stable government in a democratic republic. He has even publicly humiliated those who were once his allies, approving with dispatch and caprice the arrest and jailing of any individual who evinces even the slightest signs of opposition or criticism. Property is expropriated, and individuals are being forced to leave the country. His advisers do not challenge him, acting as sycophants who encourage Erdoğan that he knows best the interests not only of Muslims in Turkey but also across the entire Muslim world. By establishing an *àlla Turca* presidential system, Erdoğan acts like the last absolutist Ottoman sultan, Abdulhamid II.

Turkish society has been polarised between the secular and Islamist communities of the population but now this divide is split between pro-Erdoğan and anti-Erdoğan camps. However, each camp is also heavily fragmented within itself, which makes bipartisanship or poly-partisanship more unlikely to be achieved, or for the political playing field to be levelled to accommodate the full spectrum of political participation and ideology so essential to a normally functioning democratic republic. In the aftermath of the constitutional referendum that gave Erdoğan super-presidential powers, it seems more improbable that elections in the immediate future will be assured of being conducted fairly and freely. After the coup, a drastic paradigm shift took place in the governance of Turkey. This new post-coup governance stresses security over freedom; status quo over reform; a subservient society over an open one; majoritarianism over pluralism; and conspiratorial thinking over fact-based critical thinking.

Among the broadest consequences of the current shift to authoritarianism is the intellectual and moral failure of Islamic movements. The actions of Gülen and Erdoğan speak louder than their rhetoric. The AKP and the Gülen movement used to control virtually every institution in Turkey's government and both indicate they have nearly zero tolerance for any challenge or opposition to their authority. The erosion of public confidence and trust in the functioning of state institutions is accelerating. This erosion leads ordinary people to ethnic or religious populism.

7.3.2 Ethno-religious populist nationalism

When Erdoğan took an impassioned, democratic tone in words and actions, along with his defence of the rule of law, he never hesitated in identifying himself as Georgian-Muslim. But, after the events of 2013 and 2016, he started to present himself both as a Muslim and a Turkish nationalist. His conversion to Turkish nationalism is a recent development of political convenience and survival. Erdoğan's populist Turkish nationalist ideal is a rising force within his party and in the country in general. Those AKP members who criticise this strand of populist nationalism are abandoning the party rather than risking Erdoğan's retribution for challenging him. Erdoğan evidently does not have a unified, coherent story about his switch to nationalism. However, he does not hesitate to engage in divisive, disparaging rhetoric about the groups who either oppose him or who are most critical of what he has become in the aftermath of the seduced coup. These targets include the Kurds, Alevis, leftists and, more broadly, the EU.

Popular Turkish television series, such as *Diriliş*, perpetuate what has become an appealing image of a warrior leader who seeks to protect his nation against a world that is hostile to its place and position in the community. Erdoğan's nationalism is an 'aggrieved' brand comprising a strong resentment of being denied the status as a major geopolitical power (earlier, a result of

European colonial penetration into the Ottoman territories and then more recently, excluded and 'otherised' by the EU). Erdoğan is convinced that the EU will always be dishonest on the question of Turkey's full membership.

7.3.3 Erosion of the rule of law

In this process, Erdoğan has demonstrated an extraordinary ability to deepen and leverage social fears of chaos and anarchy in favour of consolidating his executive powers. The super-presidential system has sought to overcome the checks and balances of the parliament and the judiciary. Erdoğan has turned the judicial system into merely an extension of his political authority and uses the judiciary to silence his opponents.[26]

As previously mentioned, shortly after the coup, Erdoğan referred to it as 'a gift from God', an opportunity to start his war against any form of opposition.[27] Staffed by fearful and young judges, prosecutors, police and agents, and civilian vigilantes, such as Sedat Peker, a prominent mafia leader, and some political clubs, such as the Hearth of Ottomans (Osmanlı Oçakları), the AKP has set four main targets: (1) anyone who might be a sympathizer of the Gülen movement, (2) left-wing newspapers and magazines who are critical of Erdoğan, (3) any intellectual or academic who would criticise his contradicting and Islamicising policies, and (4) business professionals who do not endorse economic planning programmes that breach ethical and legal obligations. With the state of emergency powers, he discontinued Turkey's long tradition of freedom of media and freedom of academic expression in universities. Erdoğan has directly sown suspicion of anything that could be considered Gülenist as betraying his legitimacy. He regularly calls upon citizens to inform the police about sympathisers to the Gülen movement, creating a snitch and snitch-fearing society, better known to Stalinist Russia than to anything the Turkish Republic has previously known. He has claimed that Gülenist sympathisers or those who criticise his policies 'have poured the poison of disloyalty into the very arteries of our national life and these people must be punished'.

7.3.4 Violation of private property

The seduced coup provided a convenient excuse to attack the opposition and oversee the transfer of wealth and capital to pro-Erdoğan loyalist business professionals. As of May 2017, the government had seized the assets of 965 companies, totalling around $11 billion.[28] Some of these firms were centred in Anatolia and nearby areas that have been part of Turkey's recent period of economic growth. The dismantling of these firms will have a major long-term impact on Anatolia's economic development. The usurping of capital assets is unsettling, particularly to many of Turkey's younger entrepreneurs whose business careers were starting as the country's economic boom took hold. Now fearing the lack of financial security, many potential investors are avoiding the backing of new private enterprise in the country.[29] Many seized business firms and commercial properties that were connected to Gülenists have been confiscated and transferred without challenge or compensation and sold off far below their respective market value to Erdoğan loyalists.

7.3.5 Foreign policy

The conflict involving Erdoğan and the Gülenists has profoundly impacted Turkey's foreign policy, particularly in its contentious relationship with the EU as well as with members of NATO. The rise of authoritarianism – which has coincided with measures violating internationally accepted standards of human rights – has emboldened opponents who have always rejected Turkey's full membership in the EU. As Turkey has moved steadily from its commitment to democracy in its fight against the Gülenist networks, it also has distanced itself ever further from the EU. Due to entrenched perceptions about an American 'role' in the coup attempt of 2016 and the corresponding failure to support the civilian government during the fateful hours of events on 15 July, a major gap in confidence continues to widen between Turkey and the US. Russia was the first nation to condemn the coup attempt and articulate its full support of Erdoğan. Not surprisingly, Russia has exploited the situation for strategic advantage, as evidenced in Turkey's recent decision to purchase an advanced Russian-made, anti-missile defence system. The decision is one of the clearest signs of the Turkish government's disappointment in the US and Europe and the coincidental circumstances of Ankara becoming more comfortable as a 'strategic partner' of Russia.

7.4 Conclusion

The July 2016 coup attempt was the single most important event in republican history. By portraying it as a 'gift from God', Erdoğan used it as an opportunity to reshape Turkey as an Islamic republic with a pan-Islamist foreign policy. He also used the coup to purge the secular elite, forcing them into silence, and he successfully dismantled the Republic's state institutions. Erdoğan has transformed an old secular, pro-Western Turkey into a self-absorbed republic of kleptocracy in which Islam is used to cover his unethical practices as well as those of his associates. Erdoğan's Turkey is more Islamist, nationalist, revisionist and recklessly aggressive, both inside and outside its borders. Erdoğan used the coup to overhaul the political system and establish a super-presidential system without checks or balances. My research on the coup has evolved with the available and emerging evidence. I once considered it as a Gülenist coup, but I have modified this view on the basis of the court testimonies, interviews and evidence of the cover-up by Erdoğan and his innermost circle about what happened that fateful night. To understand that July night in 2016, one needs to understand the political environment Erdoğan and Akar gradually cultivated after the 2013 corruption probes.

The seduced coup and the subsequent policies enacted by Erdoğan reveal a deeply disturbing manifestation of political Islam, one that many informed observers thought had disappeared with the moderation of Islamic movements in Turkey. Both the AKP and the Gülen movement not only instrumentalised Islam and Islamic symbols for political ends but they also destroyed the rule of law, along with public faith in state institutions. The post-coup suppression, which was 'legalised' with Erdoğan's declaration of the state of emergency, has been observed with heightened trepidation by Turkey's besieged civil society. As of late 2021, Erdoğan's grip on power is firm, significantly strengthened from that which he had immediately prior to the 15 July 2016 coup. The legacy of political Islamic movements in Turkey, a country with a long and painful history concerning the tensions between secularism and religion, along with five military coups, an ongoing ethnic war between the state and the Kurdish separatists, rejection by the EU, and its unsettled relationship with the US, particularly with respect to the presence of American military bases, have all created a perfect storm for a grave political and constitutional crisis in Turkey, and the outcome is difficult for anyone to predict. Unfortunately, the image of future possibilities is currently eclipsed by a disturbing embrace of the past and its irretrievable glories. The prospective result would be a neo-Ottoman imagined homeland capable of only breeding an aggressive yet debilitating form of authoritarianism.

Erdoğan, echoing Sultan Abdulhamid II's rule, treats Islam as a convenient instrument to consolidate power, dismisses European criticism as anti-Islamic, and leverages the suffering of Muslim communities in Palestine, Syrian refugees, and among the Rohingya in Myanmar to enhance his Islamist credentials. The corruption probes of 2013 and the coup of 2016 radically transformed Erdoğan into a leader who is continuously besieged by his own fears.[30] His main preoccupation is the murder of his family members and himself. Ironically, he is feared more by those who were once in his inner circle than his external political opponents. After the coup, Erdoğan became the unchallenged and unconstrained autocrat at the expense of the country's long-established political institutions for a democratic republic. A former AKP parliamentarian said in an interview with the author, 'After the Gezi protests, there was no consultation or any open policy discussion within the party. No more shared reasoning over policies but rather Erdoğan decides whatever is in his and his family's interest.'[31]

Notes

1. Taş, 'The 15 July abortive coup and post-truth politics in Turkey', pp. 1–19. One of the best analyses which raises a number of questions about the Turkish official narrative was released by a group of Turkish military officials, 'A search for truth: 15 July 2016 of Turkey', 28 April 2017, available at <https://www.dropbox.com/s/tn7pjb3ij5ptewy/_A_Search_for_Truth_28_April_2017.docx?dl=0> (last accessed 20 November 2020).
2. The most succinct pro-government account of the lead-up to the coup is provided by the investigative team of *Türkiye Gazetesi*, Oğur and Keren, 'Who was behind the 15th July coup?', 21 March 2017. The counter argument, pro-Gülenist, is presented in The Stockholm Center for Freedom, 'Erdoğan's July 15th coup', July 2017.
3. *Hürriyet Daily News*, 'Elements other than Gülenists also supported coup attempt: Justice Minister Bozdağ', 6 July 2017.
4. A group of well-organised activists have been publishing and disseminating reports, papers and fabricated news reports to put the blame entirely on Erdoğan. For more, see <https://www.dropbox.com/s/tn7pjb3ij5ptewy/_A_Search_for_Truth_28_April_2017.docx?dl=0> (last accessed 20 November 2020). In an

interview with a reporter from *The Guardian*, Gülen claims that the coup could have been staged by Erdoğan. He also claims that this is a 'scenario prepared by Erdoğan'. See Fontanella-Khan, 'Fethullah Gülen: Turkey coup may have been "staged" by Erdoğan regime', 16 July 2016.
5. *Hürriyet*, 'General Hulusi Akar'in ifadesi', 25 July 2016.
6. All of the investigations, especially the one by the parliament, aimed to identify or label officers, bureaucrats, businessmen and journalists as members of the Gülen movement. There has not been a single investigation to understand what took place that fateful night and who carried out the coup. General Akar and Fidan, along with those generals who are still in active duty, have refused to testify at the court.
7. Popp, 'Revisiting Turkey's failed coup attempt', 6 July 2017.
8. *Reuters*, 'German spy agency chief says does not believe Gülen behind Turkey coup attempt', 18 March 2017.
9. Fitsanakis, 'Leaked EU intelligence report says Islamists were not behind Turkey coup', 18 January 2016.
10. Başbuğ, *15 Temmuz oncesi ve sonrasi*, pp. 21, 22. Erdoğan and his cohorts did not like this book, and they targeted Başbuğ.
11. Interview with IH, Ankara, 6 June 2019.
12. Interview with AG, Chicago, 7 July 2020.
13. In the first popular presidential election on 10 August 2014, Erdoğan won with 51.79 per cent of the vote. Ekmeleddin İhsanoğlu, who ran as the joint candidate of thirteen opposition parties including the CHP and right-wing MHP, came in second with 38.44 per cent. The imprisoned Selahattin Demirtaş of the pro-Kurdish party won 9.76 per cent of the vote.
14. Interview with NO, Ankara, 6 June 2019.
15. Interview with MB, Ankara, 5 June 2019.
16. Erol Olcak's case is complicated. Before the coup, he was involved in a series of corruption cases with state-owned TRT programmes. He was under investigation and some claim that he had US$90 million and had tensions with Erdoğan.
17. *PressTV*, 'Turkey coup staged with government knowledge: Opposition leader', 3 April 2017.
18. Ergin, 'July 15 and Akıncı Air Base (7): the general on Adil Öksüz's phone records', 21 July 2017.
19. House of Commons Foreign Affairs Committee, 'The UK's relations with Turkey, tenth report of session 2016–2017'.
20. Uludağ, 'The enigma of the coup tip-off officer', 18 May 2017.

21. Ergin, 'How did Major General Dişli get arrested at the prime ministry?', 18 July 2017.
22. Reports on torture and human rights violations in Turkey continue to stream across many channels. One report by Amnesty International summarised the instances: 'Turkey: independent monitors must be allowed to access detainees amid torture allegations'.
23. Amanda Paul and Demir Murat Seyrek, 'Constitutional changes in Turkey: a presidential system or the president's system?' 24 January 2017, available at <http://aei.pitt.edu/83866/1/pub_7374_conschangesinturkey.pdf> (last accessed 20 November 2020); Boyunsuz, 'The AKP's proposal for a "Turkish type of presidentialism" in comparative context', pp. 68–90.
24. See the report of the OSCE, 'Turkey, constitutional referendum, 16 April 2017: statement of preliminary findings and conclusions'.
25. Ruys and Turgut, 'Turkey's post-coup "purification process"', pp. 539–65.
26. Venice Commission, 'Venice Commission declaration on interference with judicial independence in Turkey', 20 June 2015.
27. *Russia Today*, '"Gift from God": Erdoğan sees coup as "chance to cleanse military" while PM mulls death penalty', 16 July 2016. Ahmet Sık has offered one of the best analyses of the coup in a series of articles in daily *Cumhuriyet*, 8–12 December 2016, available at <https://www.cumhuriyet.com.tr/haber/allahin-buyuk-lutfu-644388> (last accessed 22 November 2020).
28. Srivastava, 'Assets worth $11bn seized in Turkey crackdown', 7 July 2017.
29. *The Economist*, 'Turkey's purges are hitting its business class', 4 February 2017.
30. Kalaycıoğlu, 'Turkish popular presidential elections,' pp. 1–23.
31. Interview with ES, Istanbul, 21 May 2017.

8

ERDOĞAN'S KURDS: ALLIES AND ENEMIES

This chapter will first examine Erdoğan's political framework for dealing with the Kurdish question and then the rationale for how he has continuously shifted his stance towards the Kurds within the most recent two decades. After summarising Erdoğan's political framework of identity, in general, and Kurdish nationalism, in particular, the meanings and perceptions of the Kurdish issue in the Turkish political consciousness are discussed. The second section will focus on Erdoğan's understanding of the Kurds as Muslim brothers and the Kurdish question as the by-product of Kemalist secularism in addition to recounting his first attempt to resolve the issue by weakening the Kemalist system and bringing Islam into the public sphere. The third part of the chapter explores the reasoning that drove Erdoğan's peace initiatives (2009–15) and why they failed. The final section of the chapter will examine why Erdoğan has allied with Turkish nationalists while he has criminalised the identity claims of the Kurds and dehumanised Kurdish political actors.

To be clear, the Kurdish question refers to the legal and political status of the Kurdish minority in the unitary Turkish nation state. The Kurdish demands span from language rights to federalism and include the desire to turn Turkey into a binational confederate state. There are two competing views about Erdoğan's Kurdish policies. One group argues that Erdoğan was sincere in his peace initiative, but the process was set to fail by the Arab Spring events and the heightened sense of pan-Kurdish nationalism in Syria along with the PKK's confidence in establishing an independent or autonomous Kurdish region along the Turkish–Syrian border. Moreover, this group also argues that the HDP failed to engage transactional politics with Erdoğan by making him president with the hopeful quid pro quo of securing the cultural and political rights of the Kurds. Meanwhile, a second group contends that Erdoğan was never sincere in his peace initiative because he prioritised his political interest over that of the public. This chapter will highlight that Erdoğan's short-term interests for grabbing power and enriching himself matter more than solving any domestic crisis in Turkey.

For Erdoğan, the Kurdish problem was the by-product of Kemalist nation-building and aggressive reforms of secularism. He always treated the Kurdish issue as a way of attacking and criticising the Kemalist project. His understanding of the issue was formed within his cultivated Islamist views of society, politics and identity. Reflecting the manner in which Necip Fazıl Kısakürek, Erdoğan's central intellectual muse, leveraged the Dersim Rebellion of 1937, in which thousands of Alevi-Zazas were killed during an uprising against the Turkish government, to attack Kemalism, Erdoğan approached the Kurdish question by attacking the westernising policies of the Republic[1]. Erdoğan's views about the Kurdish issue is best summed up by Dengir Mir Mehmet Fırat, a prominent Kurdish politician who was one of the founding members of the AKP and served as the party's deputy chair before resigning from the party:

> His interest in the Kurdish question was an outcome of his hatred (*nefret*) against Kemalism, not about human right concerns. His understanding of Kemalism was formed by Kadir Mısıroğlu. It took some time for me to figure out how Erdoğan thinks. His core identity is Islam and his ideology is the Islamism of Necip Fazıl [Kısakürek] and, to some extent, the Muslim Brotherhood. Yet, he also expected identity and ideology to serve his personal power and enrichment. He looked at Kemalism as a foreign ideology brought to destroy Islam and the glory of the Ottoman Empire. His Islam was very superficial, reflecting Necip Fazıl's revanchist view of Islam. I do not believe he ever read a single scholarly book on Islam or the Ottoman Empire. His conceptual map consists of a set of emotional and agitating poems of Necip Fazıl and whatever he has heard or has been told at the meetings of the National Outlook Movement of [Necmettin] Erbakan.[2]

Erdoğan became affiliated with the Kurds by thinking that Kemalism had oppressed and brutalised Kurds, not because they were Kurds but rather because they were Muslims. From his simple cognitive map, he saw Kemalism as the source of all of Turkey's ills and therefore political Islam would solve these problems. By getting rid of the Kemalist establishment, especially the military's power, he believed that this would resolve the Kurdish issue. Erdoğan's attitude about the Kurdish issue is predicated on the assumption that because the Kurds are predominantly Muslim, they have become nationalists in their own right by incorporating into their thinking the Kemalist policies of secular nation-building.[3]

A political advisor to Erdoğan who once played a key role in the making of the Kurdish Opening said, preferring to remain anonymous, 'Erdoğan regards both Turkish and Kurdish identities as ethnic and divisive. For him, the supra-identity which has moral dimension is Islam. However, his politics also is informed by his political calculations to remain in power.'[4] By viewing Erdoğan as a revengeful Islamist, he therefore rejects the political role of ethnic identity and seeks instead to bring Islamic brotherhood forward in addressing the Kurdish problem. Another close confidant of Erdoğan who also worked on the Kurdish Opening initiative, said, 'One might conclude that Erdoğan is illiterate (*cahil*) about the power of ethnicity and nationalism. But he is fully aware of the unifying power of Islam and the functions of Islamic solidarity.'[5] However, Turkish political Islam cannot be fully separated from Turkish nationalism. Every Islamist also is, to a certain extent, a Turkish nationalist. Islamists seek to unify the Muslim world under Turkey's leadership while insisting that the early period of the Ottoman Empire constituted a Golden Age of which good Muslims can be proud and work to restore in contemporary Turkish society.[6]

In a way, Erdoğan has used the Kurdish issue as an effective sledgehammer to soften and then dismantle the Kemalist system and mobilise the Kurds to vote for the AKP. If Turkey moves away from secular nationalism by stressing Islamic norms and ways of life, the Kurds then will feel at home and this, in turn, will extinguish nationalistic desires and demands among the Kurds. Thus, Erdoğan has tried to frame secular republican policies as security-oriented while claiming to replace them with democracy-oriented measures. His emphasis on the democratic solution to the Kurdish problem was not an outcome of his faith in democracy but rather because (1) the EU membership requirements included the recognition of their cultural rights, (2) he needed the US and EU support to eliminate the power of the Kemalist military within the system, and (3) he needed the support of Kurdish voters to amend the constitution.

Although Erdoğan's social and economic policies were successful in improving healthcare, education and transportation in Kurdish populated regions, he ignored their political demands. In the early years of the Erdoğan administration, the government failed to collect taxes, payments on utility bills, and instead offered free healthcare with generous budgetary allocations.[7] By improving social and economic conditions in these regions, Erdoğan hoped to co-opt the Kurds and turn them into a voting bloc for the AKP. These policies swayed the Kurds to vote in substantial numbers for the AKP until the 2015 national elections. When Erdoğan realised that Kurdish voters would refuse to support his goals of establishing a presidential system, he gave up the Kurdish peace initiative and allied instead with the Nationalist Movement Party (MHP) to amend the constitution.

8.1 The Origin of the Kurdish Question

To understand the Kurdish question, one must know what the Kurds and the issue signify for ordinary Turks and the state bureaucracy. Also, one must grasp how the Kurds see their problem and how they regard the Turkish state. The Kurdish question embodies the ghost of the collapsed Ottoman Empire and the legacy of the Sèvres Treaty; subsequently, the Republic always has been scared and worried. The question reinforces much of the negative traumatic memories surrounding the collapse of the Ottoman Empire.[8] The shadow of history and especially how it has been reconstituted in the hand of early republican leaders must be taken into account.[9] When the Ottoman Empire was shattered forever by the Treaty of Sèvres, there was a consensus among the major powers to compel Turks to have their own little Bantustan in the middle of Anatolia.[10] The humiliating terms of the Treaty stirred Islamic and Turkish nationalist feelings.

The Treaty of Sèvres is a reminder of both the past trauma and potential of Turkey. The Ottoman state had no option but to surrender and sign the Treaty, which was the first document recognising Kurdish autonomy with the hope that Kurds would eventually have their own independent state. Although the Treaty was never ratified, its impact on the collective psychology of the Turks remains in the twenty-first century. This humiliation continues to galvanise the Muslim population of Anatolia, especially those who came as refugees from the Balkans and the Caucasus as the Ottoman state collapsed. They led a major resistance, known as the War of Independence, and used their Islamic bonds to mobilise the entire Muslim population against European Christian powers. Some Kurds also joined the rest of the Muslims in the fight.

After the Turkish War of Independence, the Treaty of Lausanne replaced the Treaty of Sèvres, which not only recognised the independence of Turkey within the current boundaries but also ignored many of the articles of the Treaty of Sèvres, such as the establishment of Kurdistan. (Moreover, this treaty divided the population in terms of Muslim and non-Muslims while ignoring their ethnicity-based categorisation. For instance, it guaranteed the language rights of the non-Muslims but not Muslim minorities, as indicated in Articles 40 and 41.) The European colonial powers divided the remaining Kurdish regions of the Ottoman Empire between the British and French-mandated states of Iraq and Syria. Thus, for the founding fathers as well as the majority of the Turkish population, the ethnic Kurds stood out as reminders of the humiliating articles comprising the Treaty of Sèvres and the partition of the Turkish homeland.

Furthermore, the main goal of the new Republic of Turkey was to create a nation state by imitating the European model of nation building. Thus, the homogenisation (for example, Turkification) became the goal of Kemalism, the founding and modernising philosophy in the Republic.[11] From the perspective of the Turkish state, the Kurds were fragmented, encompassing a rough amalgam of rural tribes and Islamic Sufi orders (*tarikats*). The state sought to assimilate the Kurdish tribes into the Turkish nation through a set of modernising reforms. In short, from the perspective of the Kemalist elite, neither Kurds as a homogenous ethnicity, nor Kurdistan as a geographic region, existed. The major landlords of the Kurdish region, who grabbed the arable land of the Armenians, remained loyal to the Turkish state as long as their interests were protected. As a result of this nation-building policy, the Republic Turkified all non-Turkish names. The dissemination of Kurdish language, music and literature was criminalised. A Kurd could only move up the ladder of power by denying one's Kurdishness and becoming instead a Turk.

There were rebellious uprisings against the Republic's homogenisation and secularisation policies, which heightened the traumatic perceptions of the Kurds as unreliable, even disloyal, to the central government. Some of these rebellious uprisings were supported by foreign states, so the Kurds were also regarded as a fifth-column enemy of the Kemalist republic. In 1925, Sheikh Said, belonging to the influential Nakşibendi order, incited Kurds to rise against the republican regime, then a considerable threat to the viability of the young Turkish nation state.[12] The unrest reached its apex with the Ararat Riot, which was organised by a Kurdish nationalist party, Xoybun, in Syria. Ihsan Nuri Pasha led the uprising by Kurdish inhabitants in the province of Ağrı against the Turkish government in 1930. In 1937, the Dersim Rebellion took place against the nation-building project of the Kemalist state.[13] The government responded by announcing efforts to attempt assimilating the Kurds into the nation's societal fabric.

Although policies of assimilation and harsh repression of Kurdish culture and language led to an awakening of Kurdish national consciousness among the majority of Kurds, some, especially the educated and well-off members, were comfortable with assimilating as Turks or identifying occasionally (and conveniently) as Kurds. Although Turkification policies remained in force and hardened after each of the coups (1960, 1971 and 1980), Turkey gradually de-emphasised previous assimilation and repressive policies when Turgut Özal became prime minister. He was the first Turkish politician to recognise the cultural rights of the Kurds. Until 1991, the Kurdish language was forbidden to be spoken or communicated in the country's public spaces.[14]

In the twenty-first century, the Kurdish population has been fragmented into at least four sectors:[15] (1) assimilated Kurds – that is, those who identified formerly as Kurdish and who may still claim to be Kurdish, but they have no desire for political autonomy and prefer to be integrated into the Turkish national community; (2) Islamically oriented conservative Kurds, who support Erdoğan and those Alevi Kurds who support Kılıçdaroğlu. For these Kurds, religion is much more important than ethnic identity and they are against the PKK (Kurdistan Workers' Party); (3) democratic Kurds, who demand expanded democratisation of Turkey and the full recognition of

Kurdish cultural rights; and (4) nationalist Kurds who seek autonomy or full independence and support the struggle of the PKK.

According to Altan Tan,

> Erdoğan's politics are led by the needs of his 'customers' and this is 'customer-oriented politics' (*müşteri-odaklı siyaset*). He has no core intellectual ideas or conviction. He is extremely opportunist. He is Islamist but Islam for him is the most effective instrument to bring him to power. So, Erdoğan's Islam is an instrument for other ends such as becoming rich or staying in power.[16]

Many Kurds recognise Erdoğan as a political chameleon, who will become whatever the circumstances dictate in order to preserve his governmental powers. On the basis of my interviews with Kurds in Istanbul, they emphasise three characteristics of Erdoğan: ruthless, cunning and selfish. Today, many nationalist Kurds, who voted for the HDP, coined the term '*Kerdoğan*'; '*ker*' means donkey in Kurdish, so they call him 'donkey Erdoğan' to express their dislike of him.

8.2 The Kurds as Muslim Brothers[17]

Erdoğan has never believed in the ideal of a separate Kurdish ethnicity, nor has he agreed with the claims of Kurdish autonomous rights. When Erdoğan visited Moscow in December 2002, a Kurdish worker told him: 'The Kurdish problem must be addressed and the people should not suffer anymore.' Erdoğan replied:

> There is no Kurdish question in Turkey. If you believe there is a problem, only then the problem emerges; if you believe there isn't any problem, then the problem disappears. If we assert that there is a Kurdish question, we become part of a virtually created problem. No such problem exists for us.[18]

Fırat explains why Erdoğan sympathised with the Kurdish question after becoming prime minister. He argues:

> First, Erdoğan wanted to undermine the Kemalist establishment by utilising the Kurdish issue. Moreover, Erdoğan was dissatisfied with the role of the military in the system. In his mind it was the Kurdish conflict that kept the

military in the dominant question. Finally, he needed the support from the EU and the US against the military along with their support for external legitimacy. In order to obtain their support, he said what they wanted to hear. He indicated that that he would grant some form of cultural rights to the Kurds.[19]

Erdoğan, coming from Erbakan's Islamic movement, has always stressed religious identity and confessional solidarity, while he has criticised ethnic identity and ethnicity-based political communities. In 1991, when he led the Istanbul branch of the Welfare (Refah) Party, he commissioned a position paper about how to address Turkey's Kurdish problem,[20] known as the Kurdish Report, which he presented to Erbakan. After declaring that the Kemalist project of nation-building had failed, the report referred to Kurdish-inhabited areas as Kurdistan and stressed the need for education in the Kurdish mother tongue, and also called for establishing local parliaments and decentralising the administration. This bold report argued that the issue focused on the most appropriate options for accommodating the national aspirations of the Kurds. It also dismissed national security concerns surrounding the Kurdish identity claims. The report defended cosmopolitanism and Islamic solidarity while discounting ethnic and nationalism-based solutions. It identified secular nationalism as the problem and suggested Islamic brotherhood as the alternative, along with recognising Kurdish cultural rights.

When Erdoğan was elected mayor of Istanbul in 1994, he surrounded himself with capable Kurdish advisors. He was elected to the parliament from the overwhelmingly Kurdish/Arab mixed Siirt province in 2002. He always had maintained close ties with those who were anti-establishment groups and actors, including Kurds. As prime minister, his cabinet appointees included Kurdish ministers. Given his favourable position towards the Kurds, the AKP could count on receiving at least one-third of the Kurdish votes in elections. As Erdoğan managed to penetrate the conservative (Islamic) Kurdish networks, he developed a new political language to contain the Kurdish identity claims within Islam while emphasising Turkey as a mosaic nation with Islam as the cohesive centre of this diversity. Yet, Erdoğan never developed a coherent and consistent language about the

Kurdish issue. Instead, he has shuttled back and forth between his Islamist and opportunistic positions that emphasised his political self-interests. Among the quotes exemplifying his rhetoric:

> If we really have to name this problem, then it is the Kurdish problem. Whether you name this 'the demands of our Kurdish-origin citizens' or 'south-eastern problem' or 'Kurdish problem' . . . these have to be resolved constitutionally, within a democratic-republican system and with greater democratisation.[21]

> [Turkey has many] ethnic identities. Kurds, Laz, Circassian, Georgian, Albanian, Bosnian, Turkish. There all belong to us. They have one supra identity and that is citizenship to the Turkish Republic.[22]

> It is wrong to dictate to our Kurdish citizens that 'you are not Kurdish'. The same goes for Laz, Georgian, Circassian, Abkhaz, Bosnian and Albanians.[23]

> People have the right to declare 'I'm Georgian', or 'I'm Laz'. You can't prevent people over there from declaring 'I'm Kurd'. If you say, 'you can't say you are a Kurd', then rebellion will begin.[24]

> I am also a Georgian. My Georgian family migrated from Batum to Rize.[25]

In 2005, as prime minister, by realising the voting potential of the Kurds, he said in Diyarbakır:

> The Kurdish problem is not the issue of part of the population but rather it's the problem of the entire nation! It is my problem. Within the constitution, we have to address all these problems and solve them with more democracy, more rule of law and the recognition of the rights of the citizens and increasing the welfare of the people.[26]

After the 2007 general election in which a large segment of Kurds voted for Erdoğan, he introduced the Kurdish Initiative (later renamed as the National Unity and Fraternity Project) in 2009 with the goal of recognising and supporting Kurdish cultural and linguistic rights. Later, he initiated the Peace

Process in 2012 with the main goal of disarming the PKK, which was seen as a terrorist guerrilla organisation using violence to achieve its goal of national independence.[27]

On 21 February 2009, speaking in Diyarbakır, Erdoğan announced that his government was working on the issue, labelling the efforts as 'the Kurdish Opening process'.[28] Erdoğan told a cheering crowd:

> As far as I am concerned, there is neither Turkish nor Kurdish nationalism. They are all my dear brothers. This is what makes us different from other parties. I am asking you: did these parties solve any problems of my Kurdish brother? I know their rejectionist, assimilationists and denialist policies.[29]

The year 2009 was important because the secret meetings with the PKK and the MIT (Turkish Intelligence Service) were set to culminate in a deal. Details of these secret meetings, also known as the Turkish version of the Oslo peace talks between the Israelis and Palestinians, were leaked only in 2011.[30] In May 2009, Besir Atalay, then the minister of interior and a close friend of the former Turkish president Abdullah Gül, organised brainstorming sessions with academics, opinion leaders and journalists about solving the Kurdish problem. Kurdish political activist Abdullah Öcalan responded by calling upon PKK militants to disarm and participate in the civilian political processes in October 2009. As a result, thirty-four PKK militants crossed the Habur border checkpoint into Turkey, as thousands of Kurds waving Kurdish flags and posters with Öcalan's image welcomed them. This rally, however, angered the state security establishment and the public voiced its disapproval at the Habur display, believing that it showed the state's weakness.

Realising that the military might vehemently react to these negotiations, Erdoğan decided to force the military into a defensive posture. For this purpose, he used the Gülen movement to initiate a series of kangaroo courts, charging top generals with charges of espionage, coup incitement and the killing of its own soldiers. The purpose was to weaken and discipline the military. Just before the March 2009 local election, Gül announced that 'in the following days, good things will happen on the Kurdish question'.[31] On 18 February 2010, the Republican People's Party (CHP) submitted a parliamentary inquiry against Atalay, claiming that 'ministers cannot conduct secret negotiations with terrorist organisations'. Trying to mitigate growing criticism, Erdoğan mobilised Turkey's prominent actors and political stars to support his peace initiative. Another major development was the 2010 constitutional referendum, in which the Gülen movement, along with the AKP, collaborated on ensuring its passage. It is important to acknowledge that the votes for the referendum were in a strong majority in Kurdish municipalities. With the high-profile meetings set to resolve the Kurdish questions, Erdoğan desired two objectives:

> He wanted to distribute the burden of the Kurdish Opening process to the rest of society through these famous public people and obtain their support to avoid charges of treason and instigating division in the country; and to obtain Kurdish sympathies as if he was taking actual risks to solve the problem.[32]

On 13 September 2011, a conversation was leaked online, attributed to the Oslo Talks between Fidan, then the undersecretary of the MIT, and PKK figures, which was a major security breach, as MIT's secret talks with the PKK apparently were recorded by a then unknown source.[33]

While the debate continued about the Kurdish Opening, Turkey found itself in the middle of the Arab Spring. Although Turkey supported the Arab Spring protests, the events carried devastating consequences for the country and its Kurdish problem. The peace process was derailed and state concerns about security with regard to the Kurds were reinvigorated. The PKK capitalised upon the leadership of the Syrian Kurds, treating the uprising in Syria as an opportunity for establishing an independent Kurdish state.

In 2012, Erdoğan announced the government would open negotiations with Öcalan and, in turn, the Kurds stayed away from the Gezi Park protests in 2013. Erdoğan realised his need for Kurdish support in the aftermath of the protests and became more accommodating towards the Kurdish demands. When Erdoğan visited Diyarbakır, along with Ibrahim Tatlises, Sivan Perwer, and Masoud Barzani, the president of the Kurdistan Regional Government (KRG), Erdoğan referred to Kurdistan for the first time when he introduced Barzani. In this meeting, Erdoğan's emotional tone was tempered by his strategic savviness:

A century ago, they artificially drew the borders in this region. Yet they failed to draw the borders on our deep and brotherly conversation. They cannot draw borders on our shared history and shared future. You cannot separate Turk from Kurd and Kurd from Turk. It would be the worst pain when a mother cannot speak with her child in their mother tongue? I knew those days when people would secretly list the cassette of Sivan Perwer. I knew how painful the exiles, extrajudicial killings, tortures were. We will realise that those in the mountains will come down, the prisons will be empty, and seventy-six million will come together to constitute a new Turkey.[34]

During the first decade of his government (2003–13), Erdoğan introduced policies to normalise the relations between the state and Kurdish nationalists. He lifted restrictions on Kurdish music, allowed the establishment of Kurdish language institutes, ensured freedom of expression for Kurdish media, started the peace process and improved the economic conditions of the region. Erdoğan built a university in nearly every Kurdish-inhabited province and this, in turn, helped to integrate these cities with the rest of the world.

8.3 Peace Process and Erdoğan

After Erdoğan's declaration on 28 December 2012 that the MIT had conducted talks with Öcalan to find a solution to the Kurdish question, there were concerted efforts by the AKP media to humanise and sanitise Öcalan as, to quote, a 'wise, moral, charismatic man'. The new year (2013) started with great hopes that the issue would be solved. Erdoğan tried to diffuse criticism from the nationalist circles and popularise the process by establishing a group popularly known as the 'wise people' (*akil insanlar*), which included some Islamists, Gülenists, liberals, prominent actors and Marxists. Their charge was to prepare the public for the peace process and to inform Erdoğan about the expectations of the people affected.

In 2013, Erdoğan suggested federalism as a basis for resolving Kurdish issue. In a Kanal-D TV interview, he said, 'Powerful countries do not fear federalism . . . In the Ottoman Empire, there was a province which used to be called Kurdistan. A powerful Turkey should not fear a federal system.'[35] Erdoğan cited successful federal systems such as those in Germany and the US. Yet, he has ignored mentioning that these two examples represent administrative, rather than ethnic, federalism. During the 2013 negotiation between the PKK and Erdoğan, Cengiz Çandar claimed that Öcalan and Erdoğan agreed to change the administrative system of Turkey into a federal entity along with a power-sharing agreement for the Kurds.[36] Yalçin Akdoğan, Erdoğan's closest advisor, explained that 'Öcalan was evaluating and interpreting the peace process better than other Kurdish actors'.[37] Öcalan responded with a public statement:

> Those thousands, millions of people who are pouring into these arenas are burning with the passion of Newroz. They cry for peace and amity, and they are demanding a solution. Today we are awakening to a new Turkey and a new Middle East. The youth who have welcomed my call, the eminent women who heeded my call, friends who have accepted my rhetoric and all people who can hear my voice: today, a new era is beginning. The period of armed struggle is ending, and the door is opening to democratic politics. We are beginning a process focused on political, social and economic aspects; an understanding based on democratic rights, freedoms and equality is growing.[38]

After Öcalan's statement, Erdoğan hoped to formalise the process through the Dolmabahçe Declaration.[39] On 28 February 2015, Erdoğan's deputy prime minister, Yalçin Akdoğan, met with key Kurdish politicians at the prime minister's office at Dolmabahçe, where they issued a joint statement. The most critical article was: 'Redefining the democratic republic, common homeland, nation with democratic measures and in a pluralistic system giving them legal and constitutional guarantees'.[40] Many commentators, including those I interviewed, understood this declaration as a step towards the 'formation of a binational federal state'.[41] The most serious development was the public declaration of the co-leader of the Peoples' Democratic Party (HDP), Selahattin Demirtaş, who, on 17 March 2015, spoke in his parliamentary group meeting:

> I will keep today's parliamentary group very short. I will in fact express my message in just one sentence: Mr Recep Tayyip Erdoğan, you will never be able to be the head of the nation as long as the HDP exists and as long as the HDP people are on this soil.[42]

Demirtaş repeated, 'We will not make you the president' three times and was firm that his party would not trade the Kurdish peace process for Erdoğan's aspiration to establish a supreme presidential system.[43] This speech angered Erdoğan and he started to backtrack from the previous commitments to address the Kurdish issue. Because of the dismissive and aggressive tone of Demirtaş, two weeks after the Dolmabahçe Declaration was announced, Erdoğan said, 'There is no Kurdish problem anymore. What else do you [Kurds] want?'[44]

Demirtaş' speech closed the possibility of 'give and take' negotiation and Erdoğan gave up the process. It was Demirtaş who acted on the basis of principle and rejected the trade-off. Erdoğan then declared there was no 'Kurdish problem' in the country. This is the same Erdoğan who used to exhort in public rallies in Kurdish cities that 'the Kurdish issue is my issue' or 'I would drink poison hemlock, if necessary, to solve the age-old Kurdish problem'. How could one explain this reversal in Erdoğan's policies? According to a minister who was in charge of the process:

> Erdoğan wanted the PKK to disarm before the election and this is what the military also wanted. Öcalan did not call for disarmament of the PKK and indicated that this could only take place after the constitutional changes. Moreover, Erdoğan realised the fact that the HDP [People's Democratic Party] is not going to help him to change the constitution.[45]

The 7 June 2015 election was a turning point in the way Erdoğan distanced himself from any possibility of compromise on the Kurdish issue. For the first time the composition of the parliament represented the diverse voices of the population. During the election, both sides (Erdoğan and the HDP) targeted each other: Erdoğan played up nationalism, while the HDP amplified the popular opposition against Erdoğan. They both avoided strong inroads in their campaign strategic messaging, thereby knocking around each other while eroding whatever common political ground had been established. The election of 2015 ruined the possibility of revising the process, as during the campaign, Selahattin Demirtaş told Erdoğan, 'We will not make you the president', referring to his planned constitutional reform.[46] Erdoğan's peace initiative triggered losing the support of Islamo-Turkish nationalists and that of Kurdish voters.

Thus, the biggest loser in the June 2015 elections was Erdoğan. The conservative Turkish nationalists, who had previously voted for Erdoğan, instead supported the Nationalist Movement Party of Devlet Bahçeli, and the majority of Kurds also voted for the HDP. As the HDP raised its share of total votes from 6.5 per cent in 2011 to 13 per cent in 2015, Erdoğan concluded, 'Only the HDP benefited from the political opening and liberalisation of the Kurdish issue. What did we get? Nothing!' The worst development was that the HDP built its political platform as being anti-Erdoğan and determined not to allow him to change the political system. Thus, the HDP received additional support from Turkey's liberals, leftists and nearly every other social group, including the LGBTQ community, to halt Erdoğan's attempt to implement a presidential system.

Erdoğan, who sees politics as mainly transactional, did not see anything for himself and there was no reason to continue the process. Remember that Erdoğan, not Öcalan, set the tone and the boundaries of the peace process in 2013. Thus, after the June election, Erdoğan searched for an alliance with the nationalist MHP to realise his goal of establishing a supreme presidential system without constitutional checks and balances. Bahçeli saw this an opportunity to move Erdoğan away from the Kurdish Opening and agreed to give full support for Erdoğan to establish his authoritarian presidency.

There are several domestic and regional contextual reasons why the process failed. It collapsed because there was not much public support for the initiative, as it was not clear what the government wanted. The opposition parties were sceptical and the Kurds did not know for sure what the government's objectives were. Moreover, the process was mishandled on both sides. For instance, when the thirty-four PKK members from northern Iraq entered Turkey with a major show of force and celebrated at the Habur border crossing, this display was broadcast on television and this, in turn, angered many Turks, as the pro-PKK groups treated their entrance as a PKK victory parade. The PKK interpreted the government's peace initiative as a sign of weakness and took control of Kurdish populated cities and challenged the legitimacy of the state. In addition to domestic factors, there was the negative impact of the Arab Spring, especially the failed state of Syria on the radicalisation of the PKK-led pan-Kurdish movement.

The Arab Spring of 2011 and the civil war in Syria triggered numerous security threats for Turkey. In the evolution of the civil war and the weakening of the state authority in Syria, Erdoğan played the most destructive role by supporting the Muslim Brotherhood-affiliated militias against the central government. Assad, in turn, pulled his troops from the Kurdish population border areas with Turkey and left the region to Turkey's erstwhile enemy: the PKK. By controlling huge swathes of land in Syria, the PKK gained confidence in achieving its dream of a unified pan-Kurdish state. This deepened the fears of the Turkish state, especially among the military and the Turkish nationalists.[47]

The PKK supported the Syrian Kurdish groups which declared their autonomy and developed military and political ties with the Kurds across the Turkish border. The PKK also requested a partition of sovereignty in Turkey through Kurdish autonomy. The Turkish government regarded these statements and initiatives as existential threats to its security. After receiving US support against ISIS in Syria, the PKK overplayed its hand. As relations between Erdoğan and the HDP became polarised, the PKK was determined to confront the Turkish state in Kurdish-populated urban centres in the summer of 2015. Erdoğan treated this challenge as an opportunity to display his nationalist credentials and rally the public on his side.

Thus, he issued a carte blanche order to destroy the PKK presence in the region. An initiative with historic potential collapsed and the cycle of violence worsened with the PKK-led urban insurgency. The government reacted with overwhelming destructive power and major Kurdish-inhabited cities were devastated. As a result of the confrontation between the state and PKK, 3,302 people were killed, including at least 435 civilians. More than 120,000 people lost their homes and close to 500,000 people were displaced. Meanwhile, Erdoğan gained public support in his efforts to subdue PKK militias and stabilise state sovereignty.[48] As Michael Gunter, a leading expert of the Kurdish issue, summarises:

> Erdoğan as a pragmatic and 'me-first politician' approached the Kurdish issue from a transactional perspective. Some people around him referred it as a 'grand bargain'; namely, Erdoğan expected the HDP to support his goal of establishing a presidential system in exchange for recognition of Kurdish

cultural and political rights, along with constitutional changes. Demirtaş openly rejected this idea, who said, 'the Kurds will never make you supreme president'. Thus, Erdoğan stopped the peace process and allied himself with the Nationalist Movement Party of Bahçeli.[49]

By instrumentalising Öcalan and turning him into a power broker for Kurdish society, Erdoğan has also prevented the development of a more pluralist Kurdish society. The biggest mistake was reducing this complex issue to the political futures of Erdoğan and Öcalan, who have now complicated the crisis further and have polarised the society along ethnic lines. The Kurds had no option but to subordinate themselves to the wishes of the PKK and Öcalan. Erdoğan has always imagined a solution on the basis of Islamic brotherhood and has never understood the entrenched power of ethnicity.

Altan Tan offers two reasons for the failure of the peace process:

> The PKK failed to keep its promise of disarming itself; and the peace process empowered the HDP and the local Kurdish organisations. When Erdoğan came to the conclusion that the process is empowering the HDP, not his party, he had no intention to maintain it.[50]

8.4 No Kurdish Problem in Turkey and No Kurdistan

Erdoğan ended the peace process and removed the immunity of the HDP's co-chairs, Selahattin Demirtaş and Figen Yüksekdağ (a parliamentarian), imprisoning both of them. After 2015, Erdoğan used dehumanising rhetoric against Kurdish politicians and deployed force to suppress the Kurdish political movement. As of 2020, as a result of his systematic campaign against Kurdish political demands and actors, it has become an extremely risky issue of domestic security significance, should anyone support or ally with Kurdish demands. When the issue concerns Kurdish political demands, or the Kurds in general, political and ideological differences among Turkish political parties disappear as they form a national coalition against Kurdish interests. After the bloody urban war against the PKK, Erdoğan has articulated three goals: destroy the embryonic Kurdish state along the Turkish border with Syria; work closely with Iran and Iraq to block the development of Iraqi Kurdistan into an independent state as a result of a referendum in northern

Iraq; and criminalise Kurdish political actors and networks and destroy the PKK-led urban and rural insurgency.[51]

Erdoğan has been the most consequential leader in achieving the objective of denying the Kurds their dream of autonomy in Syria and independence for the Iraqi Kurds and turning them into objects of derision in political circles.

In 2017, when Erdoğan's endorsed constitutional amendments were criticised as an attempt to establish an opportunistic federal system for his interests, he said, 'Turkey does not need to debate federalism. It is not on our agenda. We always defend the unitary structure of the state.' Compare this with his statement in 2013 when he defended federalism as a solution to the Kurdish problem. In 2019, Erdoğan said:

> I asked the same question in the cities of Van and Adiyaman yesterday: Is there a region in this country called Kurdistan? This man [the leader of the HDP] calls some region Kurdistan. If you love Kurdistan so much, get the hell out of Turkey and go to northern Iraq where there is a Kurdistan. We will never let anyone divide our country.[52]

This is the same Erdoğan who needed the Kurds when he stood in the political opposition camp and argued for their interests in resolving the Kurdish question. This also is the same Erdoğan, as president, who denied the term of Kurdistan after embracing it previously and then rejected the existence of the Kurdish question. Fırat explains the shape-shifting nature of Erdoğan's politics:

> He is a pan-Islamist but if it serves his interests and would have other benefits, he would even become more Kurdish nationalist than Kurds themselves. When he achieves his goals, he immediately backs away. In short, the Kurdish problem has been sacrificed between ideological Erdoğan and opportunist Erdoğan. He is a pan-Islamist and has a romantic view of Ottoman nostalgia. After 2015, he started seeing the Kurds as a nuisance and a hindrance against Turkey's development.[53]

As Erdoğan consolidated his alliance with the nationalist parties, he adopted a new policy: otherisation of the Kurdish political parties. He told a crowd in Diyarbakır: 'This city will penalise the HDP since they betray the city. If you vote for the CHP, HDP or MHP, those votes will go to support the old Turkey. A vote for myself will be an investment for the "Kurdish Opening" process.'[54] Erdoğan gradually turned the Kurds into an enemy by criminalising even a mention of the Kurdish issue. In Balıkesir, a city with nationalistic political leanings, he told the crowd:

> Now their only concern is the Kurdish issue, as if there is no other problem in this country. My brother: what is that nonsense of the Kurdish problem? There is no such problem in this country. I am asking those who insist on this problem: what do you lack?[55]

To recapitulate, Erdoğan started with the position of 'no Kurdish problem in Turkey' and then recognised the Kurdish problem as the problem caused by the Kemalists establishment and later exploited Kurdish concerns and sensitivities. Today, he is the most anti-Kurdish politician who has denied the basic human rights of the Kurds.[56] Erdoğan's rhetoric against the Kurds is now filled with rage. He called the HDP a '*dinsiz parti*' (a party without religion). Sezai Temelli reacted to Erdoğan's accusation, explaining that,

> he first called us terrorists and now he calls the supporters of the HDP, the mostly Kurdish people, '*dinsiz*' (atheist). What does he mean by referring to us in this way? He does not know this country. You should learn how to respect people's religion and faith. We call on him to return to common sense and human decency.[57]

8.5 Conclusion

Erdoğan's policies on the Kurdish issue have been instrumentalist, short-sighted, and based solely on his hunger for power and personal enrichment. His image of a good Kurd model is Mehmet Metiner, whose loyalty was evident in the following: 'If it is homage, be it homage, if it is obedience, be it obedience. We stand by him till death. We pay allegiance to him. In absolute loyalty and devotion we follow our leader.'[58] However, Erdoğan 'has used the Kurdish issue as a weapon against' the secular nation state system in Turkey and has identified 'secularism as a cause of division between Turks and Kurds'.[59] Erdoğan offered his own solution – Islam as the metaphorical cementing bond – to silence the Kurdish nationalists' demands.[60] His policy not only ruined state institutions in order to get rid of the secular Kemalist system, it also failed to win the hearts and minds of Kurds.

Erdoğan has failed miserably in addressing the Kurdish question, as he has never fully grasped the power of ethnic or nationalist loyalties. First, he has exaggerated the bonding role of Islam and erroneously treated religious identity as an alternative to Kurdish nationalism.[61] Second, he always tried to create obedient Kurdish constituencies, who were devoted to Erdoğan in return for financial and political support. By putting his own political survival and enrichment at the centre of his politics, Erdoğan hardly cares for the Kurds or any other group. Third, Erdoğan has cared more about the next election, whenever that may occur, than about the future of the country. If necessary to serve his goals, he directly engaged with the PKK or Öcalan mainly to delegitimise other Kurdish groups. Whenever he did not get what he wanted, he would prefer to deal with the so-called 'good Kurds', who were slavishly loyal to him. Erdoğan's short-sighted policies have dismantled essential crosscutting cleavages among Turks and Kurds and have reified ethnic boundaries in the country.

Although the Kurdish question became the casualty because of his flip from a genuine Islamist perspective to a purely opportunistic emphasis, Erdoğan's convenient rhetoric was effective in expanding the boundaries of discussion. It was Erdoğan's bold 1991 report which introduced the terms of Kurdistan, Kurdish autonomy and the Kurdish question to discuss the long-running domestic crisis. Moreover, it was the same Erdoğan who opened the avenue in 2013 espousing federalism. While Erdoğan played an important role in expanding the Kurdish question debate to consider normalisation, he also led the rhetorical charge, especially after the 2015 elections, to denigrate and isolate Kurdish political actors while making it possible to accuse anyone of treason who cooperated or associated with the pro-Kurdish HDP.

Turkey has been beset by many contentious issues: Kurdish political demands, the Alevis' demand for equality and recognition as a religious minority, widespread political corruption, erosion of the rule of law, and persistent economic problems. More broadly, Turkey needs a new social contract, but there is also no consensus on a shared language or set of principles that would bring the divided society together. As long as demands are based on identity issues, it is less likely that a functioning coalition will take hold. As no party appears willing to give up its identity-based demands, some ethnic groups, especially nationalist Kurds and Turks, will likely propose the territorial partitioning of the country, thereby bringing back the most traumatic memories of the violent period when the Ottoman Empire collapsed and the War of Independence took place, setting up the Republic that Erdoğan now threatens to damage beyond repair.

Notes

1. Göner, *Turkish National Identity and Its Outsiders*.
2. Interview with Dengir Mir Mehmet Fırat, Ankara, 6 March 2016.
3. Ince, 'Kürtler Kemalistlerin yaptıklarını unutmayacak', 14 January 2013.
4. Interview with YA, Ankara, 8 July 2019. For more on the Kurdish Opening, see Gunter, 'Reopening Turkey's closed Kurdish Opening,' pp. 88–98.
5. Interview with BA, Ankara, 8 July 2019.
6. Kurt, 'My Muslim Kurdish brother', pp. 350–65.
7. Diyarbakır, known as the unofficial capital of Kurdish region, made the lowest contribution to the budget and paid the lowest taxes; see <https://www.memurlar.net/haber/365612/> (last accessed 25 November 2020).
8. Yavuz, 'A preamble to the Kurdish question', pp. 9–18; Yavuz, 'Five stages in the construction of Kurdish nationalism', pp. 1–24.
9. For an excellent historical summary of the Kurdish question in Turkey, see Güneş, *Kurdish National Movement in* Turkey, pp. 49–64. See also Gürses, *Anatomy of a Civil War*, pp. 115–32.
10. By 'Bantustan' I mean homeland for the Turks who were dehumanised by the European colonial powers.
11. Al, 'An anatomy of nationhood', pp. 83–101.
12. Olson, *The Emergence of Kurdish Nationalism*.
13. Strohmeier, *Crucial Images in the Presentation of a Kurdish National Identity*.
14. For a comparative historical analysis of state policies towards the Kurds and other non-core groups in the Ottoman-Turkish political culture, see Al, *Patterns of Nationhood and Saving the State in Turkey*.
15. Altan Tan offers a look at the sociopolitical fragmentation of the Kurdish identity, 'Günümüzde Kürtlerde üç tarzı siyaset', 16 April 2020.
16. Phone interview with Altan Tan, Diyarbakır, 16 May 2020.
17. For a review of Islam and the Kurdish question in Turkey, see Gürses, 'Is Islam a cure for ethnic conflict?', pp. 135–54; Kurt, 'My Muslim Kurdish brother', pp. 350–65; Gürses and Öztürk, 'Religion and armed conflict', pp. 327–40.

18. Özgül, 'Erdoğan ile Kurt İşçisi Boran'in tartişması', 27 December 2002.
19. Interview with Fırat, Ankara, 6 March 2016.
20. The report, which was prepared by Mehmet Metiner, is titled 'The Kurdish question and the suggested solutions'. For the report see, Çakır, 'Erdoğan'ın 1991 yılında Erbakan'a verdiği Kürt raporu', 12 December 2007.
21. *Radikal*, 'Erdoğan: Kürt sorunu demokrasiyle çözülür', 11 August 2005.
22. Sarıoğlu, 'Kimlik Değişimi', 13 December 2005. Due to the reaction from Erdoğan, when *Milliyet* was sold to a pro-Erdoğan businessman, this study was removed from the archive of the newspaper. The same study was reproduced online by *siyasetcafe*.
23. Sarıoğlu, 'Kimlik Değişimi', 13 December 2005.
24. Sarıoğlu, 'Kimlik Değişimi', 13 December 2005.
25. Erdoğan's statement when he visited Georgia on August 11, 2004.
26. *Milliyet*, 12 August 2005, Erdoğan's speech in Diyarbakır.
27. For more on the foundational history of the PKK, see Özcan, *PKK*. For more on the political implications of the counterinsurgency of the Turkish military, see Aydin and Emrence, *Zones of Rebellion*, pp. 17–72.
28. *Milliyet*, 22 February 2009.
29. *Milliyet*, 1 June 2011.
30. *Taraf*, 'PKK-MİT görüşmeleri Tam Metin', 14 September 2011. Ural, *Bir Emniyet Müdürünün Kaleminden Oslo Görüşmeleri*.
31. NTVMSNBC, 'Gül: Kürt sorunu cözülmeli, fırsat kaçmasın', 9 May 2009.
32. Interview with BA, Ankara, 10 March 2016.
33. Hakan Fidan, the chief of the Turkish Intelligence Service (MIT), a Kurd from Van province, became Erdoğan's confidant and a point man to negotiate with the PKK in Oslo, and directly with Öcalan.
34. For Erdoğan's speech, see *World Bulletin*, 'Erdoğan calls for peace in Turkey's south-east', 16 November 2013.
35. See the criticism of this interview in Güzel, 'Federatif sistem ülkeyi böler', 4 April 2013.
36. See Cengiz Çandar's interview with Neşe Düzel, 'Cengiz Çandar ile Mülakaat: Sansür sürerse çözüm olmaz', *Taraf*, 11 March 2013. Çandar expected to play a mediating role and when Erdoğan refused to work with him because the state institutions did not trust him, he became a critic of Erdoğan. Many Kurds and the state officials I have interviewed all rejected the claims of Çandar. Altan Tan said, 'Çandar usually makes up stories to inflate his role and loves to drop names to show his importance. He never understood the causes of the tensions in Turkey.'
37. Akdoğan, 'Öcalan süreci doğru okuyor', 7 June 2014.

38. The words above are from Öcalan's Newroz call in 2013. The complete text of the declaration is available in the media. See *Bianet*, 'Öcalan'ın Açıklaması: "Silahlı Güçler Sınırdışına, Artık Siyaset Dönemi"', 21 March 2013.
39. *Cumhuriyet*, 'Dolmabahçe anlaşması', 28 February 2015. These included: (1) to make a new, pluralistic and inclusive constitution; (2) to open a way for Kurds to be part of democratic, legal politics and to remove the current 10 per cent threshold; (3) to disarm the PKK; (4) to decentralise Turkey; (5) to develop a new, more inclusive identity for the Turkish state; (6) to create a truth and reconciliation committee; (7) to strengthen the rule of law, to respect freedom of speech and free media; (8) to give amnesty for political prisoners; (9) to remove social and economic inequalities between different parts of Turkey; and (10) to improve gender equality and mitigate ecological damage.
40. The whole text of the declaration is available online. See *Al Jazeera Turk*, 'Ortak açıklamanın tam metni', 28 February 2015.
41. Interview with Nihat Ali Özcan, Ankara, 10 July 2019.
42. *Hürriyet News Daily*, 17 March 2015.
43. *Hürriyet News Daily*, 17 March 2015.
44. 'Erdoğan: Dolmabahçe toplantısını doğru bulmuyorum', NTV, 22 March 2015.
45. Interview with YA, Ankara, 8 July 2015.
46. The hashtag '#SeniBaşkanYaptırmayacağız' became a worldwide trend. *Hürriyet Daily News*, 17 March 2015.
47. Al, 'Human security versus national security', pp. 57–83.
48. The International Crisis Group's infographic is available at <https://www.crisisgroup.org/content/turkeys-pkk-conflict-visual-explainer> (last accessed 25 November 2020).
49. Interview with Michael Gunter, Salt Lake City, 24 January 2020.
50. Phone interview with Altan Tan, Diyarbakır, 16 May 2020.
51. See, for instance, Baser and Özerdem, 'Conflict transformation and asymmetric conflicts', pp. 1–22.
52. Erdoğan's speech at the rally in Bilecik, *Milliyet*, 27 March 2019. The new discourse became 'get the hell out of Turkey' and this was used in the 2019 election, as Erdoğan cultivated a close alliance with the Turkish nationalist MHP.
53. Interview with Mir Dengir Fırat, Ankara, 6 March 2016.
54. *Milliyet*, 26 July 2014.
55. *Milliyet*, 2 May 2015.
56. Özdal, 'Erdoğan'in Diyarbakır karnesi: Kardeşim ne Kürt sorunu ya!', 1 April 2017.

57. *VofAmerica*, 'Temelli'den Erdoğan'a: "Şimdi de Kürtler'e dinsiz diyor"', 19 March 2019.
58. *Hürriyet*, 'Mehmet Metiner: "Biatsa, biat, itaatsa itaaat"', 6 January 2014.
59. Yavuz and Özcan, 'The Kurdish question and the AKP', p. 103.
60. The following article claims that religious Kurds are more nationalistic and anti-Turkish state than secular Kurds: Sarıgil and Fazlıoğlu, 'Exploring the roots and dynamics', pp. 436–58.
61. Yavuz, *Secularism and Muslim Democracy*, pp. 188–90.

9

ERDOĞAN'S NEO-OTTOMAN FOREIGN POLICY

Erdoğan's foreign policy has been shaped by diverse precepts, including his Ottoman Islamic identity. In addition, his vision has been supplemented by nostalgia for Ottoman-Islamic heritage, which has reinforced his ideological attachments. Consequentially, he has shrunk the range of bilateral relations with certain countries while he has strengthened his personal ties to leaders who he believes would serve the ulterior purposes arising from the ideological preferences that echo his identity.[1] Erdoğan's foreign policy is simultaneously ideological and opportunist. In order to realise his domestic political and personal ambitions, he has never hesitated to instrumentalise foreign and security policies.[2] For instance, he has labelled virtually every European head of state as either Nazi or representing the remnants of Nazism because they refused Erdoğan's request to organise political rallies in European countries.[3]

Erdoğan's identity inflicts serious consequences on Turkey's national interests and this perception, in turn, drives the nature of Turkish foreign policy. His 'definition of the national interest' in foreign relations is carried out within the context of his ideals and identities to the exclusion of other viewpoints. After a summit involving three European leaders and himself, Erdoğan described the meeting to Turkish journalists as 'England, France, Germany and myself had a summit to discuss the regional problems'.[4] After restoring the supreme presidential system in 2018, Erdoğan has not shied away from equating himself to embodying the state and sees himself as the incarnation of the flesh for the will of the Turkish people. By distinguishing himself as such, he also defines his preferred vision of Turkish national identity and its role in the international system. Thus, his foreign policy fluctuates, sometimes with volatile circumstances, which mirrors the correlation between his self-identity and national interests. Similarly, he changes how he defines others and their views, which is reflected in shifts in his own orientation and his assessment of risks and threats that the country faces.

This is essential to comprehending Turkey's foreign policy evolution during the last decade. Erdoğan's foreign policy is a story of contradiction between his ambitions to become a regional leader and his lack of intellectual and leadership capacity that has hampered his desires to unify his own country. While he has espoused the role of an integrative leader, he has accomplished the opposite as a divisive figure. Erdoğan seeks to defend the rights of Muslim minorities abroad while simultaneously denying similar rights for the Kurds. Moreover, a disturbing record of human rights abuses, political authoritarianism, media censorship and massive economic corruption have crippled his foreign policy initiatives.

9.1 Erdoğan's Image of Turkey as a Major Power

Erdoğan does not see Turkey as a country torn between the West and the East in terms of allegiances, but he also wants to highlight Turkey's Ottoman Islamic heritage over and above any other contending identities. Yet, this contentious debate over Turkey's national orientation between the East and the West, and between the secular Republican elites and the pious Anatolian Sunni majority, has intensified during his time in elective office. Turkey's dualities are rooted in its demographic make-up, history and culture, stretching over many centuries. Located between Asia and Europe, Turkey's identity continually fluctuates between both Islamic and European tastes, practices and desires. The dynamism in its Eastern and Western identity usually corresponds to how it is being defined for the purposes of its people or for others outside Turkey. Erdoğan and the AKP's nearly twenty-year period of rule have narrowed the gap between the perceptions of an imagined community, as defined respectively by traditional Turkish society and the country's elite.

Yet, in each group, their policies and instrumentalisation of Islam fragmented society to the same degree but also in different ways. The Kemalist elite once emphasised the nation's fundamental Western orientation and destiny as a foundational basis for their legitimation; whereas the majority of the Anatolian Muslim population stressed its Ottoman Islamic identity without fully rejecting important modernist and Western-based political and social reforms. An additional nuance should be appreciated, as explained by the legitimising acceptance of Ottoman Islamic heritage that has gradually grown since the neo-liberal economic reforms of Özal. This shift engendered a major impact on the republican political, military and bureaucratic elite as well and tempered the elite's reflexive embrace of all things Western and its aversion to all things connected to Islam and the Middle East.

Erdoğan's vision of Turkey is not a bridge between East and West, as some believe, or as a country trying to reconcile being between secular and Islamic cultures. Rather, it is a Muslim country with a secular political system. Although a considerable portion of Turkish society sees their country as embodying a mix of secular and Islamic culture, there is a strong desire to move westward by leaving Islamic and Eastern aspects of the identity behind in order to become modern. However, in recent years, the West (that is, the EU and the US) is not the sort of idealised community Turkey wanted to join but rather regarded either as an opportunistic market or as a hostile rival, a modern-day Crusades enemy that would squelch Turkey's economic development. Ironically, Europe also has become a mirror upon which to examine Turkey's own identity and its sense of being. In the end, many Turkish nationals are steadily coming to terms with their Eastern roots without rejecting the legacies of their westward lurch over the last century.

To comprehend Turkey's foreign policy after 2013, one has to unpack Erdoğan's identity and personality since he has single-handedly made and executed Turkey's foreign and defence policies. There are several unique attributes in Erdoğan's foreign policy. It is more daring and willing to project military force to realise its foreign policy goals.[5] It is more transactional in nature – foreign policy based on immediate opportunities and interests more than long-term norms or shared values. Foreign policy has been instrumentalised primarily for Erdoğan's domestic and personal interests. He is guided by a sense of restoring the past Ottoman grandeur or making Turkey a leader of the Muslim world. His deep nostalgia for the Ottoman Empire is combined with his principal grievance that the empire was destroyed by Western powers. From Erdoğan's perspective, Turkey cannot survive in the post-Ottoman historic limbo, where the elite ally themselves to Western civilisation but the greater nation belongs to Islamic civilisation, as described by the late Samuel Huntington. Erdoğan's domestic and foreign policy has focused on abolishing the duality in favour of Turko-Islamic civilisation. Murat Önsoy, a leading foreign policy scholar, aptly sums up the AKP's foreign policy, which is really Erdoğan's:

> [I]n the pre-AKP period, international and domestic politics were two distinct domains; while influencing each other, they operated differently. Upon taking power in 2002, the AKP embarked on an ambitious foreign policy. Parallel to the diversification of Turkey's political and economic interests, the AKP strove to make the country an influential actor on the world stage. Domestic and international politics have been tightly interlaced ever since. Foreign policy has been utilized to reach certain goals in domestic politics, this providing an opportunity to manipulate public opinion. The AKP has been successful in linking foreign issues to religious sentiments.[6]

Erdoğan never has tried to explicitly challenge the international or regional system. Cautious enough to fear being embarrassed on a global platform, he switched rhetorical codes to suit his audiences, whether they represented Eastern or Western interests. Looking eastward, he has stressed anti-imperialism, the consequences of colonialism, the oppressive policies of the Israeli state, and rising Islamophobia in the West. Looking westward, he has stressed the virtues of the dialogue of civilisations, democracy, human rights and freedoms. However, he is anti-Western and has played an important role in consolidating anti-American attitudes in Turkey; he regards the US as a colonial and destructive power, seeking to grab the resources of Muslims countries. He does not believe in Western values as being more humanistic and therefore has seen them as opportunistic for his purposes. Thus, he has enjoyed the comfort and welfare these values helped to create. He has developed little more than contentious or frosty relations with key European heads of state, and he has avoided bringing in prominent international affairs experts, scholars or analysts to his circle of advisors.

As a summary of interviews conducted with observers of Turkish politics, Erdoğan's behaviour reflects the fact that he does not have the same calibre or pedigree of education as his Western counterparts, and by being prospective of his own ego, he sees this as minimising the risks of creating situations that would embarrass or humiliate him. European public officials have spoken about their perceptions of his ignorance and his lack of understanding of democracy and human rights. He enjoys good relations with Putin of Russia, Aliyev of Azerbaijan, Thaçi of Kosovo, Izetbegović of Bosnia, Orbán of Hungary and Berlusconi of Italy. Erdoğan is not a man of cosmopolitan tastes or interests and his understanding of culture is limited to reading the Qur'an, reading poetry from a limited body of writers that he encountered during his education in İmam Hatip school, listening to Ottoman military music, and having photo-ops with prominent pop stars of Turkey.

As Erdoğan sidelined and eventually decimated the power of Turkey's well-established and highly cultured diplomatic corps, his rough, uncultured and insulting language punctuated Turkey's foreign policy, not unlike that of the former US President Trump. Erdoğan has advanced in remaking the diplomatic and ambassadorial corps to his selfish preferences. Today, more than 15 per cent of Turkey's ambassador-level representatives in 151 missions are political appointees who either are loyal supporters or have been named as co-conspirators in corruption investigations, such as Egemen Bağış.[7] His transactional foreign policy is also based on short-term reciprocity. For instance, after defining Gülen as his enemy and a 'virus', he proposed to Trump to swap Gülen for Andrew Craig Brunson, an American pastor who was jailed in Turkey and spent two years in jail on charges of alleged links to terrorist organisations.[8] Erdoğan also proposed to Germany to swap jailed German journalist Deniz Yücel and other German citizens for Turkish officers who were accused of having ties with the Gülen movement.[9]

9.2 Erdoğan's Europeanisation and Market-led Foreign Policy (2002–10)

Turkish foreign policy under Erdoğan can be analysed in three stages as a result of evolving risks and opportunities. Although Ahmet Davutoğlu served first as an advisor (2003–9) and then as foreign minister (2009–14), the direction of foreign policy has remained under Erdoğan's tight control.

This period was dominated by two objectives: the desire to join the EU and the elimination of problems in relations with Turkey's neighbouring countries. These two objectives aimed at deepening and expanding the legitimacy of the AKP government and creating business opportunities for the Turkish economy. When Erdoğan came to power in 2002 under persistent questioning and sceptical perceptions about his legitimacy in the international system due to his involvement in Islamist politics, he framed his policies in terms of EU standards and was a committed Europhile with the full support of liberals and the pro-EU sector of the population. During this period, important milestones in Turkish foreign policy included Turkey's EU membership application process, Turkey's reaction to the US occupation of Iraq of 2003, the Cyprus negotiations and the Annan Plan of 2004, the Turkish–Armenian reconciliation agreement of 2009, Turkey's initiative for the Levant Quarter of 2010, and worsening political relations with Israel.

The 2002 EU Copenhagen Summit became the Turkish summit, with the country's insistence on a date for accession talks as defined at the time. Turkish commentators claimed that this was as important as the Tanzimat Reforms of 1839 and the Helsinki summit of 1999, in which the EU accepted Turkey as a candidate country for membership. The new AKP government worked quickly to secure a date for Turkey's accession talks on 3 October 2005. The move would consolidate democracy against the ongoing threat of another Turkish military intervention and build confidence into the Turkish economy. The EU process compelled Ankara to overhaul its political and judicial structure that had lasted for more than eighty years under the ideology of Kemalist modernisation, which had depended heavily upon an authoritarian vision of politics and society. Moreover, as a further concession to Europe, the Erdoğan government was keen to solve the Cyprus problem within the context of the Annan Plan reached in 2004.[10]

As Turkey strived to meet the Copenhagen criteria, the debate about the meaning of European identity moved to the front of public discourse and continues to this day. What does European identity entail? Do the membership of Turkey and the presence of Muslim communities in Europe challenge European identity or empower it? How should we read widespread European negative reaction to Turkey's membership? Does it stem from the anxiety over the weakness of European identity or historical hostility against

Islam and the Turks? There is no clear definition of European identity. Yet, many argue that Greek heritage, Roman law and Christianity (certainly for some) or Enlightenment values (certainly for many who see themselves as cosmopolitan) define the contextual frame of European identity. Therefore, it is a fluid identity in process, if one is to consider the implications and outcomes of Turkey reaching full membership status in the EU. As far as Turkey's Muslims have been concerned, Europe represents democracy and economic prosperity. Thus, they have not seen these identities as mutually exclusive but rather look forward to being both European and Muslim within the framework of the EU. However, the situation at the onset of the 2020s is starkly different than in the early 2000s.

With Cyprus, Erdoğan leveraged his political capital to sideline nationalist Turkish leaders such as Rauf Denktas along with the Turkish military that supports him to solve a conflict that has lasted for more than forty years.[11] EU leaders supported the new round of negotiations and Erdoğan intervened and forced the Turkish Cypriot leadership to sign up to the UN-led peace plan, also known as the Annan Plan, or the Cyprus reunification plan.[12] The plan called for restructuring the Republic of Cyprus as a United Republic of Cyprus – a federation of two states. The plan was put to a referendum in 2004 and 65 per cent of Turkish Cypriots supported it, while a majority of Greek Cypriots voted against it. The EU decided to accept the Greek Cypriot side as a full member and representative of Cyprus. This decision, in turn, disappointed Erdoğan and he concluded that the EU was neither fair nor had an ability to solve any conflict.[13]

Turkish public opinion became more sceptical of the EU's ability to address regional and national problems. Moreover, a majority of Turks believe that European leaders define European identity in opposition to Islam and Turkey so therefore Turkey's entry into the EU is an impossible mission. The former French President Giscard d'Estaing, then the president of the European Convention, publicly stated what others in Europe have long maintained privately: Turkey is 'a different culture, a different approach and a different way of life', and its admission would quite simply mean 'the end of the EU'. The remarks by d'Estaing appeared to shift the debate from what Turkey does to the reductionist construct of what Turkey was. He told *Le Monde* that Turkey's 'capital isn't in Europe, 95 per cent of its population is outside

Europe – this isn't a European country'.[14] His remarks were not anomalous and reflected what a sizeable part of the elite as well as the public thought.

As the US pushed to anchor Turkey in the EU camp as part of its own war on terrorism, some Europeans became even more suspicious of Turkey as a Trojan Horse employed by Washington to forestall deeper integration within the EU. At the heart of the debate, although few of those opposed to Turkey's accession dare to say as much, is the sensitive issue of Europe's cultural and religious identity. Edmund Stoiber, the former conservative minister president of the state of Bavaria, told a Christian Social Union (CSU) party conference that, 'Europe is a community that is based on Western values. As a community of shared values, Europe has to deal with the question of its borders. These borders must be based on shared values, culture and history. Turkey's membership would breach these borders.'[15] The British, led by then Prime Minister Tony Blair, argued in contrast that an increasingly multicultural Europe and a post-September 11 world threatened by a clash of civilisations would benefit mutually from EU membership for a democratic Muslim country such as Turkey.[16]

Erdoğan's policies until 2010 were built on expanding human rights, and liberalising society and the economy. The EU-oriented discourse expanded his domestic and international legitimacy and made him a rather popular politician throughout the Arab world, whose own leaders shunned democracy and liberalism. The EU process allowed the AKP to position itself as pro-democracy and pro-liberalism vis-à-vis the opposition secularist parties. While Turkey's admittance to the European club was never a sure thing, given the veto votes of both Greece and Cyprus, and with the electoral victories of Nicolas Sarkozy (2007–12) and Angela Merkel (2005–present), it became clear that EU had no intention of negotiating in good faith. During his 2006–7 presidential campaign in France, Sarkozy's main foreign policy theme was his opposition to Turkey joining the EU by arguing that Turkey was geographically and culturally not part of Europe.[17] Sarkozy said:

> Negotiations began in 1964. We are in 2007. The time has rather come to tell the Turks whether we want them or if we do not want them. For me actually, it is not a question of democracy, it is not at all a question of Muslims, of Islam. It is to say that it's Asia, it is not Europe. One must tell clearly to this

great nation that is Turkey that they are meant to be the heart of the Union of the Mediterranean but not the heart of the European Union.[18]

Sarkozy also rejected Turkey's membership on the basis of cultural and religious differences. He said:

> Because we do have a problem of integration, which points to the question of Islam in Europe. To pretend that this is not a problem would be to hide reality, if you take in 100 million Muslim Turks, what will happen?[19]

Meanwhile, Merkel insisted on a 'privileged partnership' and rejected the possibility of full membership in 2009.[20] Hugh Pope, a prominent journalist who has reported on Turkey, aptly concluded that, 'talk of "privileged partnership" thus looks more and more like a scapegoat for popular European fears about jobs, immigration and Islam'.[21]

It was a hard realisation in Ankara that there was no way to overcome the perceived EU racism for Turkey to realise a goal of full membership. The de facto exclusion of Turkey fostered a period of confusion and disappointment, and eventually Turkey lost its enthusiasm for joining the EU. It has become clear that the EU treats Turkey as a buffer zone and wants Turkey to work with the EU on energy, immigration and the fight against terrorism. However, the EU rejection of Turkish membership engendered a shattering impact on the secular nation state identity of the country and it has gradually drifted ever closer towards the Middle East and the Balkans while buoyed by a spirit of neo-Ottomanism, which Erdoğan has amplified.

The dynamic of interaction between Turkey and the EU has done much to shape the identity and position of the AKP's leadership and the EU is now viewed broadly as an untrustworthy partner. Some scholars tend to view Erdoğan's EU efforts as cynical and insincere by arguing that his real intent was to weaken and subordinate the guardians of secularism (for example, military, judiciary and university), so that he could implement his Islamisation policy without any resistance. These scholars contend that since Erdoğan and his AKP shared anti-Western Islamist and Ottomanist worldviews they pretended to pursue EU membership in order to receive external support to use against their domestic secularist opponents. Erdoğan's primary foreign policy goal was to join the EU and this orientation continued until 2009. Robert Gates, former US defence secretary, said that if Turkey is moving eastward, it is 'in no small part because it was pushed by some in Europe refusing to give Turkey the kind of organic link to the West that Turkey sought'.[22]

One of the key foreign policy initiatives that fell victim to the deteriorating relations with the EU was the possibility of establishing diplomatic relations with Armenia. Abdullah Gül, then Turkey's president, visited Armenia in September 2008 to attend a football game between the teams of the two countries, a potential confidence-building opener for relations. As a result of a series of secret meetings between Turkey and Armenia, representatives agreed to establish diplomatic relations, open the borders and convene a joint commission of historians to examine the Armenian claims of genocide. The Armenian–Turkish Protocols were signed on 10 October 2009 by the foreign ministers of Turkey and Armenia. US Secretary of State Hillary Clinton; Javier Solana, EU high representative for common foreign and security policy; French Minister of Foreign Affairs Bernard Kouchner and Russian Foreign Minister Sergey Lavrov were also present during the signing ceremony. However, the decision by the Armenian Constitutional Court to reinterpret the protocols and the reaction from the Republic of Azerbaijan turned Turkish public opinion against the ratification of these protocols.[23]

9.3 Erdoğan's Relations with US, Israel and the Arab World

Changing circumstances in the region compelled the Turkish government to reorient its foreign policy, especially in affairs involving the Middle East and Russia. The American decision to occupy Iraq was especially consequential. During the Erdoğan era, relations with the US worsened, as defined by the Turkish parliament's decision not to allow American forces to occupy Iraq, disagreement over the Iranian nuclear deal, the unquestioned US support for Israel, divergence over the 2013 coup in Egypt, and the civil war in Syria and American support for the Kurdish insurgency.

In 2002, the first crisis the newly elected AKP government had to deal was the US decision to launch a military operation to overthrow Saddam Hussein in Iraq. The Bush administration planned the invasion, believing that Turkey would open its territories to American forces to facilitate the occupation. However, on 1 March 2003, the Turkish parliament denied the request, forcing the American government to change its occupation strategy and tactics.[24] The parliament acted more or less on the basis of Turkish public opinion as many were against allowing US troops to enter Turkish territory, fearing that such a move would destabilise the entire region. Erdoğan blamed this early political failure on the Turkish military, which did not support his proposal in the parliament. Erdoğan used every opportunity to weaken the Turkish military's prestige. Paul Wolfowitz, then US deputy secretary of defence, openly criticised the Turkish military for not convincing Turkish politicians of the resolution's purpose.[25] This decision instigated the end of Turkish–American relations as both partners had known it for decades. The American government and its top military echelons did not forget or forgive this decision.[26] After 2003, the various American presidential administrations approached Turkey sceptically, as the respective interests of both countries continued to diverge.

During the Obama administration, despite Erdoğan developing closer ties with the American president, fundamental disagreements between the two countries were not resolved. Erdoğan failed to understand the role of the US Congress and American public opinion. He attempted to build relations only on a personal level while keeping the security bureaucracy in the dark. Erdoğan cultivated relations with Syria and the Palestinian authorities, especially with Hamas. The Obama administration was adamantly against this because of Israel. The visit to Ankara by a Hamas delegation after elections in Gaza angered the US Congress and the Obama administration.[27] In April 2009, Barack Obama visited Turkey and addressed the Turkish parliament, praising the country's democratic advances and signalling his support for its full membership in the EU. However, the 2011 Arab Spring, along with coups and civil wars in the region, would destabilise the once-strong sense of comity that marked US–Turkey relations.

Erdoğan did not hesitate to express shared cultural and historic ties with the Middle East as a driving force for his foreign policy and his attempts to engage with the regional crises. During an interview with Charlie Rose on the American Public Broadcasting Service network in 2011, Erdoğan defended Turkey's presence in the Middle East, adding, 'France, Germany and the US are there; why can't we be there? It's very logical for us to be there because we have a common history, culture and long borders with these countries.'[28]

Erdoğan's actions underscored his sentiment. With Turkey's assistance, Professor Ekmeleddin İhsanoğlu was elected as the secretary-general of the Organisation of Islamic Cooperation in 2004 – the first time a Turk had led the group. In 2006, Erdoğan became the first Turkish leader to address an Arab League Summit, in which Turkey was granted permanent guest status. The Arab public supported Erdoğan's charismatic leadership in the belief that it would help reconcile Islam and democracy in their own countries. In 2009, Turkey was elected to a rotating seat on the United Nations Security Council with the support of Arab, Asian and African countries. Erdoğan's popularity was not only at the grass-roots levels in Arabic countries but he also was recognised officially by various governments and heads of state. Saudi Arabia awarded Erdoğan with its highest honour, the King Faisal Award, for his service to Islam and Islamic causes. In 2010, Erdoğan received the Ghaddafi Award for Human Rights in recognition for his candid courage and support for the Palestinian people, his defence of the poor and disadvantaged, and his continuous struggle for the rights for underrepresented countries and communities and their cultures and values.

Erdoğan sought to convert these cultural affinities into regional economic gains by trying to use the EU model to push towards economic interdependence in the Middle East. Erdoğan was aware that the European Customs Union had a positive impact on the continental economy and prioritised economics-based foreign policy orientation. Turkish officials believed that increased economic interdependency with the regional countries would enhance the economy and strengthen Turkey's influence in the region.

One major country, which would have played a key role in Turkey's desires for regional integration, was Syria. Likewise, Erdoğan believed Jordan and Lebanon were crucial to his geopolitical project. In 2010, under the Turkish lead, these countries formed the Levant Quartet to create something similar to the EU.[29] Turkey unilaterally lifted visa restrictions for citizens in Syria, Jordan and Lebanon.

Turkey supported the reform measures of Bashar Assad, who, in January 2004, became the first Syrian president to visit Turkey. Later that year in December, Erdoğan reciprocated by visiting Damascus to address an ongoing border dispute with Syria and sign a bilateral free-trade agreement, which became effective in 2007. In 2005, Erdoğan visited Syria again and Turkey removed the minefields at the Syrian–Turkish border, lifted visa requirements, and signed a free-trade agreement. Both countries agreed to establishing a 'friendship dam' on the Orontes/Asi river along the Hatay border between Syria and Turkey, which also secured Syrian recognition of Hatay as a Turkish territory.

When Erdoğan came to power, he developed closer ties with the Israeli lobby in America and tried to court Israel's blessings to overcome the perception of being seen as simultaneously Islamist and anti-Israel. Before Erdoğan won the election, the previous government extended relations with Israel in military, economic and technological circles. When Erdoğan became prime minister, he did not try to interrupt the process but later he recalled the Turkish ambassador when Israel assassinated Shaykh Ahmed Yassin, a Palestinian political leader, in March 2004. Erdoğan accused Israel of terrorism, as he condemned the killing. Whatever constructive relations with Israel had been cultivated, the tone changed when he visited Israel in 2005 and toured the occupied territories. According to one of Erdoğan's advisers, what he witnessed in the occupied territories and the dispossession of Palestinians transformed his view.

As Israel became more aggressive towards its neighbours, it became harder for Erdoğan to remain silent and maintain civil relations with Israel. For instance, Erdoğan sharply criticised Israeli repressive policies against the Palestinians and its attack on civilian targets in the Lebanese war in 2006. Because of pressure from the military, he remained hopeful of mediation between the state of Israel and Palestinians and supported Gül's 2007 proposal to invite Shimon Peres and Mahmoud Abbas to Ankara and allow both leaders to address the Turkish parliament. Turkey also developed closer ties with Hamas and invited its leader Khalid Mishal to visit Ankara. Although some Israelis, and especially the Israeli lobby in Washington, were angry at Mishal's visit to Ankara, relations between Ankara and Tel Aviv were sour but not bad enough to be cut. Erdoğan was happy to mediate between Israel and Syria, and Ankara organised a series of indirect talks in 2008. While Erdoğan invested his political capital to achieve peace between Israel and Syria, Israel, without informing Turkey, unleashed a military campaign, known as the Operation Cast Lead massacre against Gaza civilians in late 2008 and early 2009. These brutal attacks on the civilian population resulted in the deaths of 1,423 Palestinians and thirteen Israelis.[30]

In nearly every major city in Turkey there were demonstrations against the Israeli attack on Gazan civilians and the unanimous silence from major Western powers. Erdoğan was furious because he had just met with then Israeli Prime Minister Olmert four days before the attack in December 2008 and nothing about the impending tactics was mentioned. Erdoğan, according to one of his advisers, believed he was being used by Israel to gain legitimacy in the region while at the same time it planned to attack Palestinians. Erdoğan suspended his mediating role between Israel and Syria. He was disrespected and humiliated before the Turkish and Muslim public and he, in return, became harsher in his criticism of Israel and its policies. He accused Israel of turning Gaza 'into an open-air prison' and called on Muslims to support the Palestinian cause. After the Gaza war, Erdoğan toured Jordan, Syria, Egypt and Saudi Arabia, and asked those countries to support the just cause of the Palestinians, accusing Israel of crimes against humanity.

In January 2009, Erdoğan lashed out against Shimon Peres, then Israel's popular president, at the World Economic Forum in Davos, Switzerland, a move that emboldened the Turkish leader's role as ally to Arab causes in the international relations arena.[31] Erdoğan maintained his criticism of Israel especially after the raid of the Gaza-bound Mavi Marmara flotilla in which Israeli commandos killed nine Turkish activists in 2010. At this point, he became the most popular politician in Arab streets as well as with governments that had long-standing problems with Israel. Israel reacted to Erdoğan's policies by humiliating the Turkish ambassador at the time, Ahmet Oguz Celikkol, when in January 2010, Israeli Deputy Foreign Minister Danny Ayalon summoned the envoy to his office and humiliated him before the Israel television news crew covering the event. When Turkey recalled its ambassador, Ayalon apologised, but this act exacerbated the already soured relations between the two countries.

Erdoğan was disturbed by Israeli policies of ethnic and cultural cleansings against the Palestinian presence in their ancient homeland and, as one interview subject explained, 'he was even more pained to witness the weakness of the Palestinians in particular and Arabs in general'. Erdoğan concluded in 2011 that 'Israel does not want peace and it can only survive if it keeps the region fragmented with the US support. The US military and economic aid to Egypt is key to keep the Arabs fragmented and weak vis-à-vis

Israel'.[32] Erdoğan has consistently criticised the status quo in the Middle East, believing that the will of the ordinary people has also been suppressed by the respective Arab governments.

9.4 The Arab Spring and Islamisation of Foreign Policy (2011–Present)

Erdoğan and his key advisors welcomed the popular uprising in the Middle East by hoping they would create favourable international contexts for Turkey's geopolitical leadership.[33] The collapse of various Arab governments led to an institutional and legitimacy vacuum and the AKP wanted to lead Muslim Brotherhood-related parties to fill the space. The 2012 election victory of the Muslim Brotherhood in Egypt was a catalyst for Erdoğan to project his influence. However, his hopes were dashed quickly. The July 2013 coup in Egypt resulted in the overthrow of Mohamed Morsi, which ended the Muslim Brotherhood's brief hold on political power. As a result of this coup, Turkey lost a major prospective partner in shaping politics in the region. The coup shattered Erdoğan's dreams of leading the diaspora of Sunni Muslims. Meanwhile, ISIS expanded its power into Raqqa in early 2014 and carried out terrorist attacks in major European capitals. Western public opinion and governments turned to defending the region's secular and authoritarian regimes against any Islamic-inclined political formations. Thus, the uprisings against the governments were not welcomed and portrayed instead as a terrorist or radical Islamic initiative, which led to a new cold war in the region.

The civil war in Syria also had spilled into Turkey. ISIS carried out suicide attacks inside Turkey, including at a peace rally in Ankara in October 2015 that killed 102 activists. The ongoing erosion of the sovereignty of the Syrian government enabled the PKK-led Syrian Democratic Union Party (PYD) to control northern Syria, across the Turkish border. Many Western governments, especially the US, welcomed the PYD as a counter-force against ISIS. Erdoğan's short-sighted policy in Syria created many security risks for Turkey. It also isolated Turkey in the West, and Turkey became hostage to Russian demands and ambitions in the region.

In addition to the EU's rejection of Turkey, Erdoğan relapsed to his strict Islamist position in his efforts to achieve authoritarian and kleptocratic interests. Turkey's rising confidence in its military strength along with economic growth fed the favourable environment for Erdoğan to become a regional power through the use of Islam and the Muslim Brotherhood networks. As the AKP consolidated its power as a result of the 2010 constitutional reform which practically ended the secular-Kemalist constraints around the system, Erdoğan was free to establish his imagined autocratic system.

In addition to these developments, Davutoğlu became foreign minister (2009–14) and he had the opportunity to put his ideology into practice, determined to make Turkey a central state that controls its own foreign policy and leads these efforts in the region. As an ideologue best described as a reverse-Huntingtonian who strongly believed in the clash of civilisations and civilisational approach to politics, he is compelled by a fantastical idea that the Muslim communities of the former Ottoman Empire maintained their 'Ottoman spirit' and they all look towards Turkey as a leader country.

Thus, he wanted Turkey to exploit this latent cultural landscape to Turkey's advantage, a position that appealed to Erdoğan. Davutoğlu formulated the concept of *tarihdaş*, defined as sharing Ottoman history with Turkey and redeveloping Ottoman civilisation in tandem with regional partners. He argued that these communities who share the same Ottoman past with Turkey constitute Turkey's legitimate sphere of influence and the nation should lead the project of regional unification of these countries. Erdoğan and Davutoğlu in tandem stressed the value of civilisational (Islamic) leadership, which shifted Turkey's pro-Western foreign policy and repositioned on broader terms Islamic civilisation against its Western counterpart. Erdoğan gradually mobilised the Muslim Brotherhood networks in the Arab World to become master of this new order of regional politics.

In this process, he identified Saudi Arabia and Egypt as the viable contenders and the challengers to Erdoğan's claim to speak for the Muslim world. Although Erdoğan embodies a conservative-Islamic orientation in his thinking, he also became vocal in criticising the EU because of what he perceived as short-sighted, racist policies of Europe, especially Sarkozy, Macron and Merkel, who rejected Turkey's membership in the EU on the basis of religious and cultural differences. This exclusion and humiliation led to Erdoğan's disillusionment with the West and this, in turn, prompted him to redefine and restore Turkey's relations with Muslim countries, for the purpose of becoming a regional leader in the Middle East, Balkans and the Caucasus. Many scholars and journalists describe this new orientation as neo-Ottomanism.[34]

By late 2010, Middle Eastern and North African dictatorships sharply encountered the challenges posed by the demands of their own citizens. The first uprising began in Tunisia on 18 December 2010 and resulted with the collapse of the Ben Ali regime, which had lasted twenty-three years. Mass protests spread throughout Arab countries, in Bahrain, Algeria, Egypt, Jordan and Syria. Erdoğan had warned Hosni Mubarak that the time would come for him to step aside, and Egyptians duly toppled the Mubarak regime, which had ruled since 1981. Erdoğan fully supported the Muslim Brotherhood-led elections and their new government in Egypt, and the AKP hoped to be a mentor to it, as it presented the Turkish case as a model for the compatibility of Islam and democracy.[35]

Erdoğan and Davutoğlu, along with the pro-government think tank known by its acronym of SETA, welcomed these popular uprisings as an opportunity for Turkey to restore Islamic civilisation, reconfigure the Middle East and become a spokesperson of the Islamic world.[36] The rise of Turkey as a regional Islamic leader, as the seat of the last Ottoman Caliphate, came to an end with the military coup in Egypt, Syria's intractable civil war, Russia's growing presence in the region and the fear of Kurdish separatism.

The major casualty of the Arab Spring encompassed Turkish–Syrian relations, which were the most important in terms of establishing ties with ex-Ottoman Arab societies. When the youth took to the streets in Syria, Erdoğan worked hard to get Assad to open up the system.[37] Despite Turkey's encouragements, Assad refused to give in to the demonstrators. Then, Ankara made a 180-degree turn and instead supported the popular uprising against the Syrian president. Turkey supported the Syrian National Council in logistics and military terms to resist the Syrian government. Erdoğan, by supporting armed opposition in Syria, helped to weaken the central government and this, in turn, created an opportunity for secessionist Kurds to carve out the large territory on the border with Turkey. This forced Assad to rely on Iran and Russia while Turkey became more sensitive to the needs of these two states in order to have a limited role in Syria. The civil war in Syria produced more than nine million refugees – the majority moved to Turkey.

What explains Turkey's arguably irrational policy towards Syria? What motivated Erdoğan to support the opposition against the central government? Turkey wanted to engage with the international community, but it also believed that it must support the legitimate demands of Syrian Sunni Muslims. The rebellions in other Arab countries resulted in the overthrow of the governments and Turkey expected the same result in Syria. The war had two major effects on Turkey. First, it killed the Turkish dream of realising the Levant Quartet as a free-trade zone and reconnecting with the ex-Ottoman Arab communities. Eventually, Turkey ended up with five million Syrian refugees. Second, the Syrian civil war combined with the sectarian government in Iraq created a fertile ground for the emergence of ISIS.

These outcomes indicate that the shift in Turkey's foreign policy was less strategic and more of a tactical response to emerging geopolitical challenges and opportunities. The rejection by the EU and US support for Kurdish autonomy and independence in Iraq and Syria have turned Turkish public opinion decidedly against the West – in essence pulling the rug out from pro-West secularists in Turkey. The AKP's foreign policy has aligned with this new public mood of optimism in the country and a belief in Turkey's indispensability in world affairs. However, it would also be a mistake to treat the AKP's foreign policy as the manifestation of the public's will because, as polling and elections have shown on numerous occasions, a sizable number of people have disagreed with Erdoğan's adventurist foreign policy direction. The most important instigator of the foreign policy during this period was the identity and ideological conviction of Erdoğan. In 2014, especially after he was elected president in a popular vote, he convinced himself that he represents the will of the people and, therefore, he is the supreme authority to make domestic and foreign policy. Unfortunately, Turkish foreign policy has become more personalised, militarised and daring against its neighbours, consistently with negative effects.

Erdoğan has become more Islamo-Turkish nationalist and much more confrontational. The AKP ceased to be an agent of conservative democracy but rather emerged as an agent of authoritarianism and Islamo-Turkish restoration.[38] In 2014, *The Economist* summed up the situation in Turkey:

> When the Arab Spring burst onto the Middle East three years ago, hopeful democrats in search of a model were drawn to Turkey as a country that seemed to combine moderate Islam with prosperity and democracy. Unfortunately, the Arabs did not follow the Turkish path. Instead, Turkey has set off down the old Arab road to corruption and autocracy.[39]

Over time, Erdoğan shed his liberal, democratic skin and returned to his old Islamic identity that was developed intellectually by Kısakürek. He used Islamism-cum-Turkish nationalism to consolidate his power. After the events of 2013, Erdoğan first purged those who would challenge his authoritarian tendencies and gradually regressed to the Islamist ideology of the Muslim Brotherhood from his pro-EU and democratic rhetoric.[40] At the height of the Arab Spring, Erdoğan presented himself as a model for the powerful Islamic groups and became their main supporter. In many countries the Muslim Brotherhood was in a better position to control the government through the ballot box. Initially, demonstrations in Syria, Turkey and the US encouraged Assad to carry out political reforms.[41] Erdoğan supported the Muslim Brotherhood, asking Assad to share power with the movement, hoping this would eventually lead to total victory for the Muslim Brotherhood.

However, when Turkey and the US failed to convince Assad to carry out the political reform and the government opened fire against the demonstrators, both countries called for Assad to step down in November 2011.[42] Neither the US nor Turkey had any coherent strategy to remove Assad from power and both governments underestimated Russian and Iranian commitment to the regime in Damascus. The rise of ISIS in Iraq and then its expansion into Syria transformed the priorities and policies for regional and international actors. Turkey treated ISIS as an outcome of the failed and oppressive states in Iraq and Syria, whereas the US and the EU regarded ISIS as a terrorist organisation and tried to contain the problem through counterinsurgency strategies. Turkey's reading of the problem diverged from its Western allies and thus, Erdoğan pursued divergent strategies to cope with the regional problems.

Erdoğan was reluctant to fight against ISIS because Turkey's main concern was the PKK, not ISIS. Although the Turkish public was vehemently against ISIS, Erdoğan was hopeful that ISIS could weaken the PKK and help to overthrow the Assad government. The US decided to ally with Kurdish insurgent groups to fight and defeat ISIS – essentially choosing one terrorist group over friendlier terrorist counterparts to control the situation. The Obama administration's decision to support the YPG, the Syrian branch of the PKK, which is considered as a terrorist organisation, was the last straw for friendly Turkish–American relations.[43] Washington ignored Turkey's security concerns and allied with the YPG by providing military training and arming insurgents to fight against ISIS.[44] This created an opportunity for Erdoğan to develop a new security-first political language; use nationalism to mobilise the masses; and mend the ties with the Turkish military by fighting against its erstwhile enemy of the Kurdish insurgency.

As the Obama and Trump administrations increased their military support for the Kurdish fighters, the YPG controlled the Turkish–Syrian border. This, in turn, heightened fears of the Turkish military establishment. When the YPG carried out an ethnic cleansing campaign against Arabs and Turkomans, Ankara shared its concerns with Washington, which saw its main purpose as defeating ISIS. Meanwhile, the Kurds regarded this American support to consolidate their military and territorial power by expanding to control one-third of the Syrian landscape. The American weapons eventually ended up in the hands of PKK fighters in Turkey and the government did not hesitate to share this information with the public. Washington unintentionally provided a new space for Erdoğan to rally the public around Turkish nationalism, allowing him to characterise the Kurds as the fifth column that could be weaponised against the Turkish state.

Erdoğan is the only one who benefited from unforced American errors and short-sighted American policies and was able to raise nationalist and security concerns to rally the public. When Erdoğan declared the west bank of the Euphrates River would be the 'red line' and asked the US-led YPG to retreat, the US government ignored his call. In turn, Erdoğan allied with Russia and carried out Operation Euphrates Shield in 2016 to cleanse the YPG groups from the region. Although a new administration took office in 2017, the US policy did not change under President Trump. On the contrary, the Trump administration offered heavy weapons to the YPG and this, in turn, reinforced the anger in Ankara. In May 2017, when photographs showing Brett McGurk, a senior American diplomat who coordinated military efforts against ISIS, with the YPG militants were published in several major Turkish newspapers, it angered the public and Erdoğan had no option but to respond formally as president.

To conclude, the civil war in Syria resulted in several impacts that besieged Turkey's domestic and foreign policy options. First, it produced a significant refugee problem and Turkey ended up taking close to five million refugees, a number that has raised concerns about maintaining domestic stability. Second, it led to the Pakistanisation of Turkey and Islamisation of Turkey's security establishment. Third, it turned relations between Turkey and the US upside down because of their divergent interests. Fourth, the Kurdish issue has been internationalised and has generated international sympathy for Kurdish independence. Fifth, the divergence and tension with the US compelled Ankara to ally more closely with Russia. Finally, the civil war in Syria and the American collaboration with PKK Kurds deepened Erdoğan's fears about his grip on power and he, in turn, has projected his fears on to the nation. He has convinced the people that the country faces an existential threat from its internal and external enemies. This survival mode sentiment has made security an absolute necessity in foreign policy considerations, along with strategies to deal with domestic opponents, especially the Kurds.

9.5 Erdoğan–Muslim Brotherhood Relations

The marriage between Erdogan's AKP and the Muslim Brotherhood may have enjoyed a prolonged period of ideological flirtation, but it was consummated at a time and place when both parties desperately needed each other. Although both are Islamists, the Muslim Brotherhood remains a distinctly Arab phenomena whose instincts are deeply conservative and stand at odds with Erdoğan's relatively more secular leaning. Despite them being on the same side in terms of the regional conflict, the Muslim Brotherhood organisation has not always been able to fit neatly within Erdoğan's neo-Ottoman designs and has struggled to translate Turkey's foreign policy to Arab audiences without appearing slavish and subservient. The relationship between the two is most certainly not one of equals; it is also not an exclusive one. The third partner in the relationship is Qatar, the Gulf state that has furnished the financial resources to Muslim Brotherhood networks worldwide, and particularly those that operate in Turkey. Having done business with a wide array of governments in the past, mutual utilitarianism has been the defining feature of Muslim Brotherhood strategy. In its dealings with Erdoğan's Turkey, the Muslim Brotherhood has demonstrated the same instincts for opportunism and survival and will likely continue to do so as long as it furnishes the Turkish–Qatari agitation machine with the useful manpower that it so badly needs.

Although both Erdoğan and the Muslim Brotherhood share a broad vision inspired by a certain understanding of Islam, there remain important differences. Erdoğan does not appear to favour implementing sharia law, a question that is settled in his mind,[45] while in Muslim Brotherhood organisations the issue still resonates as a priority. Moreover, Erdoğan is a distinctly Turkish-Islamist nationalistic where the role model is not so much the early period of Islam in the Arabian Peninsula (as is the case with the Muslim Brotherhood), but rather the classical age of the Ottoman Empire. Identifying as neo-Ottomanists, the AKP elite regards the fall of the caliphate as a political catastrophe for Turkey because it meant a loss of influence in the Muslim world. Erdoğan does not seek military conquest like his Ottoman forefathers, but rather political, economic and cultural cooperation of Muslim countries where Turkey plays the leading role and draws the lion's share of benefits. The Muslim Brotherhood is not ideologically wedded to this neo-Ottoman fantasy, but it does support the objective of reviving the spirit of the Ottoman Empire as part of a broad neo-Islamic revivalism.

While ideology may have brought Erdoğan and the Muslim Brotherhood closer together, it is Erdoğan's goal of restructuring the Middle East that has created the terms for actual partnership with the Muslim Brotherhood. Erdoğan's regional vision is informed by a deep resentment at the post-World War I political order.[46] In his early political indoctrination, Erdoğan was influenced by the National Outlook Movement of Necmettin Erbakan that criticised the Kemalists as having abandoned Turkey's historic rights in the region.[47] Erbakan preached that the West only allowed Turkey to become an independent state in return for dismantling its Muslim identity. He also saw Turkey's current borders, as well as those of neighbouring states, as 'colonial inventions'. This line of thinking paved the way for a more radical idea that would be adopted by Erdoğan, that the entire state system in the region was skewed against Turkey and that Turkish secularism was primarily a concession to the West that could, and should, be reversed.

Erdoğan's foreign policy towards the Middle East region is based on four main assumptions. The first is that the source of the problems in the region is the collapse of the Ottoman Empire and the formation of the Sykes–Picot borders, and what followed on from that in terms of client regimes being installed by colonial powers. The states of the region are 'artificial constructs' that do not represent Muslim interests. Second, the only effective integrative force is political Islam. The region can only come together based on Islamic identity and not ethnicity, and through the work of Islamically inspired political parties such as the Muslim Brotherhood. Third, the current regimes of the Middle East, especially those led by royal families in oil-rich monarchies, represent the biggest problems barring the re-integration of the region under Turkish leadership. Those regimes function as garrisons of Western interests to perpetuate twenty-first-century colonialism. Fourth, the Palestine issue exemplifies the worst outcome that could have happened as a result of the collapse of the Ottoman order.[48] For Erdoğan and Turkish Islamists generally, the Palestine issue is the 'shame of the *umma*', and symptomatic of the abject failure and treachery of Arab governments.

Erdoğan's support for the Muslim Brotherhood and willingness to provide a safe haven to carry out their campaign from Istanbul has angered many Arab countries, especially Saudi Arabia and the United Arab Emirates. The 2017 Qatar crisis provided a new opportunity for Erdoğan to establish a military base in Doha and gradually it became involved in intra-Arab squabbles. Initially, the killing of Saudi Arabian journalist Jamal Khashoggi was not seen as a major geopolitical event, but with the Qatar crisis, with the help of Iran, it became a major regional issue to undermine the position of Saudi Arabia. Erdoğan seized this opportunity to wound Turkey's regional rival. He temporarily delayed sharing the video and audio recordings of Khashoggi's murder because it would expose Turkish capabilities of covert surveillance in diplomatic buildings, which runs against international norms. However, as Saudi officials denied the charges, Erdoğan leaked the information to embarrass the Saudi Crown Prince Mohammad bin Salman. Through these incremental leaks he kept a steady drip-drip of pressure on Saudi Arabia, which forced ongoing changes in their narratives about the circumstances surrounding Khashoggi's death.

Erdoğan's goal was to ruin the credibility and reputation of Mohammad bin Salman, who is known for meticulously crafting a positive, favourable image in the international community. By targeting the crown prince, Erdoğan decimated Turkish–Saudi relations and turned a once-friendly country against Turkey. In an interview with an adviser of Erdoğan about why the Turkish president took this destructive path against Saudi Arabia, he said:

Yes, we could not get him removed but we at least clipped the wings of Muhammed bin Kushner [referencing the close ties with Jared Kushner, the son-in-law of former President Trump]. The main problem in the region is Saudi Arabia and their version of Wahhabi Islam.

Because of his personal relations with the Emir of Qatar, Erdoğan has not covered up his dislike of the Saudi crown prince and welcomes every opportunity to expose Saudi weaknesses. As this case indicates, Erdoğan's foreign policy has been less about the national interests of Turkey and more about his personal preferences, such as having joint ventures with the Emir of Qatar, which involves receiving gifts that violate all legal and ethical norms that were designed to prevent graft and corruption.[49] In November 2018, for example, Qatar's emir approved a package of economic projects, investments and deposits worth $15 billion to support Turkey's economy.

As the EU dealt with the massive influx of refugees from the Syrian civil war while Turkey took a large number of Syrians into the country, Erdoğan tried to use the refugee issue as a bargaining chip against the EU. German Chancellor Angela Merkel, who led the EU's efforts on Syrian refugees, faced political opposition at home. Initially, the humanitarian focus made Merkel popular, but domestic opposition soon used the issue to challenge her popular standing in German public opinion. Erdoğan saw the situation as an opportunity to project himself as a powerful Ottoman-like sultan and a defender of Turkey against its enemies.

Erdoğan's standing, however, in Europe only worsened as heads of state worried about growing authoritarianism in Turkey and refused his requests to allow mass rallies in support of Turkish citizens. He accused Germany of resurrecting Nazism, adding that other European countries operated as remnants of the 1930s. On 10 March 2017, Turkey's relations with the Netherlands hit the lowest point since the history of the Republic when the Dutch government refused to let the Turkish foreign minister fly into the country to hold a campaign at the Turkish consulate in Rotterdam. Erdoğan fired back, comparing the Dutch to fascists. Erdoğan's dictatorial tactics enhanced ultra-right arguments against the Turks in Europe. However, moderate Europeans raised questions about the commitment of Euro-Turks to democracy and human rights because the overwhelming majority recently had voted for Erdoğan to build an autocratic state.

At the same time, the conflict involving Erdoğan and the Gülenists has profoundly affected Turkey's foreign policy, particularly in its contentious relationship with the EU as well as with members of the NATO. The rise of authoritarianism, which has coincided with the measures violating internationally accepted standards of human rights, has emboldened European circles who always have opposed to Turkey's full membership in the EU. As Turkey has moved steadily from its commitment to democracy in its fight against the Gülenist networks, it also has distanced itself further than ever from the EU. Due to entrenched perceptions about an American role in the coup attempt of 2016 and the corresponding failure to support the civilian government during the fateful hours of events on the night of 15 July, a major gap in confidence continues to widen between Turkey and the US. Even before the coup attempt, Turkish public opinion regarding the US had already turned negative. Since the collapse of Iraq and later Syria, Washington's support for the Syrian branch of the PKK, (itself officially recognised as a terrorist organisation), in its efforts to find proxies to combat ISIS, has gravely undermined its relationship with Turkey. The US had assured Turkey that the Syrian PKK affiliate, known as the Democratic Union Party (PYD), would not be allowed to move to the west of the Euphrates River. However, it has been clear that the US helped the PYD to occupy the town of Manjib and ethnically cleanse the Arab and Turkoman population in the broader area.

Russia was the first nation to condemn the coup attempt against Erdoğan and reaffirm its support for him. Not surprisingly, Russia has exploited the situation for strategic advantage, as evidenced in Turkey's recent decision to purchase an advanced Russian-made, anti-missile defence system. The decision is one of the clearest signs of the Turkish government's disappointment in the US and Europe and the coincidental circumstances of Ankara becoming more comfortable as a 'strategic partner' of Russia.[50]

Washington's failure to utilise the promise of the Arab Spring and move away from ISIS and perpetual crisis, as Ankara had warned, has threatened Western democracies with the rise of neo-fascist movements in the US and the EU. For Turkey, this Western strategic failure has led to increased strategic cooperation with Moscow and Beijing as a counterweight to the West. The aftermath of the coup was used to expedite Russo-Turkish reconciliation following the November 2015 shooting of a Russian SU-24.

In addition to Russia, Turkey has looked for rapprochement and increased strategic and economic cooperation with Iran. If this new configuration – Russia, Turkey and Iran – works effectively, these three nations could significantly reshape the strategic map of the Middle East without deferring to Washington. Russia has been the largest winner of the aftermath of the coup by repositioning itself as an honest broker vis-à-vis Turkey. Many Turks believe that the North Atlantic Treaty Organization (NATO) failed to support the democratic government in Turkey, nor has it done much to assist meaningfully in the struggle against both PKK and ISIS terrorism.

However, a Eurasian turn towards Russia also is problematic for Ankara. There are Turkey's memories of the Russian Empire seizing Ottoman territories in the Balkans and the Caucasus, and even in Anatolia. Forces from Moscow in the Caucasus and the Balkans were instrumental in the genocidal ethnic cleansing of the Ottoman-Muslim population of the region and Turks have neither forgotten nor forgiven Moscow's support or involvement in the recent genocidal onslaughts against Ottoman Muslim populations in Bosnia, Kosovo and Chechnya. It was as recent as the end of the Soviet Union in the early 1990s when the Russians were seen as Turkey's enemy. The relations between the two countries were also diametrically opposed in the Russian occupation of Crimea because Turkey supports the territorial integrity of Ukraine and rejects recognising Crimea as a part of Russia. Turkey also supports Azerbaijan's territorial integrity and keeps its border closed to Armenia due to its occupation of 20 per cent of Azerbaijani territories (returned to Azerbaijan after the Second Karabakh War in 2020). The largest impediment continues to be Russia's unstinting support for the genocidal minority regime of Assad in Syria.

There were also several foreign policy consequences flowing from the aborted coup attempt of July 2016. Its first impact was the rise of anti-Western, specifically anti-American, attitudes in the country. Many Turks have accused the US of masterminding the coup attempts. This accusation stems from the American role in past Turkish coups and especially the US acceptance of the Egyptian coup. The Turkish public believes that the US, like past Western imperialist powers, does not support democracy and economic development in the Muslim world but rather favours despotic client regimes in order to exploit the region and keep it fragmented. The fact that during the Obama administration, then Secretary of State John Kerry's initial reaction to the coup was not to defend Turkish democracy but, as in the case of Egypt, call for 'peace, continuity and stability', along with the dismissal of evidence that the Gülen movement was at the centre of the plot, also inflamed Turkish public opinion.[51] The surge in anti-Western sentiment is now widely shared. One poll found that 84 per cent of Turks believe that the coup plotters received help from abroad; more than 70 per cent suspect the US of having a hand.[52]

Tensions between Turkey and the US are likely to deepen, given the fact that the interests of the two countries do not overlap, especially as the US policy towards Turkey is generally an extension of its regional policy long-centred on serving Israeli interests and safeguarding energy resources. The US has never developed a policy specifically dedicated to transforming the structural–systemic causes of war and authoritarianism in the broader region in which Turkey is poised to play a central role in ameliorating given its historical and geopolitical weight in the region.[53] Instead, Turkey has been treated as a frontline state either against communism (1950–91), against Iran, or Iraq (1991–present). For example, it has been seen primarily as a military base (that is, İncirlik) in the war against ISIS. These regional conflicts have not presented a base for delineating common interests or values. Moreover, as noted before, so-called Turkey experts inside Washington tend to have a pronounced Israel-centric ideological bias and remain largely ignorant of the evolving internal dynamics of Turkish state and society, not least because they have limited linguistic–cultural expertise in carrying out serious field work in the country.[54]

Turkey, for her part, as the emerging regional power, is no longer interested in serving as a US client state but as a regional power seeking to bring order and development to a region deliberately fragmented by post-Sykes–Picot Western imperial politics and interventions. The US needs Turkey's cooperation in the fight against ISIS and broader concerns for regional stability, while the EU needs Turkey to help stem the flow of Syrian and Iraqi refugees and to provide balance against a revanchist Russia. Turkey, as the seventeenth largest economy in the world and as the historic pre-eminent and re-emerging Muslim power, retains the capacity to significantly shape global balances of power and one ignores it or treats it with disdain at one's own peril.

9.6 Conclusion

Turkey's foreign policy's effectiveness depends upon the context in which it is viewed. At one time, it was autonomous of Turkey's daily political debates and was conducted by an experienced, professional diplomatic corps. Erdoğan essentially has no foreign policy but only domestic policy to keep himself in power, control the resources and criminalise his opponents. Thus, the lines have been blurred between both realms of policy.

Turkey occasionally is described as gloomy, as becoming more like Pakistan, in which there is a growing Islamic nature and influence in the operations of the state's security services.[55] The AKP has focused on Islamic issues, becoming the champion of Islamic causes from Burma to Bosnia; from Kashmir to Palestine; from the Moro Liberation movement in the Philippines to mosque building in sub-Saharan Africa. Due to his criticism of the military coup in Egypt, which resulted in the overthrow of Mohamed Morsi as president, Erdoğan soon became the new popular figure on Arab streets, as Turkey turned itself into the hub of the Muslim Brotherhood in the Arab world while allowing the opening of offices to a multitude of Islamic groups within its borders. It offers safe haven for many leaders and thinkers in the Muslim world, a fact not in contradiction with its Ottoman past. Abdulhamid II also welcomed Islamic thinkers (that is, al-Afghani, and Muslim political refugees).

Erdoğan's policies have been criticised consistently by Kemal Kılıçdaroğlu, the head of Turkey's biggest opposition party, the Republican People's Party (CHP). Kılıçdaroğlu said:

> Erdoğan's real aim is to take Turkey out of the Western bloc, out of the civilized world, and to turn Turkey into a Middle Eastern country where he can continue to rule without any obstacles. He wants to turn Turkey into a country where there is no secularism and where people are divided along their ethnic identity and their beliefs. It is becoming a nation that faces internal conflict, just as we have seen in Iraq, Syria or Libya.[56]

In the new decade, which coincides with the forthcoming centennial of the founding of the Turkish Republic, the question is how long Erdoğan will remain in power, and what are the risks of permanent damage to the state's constitutional integrity if his powers continue to expand without checks or balances.

Notes

1. Yavuz, *Nostalgia for the Empire*.
2. Haugom, 'Turkish foreign policy under Erdoğan', pp. 206–23. This article examines the sources of the change in the foreign policy of Turkey after Erdoğan became president in 2014.
3. Kramer and Mellen, 'Turkish president Erdoğan calls Dutch "Nazi remnants"', 13 March 2017; Osborne, 'Erdoğan has called Europe "the racist, fascists and tyrannical"', 22 March 2017.
4. Sevinç, 'Ingiltere, Fransa, Almanya ve Şahsı üzerine', 12 December 2019.
5. For the theoretical debate between 'caution' and 'daring' in Turkish foreign policy, see Mufti, *Daring and Caution in Turkish Strategic Culture*, pp. 1–8, 17–28. Erdoğan's foreign policy has been more daring and aggressively assertive. Turkey shot down a Russian plane in November 2015; organised a major military intervention into northern Syria, known as Operation Euphrates Shield in August 2016, and Operation Olive Branch in January 2018. In 2020, Erdoğan sent troops to Libya to change the balance of power in favour of the Sarraj government. Turkey has also been very assertive in the Mediterranean Sea. Moreover, Turkey has major military bases in Somalia and Qatar, and is actively involved in the training of Azerbaijani troops.
6. Önsoy, 'Caught on the horns of a diplomatic dilemma', p. 259.
7. Demirtaş, 'Explained: AKP fails to keep unity over corruption', 21 January 2015; Ayasun, 'Egemen Bagis the ambassador exposes moral rot in Turkey's diplomatic service', 14 November 2019.
8. *Reuters*, 'Turkey's Erdoğan links fate of detained US pastor to wanted cleric Gülen', 28 September 2017.
9. Schenkkan, 'Turkey's new foreign policy is hostage-taking', 2 March 2019; Yücel, 'Inside and outside: on the 100th day of Deniz Yucel's imprisonment', 24 May 2017.
10. The Turks voted for the plan and the Greek side voted against the unification on 21 April 2004. Only the Greek Cypriot part of the island joined the EU.
11. For more on the political history of the Cypriot conflict, see Mehmet, *Sustainability of Microstates*, pp. 1–39.
12. *The Annan Plan*, 'The comprehensive settlement of the Cyprus problem', available at <http://www.hri.org/docs/annan/Annan_Plan_April2004.pdf> (last accessed 26 November 2020).

13. When Nicolas Sarkozy, as a term president of the EU, mediated the Russian occupation of Georgian territories, he failed to force Russia to withdraw and instead demanded that Georgia sign on the Russian terms. This was a clear sign to Ankara that the EU has no teeth or vision to solve any conflict.
14. *Le Monde*, 8 November 2002. Many European leaders argue that 'Turkey has no place in Europe' and that admitting Turkey to the EU would mark the 'end of Europe'. These statements are made by former German Chancellor Helmut Kohl in *The Guardian*, 7 March 1997.
15. For the statements of Stoiber, see *The Guardian*, 27 November 2002.
16. Baldwin, 'Blair promotes Turkish EU membership', 20 January 2007.
17. Vaisse, 'Slamming the *Sublime Porte*? Challenges in French–Turkish relations from Chirac to Sarkozy', 6 December 2007; Bilefsky, 'Sarkozy blocks key part of EU entry talks on Turkey', 25 June 2007.
18. Bernard, 'Quotes from, and about Nicolas Sarkozy', 7 May 2007.
19. Vaisse, 'Slamming the *Sublime Porte*?', p. 8.
20. *Reuters*, 'Merkel says still against Turkey joining the EU', 8 October 2015. For Merkel's earlier statements on privilege membership, see Guttenberg, 'Preserving Europe: offer Turkey a "privileged partnership" instead', 15 December 2004. See also Altay, 'Toward a "Privileged Partnership"', pp. 179–98.
21. Pope, 'Privileged Partnership offers Turkey neither privilege nor partnership'.
22. Zand, 'The Anatolian Tiger: how the West is losing Turkey', 15 June 2010.
23. Mikhelidze, 'The Turkish–Armenian rapprochement at the deadlock', 5 March 2010.
24. Filkins, 'Threats and responses: Ankara; Turkish deputies refuse to accept American troops', 2 March 2003.
25. *Hürriyet*, 'Wolfowitz: Accept your mistake, our partnership shall continue', 7 May 2003.
26. The worst confrontation which took place between the US and Turkish military was on 4 July 2003, when American soldiers raided the Turkish military post in Suleymania and hoods were placed on the heads of Turkish soldiers. This event, known as the 'hood incident', deepened the crisis between the two militaries. Howard and Goldberg, 'US arrest of soldiers infuriates Turkey', 7 July 2003.
27. *United Press International*, 'Hamas leaders visit Turkey', 16 February 2006.
28. Charlie Rose, 'Interview with Recep Tayyip Erdoğan', 22 September 2011, available at <https://www.youtube.com/watch?reload=9&v=N-v1tfGXY6U> (last accessed 26 November 2020).
29. Tocci and Walker, 'From confrontation to engagement', pp. 35–60.

30. The Israeli military destroyed the infrastructure of Gaza and indiscriminately bombed the civilian centres. The UN special mission to investigate the killings accused the Palestinian militants and the Israel Defence Forces of war crimes and possibly crimes against humanity. The government of Israel dismissed the report and refused to cooperate with the UN. BBC, 'The UN condemns the "war crimes" in Gaza', 16 September 2009.
31. *Al Arabiya*, 'Erdoğan hailed as new champion for Arabs who hope to emulate the Turkish model', 14 September 2011.
32. Interview with retired Turkish ambassador, NT, 12 June 2018.
33. Günay, 'The roles Turkey played in the Middle East', pp. 195–211.
34. Yavuz, 'Social and intellectual origins of neo-Ottomanism', pp. 438–65; Yanik, 'Bringing the empire back in', pp. 466–88.
35. Mufti, 'The AK Party's Islamist realist political vision', pp. 28–42.
36. See Ahmet Davutoğlu's interview with İbrahim Karagül, *Yeni Şafak*, 'Yüzyıllık parantezi kapatacağız', 1 March 2013. See also Yeşiltaş, 'The transformation of the geopolitical vision', p. 678. Yeşiltaş is the leading security expert of the Foundation for Political, Economic and Social Research (known as SETA). This foundation is funded by the AKP government and its function is to justify the policies of Erdoğan.
37. d'Alema, 'The evolution of Turkey's Syria policy', 17 October 2017.
38. Insel, 'Tarihi rövanş hırsı ve muhafazakâr restorasyon', 21 June 2016.
39. *The Economist*, 'The Arab road', 4 January 2014.
40. Istanbul has become the headquarters of the Muslim Brotherhood and this, in turn, has angered many Arab governments.
41. 'Readout of the president's call with Prime Minister Erdoğan of Turkey', *The White House Archives – President Barack Obama*, 11 August 2011, available at <https://obamawhitehouse.archives.gov/the-press-office/2011/08/11/readout-presidents-call-prime-minister-Erdo%C4%9Fan-turkey> (last accessed 26 November 2020)
42. Myers, 'US and allies say Syria leader must step down', 18 August 2011; Burch, 'Turkey tells Syria's Assad: Step down!', 22 November 2011.
43. In order to avoid Turkish criticism of working together with the terrorist organisation, the PKK, a Kurdish nationalist-secessionist group, designated as a terrorist organisation by Washington, a new name was invented for the YPG: the Syrian Democratic Forces. However, the group remained overwhelmingly Kurdish and maintained its ties with the PKK.
44. BBC, 'Kobane: US drops arms and aid to Kurds battling IS', 20 October 2014.

45. Erdoğan said: 'I hope the new Egyptian regime will be secular', adding that while he personally was a Muslim, the nation which he headed was a secular one. 'I recommend a secular constitution for Egypt', declared Erdoğan, emphasising that secularism was not an 'enemy of religion'. *Hürriyet Daily News*, 'If only Morsi had listened to Erdoğan', 29 August 2013; *Al Arabiya*, 'Egypt's Muslim Brotherhood criticizes Erdogan's call for a secular state', 14 September 2011.
46. Beck, 'Turkey's global soft-power push is built on mosques', 1 June 2019.
47. Erbakan, *Erbakan Kulliyatı*.
48. In his speech on July 11 to reconvert the Hagia Sophia into a mosque, Erdoğan said: 'The resurrection of Hagia Sophia heralds the liberation of Al-Aqsa Mosque', available at <https://www.jpost.com/middle-east/turkey-vows-to-liberate-al-aqsa-after-turning-hagia-sophia-to-mosque-634700> (last accessed 26 November 2020).
49. BBC, 'Qatar's emir "gives $500 m private jet to Turkey"', 17 September 2018.
50. Đidić and Kösebalabanh, 'Turkey's rapprochement with Russia', pp. 123–38.
51. Luttwak, 'Why Turkey's *coup d'état* failed', 16 July 2016.
52. *The Economist*, 'Turkish anger at the West: duplicity coup', 20 August 2016.
53. Yavuz and Khan, 'Turkey asserts its role in the region', 11 February 2015.
54. A telling example of such limited and Israel-centric 'expertise' on Turkey is evidenced by Cook and Koplow, 'Turkey is no longer a reliable ally', 10 August 2016. For more on the article of Koplow, see <https://www.foreignaffairs.com/authors/michael-j-koplow> (last accessed 26 November 2020).
55. Yildirim, 'The reality of Turkey's Pakistanization', 17 March 2017.
56. Trofimov, 'Turkey's autocratic turn', 9 December 2016.

CONCLUSION

Far from being a selective and gradual process, instead Turkey's westernisation was a holistic undertaking with the ultimate goal of becoming fully Europeanised. This imitation was no casual choice, but rather a deliberate one, seen as an existential necessity for a sovereign state hoping to protect and preserve the rest of the Muslim population of Anatolia. Although some nationalists and Kemalists have insisted that this project was a process of self-discovery, in fact it risked the self-annihilation of an Islamo-Ottoman identity. The Kemalist version of imitative modernisation was the outcome of a justifiable fear of being further partitioned by the major European powers. Westernisation *in toto* was based on survival. In fact, many Kemalists, especially those observed at the Mekteb-i Mülkiye (the Faculty of Political Science at the University of Ankara), were similar to Naipaul's characterisation of the 'supreme mimic man'. They believed that 'we never are what we want to be . . . but what we must be.'[1] In fact, westernisation was a process of borrowing and learning to live within a borrowed culture. It was a simultaneous process of voluntary self-annihilation and self-discovery.

Erdoğan's democratic image is likewise an incomplete imitation where he has never sincerely understood the core meaning of democracy. He has treated it as a necessary vehicle, or as he calls it a 'train', to arrive at his authoritarian destination. As a political chameleon, his character has always adapted to the external pressures and internal needs in order to suit his purpose at a given moment, which always entails accumulating more power and control for himself. What has become apparent in 2021 is that Erdoğan acted outwardly as a democrat but internally remained a committed autocrat, and as soon as the constraints were removed, his true inner autocratic identity shined. One aim in this book is to explore whether this broad project of imitation is a casual choice, a necessity, or a means of survival for the key characters. Does imitation of this sort imply a simulation of self-discovery and ultimate self-annihilation? Can the characters create something new or just be satisfied with imitation alone, thereby perpetuating the sense of living in the illusion of a constructed reality that serves the limits of one's selfish interests, which reach no further than one individual and the narrowest of the elite class?

In this book I have examined the three stages defining the Erdoğan era: the first encompasses the rise of the powerful AKP and coordinated leadership of Abdullah Gül, Abdullatif Şener and Bülent Arınç (2001–7); the second signifies an alliance with the Gülen movement to destroy the Kemalist establishment, especially the military (2007–13); and the third and current indicates the emergence of the autocrat Erdoğan who embodies the party and equates himself to the state (2013–present). Yet, each stage has its own dominant discourse. For instance, the first, in which the AKP sought to establish internal and external legitimacy, the dialogue was dominated by the concepts of democracy, the rule of law, human rights. The AKP had a clear path committed to joining the EU. Erdoğan and his colleagues stressed the fact that they had shed their previous Islamist ideology and had now become born-again Europhiles and recovering Islamists, with the goal of making Turkey a full member of the EU. Erdoğan portrayed himself as pro-Western, emphasising the concept of conservative democracy as the identity of the party to distance itself from Islamism. This moderation was the outcome of the February 28 process, the still prevailing Kemalist establishment, and the balance of forces within the AKP itself, and an ongoing search for internal and external political legitimacy. During this period, Erdoğan and his colleagues' primary domestic goal was the promotion of economic liberalisation and the rebuilding of the economy's infrastructure.

The second stage was shaped by confrontations between the AKP and the Kemalist establishment. These confrontations not only compelled Erdoğan to ally with the Gülen movement but also start to recall his Islamist identity into the public sphere. The string of events included the 2007 presidential election crisis, republican rallies, the Constitutional Court decision to penalise the AKP for charges of violating the principles of secularism of the state, the Balyoz and Ergenekon cases involving the military by using the courts, the 'one-minute incident' at the 2009 Wolrd Economic Forum in Davos, the 2010 Mavi Marmara assult, and the 2011 Arab Spring movement. All of these events aggravated and deepened Erdogan's anxieties and insecurity and he subsequently allowed the Gülen community to protect itself against the Kemalist establishment.

The Gülenists opened a multifront assault against the Kemalist establishment and gradually gained control of state institutions. Erdoğan dropped the rhetoric of democracy, civil society and the EU, and brought out his old Islamist cloak from the closet which he dusted off and donned. His political discourse was increasingly punctuated by Islam, especially with flighty homages to Islamic – read Ottoman – civilisation. For instance, on 30 September 2012, then prime minister, Erdoğan spoke at the AKP's Fourth Ordinary Grand Convention. His speech highlighted the transformation of his new political language. In this speech, he used the term 'our [Islamic] civilisation' thirteen times as signifying the core of values and spirit of the nation. His speech focused on Islamic values and Islamic civilisation and hardly mentioned the EU or the discourse of human rights. In the same speech, Erdoğan reminded the audience of the importance of a shared Islamic past and stressed the common mission of the Turks and Kurds. He stressed the promises of a 2071 vision – which reminded the people of the 1000th anniversary of the Battle of Manzikert – and emphasised the Islamisation of Anatolia as the key mission of the 1071 battle. So this speech not only represented a break from the rhetoric of democracy, the rule of law and the EU orientation, but it also dropped the appearance of being the party of *service* (that is, improving economy and life standards of the citizens) and replaced it by becoming the party of *mission* (*dava*) to 'make Turkey great again' and to lead the Muslim world.[2]

The third stage (2013–present) is the most significant because the party has become fully assimilated into the body of Erdoğan and he has become the autocrat and the party itself. This period was triggered by his fear of being caught up in charges of corruption and experiencing the same fate of Muhamed Morsi in Egypt. The Gezi Park incident and the corruption probes only served to enhance his paranoia. External events such as the overthrow of Morsi, the Russian intervention in the Syrian civil war, the PKK/PYD efforts to open a corridor in northern Syria, and the US support for the PYD to fight against ISIS all pushed Erdoğan to centralise his power on unconditional terms. During this period, his discourse turned increasingly nationalistic and even at times fascist in tone. He stressed the native (*yerli*) and national (*milli*) values and discourses. This became the period dominated by the Rabaa sign: one nation, one flag, one homeland, one state, and all these represented by Erdogan as a *başyüce*.[3]

Erdoğan used the seduced coup of July 2016 not to underscore native-national policies and orientation but instead to build a new national spirit at the Yenikapı Convention, which took place after the coup to demonstrate national unity and solidarity. Because of Erdoğan's transformation as a nationalist, Devlet Bahçeli decided to support Erdoğan's vision of establishing a Turkish style presidential system (that is, reincarnation of the Ottoman sultan). Erdoğan's following statement sums up the political language of this stage:

> Although the AKP is a seventeen-year-old movement, we represent a glorious Islamic civilisation. As you all know now, we are the only one who represents this Islamic civilisation, which has one eye in the past and another in the future. Our movement and mission spring from Mount Hira, Manzikert, Dumlupınar, Sakarya and Çanakkale . . . As you all know, we are the grandchildren of Sultan Mehmed the Conquerer. It was the Conquerer, who, at the age of twenty-one, said, 'Either I shall take Byzantium or it shall take me.' Indeed, we still represent that Islamic civilisation and we belive that there is no victor but God.[4]

Erdoğan has appropriated the language of Islamism, nationalism and communitarian nativism to justify his authoritrian rule and widespread kleptocratic practices. He unquestionably has put his personal interests before that of his nation and citizens, thereby opening the door to unchecked abuses.

Erdoğan has destroyed several myths which have dominated scholarly assumptions about Turkey. The first of these shattered myths was that the democratisation of Turkey requires the withdrawal of the military and the empowerment of civilian politicians. Many scholars explained the lack of democratisation in Turkey by the overly powerful position of the military within the country.⁵ They suggested that Turkey could only become more democratic if, and only if, the military was forced out of the political domain and its power radically curtailed. In reality the military's involvement in politics is indeed against democratic principles, but as the Turkish military was forced out of state institutions and eventually became weaker in its ability to shape political affairs, this process did not lead to consolidation of democracy but rather Turkey has ended up with the most oppressive illiberal democracy in the history of the Republic, arguably much worse than even the aftermath of any of the military coups. In fact, as of 2019, Turkey has not become a democratic state after the military's political role was demolished and its rank and file demoralised. Rather, Turkey has been sliding towards a textbook case of an authoritarian state and a government of kleptocracy.⁶

The Turkish military, self-appointed guardians of the Kemalist ideology, along with the judiciary, were all instrumental in constraining majoritarian democracy by stressing the rule of law. As soon as he realised that these checks and balances constricted his own ambitions, Erdoğan loathed them. He destroyed the parliamentary system and built a neo-patrimonial '*àlla Turca*' presidential system defined by kleptocracy, intolerance and obsequiousness. Moreover, it was Erdoğan who reconstituted the AKP in his own image by ordering the purge of its key members such as Abdullah Gül, Besir Atalay and Ali Babacan. As of 2019, the AKP has become impotent in Erdoğan's shadow; in effect, it has been turned into an ineffective empty shell to keep Erdoğan in power. Erdoğan never had any commitment to institutions or norms but rather he placed his beliefs in personal enrichment and the idea that the ends justify the means. In fact, Erdoğan, not unlike the absolutist monarch Louis XIV, believes that he 'is the State' ('*L'État, c'est moi*'). After purging key personalities of the AKP such as Gül, Şener, Davutoğlu and Babacan, he envisioned himself as embodying the nation and the state, and his policies, respectively, as the will of the people. Within this thinking, the normalising boundary between the state and society has been replaced by one segregating his unconditional loyalists and those who dare oppose or challenge his power or governing strategy. The latter group encompasses secularists, the Other (*bunlar*) and aliens as illegitimate members of the nation, as he perceives it. That is, only the former group (the loyalists) are full-fledged members of the Turkish nation, in his mind.

Ominously, the Venice Commission, an advisory body of constitutional law experts under the Council of Europe, has described a 'dramatic decline in the standard of democracy' in Turkey and pointed out that the proposed changes to the constitution would lead Turkey to 'an autocracy and a one-person regime'.[7] By utilising the post-coup political environment, Erdoğan has entirely ignored all these criticisms and organised a neither free nor fair referendum to force his new constitution through. After the coup attempt, Erdoğan freed himself from the shackles of the Constitutional Court and the parliament by declaring a state of emergency. With these decrees, he created a legal framework for one-man rule by undermining the rule of law and state institutions, and creating an obedient political structure.

Today, Turkey has an autocratic constitution which empowers the executive, in the person of Erdoğan, at the expense of all other branches of government. During the referendum campaign, held under a state of emergency, Erdoğan mobilised all of the resources of the government, including its finances and its power over the media, to promote the 'Yes' campaign, while working to intimidate and disrupt the opposition. Over the course of the nine months after the state of emergency was imposed following the seduced coup of July 2016, Erdoğan shuttered scores of opposition media outlets and jailed thousands of people, including thirteen MPs of the pro-Kurdish Peoples' Democratic Party (HDP) and some 150 journalists for suspected links to terrorist organisations. No leader in the history of Turkey has criminalised the opposition to such an extent as Erdoğan has. Timothy Ash summed up the changes in the following way:

> The repertoire of this new generation of authoritarians is by now familiar. You control the media through the oligarchs and business conglomerates that own them. You [then] knit a patchwork quilt of elastic legal provisions under which you can prosecute almost anyone.[8]

The second myth now debunked by Erdoğan's stint in power was that Islam is the cohesive moral bond of the Turkish society. Although Erdoğan framed Islam as a 'cement' for the ethnically diverse (Turkish and Kurdish) Muslim communities, he has failed miserably to assimilate and contain the Kurdish political demands within Islam. Erdoğan has never fully grasped the power of ethnicity. In the hands of Erdoğan, Islam is an instrument to hold on to power and cover up corrupt practices. As Erdoğan successfully expanded his power and sidelined the military from politics, bottled up the judiciary and won the first popular election for presidency, he adopted a different course of governance by cracking down on dissent, criminalising his opponents and intimidating the news media.[9]

Religion, for Erdoğan, was a rug under which he could sweep his kleptocratic practices away from the attention of his followers. He thus instrumentalised Islam to mobilise the masses and seek personal gain. In other words, Erdoğan reduced the profound teachings and moral vision of Islam into insipid political slogans to mould state and society according to his whims. The worst impact of his Islamisation policy has been in the domain of education. The education system under the AKP governments went through several transformations and has been constantly underfunded, although now mandated with heavy doses of religious instruction at every level.

The government has limited the number of secular schools and turned almost all those schools owned by the Gülen movement into İmam Hatips. The stated goal of the education system has been to raise a 'pious generation'. Ceylan Yeginsu, the leading investigative journalist of *The New York Times*, argues that the İmam Hatip schools have

> seen a sharp rise in [their numbers] . . . under the leadership of Mr Erdoğan, himself an İmam Hatip graduate. At a recent school inauguration, he celebrated the fact that enrollment in the schools had jumped to almost a million from just 63,000 during his 12 years in power.[10]

Today, religious instruction starts as early as six years old and takes place at every level of the educational curriculum. The education system in Turkey today is much worse than any OECD country, especially in mathematics, biology and physics. Critical thinking has more or less been removed from both high school and university education and is negatively viewed by the system.

Erdoğan's Islam or Islamism are divorced from morality and both are treated as an instrument of power. In fact, Islam, for Erdoğan, comprises a set of ideals, goals and practices on how to keep power within his own grip and how to manipulate and mobilise public opinion, while drawing on and preserving Turko-Ottoman Islamic culture and tradition. It is more about his personal power and enrichment and less about the interests of Turkey. Yet, Erdoğan is a skilled politician who knows the emotional codes and signals of his people. He is in touch with the religio-national instincts of the majority of the Turkish population, especially the more conservative rural masses. Just like ordinary Turks, Erdoğan is aware of (although not necessarily educated on) the past of the Ottoman Empire and the way in which it was partitioned by the major European powers. His uncomplicated vision of the past and his heady aspirations for the future resonate with ordinary Turks. Islam in Turkey is a repository not just of past mistakes and deep wounds but also the emotions, habits and ideals of a country. Erdoğan believes that a more democratic (by which he means majoritarian democracy) Turkey might be a more conservative (Islamic) state. By understanding Erdoğan and his worldview, we might come to decipher Turkey's strengths, weaknesses and fault lines. It took a long time for Erdoğan to understand and appreciate the concept of the state in Turkish political culture. He, just like most Turks, stressed the need for a strong state to protect Turkey and its religion against real and imaginary internal and external enemies. Also, Erdoğan and many Turks believe that Turkey must be a great regional power, not because of its economic or military strength but because of its Ottoman past, which implies some sort of vaunted destiny.

If the democratisation of Turkey was the first myth shattered by Erdoğan, the third myth is that the problems of Turkey all originated in the strict ideology of Kemalism and as soon as Kemalism was removed Turkey would become more democratic and civic, and would learn to recognise and take pride in its diversity.[11] Atatürk transformed the truncated remains of the Ottoman Empire into a new secular (Western) nation state. Atatürk was determined to overcome the economic and social backwardness of the Ottoman past through a forced modernisation project for Turkey. He was a Jacobin modernist who wanted to create a modern society free of religion. He said:

> I have no religion, and at times I wish all religions at the bottom of the sea. He is a weak ruler who needs religion to uphold his government; it is as if he would catch his people in a trap. My people are going to learn the principles of republicanism, the dictates of truth and the teaching of science. Superstition must go.[12]

Contrary to Atatürk's expectations, as Turkey modernised under Kemalism, religion was moved to the forefront of public life with a vengeance. With the advent of AKP power, however, Erdoğan reproduced Islam and its role in politics to consolidate his authoritarian rule. He mobilised the deep sense of the grievance of the Anatolian people, which is not unfamiliar throughout the Muslim world, that the Ottoman Empire, as an Islamic power, was destroyed by Western imperialist powers. This deep sense of victimhood is the driving force for revanchist feelings throughout the country, and Erdoğan has never hesitated to exploit these past wounds of the Muslims. As a first-rate political demagogue, he has shamelessly polarised society and attacked the shared values and memories of the people in order to keep himself in power. While he claims that Muslims are incapable of carrying out a genocide, he calls on the opposition party, the CHP, to confront its genocidal campaigns against the Kurdish Alevis.[13] No political leader in Turkey has cheapened the moral concepts held by society as much as Erdoğan. From his perspective, the Christian West has been responsible for the failures of Muslim countries. He represents the strong residue of anti-Western sentiment remaining among the Anatolian population nostalgic for the grandeur of the Ottoman Empire.

The fourth myth debunked by Erdoğan is that Islamically oriented politicians are more ethical and less prone to corruption. Erdoğan talks the rhetoric of restoring the dignity of Muslims, distribution of resources, and the establishment of a moral and just system. And yet his entire term in power is punctuated by the destruction of the rule of law and the dignity of innocent people, jailing large numbers of journalists and opponents, and the corrupting of the state by himself and his ministers. He talks about the oppression of Palestinians, Muslims in Myanmar, or in Kashmir (even though he fails to be the champion for the oppressed Uighurs, as it would entail butting heads with China), but he denies the basic rights of the Kurds, jails his opponents and destroys the dignity of ordinary (Muslim) citizens. He has hardly developed a meaningful idea as to how to solve the sufferings of Muslim communities in the region. Yet, he wants to be the leader and the voice of the Sunni Muslim world and accuses the Kingdom of Saudi Arabia of being a divisive force in the Muslim world. Erdoğan talks about the security of the state, but he is more worried about the security of his regime and denies any form of democracy within his own party. Erdoğan's construction of a giant new

1,000-room palace in the Beştepe district of Ankara further convinced the public, and even many AKP voters, that the 2013 corruption charges might have been true. The cost of the palace, approximately $620 million, was the major subject of an embarrassing debate in the run-up to the elections.[14] Some Islamic groups who stress the ethical aspect of religion have sharply criticised Erdoğan's kleptocratic practices as non-Islamic and destructive for the understanding of religion in Turkish society.

Erdoğan's crony capitalism has moved Turkey from a system of market economy to one of kleptocracy. This version of kleptocracy, however, is ironically legitimated and justified by some prominent Islamic scholars such as Hayrettin Karaman.[15] Thus, Erdoğan has managed to nurture and legitimise an 'Islamic kleptocracy' under a religious shawl. He has successfully dismantled some secular-oriented business leaders and created his own Islamic-shaped oligarchy (that is, groups of business leaders enriched through public procurement). His economic policies have hampered real and sustainable growth and creative entrepreneurship, and have hurt Turkey's image abroad as a safe place to do business. The Turkish state has been captured by a small group of business executives and politicians who support Erdoğan. Erdoğan and this group's only objective has been their own enrichment at the expense of the state and society. They use Islam and Islamic issues to cover their kleptocratic practices. What bonds the people around Erdoğan is not ideals but rather a hunger to feed at the state trough. Corruption has become the new glue of this mafia-like group to use their resources to criminalise the opposition and silence critical voices. Erdoğan's working strategy is to get those who work for him to be his accomplices in crime, as everyone gets muddied in it and no one can point an unsullied finger.

After the July 2016 coup attempt, Erdoğan began harassing his opponents, seizing their properties and banning alternative news outlets. The reputation of Turkey's rule of law and stability has been further undermined as Erdoğan ordered the state agencies to arrest hundreds of businessmen and seize more than 600 companies – with assets in excess of $10 billion – suspected of Gülenist sympathies. On 5 February 2018, Erdoğan established the Sovereign Wealth Fund, into which billions of dollars in the Turkish treasury's stakes in blue-chip companies were to be transferred. On the fund's board is Yigit Bulut, an adviser who once warned that Erdoğan may be targeted for assassination by telekinesis. Its assets would be used to raise funds for what Erdoğan has described as his 'crazy projects', such as the landscape-changing infrastructure works that have marked much of his premiership: the world's largest airport, a canal to rival the Bosporus and high-speed railways. These government bids are given to those who either support Erdoğan or to companies in which Erdoğan owns a stake. The *Financial Times* has regularly criticised the grab of private property in Turkey:

> Now, with Mr Gülen and his followers declared terrorists, their businesses belong to the state, to be auctioned to bidders eager to proclaim their loyalty to Mr Erdoğan. Galip Ozturk, owner of a bus company with a market capitalisation of about $100m, aims to bid for the assets of Koza Ipek, a conglomerate whose listed units once had a market cap of nearly $6bn. His biggest qualification: his desire to please Mr Erdoğan and to do his will, he bragged to local media.[16]

Under Erdoğan's rule, the Public Procurement Law (PPL) went through 150 amendments to, in essence, legalise such corruption and kleptocracy.[17] The public procurement process – the purchase of goods and services, such as roads, schools, social housing, electricity, airports and hospital buildings – by the central government from the private sector is the key path to corruption under Erdoğan government. The assumption that a pro-Islamic party would be cleaner and more just has been tested under Erdoğan and it is possible to conclude that Turkey has never seen such widespread corruption at every level of the state. Billions of dollars were wasted on Erdoğan's infamous megaprojects and these projects all had one aim: transfer wealth to a new economic crony class. The transfer of wealth to those who support Erdoğan's regime, and in some cases to companies in which Erdoğan has been a partner, managed to legalise the corruption by amending the PPL to carry out their corrupt practices. Not more than fifteen companies received the lion's share of these lucrative public contracts.

Finally, there is another shattered myth: many believe that dictators rule despite their population; if the masses were given the opportunity, they would vote against these quasi-fascist and corrupt regimes. This assumption is not true for many countries, in particular in the era of populism, especially in Turkey. Erdoğan's regime was not imposed on the people but rather jointly constructed by him and a large sector of the conservative Muslim Turkish citizenry, themselves. Erdoğan is more or less synonymous for this large sector of the population. He has managed to produce a shared fiction for his followers. With movies and public spectacle, Erdoğan takes conservative Turks on a glorious journey away from their current humiliating conditions. We also need to think not about 'Erdoğan's Turkey' but more so about 'Turkey's Erdoğan', because there are deep organic sources to support Erdoğan-like populist leaders.

Erdoğan has been the most polarising personality in the history of Turkish politics. Moreover, he is the most authoritarian, ruthless and reckless leader in recent history. The main characteristic of his politics is that everything for him is transactional. There is no loyalty but rather how 'useful' one can be. His liberal ex-allies have criticised him for promoting corruption, destroying the free media and established institutions, creating a police state, and Islamising the society and the state simultaneously. They claim that they just now realised that Erdoğan had a secret agenda to enrich himself with state resources, and use Islam to cover up his corrupt practices. The Kurds also accuse Erdoğan of 'using them' and in reality 'seeking to deny their national rights by empty talk of "Islamic brotherhood"'. Moreover, as a result of Erdoğan's policies, today Kurdish identity has been dehumanised; it has once again become 'shameful' and 'risky' to claim Kurdishness. Furthermore, Turkey's Alevi community has also been marginalised, persecuted and in essence forced to become Sunni as a result of mandatory religious education in schools.

To conclude, Erdoğan has been the most consequential leader of modern Turkish history. He has destroyed the Kemalist state institutions, especially the military and the judiciary, and created a kleptocratic authoritarian political system. It will not be easy for Turkey to rebuild what Erdoğan has dismantled. The Turkish state needs to prioritise societal reconciliation and act within the rule of law in order to unify the divided country. Turkey's geostrategic location at the crossroads of East and West will always give the country great importance, as seen in the current competition over energy routes, and thus no competing centres of global power can afford to alienate it. For Turkey to survive in this sensitive region, it needs powerful institutions. Today, Turkey is morally naked and politically weak. The chaos in Turkey will have a seismic impact on the EU and the balance of power in the Middle East and Eurasia.

Notes

1. Naipaul, *Three Novels*, p. 55.
2. Erdoğan, 'Address to the AK Party's 4th Ordinary Grand Convention', 30 September 2012.
3. The Rabaa sign was originally invented to support the resistance of the Egyptian people to the Sisi regime.
4. Erdoğan, 'Genel Başkan ve Cumhurbaşkanı Recep Tayyip Erdoğan, Yenikent Spor Salonu'nda düzenlenen Eskişehir 6. Olağan İl Kongresi'nde partililere hitap etti' (speech, 17 February 2018).
5. Sakallioglu, 'The anatomy of the Turkish military's political autonomy', pp. 151–66.
6. Başer and Öztürk, *Authoritarian Politics in Turkey*; Tziarras, 'Erdoğanist authoritarianism and the "new" Turkey', pp. 593–8.
7. For more on the Venice Commission's report on the constitutional changes in Turkey, see <http://www.venice.coe.int/webforms/events/?id=2369> (last accessed 27 November 2020). The commission made the following conclusions:
    - letting the new President exercise executive power alone, with unsupervised authority to appoint and dismiss ministers, and to appoint and dismiss all high officials on the basis of criteria determined by him or her alone
    - allowing the President to be a member and even the leader of his or her political party, that would give him or her undue influence over the legislature
    - giving the President the power to dissolve parliament on any grounds whatsoever, which is fundamentally alien to democratic presidential systems
    - further weakening the already inadequate system of judicial oversight of the executive
    - further weakening the independence of the judiciary.
8. Garton Ash, 'As Erdoğan turns the screw, we must stand up for human rights in Turkey', 2 March 2017.
9. Arsu, 'In push against Muslim cleric, Turkey detains police officers and journalists', 14 December 2014.
10. Yeginsu, 'Turkey promotes religious schools, often defying parents', 16 December 2017.
11. For a succinct summary of this myth, see Aytürk, 'Post-post-Kemalizm', pp. 34–48.
12. Ellison, *Turkey Today*, p. 24.
13. Ayata and Hakyemez, 'The AKP's engagement with Turkey's past crimes', pp. 131–43.

14. On the coverage of the new palace, see Arango, 'Turkish leader, using conflicts, cementing power', 31 October 2014; for a more critical review, see Mishra, 'The Western model is broken', 14 October 2014.
15. Karaman provides all necessary Islamic edicts (*fetwa*s) for Erdoğan to justfy his authoritarian and corrupt regime. Karaman also sits on numerous state-owned bank boards of directors. For more on Karaman and his corrupt practices, see Kenes, 'Instrumentalization of Islam: Hayrettin Karaman's role in Erdoğan's despotism', 30 July 2018; Kenez, 'Hired for religious fatwa: Erdogan's chief edict provider Hayrettin Karaman', 7 January 2019; Yenigün, 'Hayrettin Karaman'la "Laik Düzende Dini Yaşamak" yahut Siyaset Fıkhının Sınırları', pp. 203–10; Akyol, 'Erdoğan counts on Karaman's Islamic counsel', 29 January 2014.
16. Available at: <https://www.ft.com/content/6337eb16-f85a-11e6-bd4e-68d53499ed71#comments> (last accessed 27 November 2020).
17. For the best book on the corruption of the AKP government, see Esra Ceviker Gürakar, *Politics of Favoritism in Public Procurement in Turkey*.

BIBLIOGRAPHY

Abbas, Tahir (2017), Abbas, *Contemporary Turkey in Conflict: Ethnicity, Islam and Politics* (Edinburgh: Edinburgh University Press).

Ackerman, Xanthe and Ekin Calisir (2015), 'Erdoğan's assault on education: the closure of secular schools', *Foreign Affairs*, 23 December, <https://www.foreignaffairs.com/articles/turkey/2015-12-23/erdogans-assault-education> (last accessed 11 November 2020).

Aghaie Joobani, Hossein and Umut Can Adısönmez (2018), 'Turkey's volte-face politics: understanding the AKP's securitization policy toward the Syrian conflict', *New Middle Eastern Studies*, 8(1), pp. 42–62.

Akçalı, Cevdet (2004), 'Başbakan Erdoğan'ın bir itirafı, Türkiye'de kanunları kim yapıyor?', *Yeni Safak*, 27 July.

Akdoğan, Yalçın (2011), 'Dersim 2011', *Star*, 28 November.

Akdoğan, Yalçın (2014), 'Öcalan süreci doğru okuyor', *Al Jazeera Turk*, 7 June, <http://www.aljazeera.com.tr/haber/ocalan-sureci-daha-dogru-okuyor> (last accessed 25 November 2020).

AK Party (2004), *Uluslarası Muhafazakarlık ve Demokrasi Sempozyumu, 10–12 Oçak 2004* (Ankara: AK Parti).

Aksu, Fatma (1995), 'Kasımpaşa sokaklarından başkanlık koltuğuna', *Meydan*, 26 September–12 October.

Akyaz, Doğan (2002), *Askeri Müdahalelerin Orduya Etkisi, Hiyerarşi Dışı Örgütlenmeden Emir Komuta Zincirine* (Istanbul: İletişim Yayınları).

Akyol, Mustafa (2014), 'Erdoğan counts on Karaman's Islamic Counsel', *Al-Monitor*, January 29, <https://www.al-monitor.com/pulse/originals/2014/01/erdogan-karaman-counsel.html> (last accessed 27 November 2020).

Akyol, Mustafa (2015), 'Turkey's authoritarian drift', *The New York Times* 10 November, <https://www.nytimes.com/2015/11/11/opinion/turkeys-authoritarian-drift-election-erdogan.html> (last accessed 19 November 2020).

Al, Serhun (2015), 'An anatomy of nationhood and the question of assimilation: debates on Turkishness revisited', *Studies in Ethnicity and Nationalism*, 15, pp. 83–101.

Al, Serhun (2018), 'Human security versus national security: Kurds, Turkey and Syrian Rojava', in E. E. Tuğdar and S. Al (eds), *Comparative Kurdish Politics in the Middle East: Actors, Ideas, Interests* (New York: Palgrave), pp. 57–83.

Al, Serhun (2019), *Patterns of Nationhood and Saving the State in Turkey: Ottomanism, Nationalism and Multiculturalism* (New York: Routledge).

Al Arabiya (2011), 'Egypt's Muslim Brotherhood criticizes Erdogan's call for a secular state', 14 September, <http://www.alarabiya.net/articles/2011/09/14/166814.html> (last accessed 26 November 2020).

Al Arabiya (2011), 'Erdoğan hailed as new champion for Arabs who hope to emulate the Turkish model', 14 September, <http://www.alarabiya.net/articles/2011/09/14/166780.html> (last accessed 26 November 2020).

Al Jazeera Turk (2015), 'Ortak açıklamanın tam metni', 28 February, <http://www.aljazeera.com.tr/haber/ortak-aciklamanin-tammetni> (last accessed 25 November 2020).

Alaranta, Toni (2014), *Contemporary Kemalism: From Universal Secular-Humanism to Extreme Turkish Nationalism* (New York: Routledge).

Alaranta, Toni (2015), *National and State Identity in Turkey: The Transformation of the Republic's Status in the International System* (Lanham: Rowman & Littlefield).

d'Alema, Francesco (2017), 'The evolution of Turkey's Syria policy', *IAI Working Papers*, 17 October, <http://www.iai.it/sites/default/files/iaiwp1728.pdf> (last accessed 26 November 2020).

Alpan, Başak (2012), 'AKP's "conservative democracy" as an empty signifier in Turkish politics: shifts and challenges after 2002', IPSA 22nd World Congress of Political Science, 8–12 July.

Altay, Serdar (2018), 'Toward a "privileged partnership": the EU, Turkey and the upgrade of the customs union', *Insight Turkey*, 20(3), pp. 179–98.

Amnesty International (2016), 'Turkey: independent monitors must be allowed to access detainees amid torture allegations', <https://www.amnesty.org/en/latest/news/2016/07/turkey-independent-monitors-must-be-allowed-to-access-detainees-amid-torture-allegations/> (last accessed 20 November 2020).

Arango, Tim (2014), 'Turkish leader, using conflicts, cementing power, *The New York Times*, 31 October, <https://www.nytimes.com/2014/11/01/world/europe/erdogan-uses-conflict-to-consolidate-power.html> (last accessed 18 November 2020).

Arat, Yeşim and Şevket Pamuk (2019), *Turkey: Between Democracy and Authoritarianism* (New York: Cambridge University Press).

Armstrong, William (2017), 'The sultan and the sultan', 8 November, <https://armstrongwilliam.wordpress.com/2017/11/08/the-sultan-and-the-sultan/> (last accessed 16 November 2020).

Arsu, Sebnem (2014), 'In push against Muslim cleric, Turkey detains police officers and journalists', *The New York Times*, 14 December, <https://www.nytimes.com/2014/12/15/world/europe/turkish-police-officers-and-media-workers-are-detained-in-roundup.html> (last accessed 27 November 2020).

Atasoy, Yildiz (2003), 'Cosmopolitan Islamists in Turkey: rethinking the local in a global era', *Studies in Political Economy*, 71/72, pp. 133–61.

Atay, Fatih Rıfkı (1943), *Zetindağı* (Istanbul: Remzi Kitapevi).

Avcı, Arife (1998), 'Erdoğan: Plaka Okusam da Suçlanırdım', *Milliyet*, 9 October.

Ayasun, Abdullah (2019), 'Egemen Bagis the ambassador exposes moral rot in Turkey's diplomatic service', *Medium*, 14 November, <https://abyasun.medium.com/egemen-bagis-the-ambassador-exposes-moral-rot-in-turkeys-diplomatic-service-cb17277c87a> (last accessed 25 November 2020).

Ayata, Bilgin and Serra Hakyemez (2013), 'The AKP's engagement with Turkey's past crimes: an analysis of PM Erdoğan's 'Dersim apology', *Dialectical Anthropology*, 37(1), pp. 131–43.

Ayata, Sencer (2007), 'Meydanlardakiler 'yeni orta sınıf'tır', *Milliyet*, 21–2 May, <https://www.milliyet.com.tr/siyaset/meydanlardakiler-yeni-orta-siniftir-200259> (last accessed 13 November 2020).

Aybak, Tunc (2017), 'The Sultan is dead, long live "Başyüce" Erdoğan Sultan!', *Open Democracy*, 31 May, <https://www.opendemocracy.net/tunc-aybak/sultan-is-dead-long-live-ba-y-ce-Erdoğan-sultan> (last accessed 8 November 2020).

Aydin, Aysegül and Cem Emrence (2015), *Zones of Rebellion: Kurdish Insurgents and the Turkish State* (Ithaca: Cornell University Press).

Aytürk, İlker (2015), 'Post-post-Kemalizm: Yeni bir paradigmayı beklerken', *Birikim*, 319, pp. 34–48.
Azeri, Siyaves (2016), 'The July 15 coup attempt in Turkey: the Erdoğan–Gülen confrontation and the fall of "moderate" political Islam', *Critique*, 44(4), pp. 465–78.
Bacık, Gökhan (2008), 'The parliamentary elections in Turkey, July 2007', *Electoral Studies*, 27(2), pp. 377–81.
Bal, Idris (2013), 'AK Party parliamentarian, issued a report criticizing government policies', *Radikal*, 13 August, < http://www.radikal.com.tr/gezi_raporu.doxc/> (last accessed 16 November 2020).
Balbay, Mustafa (2003), 'Genç subaylar tedirgin', *Cumhuriyet*, 23 May.
Baldwin, Katherine (2007), 'Blair promotes Turkish EU membership', *Reuters*, 20 January, <https://uk.reuters.com/article/uk-turkey-blair-eu/blair-promotes-turkish-eu-membership-idUKL1688602520061216> (last accessed 26 November 2020).
Baran, Zeyno (2010), *Torn Country: Turkey between Secularism and Islamism* (Stanford: Hoover Institution Press Publication).
Bardakcı, Murat (2013), 'O kışla neler gördü', *Sabah*, 9 June.
Barkan, Elazar (2000), *The Guilt of Nations: Restitution and Negotiating Historical Injustices* (New York: Norton).
Barkey, Karen (1996), *Bandits and Bureaucrats: The Ottoman Road to State Centralization* (New York: Cornell University Press).
Barkey, Karen (2008), *Empire of Difference: The Ottomans in Comparative Perspective* (Cambridge: Cambridge University Press).
Başer, Bahar and Alpaslan Ozerdem (2019), 'Conflict transformation and asymmetric conflicts: a critique of the failed Turkish–Kurdish peace process', *Terrorism and Political Violence*, 31(2), pp. 1–22.
Başer, Bahar and Ahmet Erdi Öztürk (eds) (2017), *Authoritarian Politics in Turkey: Elections, Resistance and the AKP* (London: I. B. Tauris).
Başbuğ, İlker (2013), *Suçlamalara Karşı Gerçekler* (Istanbul: Kaynak).
Başbuğ, İlker (2015), *15 Temmuz öncesi ve sonrasi* (Istanbul: Doğan Kitap).
Bayat, Fuzuli (2009), *Köroğlu Destanı, Türk Dünyasının Köroğlu Fenomenolojisi* (Istanbul, Ötüken).
Bayburtlu, Mustafa (1969), *Kızıl Pençe* (Çorum: Toker Matbaası).
Baykal, Arda (2009), 'Recep Tayyip Erdoğan', *The House of Commons Library*, 22 December, <https://commonslibrary.parliament.uk/research-briefings/sn05257/> (last accessed 6 November 2020).

BBC (2009), 'The UN condemns the "war crimes" in Gaza', 16 September, <http://news.bbc.co.uk/1/hi/world/middle_east/8257301.stm> (last accessed 26 November 2020).

BBC (2014), 'Berkin Elvan: Turkish PM accuses dead boy of terror links', 15 March, <https://www.bbc.co.uk/news/world-europe-26594922> (last accessed 16 November 2020).

BBC (2014), 'Kobane: US drops arms and aid to Kurds battling IS', 20 October, <https://www.bbc.co.uk/news/world-middle-east-29684761> (last accessed 26 November 2020).

BBC (2018), 'Qatar's emir "gives $500 m private jet to Turkey"', 17 September, <https://www.bbc.co.uk/news/world-middle-east-45550537> (last accessed 26 November 2020).

Beck, John M. (2019), 'Turkey's global soft-power push is built on mosques', *The Atlantic*, 1 June, <https://www.theatlantic.com/international/archive/2019/06/turkey-builds-mosques-abroad-global-soft-power/590449/> (last accessed 26 November 2020).

de Bellaigue, Christopher (2001), 'Turkey's hidden past', *New York Review of Books*, 8 March.

de Bellaigue, Christopher (2017), 'Turkey: the return of the sultan', *New York Review of Books*, 9 March, <http://www.nybooks.com/daily/2017/03/09/turkey-the-return-of-the-sultan/> (last accessed 9 November 2020).

Berkes, Niyazi (1998), *The Development of Secularism in Turkey* (New York: Routledge).

Bernard, Ariane (2007), 'Quotes from, and about Nicolas Sarkozy', *The New York Times*, 7 May, <https://www.nytimes.com/2007/05/07/world/europe/07francequotes.html> (last accessed 26 November 2020).

Besli, Hüseyin and Ömer Özbay (2014), *Bir Liderin Dogusu: Recep Tayyip Erdoğan* (Istanbul: Yeni Türkiye Yayınları).

Bianet (2013), 'Öcalan'ın Açıklaması: "Silahlı Güçler Sınırdışına, Artık Siyaset Dönemi"', 21 March, <http://bianet.org/bianet/ siyaset/145269-silahli-gucler-sinirdisina-artik-siyaset-donemi> (last accessed 25 November 2020).

Bianet (2017), 'Erdoğan calls Osman Kavala "domestic Soros"', 24 October, <https://m.bianet.org/bianet/politics/190908-erdogan-calls-osman-kavala-domestic-soros> (last accessed 16 November 2020).

Bila, Fikret (2003), *Sivil Darbe Girişimi ve Ankara'da Irak Savaşları* (Ankara: Ümit Yayıncılık).

Bilefsky, Dan (2007), 'Sarkozy blocks key part of EU entry talks on Turkey', *The New York Times*, 25 June, <https://www.nytimes.com/2007/06/25/world/europe/25iht-union.5.6325879.html> (last accessed 26 November 2020).

Bilgiç, Ali (2018), 'Reclaiming the national will: resilience of Turkish authoritarian neoliberalism after Gezi', *South European Society and Politics*, 23(2), pp. 259–80.
Binder, David (2003), 'Alija Izetbegović', *The New York Times*, 20 October, <https://www.nytimes.com/2003/10/20/world/alija-izetbegovic-muslim-who-led-bosnia-dies-at-78.html?searchResultPosition=2> (last accessed 6 November 2020).
Binney, Horace (1862), *The Privilege of the Writ of Habeas Corpus Under the Constitution*, 2nd edn (Philadelphia: C. Sherman & Son).
Birand, Mehmet Ali and Reyhan Yıldız (2012), *Son Darbe: 28 Şubat* (Istanbul: Doğan Kitap).
Bora, Tanıl (2013), 'Notes on the White Turks debate', in R. Kastoryano (ed) *Turkey between Nationalism and Globalization* (New York: Routledge), pp. 87–104.
Boratav, Pertev Naili (1931), *Köroğlu destanı* (Istanbul: Evkaf Matbaasi).
Boyunsuz, Şule Özsoy (2016), 'The AKP's proposal for a "Turkish type of presidentialism" in comparative context', *Turkish Studies*, 17(1), pp. 68–90.
Bülent Keneş (2018), 'Instrumentalization of Islam: Hayrettin Karaman's role in Erdoğan's despotism', *PoliTurco*, 30 July, <https://www.politurco.com/instrumentalization-of-islam-hayrettin-karamans-role-in-erdogans-despotism.html> (last accessed 27 November).
Burch, Jonathan (2011), 'Turkey tells Syria's Assad: Step down!', *Reuters*, 22 November, <https://www.reuters.com/article/us-syria-idUSL5E7MD0GZ20111122> (last accessed 26 November 2020).
Cagaptay, Soner (2017), *The New Sultan: Erdogan and the Crisis of Modern Turkey* (New York: I. B. Tauris).
Cagaptay, Soner (2019), *Erdogan's Empire: Turkey and the Politics of the Middle East* (New York: I. B. Tauris).
Çağlar, Ismail (2013), *From Symbolic Exile to Physical Exile: Turkey's İmam Hatip Schools, the Emergence of a Conservative Counter-Elite, and Its Knowledge Migration to Europe* (Amsterdam: Amsterdam University Press).
Çakır, Ruşen and Fehmi Çakmak (2001), *Recep Tayyip Erdoğan: Bir Dönüşüm Öyküsü* (Istanbul: Metis).
Çakır, Ruşen (2007), 'Erdoğan'ın 1991 yılında Erbakan'a verdiği Kürt raporu', *Vatan*, 12 December.
Cakırözer, Utku (2014), 'Tek sorumlu cemaat değil', *Cumhuriyet*, 26 June, <https://www.cumhuriyet.com.tr/yazarlar/utku-cakirozer/tek-sorumlu-cemaat-degil-87071> (last accessed 18 November 2020).
Carkoğlu, Ali and Binnaz Toprak (2007), *Religion, Society and Politics in a Changing Turkey* (Istanbul: Tesev).
Cemal, Hasan (1990), *Özal Hikayesi* (Ankara: Bilgi).

Cemal, Hasan (2006), 'Başbakan Erdoğan'dan Amerika yolunda Komutanlara Mesajlar: İrtica diye Bir Tehdit Yok', *Milliyet*, 1 October.

Close, David (2004), *Undoing Democracy: The Politics of Electoral Caudillismo* (Lanham: Lexington Books).

Cook, Steven A. and Michael J. Koplow (2016), 'Turkey is no longer a reliable ally', *The Wall Street Journal*, 10 August, <https://www.wsj.com/articles/turkey-is-no-longer-a-reliable-ally-1470869047> (last accessed 26 November 2020).

Coşkun, Bekir (2006), 'Yol ne yana', *Hürriyet*, 7 March, <https://www.hurriyet.com.tr/yol-ne-yana-4034995> (last accessed 13 November 2020).

Cumhuriyet (2014), 'Abdullah Gul'un 16 Nisan 2003 tarihli cemaat genelgesi', 18 May, <https://www.cumhuriyet.com.tr/haber/cemaat-genelgesine-iptal-73301> (last accessed 19 November 2020).

Cumhuriyet (2015), 'Dolmabahçe anlaşması', 28 February, <https://www.cumhuriyet.com.tr/amp/haber/dolmabahce-anlasmasi-224047> (last accessed 25 November 2020).

Cumhuriyet (2017), 'Erdoğan halife olacak, Ak Saray'daki odalarda hilafet temsilcilikleri açılacak', 16 January.

Dale, Roger (1977), 'Implications of the rediscovery of the hidden curriculum for the sociology of teaching', in D. Gleeson (ed.) *Identity and Structure: Issues in the Sociology of Education* (Driffield: Nafferton Books), pp. 44–54.

Davutoğlu, Ahmet (1994), *Civilizational Transformation and the Muslim World* (Kuala Lumpur: Mahir Publications).

Davutoğlu, Ahmet (2004), 'Türkiye merkez ülke olmalı', *Radikal*, 26 February <http://www.radikal.com.tr/yorum/turkiye-merkez-ulke-olmali-702116/> (last accessed 30 November 2020).

Davutoğlu, Ahmet (2007), 'Turkey's foreign policy vision: an assessment of 2007', *Insight Turkey*, 10(1), pp. 77–96.

Davutoğlu, Ahmet (2015), *Stratejik Derinlik: Türkiye'nin Uluslararası Konumu* (Istanbul: Küre Yayınları).

Demiralp, Sead (2012), 'White Turks, black Turks? Fault-lines beyond Islamism versus secularism', *Third World Quarterly*, 33(3), pp. 511–24.

Demirtaş, Serkan (2015), 'Explained: AKP fails to keep unity over corruption', *Hurriyet Daily News*, 21 January.

Deutsche Welle (2016), 'Böhmermann: How a German satirist sparked a freedom of speech debate', 5 October, <http://www.dw.com/en/böhmermann-how-a-german-satirist-sparked-a-freedom-of-speech-debate/a-19185804> (last accessed 9 November 2020).

Đidić, Ajdin and Hasan Kösebalaban (2019), 'Turkey's rapprochement with Russia: assertive bandwagoning', *The International Spectator*, 54(3), pp. 123–38.

Diken (2017), 'Evet'çilere "hanedan" desteği: Erdoğan'ı 2. Abdülhamit Han'ın yalnızlığına bırakmamak için', 27 January, <http://www.diken.com.tr/evetcilere-hanedan-destegi-Erdo%C4%9Fani-2-abdulhamit-hanin-yalnizligina-birakmamak-icin/> (last accessed 9 November 2020).

Dindar, Cemal (2014), *Bi'at ve Öfke: Recep Tayyip Erdoğan'ın Psikobiyografisi* (Istanbul: Telos Yayıncılık).

Dogan, Yonca Poyraz (2011), 'PM Erdoğan apologises for Dersim massacre on behalf of Turkish state', *Today's Zaman*, 23 November.

Dombey, Daniel (2015), 'Turkish commission votes against the corruption case', *Financial Times*, 5 January, < https://www.ft.com/content/54ed81f8-94fa-11e4-b32c-00144feabdc0> (last accessed 18 November 2020).

Duman, Hasan (1986), 'Mehmet Akif ve Bir Mecmuanin Anatomisi', *Milli Kültür Dergisi*, 55, pp. 78–95.

Duran, Burhanettin (2001), 'Transformation of Islamist political thought in Turkey from the empire to the early republic (1908–1960): Necip Fazıl Kısakürek's political ideas' (PhD dissertation, Bilkent University).

Duran, Burhanettin (2013), 'Understanding the AK Party's identity politics: a civilizational discourse and its limitations', *Insight Turkey*, 15(1), pp. 91–109.

Duran, Burhanettin (2016), 'Comparing Erdoğan with Mustafa Kemal and Sultan Abdulhamid', *Daily Sabah*, 6 October.

The Economist (2013), 'Justice or revenge?', 10 August, <https://www.economist.com/europe/2013/08/10/justice-or-revenge> (last accessed 15 November 2020).

The Economist (2014), 'The Arab road', *The Economist*, 4 January, <https://www.economist.com/leaders/2014/01/04/the-arab-road> (last accessed 26 November 2020).

The Economist (2016), 'Getting off the train', 4 February, <https://www.economist.com/special-report/2016/02/04/getting-off-the-train> (last accessed 11 November 2020).

The Economist (2016), 'Turkish anger at the West: duplicity coup', 20 August, <https://www.economist.com/europe/2016/08/20/duplicity-coup> (last accessed 26 November 2020).

The Economist (2017), 'Turkey's purges are hitting its business class', 4 February, <https://www.economist.com/europe/2017/02/02/turkeys-purges-are-hitting-its-business-class> (last accessed 22 November 2020).

Ellison, Grace (1928), *Turkey Today* (London: Hutchinson).

Erbakan, Necmettin (2013), *Erbakan Kulliyatı*, 5 vols (Ankara: Milli Görüş Vakfı).

Erdoğan, Recep Tayyip (2001), *Bu Sarkı Burada Bitmez* (Istanbul: Nesil).

Erdoğan, Recep Tayyip (2004), 'Atatürk'ün dünya görüşünün temeli akılcılıktır', *Milliyet*, 10 November, <http://www.milliyet.com.tr/2004/11/10/son/sonsiy06.html> (last accessed 12 November 2020).

Erdoğan, Recep Tayyip (2004), *Başbakan Recep Tayyip Erdoğan'in Konuşmaları* (Ankara: AK Parti).

Erdoğan, Recep Tayyip (2004), 'Keynote speech', *Uluslarası Muhafazakarlık ve Demokrasi Sempozyumu* (Ankara: AK Parti), pp. 7–17.

Erdoğan, Recep Tayyip (2012), 'Address to the AK Party's 4th Ordinary Grand Convention', 30 September, <http://www.akparti.org.tr/site/haberler/basbakan-Erdoğanin-ak-parti-4.-olagan-buyuk-kongresi-konusmasinin-tam-metni/31771> (last accessed 27 November 2020).

Erdoğan, Recep Tayyip (2014), 'Necip Fazil Kısakürek hakkındaki konusması', 2 November, <https://tccb.gov.tr/en/news/542/3297/necip-fazil-kisakurek-awards-will-bring-us-the-genuine-voice-scent-and-soul-of-this-land> (last accessed 8 November 2020).

Erdoğan, Recep Tayyip (2015), 'Our difference is conquest, not plunder', 24 December, <https://tccb.gov.tr/en/news/542/37426/our-difference-is-conquest-not-plunder> (last accessed 8 November 2020).

Erdoğan, Recep Tayyip (2018), 'Genel Başkan ve Cumhurbaşkanı Recep Tayyip Erdoğan, Yenikent Spor Salonu'nda düzenlenen Eskişehir 6. Olağan İl Kongresi'nde partililere hitap etti', 17 February, <http://www.akparti.org.tr/site/haberler/cumhurbaskani-Erdoğan-eskisehir-6.-olagan-il-kongresinde-konustu/97422#1> (last accessed 8 November 2020).

Erdoğan, Recep Tayyip (2019), 'Bilecik Konuşması', *Milliyet*, 27 March.

Erenoğlu, Can (2015), *Aldattılar Siz Duymadınız Sesimizi, Balyoz Davasında Yalanlar ve Gerçekler* (Istanbul: Kaynak Yayınları).

Ergin, Sedat (2011), 'Erdoğan ve CHP liderinin Aleviliği," *Hürriyet*, 18 May, <https://www.hurriyet.com.tr/erdogan-ve-chp-liderinin-aleviligi-17813544> (last accessed 15 November 2020).

Ergin, Sedat (2017), 'How did Major General Dişli get arrested at the prime ministry?', *Hürriyet Daily News*, 18 July, <http://www.hurriyetdailynews.com/how-did-major-general-disli-get-arrested-at-theprime-ministry.aspx?pageID=449&nID=115623&NewsCatID=428> (last accessed 20 November 2020).

Ergin, Sedat (2017), 'July 15 and Akıncı Air Base (7): the general on Adil Öksüz's phone records', *Hürriyet Daily News*, 21 July, <http://www.hurriyetdailynews.com/july-

15-and-Akıncı-air-base-7-the-general-on-adil-oksuzs-phone-records.aspx?pageID =449&nID=115816&NewsCatID=428> (last accessed 20 November 2020).

Eroğlu, Cem (1990), *Demokrat Parti: Tarihi ve İdeolojisi* (Ankara: İmge).

Ersoy, Mehmet Akif (2014), *Safahat* (Istanbul: İnkılap Kitabevi).

Ertem, Cemil (2014), 'Erdoğan, 2. Abdülhamit misyonunun takipçisidir', *Haber7.com*, 20 December, <https://www.haber7.com/ic-politika/haber/1227287-erdogan-2-abdulhamit-misyonunun-takipcisidir> (last accessed 9 November 2020).

Esen, Berk and Sebnem Gümüşcü (2016), 'Rising competitive authoritarianism in Turkey', *Third World Quarterly*, 37(9), pp. 1581–606.

Ete, Hatem (2014), 'Gülen'in Dünü, Bugünü, Yarını', *Türkiye Günlüğü*, 117, pp. 72–84.

Fanon, Frantz (1967), 'On national culture', in F. Fanon, *The Wretched of the Earth* (Harmondsworth: Penguin), pp. 167–89.

Filkins, Dexter (2003), 'Threats and responses: Ankara; Turkish deputies refuse to accept American troops', *The New York Times*, 2 March, <https://www.nytimes.com/2003/03/02/world/threats-and-responses-ankara-turkish-deputies-refuse-to-accept-american-troops.html> (last accessed 26 November 2020).

Findley, Carter Vaughn (2010), *Turkey, Islam, Nationalism, and Modernity: A History 1789–2007* (New Haven: Yale University Press).

Finkel, Andrew (2015), 'Captured news media: the case of Turkey', October, <https://www.cima.ned.org/wp-content/uploads/2015/10/CIMA-Captured-News-Media_The-Case-of-Turkey.pdf> (last accessed 30 November 2020).

Fisher, Ian (2002), 'Turkey waits and wonders how closely bound to Islam', *The New York Times*, 7 November, <https://www.nytimes.com/2002/11/07/world/turkey-waits-and-wonders-how-closely-bound-to-islam-is-election-victor.html> (last accessed 6 November 2020).

Fitsanakis, Joseph (2016), 'Leaked EU intelligence report says Islamists were not behind Turkey coup', *intelNews*, 18 January, <https://intelnews.org/2017/01/18/01-2045/> (last accessed 20 November 2020).

Fontanella-Khan, Amana (2016), 'Fethullah Gülen: Turkey coup may have been "staged" by Erdoğan regime', *The Guardian*, 16 July, <https://www.theguardian.com/world/2016/jul/16/fethullah-gulen-turkey-coup-erdogan> (last accessed 20 November 2020).

Fukuyama, Francis (2013), 'The middle-class eevolution', *The Wall Street Journal*, 28 June, <https://www.wsj.com/articles/SB10001424127887323873904578571472700348086> (last accessed 16 November 2020).

Garton Ash, Timothy (2017) 'As Erdoğan turns the screw, we must stand up for human rights in Turkey', *The Guardian*, 2 March 2017, <https://www.theguardian

.com/commentisfree/2017/mar/02/erdogan-turns-screw-human-rights-turkey> (last accessed 27 November 2020).

Göle, Nilüfer (2013), 'Gezi – anatomy of a public square movement' *Turkish Insight*, 15(3), pp. 7–14.

Göner, Özlem (2017), *Turkish National Identity and Its Outsiders: Memories of State Violence in Dersim* (New York: Routledge).

Gottschlich, Jürgen (2011), 'Erdoğan falls short of goal in Turkish elections', *Spiegel*, 13 June, <http://www.spiegel.de/international/europe/0,1518,768175,00.html> (last accessed 15 November 2020).

Gözaydın, İştar (2008), 'Religion, politics, and the politics of religion in Turkey', in D. Jung and C. Raudvere (eds), *Religion, Politics and Turkey's EU Accession* (New York: Palgrave Macmillan), pp. 160–76.

Güler, İlhami (2019), 'İslamcı muhafazakârların ahlaki performansının teolojik-politik kökenleri üzerine', *Karar*, 26 June, <https://www.karar.com/islamci-muhafazakarlarin-ahlaki-performansinin-teolojik-politik-kokenleri-uzerine-1250998 > (last accessed 6 November 2020).

Gürsel, Kadri (2014), 'Erdoğan Islamizes education system to raise "devout youth"', *Al-Monitor*, 9 December, <https://www.al-monitor.com/pulse/originals/2014/12/turkey-islamize-education-religion.html> (last accessed 11 November 2020).

Gültekin, Levent (2014), 'AK Parti-Cemaat Kavgası Kimin ve Neyin Kavgası', *Türkiye Günlüğü*, 117, pp. 68–71.

Günay, Defne (2017), 'The roles Turkey played in the Middle East, (2002–2016)', in P. G. Ercan (ed.), *Turkish Foreign Policy: International Relations, Legality and Global Reach* (New York: Palgrave), pp. 195–211.

Güneş, Cengiz (2012), *Kurdish National Movement in Turkey: From Protest to Resistance* (London: Routledge).

Güngör, Nasuhi (2002), *Yenilikci Hareket* (Ankara: Anka Yayınları).

Gunter, Michael M. (2013), 'Reopening Turkey's closed Kurdish Opening?', *Middle East Policy*, 22(3), pp. 88–98.

Gunter, Michael M. (2020), 'Erdogan's train to authoritarianism', *Sociology of Islam*, 8, pp. 127–49.

Gür, Bilal Çetin (2003), *Türk siyasetinde bir Kasımpaşalı Tayyip Erdoğan* (Istanbul: Gündem).

Gür, Kader (2003), *Esaretten Zirveye* (Istanbul: MDS Yayınları).

Gürakar, Esra Çeviker (2016), *Politics of Favoritism in Public Procurement in Turkey* (New York: Palgrave).

Gürses, Mehmet (2015), 'Is Islam a cure for ethnic conflict? Evidence from Turkey', *Politics and Religion*, 8(1), pp. 135–54.

Gürses, Mehmet (2018), *Anatomy of a Civil War: Sociopolitical Impacts of the Kurdish Conflict in Turkey* (Ann Arbor, MI: University of Michigan Press).

Gürses, Mehmet and Ahmet Erdi Öztürk (2020), 'Religion and armed conflict: evidence from the Kurdish conflict in Turkey', *Journal for the Scientific Study of Religion*, 59(2), pp. 327–40.

Guttenberg, Karl-Theodor Zu (2004), 'Preserving Europe: offer Turkey a "privileged partnership" instead', *The New York Times*, 15 December, <https://www.nytimes.com/2004/12/15/opinion/preserving-europe-offer-turkey-a-privileged-partnership-instead.html> (last accessed 26 November 2020).

Güzel, Hasan Celal (2013), 'Federatif sistem ülkeyi böler', *Sabah*, 4 April, <https://www.sabah.com.tr/yazarlar/guzel/2013/04/02/federatif-sistem-ulkeyi-boler> (last accessed 25 November 2020).

Hakan, Ahmet (2007), 'Cemaat diyor ki: O bakan bize düsman', *Hürriyet*, 4 April, <https://www.hurriyet.com.tr/cemaat-diyor-ki-o-bakan-bize-dusman-6271771> (last accessed 13 November 2020).

Hakan, Ahmet (2007), 'Cemaat, ey cemaat', *Hürriyet*, 2 April, <https://www.hurriyet.com.tr/cemaat-ey-cemaat-6249583> (last accessed 13 November 2020).

Hale, William and Ergun Özbudun (2011), *Islamism, Democracy, and Liberalism in Turkey: The Case of the AKP* (New York: Routledge).

Handy, Nathaniel (2018), 'Has Turkey had enough of Erdoğan?', *Fair Observer*, 16 May.

Hansen, Suzy (2009), 'What remains of the Turkish press', *Columbia Journalism Review* (Summer 2019), <https://www.cjr.org/special_report/turkish-press.php> (last accessed 12 November 2020).

Haugom, Lars (2019), 'Turkish foreign policy under Erdoğan: a change in international orientation?', *Comparative Strategy*, 38(3), pp. 206–23.

Hendrik, Joshua (2013), *Gülen: The Ambiguous Politics of Market Islam in Turkey and the World* (New York: New York University Press).

House of Commons Foreign Affairs Committee (2017), 'The UK's relations with Turkey, tenth report of session 2016–2017', <https://www.publications.parliament.uk/pa/cm201617/cmselect/cmfaff/615/615.pdf> (last accessed 25 May 2017).

Howard, Michael and Suzanne Goldberg (2003), 'US arrest of soldiers infuriates Turkey', *The Guardian*, 7 July, <https://www.theguardian.com/world/2003/jul/08/turkey.michaelhoward> (last accessed 26 November 2020).

Hürriyet (2003), 'Wolfowitz: Accept your mistake, our partnership shall continue', 7 May, <http://www.hurriyet.com.tr/gundem/wolfowitz-accept-your-mistake-our-partnership-shall-continue-145127> (last accessed 26 November 2020).

Hürriyet (2006), 'Semdinli iddianamesi', 7 March, <https://www.hurriyet.com.tr/gundem/iste-semdinli-iddianamesi-4037895> (last accessed 13 November 2020).

Hürriyet (2007), 'Genelkurmay'dan çok sert açıklama', 29 April, <https://www.hurriyet.com.tr/gundem/genelkurmaydan-cok-sert-aciklama-6420961> (last accessed 13 November 2020).

Hürriyet (2009), 'Mümtaz Soysal: Erdoğan Batı'da ikinci kez çizildi', 30 January, <https://www.hurriyet.com.tr/gundem/mumtaz-soysal-erdogan-batida-ikinci-kez-cizildi-10893886> (last accessed 9 November 2020).

Hürriyet (2011), 'Başbakan gazetecilerin neden tutuklandığını açıkladı', 8 March, <https://www.hurriyet.com.tr/gundem/basbakan-gazetecilerin-neden-tutuklandigini-acikladi-17213207> (last accessed 12 November 2020).

Hürriyet (2012), 'Dindar gençlikyetiştireceğiz', 2 February, <https://www.hurriyet.com.tr/gundem/dindar-genclik-yetistirecegiz-19825231> (last accessed 15 November 2020).

Hürriyet (2012), 'MİT'ten böcek harekâtı', 25 December, <http://www.hurriyet.com.tr/mit-ten-bocek-harek-ti-22227306> (last accessed 19 November 2020).

Hürriyet (2013), 'Başbakan: Yüzde 50'yi evinde zor tutuyorum', 4 June, <https://www.hurriyet.com.tr/gundem/basbakan-yuzde-50-yi-evinde-zor-tutuyorum-23429709> (last accessed 16 November 2020).

Hürriyet (2013), 'Erdoğan'ın anket tepkisi: Fecaat', 22 February, <https://www.hurriyet.com.tr/gundem/erdo%C4%9Fanin-anket-tepkisi-fecaat-22653369> (last accessed 13 November 2020).

Hürriyet (2014), 'Mehmet Metiner: "Biatsa, biat, itaatsa itaaat"', 6 January, <https://www.hurriyet.com.tr/gundem/mehmet-metiner-biatsa-biat-itaatsa-itaat-25504058> (last accessed 25 November 2020).

Hürriyet (2016), 'General Hulusi Akar'in ifadesi', 25 July, <http://www.hurriyet.com.tr/galeri-genelkurmay-baskani-hulusi-akarin-ifadesi-40168764> (last accessed 20 November 2020).

Hürriyet Daily News (2013), '"Patience has its limits", Turkish PM Erdoğan tells Taksim Gezi Park demonstrators', 9 June, <https://www.hurriyetdailynews.com/patience-has-its-limits-turkish-pm-erdogan-tells-taksim-gezi-park-demonstrators-48516> (last accessed 16 November 2020).

Hürriyet Daily News (2013), 'İbrahim Kalın told that 'Turkey not "lonely" but dares to do so for its values and principles, says PM advisor', 26 August, <https://www.hurriyetdailynews.com/turkey-not-lonely-but-dares-to-do-so-for-its-values-and-principles-says-pm-adviser--53244> (last accessed 18 November 2020).

Hürriyet Daily News (2013), 'If only Morsi had listened to Erdoğan', 29 August, <https://www.hurriyetdailynews.com/if-only-morsi-had-listened-to-erdogan-53409> (last accessed 26 November 2020).

Hürriyet Daily News (2015), 'Surrounded by Ottoman soldiers, Erdoğan toughens rhetoric against *New York Times*', 30 May, <www.hurriyetdailynews.com/surrounded-by-ottoman-soldiers-Erdo%C4%9Fan-toughens-rhetoric-against-new-york-times.aspx?pageID=238&nID=83215&NewsCatID=338> (last accessed 9 November 2020).

Hürriyet Daily News (2017), 'Elements other than Gülenists also supported coup attempt: Justice Minister Bozdağ', 6 July, <http://www.hurriyetdailynews.com/elements-other-than-gulenists-also-supported-coup-attempt-justice-minister-bozdag.aspx?pageID=238&nID=115179&NewsCatID=338> (last accessed 20 November 2020).

Idiz, Semih (2015), 'Is the AKP shielding former ministers from the corruption charges', *Al-Monitor*, 6 January 2015, <https://www.al-monitor.com/pulse/originals/2015/01/turkey-corruption-akp-protects-former-ministers.html> (last accessed 18 November 2020).

Ince, Vahdettin (2013), 'Kürtler Kemalistlerin yaptıklarını unutmayacak', *Star*, 14 January, <https://www.star.com.tr/yazar/vahdettin-ince-kurtler-kemalistlerin-yaptiklarini-unutmayacak-yazi-797666/> (last accessed 6 December 2020).

The Independent (2019), 'Mohamed Morsi death: former Egyptian leader was murdered, says Turkish president Erdogan', 19 June, <https://www.independent.co.uk/news/world/middle-east/mohamed-morsi-murder-dead-killed-erdogan-turkey-egypt-president-muslim-brotherhood-prison-a8965436.html> (last accessed 18 November 2020).

Insel, Ahmet (2007), 'Neofeodal devlette ilerlerken', *Radikal İki*, 4 March.

Insel, Ahmet (2016), 'Tarihi rövanş hırsı ve muhafazakâr restorasyon', *Cumhuriyet*, 21 June, <https://www.cumhuriyet.com.tr/yazarlar/ahmet-insel/tarihi-rovans-hirsi-ve-muhafazakar-restorasyon-554604> (last accessed 26 November 2020).

Izetbegovic, Alija (1985), *Islam Between East and West* (New York: American Trust Publications).

Jenkins, Gareth (2011), 'Turkey's election, and democracy's shadow', *Open Democracy*, 21 June, <https://www.opendemocracy.net/en/turkeys-election-and-democracys-shadow/> (last accessed 15 November 2020).

Kadercan, Burak (2016), 'Erdoğan's last off-ramp: authoritarianism, democracy, and the future of Turkey', *War on the Rocks*, 28 July, <https://warontherocks.

com/2016/07/erdogans-last-off-ramp-authoritarianism-democracy-and-the-future-of-turkey/> (last accessed 19 November 2020).

Kafka, Franz (2002), *Kafka's 'The Metamorphosis' and Other Writings* (New York: Continuum).

Kalaycıoğlu, Ersin (2012), '*Kulturkampf* in Turkey: the constitutional referendum of 12 September 2010', *South European Society and Politics*, 17(1), pp. 1–22.

Kalaycıoğlu, Ersin (2015), 'Turkish popular presidential elections: deepening legitimacy issues and looming regime change', *South European Society and Politics*, 20(3), pp. 1–23.

Kalın, Ibrahim (2009), 'Debating Turkey in the Middle East: the dawn of a new geo-political imagination?', Insight *Turkey*, 11(1), pp. 83–96.

Kalın, Ibrahim (2010), 'US–Turkish relations under Obama: promise, challenge and opportunity in the 21st century,' *Journal of Balkan and Near Eastern Studies*, 12(1), pp. 93–108.

Kalın, Ibrahim (2013), 'AK Party in Turkey', in J. L. Esposito and E. El-Din Shahin (eds), *Oxford Handbook of Political Islam* (New York: Oxford University Press, 2013), pp. 423–30.

Kaplan, Hilal (2016), 'Abdülhamit ve Erdoğan', *Sabah*, 3 June.

Kaplan, Sefa (2007), *Recep Tayyip Erdoğan* (Istanbul: Doğan Kitap).

Karagül, Ibrahim (2013), 'Ahmet Davutoğlu: Yüzyıllık parantezi kapatacağız', *Yeni Şafak*, 1 March, <https://www.yenisafak.com/yazidizileri/yuzyillik-parantezi-kapatacagiz-494795> (last accessed 26 November 2020).

Kardaş, Saban (2006), 'Turkey and the Iraqi crisis: AKP between identity and interest', In M. H. Yavuz (ed.), *The Emergence of a New Turkey: Democracy and AK Parti* (Salt Lake City: University of Utah Press), pp. 306–32.

Kasaba, Resat and Sibel Bozdoğan (2000), 'Turkey at a crossroad', *Journal of International Affairs*, 54(1), pp. 1–20.

Kenez, Levent (2019), 'Hired for religious fatwa: Erdogan's chief edict provider Hayrettin Karaman', *Nordic Monitor*, 7 January, <https://www.nordicmonitor.com/2019/01/hired-for-religious-fatwa-erdogans-chief-edict-provider-hayrettin-karaman/> (last accessed 27 November 2020).

Kenyon, Peter (2013), 'Not everyone cheers Turkey's move to tighten alcohol rules', *NPR*, 7 June 2013, <https://www.npr.org/sections/thesalt/2013/06/07/187334924/not-everyone-cheers-turkeys-move-to-tighten-alcohol-rules?t=1605516496142> (last accessed 16 November 2020).

Kinzer, Stephen (2004), 'Will Turkey make it?', *The New York Review*, 15 July, <https://www.nybooks.com/articles/2004/07/15/will-turkey-make-it/> (last accessed 11 November 2020).

Kırmızı, Abdulhamid (2016), 'Erdoğan Abdulhamid'e değil, Mustafa Kemal'e benziyor', *Al Jazeera*, 22 September, <http://www.aljazeera.com.tr/gorus/erdogan-abdulhamide-degil-mustafa-kemale-benziyor> (last accessed 9 November 2020).

Kısakürek, Necip Fazıl (1968), *İdeolocya Örgüsü* (Istanbul: Büyük Doğu Yayınları).

Kısakürek, Necip Fazıl (1998), *O ve Ben* (Istanbul: Büyük Doğu Yayınları).

Koçak, Cemil (2003), *Türkiye'de Milli Şef Dönemi, 1938–1945*, Vol. 1, 2nd edn (Istanbul: İletişim).

Köroğu, Erol (2007), *Ottoman Propaganda and Turkish Identity: Literature in Turkey During World War I* (London: I. B. Tauris).

Kramer, Robby and Ruby Mellen (2017), 'Turkish President Erdoğan calls Dutch "Nazi remnants"', *Foreign Policy*, 13 March.

Küçükkoşum, Sevil (2010), 'European Commission wary on restructured HSYK', *Hürriyet Daily News*, 17 September, <http://www.hürriyetdailynews.com/n.php?n=eu-earlier-warned-the-government-on-the-hsyk-structure-2010-09-17> (last accessed 16 August 2015).

Kumar, Leslie Keerthi (2014), 'Examining AKP's impact on Turkey's domestic and foreign policy', *Contemporary Review of the Middle East*, 1(2), pp. 207–30.

Kurt, Mehmet (2019), '"My Muslim Kurdish brother": colonial rule and Islamist governmentality in the Kurdish region of Turkey', *Journal of Balkan and Near Eastern Studies*, 21(3), pp. 350–65.

Laçiner, Sedat (2003), 'Özalism (neo-Ottomanism): an alternative in Turkish foreign policy', *Journal of Administrative Science*, 1(2), pp. 161–202.

Laclau, Ernesto (2005), *On Populist Reason* (London: Verso).

Linden, Ronald H. (2012), *Turkey and Its Neighbors: Foreign Relations in Transition* (Boulder, CO: Lynne Rienner Publishers).

Lüküslü, Demet (2016), 'Creating a pious generation: youth and education policies of the AKP in Turkey', *Southeast European and the Black Sea Studies*, 16 (4), pp. 637–49.

Luttwak, Edward (2016), 'Why Turkey's coup d'état failed', *Foreign Policy*, 16 July, <http://foreignpolicy.com/2016/07/16/why-turkeys-coup-detat-failed-Erdoğan/> (last accessed 26 November 2020).

Machiavelli, Niccolo (1965), *The Chief Works and Others*, trans. A. Gilbert, 3 vols (Durham, NC: Duke University Press).

Machiavelli, Niccolo (1988), *The Prince*, eds Q. Skinner and R. Price (Cambridge: Cambridge University Press).

Machiavelli, Nicolo (2016), *The Prince* (Woodstock, Ontario: Devoted Publishing).

Maraniss, David (1994), 'The woman who shaped the president', *The Washington Post*, 7 February, <https://www.washingtonpost.com/wp-srv/politics/special/clinton/stories/kelley010794.htm> (last accessed 9 November 2020).

Mardin, Şerif (1989), *Religion and Social Change in Modern Turkey: The Case of Bediuzzaman Said Nursi* (Syracuse: Syracuse University Press).

Mardin, Şerif (1995), 'Civil society and Islam', in J. Hall (ed) *Civil Society: Theory, History and Comparison* (Cambridge: Polity), pp. 278–300.

Mardin, Şerif (2005), 'Turkish Islamic exceptionalism yesterday and today: continuity, rupture and reconstruction in operational codes', *Turkish Studies*, 6 (2), pp. 145–65.

Mardin, Şerif (2006), 'Cultural change and the intellectual: Necip Fazil and the Naksibendi', in Ş. Mardin, *Religion, Society and Modernity in Turkey* (Syracuse: Syracuse University Press), pp. 243–59.

Mardin, Şerif (2007), 'Mahalle havası diye bir şey var ki AKP'yi bile döver', *Vatan Gazetesi*, 15 May.

McCarthy, Justin (1995), *Death and Exile: The Ethnic Cleansing of Ottoman Muslims, 1825–1922* (Princeton: Darvin Press).

Mehmet, Ozay (2009), *Sustainability of Microstates: The Case of North Cyprus* (Salt Lake City: University of Utah Press).

Mert, Nuray (2016), 'Abdulhamid Han ve Erdoğan', *Cumhuriyet*, 23 September.

Metiner, Mehmet (2003), 'Dünden bugüne Tayyip Erdoğan', *Radikal İki*, 6 July, <http://www.radikal.com.tr/radikal2/dunden-bugune-tayyip-erdogan-870285/> (last accessed 12 November 2020).

Metiner, Mehmet (2014), 'Biatsa, biat, itaatsa itaaat', *Hürriyet*, 6 January, <https://www.hurriyet.com.tr/gundem/mehmet-metiner-biatsa-biat-itaatsa-itaat-25504058> (last accessed 12 November 2020).

Mikhelidze, Nona (2010), 'The Turkish–Armenian rapprochement at the deadlock', *Institute of International Affairs* (Rome), 5 March, <http://www.iai.it/sites/default/files/iai1005.pdf> (last accessed 26 November 2020).

Milliyet (2007), 'Kürtler AKP'ye sadece kredi açtı', 30 July, <https://www.milliyet.com.tr/siyaset/kurtler-akpye-sadece-kredi-acti-208070> (last accessed 15 November 2020).

Milliyet (2013), 'Askerden atılan personel geri döndü', 23 January.

Milliyet (2013), 'Erdoğan, Erzurum'da halka seslendi', 23 June, <https://www.milliyet.com.tr/siyaset/erdogan-erzurumda-halka-seslendi-1726742> (last accessed 16 November 2020).

Milliyet (2013), 'Yeni buluşma noktası: Gezi Parkı', 9 June, <https://www.milliyet.com.tr/yazarlar/cagdas-ertuna/yeni-bulusma-noktasi-gezi-parki-1720384> (last accessed 16 November 2020).

Mishra, Pankaj (2014), 'The Western model is broken', *The Guardian*, 14 October, <https://www.theguardian.com/world/2014/oct/14/-sp-western-model-broken-pankaj-mishra> (last accessed 18 November 2020).

Mishra, Pankaj (2017), *Age of Anger: A History of the Present* (New York: Farrar, Straus and Giroux).
Mounk, Yascha (2014), 'Pitchfork politics: the populist threat to liberal democracy', *Foreign Affairs*, 93, pp. 27–36.
Mudde, Cas (2004), 'The populist zeitgeist', *Government and Opposition*, 39(4), pp. 542–63.
Mudde, Cas (2015), 'The problem with populism', *The Guardian*, 17 February, <https://www.theguardian.com/commentisfree/2015/feb/17/problem-populism-syriza-podemos-dark-side-europe> (last accessed 30 November 2020).
Mufti, Malik (2009), *Daring and Caution in Turkish Strategic Culture: Republic at Sea* (London: Palgrave Macmillan).
Mufti, Malik (2014), 'The AK Party's Islamist realist political vision: theory and practice', *Politics and Governance*, 2(2), pp. 28–42.
Müller, Jan-Werner (2016), *What Is Populism?* (Philadelphia: University of Pennsylvania Press).
Muradoğlu, Abdullah (2003), 'Hapisten başbakanlığa', *Yeni Şafak*, 12 March, <https://www.yenisafak.com/arsiv/2003/mart/12/gundem.html> (last accessed 8 November 2020).
Myers, Steven Lee (2011), 'US and allies say Syria leader must step down', *The New York Times*, 18 August, <https://www.nytimes.com/2011/08/19/world/middleeast/19diplo.html> (last accessed 26 November 2020).
Naipaul, V. S. (1982), *Three Novels: The Mystic Masseur, The Suffrage of Elvira, Miguel Street* (New York: Alfred Knopf).
Necipoğlu, Gülru, 'The life of an imperial monument: Hagia Sophia after Byzantium', in R. Mark and A. S. Cakmak (eds), *Hagia Sophia From the Age of Justinian to the Present* (New York: Cambridge University Press, 1992), pp. 195–225.
NTV (2015), 'Erdoğan: Dolmabahçe toplantısını doğru bulmuyorum', 22 March.
NTVMSNBC (2009), 'Gül: Kürt sorunu cözülmeli, fırsat kaçmasın', 9 May, <https://www.ntv.com.tr/turkiye/gul-kurt-sorun-cozulmeli-firsat-kacmasin,rznr6amVEUOzi2KyfWU9fg> (last accessed 25 November 2020).
O'Donnell, Guillermo (1994), 'Delegative democracy', *Journal of Democracy*, 5(1): pp. 55–69.
Oğur, Yıldıray and Cener Keren, 'Who was Behind the 15th July Coup?' *The Medium*, 21 March 2017.
Okay, M. Orhan (2000), *Necip Fazıl Kısakürek* (Istanbul: Dergah Yayınları).
Okutan, M. Çağatay (2004), *Bozkut'tan Kuran'a Milli Türk Talebe Birliği (MTTB) 1916–1980* (Istanbul: Bilgi Universitesi Yayınları).

Olson, Robert (1989), *The Emergence of Kurdish Nationalism and the Sheikh Said Rebellion, 1880–1925* (Austin: University of Texas Press).

Onar, Nora Fisher (2009), 'Echoes of a universalism lost: rival representations of the Ottomans in today's Turkey,' *Middle Eastern Studies*, 45(2), pp. 229–41.

Onar, Nora Fisher (2015), 'Continuity or rupture? The historiography of the Ottoman past and its political uses', in K. Nicolaidis and B. Sebe (eds) *Echoes of Colonialism: Memory, Identity and the Legacy of Imperialism* (London: I. B. Tauris), pp. 139–52.

Onar, Nora Fisher (2016), 'The populism/realism gap: managing uncertainty in Turkey's politics and foreign policy', *Brookings Institution*, 4 February, <https://www.brookings.edu/research/the-populismrealism-gap-managing-uncertainty-in-turkeys-politics-and-foreign-policy/> (last accessed 19 November 2020).

Öniş, Ziya (2006), 'The political economy of Turkey's Justice and Development Party', in M. H. Yavuz (ed.), *Emergence of a New Turkey Democracy and The AK Party* (Salt Lake City: University of Utah Press), pp. 211–12.

Önsel, Mustafa (2014), *Silivri'de Firavun Töreni* (Istanbul: Kaynak Yayınları).

Önsoy, Murat (2014), 'Caught on the horns of a diplomatic dilemma: the Ukrainian crisis and Turkey's response', *Südosteuropa*, 62(2), pp. 250–64.

Orucoglu, Beriyan (2015), 'How President Erdoğan mastered the media', *Foreign Policy*, 12 August, <https://foreignpolicy.com/2015/08/12/how-president-erdogan-mastered-the-media/> (last accessed 16 November 2020).

Osborne, Samuel (2017), 'Erdoğan has called Europe "the racist, fascists and tyrannical"', *The Independent*, 22 March, <https://www.independent.co.uk/news/world/europe/turkey-erdogan-germany-netherlands-warning-europeans-not-walk-safely-a7642941.html> (last accessed 25 November 2020).

OSCE (2017), 'Turkey, constitutional referendum, 16 April 2017: statement of preliminary findings and conclusions', <https://www.osce.org/odihr/elections/turkey/311726> (last accessed 20 November 2020).

Öz, Asım (2015) *Necip Fazıl Kitabı, Sempozyum Tebliğleri* (Istanbul: Zeytinburnu Belediyesi).

Özal, Turgut (1991), *Turkey in Europe and Europe in Turkey* (Istanbul: K. Rustem & Brother).

Özbank, Murat (2015), 'Erdoğan'ın hükümetten isteyip de alamadığı şey "Başyücelik" olabilir mi?', *T24*, 11 April, <https://t24.com.tr/haber/Erdo%C4%9Fanin-hukumetten-isteyip-de-alamadigi-sey-basyucelik-olabilir-mi,293252> (last accessed 8 November 2020).

Özcan, Gencer and Ozum Arzik (2016), 'Haunting memories of the Great War: the Gallipoli victory commemorations in Turkey', in M. H. Yavuz and F. Ahmad (eds), *War and Collapse: World War I and Ottoman State* (Salt Lake City: University of Utah), pp. 1240–57.

Özcan, Nihat Ali (1999), *PKK (Kürdistan İşçi Partisi) Tarihi ideolojisi ve yöntemi* (Ankara: ASAM Yayınları).

Özdal, Hakkı (2017), 'Erdoğan'in Diyarbakır karnesi: Kardeşim ne Kürt sorunu ya!', *Gazete Duvar*, 1 April, <https://www.gazeteduvar.com.tr/yazarlar/2017/04/01/erdoganin-diyarbakir-karnesi-kardesim-ne-kurt-sorunu-ya> (last accessed 25 November 2020).

Özdenören, Rasim (2015), 'Yalnızlık: Erdoğan'ın Kaderi', *Yeni Safak*, 25 June.

Özdenören, Rasim (2018), 'Necip Fazıl Kısakürek', in Y. Aktay (ed.), *Modern Turkiye'de Siyasi Düşünce: İslamcılık* (Istanbul, Iletişim Yayınları), pp. 136–49.

Özel, İsmet (2012), *Bir Akşam Gezintisi Değil Bir İstiklâl Yürüyüşü* (Istanbul: Tiyo Yayınları).

Özel Volfová, G. (2016), 'Turkey's Middle Eastern endeavors: discourses and practices of neo-Ottomanism under the AKP', *Die Welt des Islams*, 56(3–4), pp. 489–510.

Özgül, Mehmet (2002), 'Erdoğan ile Kürt Işcisi Boran'ın tartışması', *Özgür Politika*, 27 December, <http://www.ozgurpolitika.org/2002/12/27/hab18b.html> (last accessed 11 November 2020).

Özgür, Iren (2012), *Islamic Schools in Modern Turkey: Faith, Politics, and Education* (New York: Cambridge University Press).

Özhan, Taha (2014), '17 Aralık Süreci: post-Kemalist Turkiye ve Gülen Grubu', *Türkiye Günlüğü*, 117, pp. 53–66.

Özkan, Behlül (2014), 'Turkey, Davutoglu and the idea of pan-Islamism', *Survival*, 56(4), pp. 119–40.

Özkök, Ertuğrul (2003), 'Kardeşiniz Bir Zenci Türk'tür', *Hürriyet*, 14 May.

Özkök, Ertuğrul (2006), 'Beyaz Türklerin Tasfiyesi mi', *Hürriyet*, 21 April.

Pamuk, Muhammed (2001), *Yasaklı Umut: Recep Tayyip Erdoğan* (Istanbul: Birey Yayıncılık).

Panizza, Francisco (2005), *Populism and the Mirror of Democracy* (London: Verso).

Peet, John (2011), 'Turkey after the 2011 election: challenges for the AK government', *Chatham House*, 5 July, <https://www.europeansources.info/record/turkey-after-the-2011-election-challenges-for-the-ak-government/> (last accessed 3 December 2020).

Pope, Hugh (2009), 'Privileged Partnership offers Turkey neither privilege nor partnership', International Crisis Group, 23 June, <https://www.crisisgroup.org/europe-central-asia/western-europemediterranean/turkey/privileged-partnership-offers-turkey-neither-privilege-nor-partnership> (last accessed 30 November 2020).

Popp, Maximilian (2017), 'Revisiting Turkey's failed coup attempt", *Der Spiegel Online*, 6 July.

Poyraz, Ergun (2015), *Musa'nın Çocukları: Tayyip ve Emine*, 3rd edn (Istanbul: Togan).
PressTV (2017), 'Turkey coup staged with government knowledge: Opposition leader', 3 April, <http://www.presstv.ir/Detail/2017/04/03/516596/Turkey-AKP-CHP-Kemal-Kilicdaroglu-Erdogan-coup-FETO-Gulen> (last accessed 20 November 2020).
Pulur, Hasan (2009), 'Davos'ta siz olsanız ne yapardınız?' *Hürriyet*, 30 January.
Radikal (2005), 'Erdoğan: Kürt sorunu demokrasiyle çözülür', 11 August.
Radikal (2009), 'Davos'da Kasımpaşa Havası', 30 January.
Reuters (2007), 'One million Turks rally against government', 29 April, <https://uk.reuters.com/article/us-turkey-president/one-million-turks-rally-against-government-idUSL2910950920070429> (last accessed 13 November 2020).
Reuters (2015), 'Merkel says still against Turkey joining the EU', 8 October, <https://www.reuters.com/article/us-europe-migrants-germany-turkey/merkel-says-still-against-turkey-joining-the-eu-idUSKCN0S12RD20151007> (last accessed 26 November 2020).
Reuters (2017), 'German spy agency chief says does not believe Gülen behind Turkey coup attempt', 18 March, <https://www.reuters.com/article/us-turkey-security-germany/german-spy-agency-chief-says-does-not-believe-gulen-behind-turkey-coup-attempt-idUSKBN16P0LQ> (last accessed 23 December 2019).
Reuters (2017), 'Turkey's Erdoğan links fate of detained US pastor to wanted cleric Gülen', 28 September, <https://www.reuters.com/ article/us-usa-turkey-cleric/turkeys-Erdoğan-links-fate-of-detained-u-s-pastor-to-wanted-cleric-Gülen-idUSKCN1C31IK> (last accessed 25 November 2020).
Robins, Philip (2013), 'Turkey's "double gravity" predicament: the foreign policy of a newly activist power', *International Affairs*, 89(2), pp. 381–97.
Russia Today (2016), '"Gift from God": Erdoğan sees coup as "chance to cleanse military" while PM mulls death penalty', 16 July, <https://www.rt.com/news/351630-erdogan-turkish-military-relationships/> (last accessed 22 November 2020).
Ruys, Tom and Emre Turgut (2018), 'Turkey's post-coup "purification process": collective dismissals of public servants under the European Convention on Human Rights', *Human Rights Law Review*, 18(3), pp. 539–65.
Şahin, Mehmet Nuri and Mehmet Çetin (eds) (2010), *Necıp Fazil Kizakürek* (Ankara: Kültür ve Turizm Bakanlığı Yayınları).
Sakallioglu, Umit Cizre (1997), 'The anatomy of the Turkish military's political autonomy', *Comparative Politics*, 29 (2), pp. 151–66.
Salt, Jeremy (1999), 'Turkey's military "democracy"', *Current History*, 98(625), pp. 72–8.
Salt, Jeremy (2019), *The Last Ottoman Wars: The Human Cost, 1877–1923* (Salt Lake City: University of Utah Press).

Sandel, Michael J. (2012), *What Money Can't Buy: The Moral Limits of Markets* (Farrar, Straus and Giroux).

Sarıgil, Zeki and Ömer Fazlıoğlu (2014), 'Exploring the roots and dynamics of Kurdish ethno-nationalism in Turkey', *Nations and Nationalisms*, 20(3), pp. 436–58.

Sarıoğlu, Bülent (2005), 'Kimlik Değişimi', *Milliyet*, 13 December.

Sarızeybek, Erdal (2009), *Ergenekon Gölgesinde İhaneti Yasamak* (Istanbul: Pozitif, 2009).

Schenkkan, Nate (2019), 'Turkey's new foreign policy is hostage-taking', *Foreign Policy*, 2 March, <https://foreignpolicy.com/2018/03/02/turkeys-new-foreign-policy-is-hostage-taking/> (last accessed 25 November 2020).

Schmitt, Carl (2007), *The Concept of the Political*, expanded edn, trans. G. Schwab (Chicago: University of Chicago Press).

Selek, Sabahattin (1987), *Anadolu İhtilali* (Istanbul: Kastaş Yayınları).

Sevinç, Murat (2015), 'Kılavuzu Necip Fazıl olanlar ve Başyücelik Devleti', *Diken*, 8 December, <http://www.diken.com.tr/kilavuzu-necip-fazil-olanlar-ve-basyucelik-devleti/> (last accessed 8 November 2020).

Sevinç, Murat (2019), 'Ingiltere, Fransa, Almanya ve Şahsı üzerine', *Gazete Duvar*, 12 December, <https://www.gazeteduvar.com.tr/yazarlar/2019/12/12/ingiltere-fransa-almanya-ve-sahsi-uzerine> (last accessed 25 November 2020).

Simmel, George (1906), 'The sociology of secrecy and of secret societies', *American Journal of Sociology*, 11(4), pp. 441–98.

Smith, Hannah Lucinda (2019), *Erdoğan Rising: The Battle for the Soul of Turkey* (London: William Collins).

Sofuoğlu, Ebubekir (2015), 'Abdulhamid'e yapılanlarla Erdoğan'a yapılanlar arasındaki benzerlikler', *Sabah*, 25 June.

Sol Haber Portalı (2020), 'Arşivden bulup çıkardık, Erdoğan'ın yıllar önce oynadığı piyesin metni', 23 May, <https://haber.sol.org.tr/turkiye/bakin-hitler-meraki-nereden-geliyor-arsivden-bulup-cikardik-Erdo%C4%9Fanin-yillar-once-oynadigi> (last accessed 8 November 2020).

Sontag, Deborah (2003), 'The Erdoğan experiment', *The New York Times Magazine*, 11 May, <https://www.nytimes.com/2003/05/11/magazine/the-erdogan-experiment.html> (last accessed 11 November 2020).

Srivastava, Mehul (2017), 'Assets worth $11bn seized in Turkey crackdown', *Financial Times*, 7 July, <https://www.ft.com/content/fed595d0-631e-11e7-8814-0ac7eb84e5f1> (last accessed 22 November 2020).

Star (2013) 'Başbakan Erdoğan Milli İradeye Saygı mitinginde halka seslendi', 16 June, <https://www.star.com.tr/politika/basbakan-erdogan-milli-iradeye-saygi-mitinginde-halka-seslendi-haber-763054/> (last accessed 16 November 2020).

The Stockholm Center for Freedom (2017), 'Erdoğan's July 15th coup', July, <https://stockholmcf.org/15-july-erdogans-coup/> (last accessed 20 November 2020).

Strohmeier, Martin (2002), *Crucial Images in the Presentation of a Kurdish National Identity: Heroes and Patriots, Traitors and Foes* (Leiden: Brill).

Talmon, Jacab L. (1970), *The Origins of Totalitarian Democracy* (New York: W. W. Norton & Co.).

Tamimi, Azzam (2001), *Rachid Ghannouchi: A Democrat within Islamism* (New York: Oxford University Press).

Tamir, Christine, Aidan Connaughton and Ariana Monique Salazar (2020), 'The global God divide', *Pew Research Center*, 20 July, <https://www.pewresearch.org/global/2020/07/20/the-global-god-divide/> (last accessed 15 November 2020).

Tan, Altan (2007), 'Kürtler AKP'ye sadece kredi açtı', *Milliyet*, 30 July, <https://www.milliyet.com.tr/siyaset/kurtler-akpye-sadece-kredi-acti-208070> (last accessed 15 November 2020).

Tan, Altan (2020), 'Günümüzde Kürtlerde üç tarzı siyaset', *Independent Türkçe*, 16 April, <https://www.indyturkish.com/node/159236/t%C3%BCrkiyeden-sesler/g%C3%BCn%C3%BCm%C3%BCzde-k%C3%BCrtlerde-3-tarz%C4%B1-siyaset> (last accessed 25 November 2020).

Tansel, Fevziye Abdullah (1991), *Mehmet Akif Ersoy: Hayati, Eserleri* (Istanbul: Mehmet Akif Ersoy Fikir ve Sanat Vakfı Yayınları).

Taraf (2011), 'PKK-MİT görüşmeleri Tam Metin', 14 September, <https://www.ilke-haber.com/haber/pkk-mit-gizli-gorusmeleri-tam-metin-18601.htm> (last accessed 25 November 2020).

Tarihi, Giriş (2010), 'The Prime Minister Erdoğan's perspective on Mehmet Akif', *Sabah*, 27 December, <https://www.sabah.com.tr/gundem/2010/12/27/basbakanin_gozunden_mehmet_akif> (last accessed 9 November 2020).

Taş, Hakki (2015), 'Turkey – from tutelary to delegative democracy', *Third World Quarterly*, 36(4), pp. 776–91.

Taş, Hakki, (2018), 'The 15 July abortive coup and post-truth politics in Turkey', *Southeast European and Black Sea Studies*, 18(1), pp. 1–19.

Taşgetiren, Ahmet (1995), 'Boğulma Hissi', *Zaman*, 18 January.

Taşgetiren, Ahmet (2020), 'Dökülme', *Karar*, 26 June, <https://www.karar.com/yazarlar/ahmet-tasgetiren/dokulme-1571270> (last accessed 16 November 2020).

Taştan, Coşkun (2013), 'The Gezi Park protests in Turkey: a qualitative research', *Turkish Insight*, 15(3), pp. 27–38.

Tavernise, Sabine (2016), 'Turkish leader Erdogan making new enemies and frustrating old friends', *The New York Times*, 4 July, <https://www.nytimes.com/2016/07/05/world/europe/turkey-erdogan-new-enemies-frustrating-friends.html> (last accessed 9 November 2020).

Tekelioğlu, Orhan (1996), 'The rise of a spontaneous synthesis: the historical background of Turkish popular music', *Middle Eastern Studies*, 32(1), pp. 194–215.

Terkoğlu, Barış (2019), 'Erdoğan'ın "Saddamlaştırılması"nın başlangıcı', *Cumhuriyet*, 9 May, <https://www.cumhuriyet.com.tr/yazarlar/baris-terkoglu/erdoganin-saddamlastirilmasinin-baslangici-1384136> (last accessed 11 November 2020).

Tharoor, Ishaan (2016), 'Turkey's Erdoğan always feared a coup. He was proved right', *The Washington Post*, 15 July, <https://www.washingtonpost.com/news/worldviews/wp/2016/07/15/turkeys-erdogan-always-feared-a-coup-he-was-proved-right/> (last accessed 18 November 2020).

Tibi, Bassam (2006), 'Europeanizing Islam, or the Islamization of Europe', in T. Byrnes and P. Katzenstein (eds), *Religion in an Expanding Europe* (New York: Cambridge University Press), pp. 204–24.

Tittensor, David (2014), *The House of Service: The Gülen Movement and Islam's Third Way* (New York: Oxford University Press).

Tocci, Nathalie and Joshua W. Walker (2012), 'From confrontation to engagement: Turkey and the Middle East', in R. H. Linden, A. O. Evin, K. Kirişci, T. Straubhaar, N. Tocci, J. Tolay and J. W. Walker (eds), *Turkey and Its Neighbors: Foreign Relations in Transition* (Boulder, CO: Lynne Rienner Publishers), pp. 35–60.

Tokdoğan, Nagehan (2018), *Yeni Osmanlıcılık: Hınç, Nostalji, Narsisizm* (Istanbul: Iletişim).

Toprak, Binnaz (1982), *Islam and Political Development* (Leiden: Brill).

Toprak, Binnaz (2010), 'Who are these White Turks?', *Hürriyet Daily News*, 15 November.

Toprak, Binnaz, Irfan Bozan, Tan MorGül and Nedim Şener (2008), *Being Different in Turkey: Otherized on the Axis of Religion and Conservatism* (Istanbul: Bogazici Universitesi Yayınları).

Tosun, Resil (2016), 'Abdulhamid Erdoğan Benzerliği', *Star*, 25 September.

Toynbee, Arnold Joseph (1948), *Civilization on Trial* (Oxford: Oxford University Press).

Toynbee, Arnold Joseph (1955), 'The Ottoman Empire in world history', *Proceedings of the American Philosophical Society*, 99(3), pp. 119–26.

Trofimov, Yaroslav (2016), 'Turkey's autocratic turn', *The Wall Street Journal*, 9 December, <https://www.wsj.com/articles/turkeys-autocratic-turn-1481288401> (last accessed 26 November 2020).

Turgut, Serdar (2004), 'AKP Beyaz Türk İktidarını Yıktı', *Habertürk*, 3 June.

Türk, Bahadır (2014), *Muktedir: Türk Sağ Geleneği ve Recep Tayyip Erdoğan* (Istanbul: Iletisim).

Turner, Bryan S. (1988), *Concepts in Social Thoughts* (Minneapolis: University of Minnesota Press).

Tziarras, Zenonas (2018), 'Erdoğanist authoritarianism and the "New" Turkey', *Southeast European and Black Sea Studies*, 18(4), pp. 593–8.

Ünsal, Fatma Bostan (2004), 'Mehmet Âkif Ersoy', *Modern Türkiye'de Siyasi Düşünce, İslâmcılık* (Istanbul: İletişim Yayınları), pp. 76–7.

Ural, Ibrahim, (2014), *Bir Emniyet Müdürünün Kaleminden Oslo Görüşmeleri* (Istanbul: Ileri Yayınları).

Ülgen, Sinan (2011), 'Is Brussels the loser in Turkey's elections?', *European Voice*, 15 June, <https://www.politico.eu/article/is-brussels-the-loser-in-turkeys-elections/> (last accessed 15 November 2020).

Uludağ, Alican (2017), 'The enigma of the coup tip-off officer', *Cumhuriyet*, 18 May, <http://www.cumhuriyet.com.tr/haber/english/743431/The_enigma_of_the_coup_tip-off_officer.html> (last accessed 20 November 2020).

United Press International (2006), 'Hamas leaders visit Turkey', 16 February, <https://www.upi.com/Hamas-leaders-visit-Turkey/42871140112629/> (last accessed 26 November 2020).

Uzer, Umut (2018), 'Glorification of the past as a political tool: Ottoman history in contemporary Turkish politics', *The Journal of the Middle East and Africa*, 9(4), pp. 339–57.

Uzgel, İlhan (2006), 'Dış politikada AKP: stratejik konumdan stratejik modele', *Mülkiye*, 252, pp. 69–84.

Uzun, Sabri (2015), *İn-Baykal Kaseti, Dink Cinayeti ve Diğer Komplolar* (Istanbul: Kırmızı Kedi Yayınevi).

Venice Commission (2015), 'Venice Commission declaration on interference with judicial independence in Turkey', 20 June, <https://venice.coe.int/files/turkish%20declaration%20June%202015.pdf> (last accessed 22 November 2020).

Vaisse, Justin (2007), 'Slamming the *Sublime Porte*? Challenges in French–Turkish relations from Chirac to Sarkozy', 6 December, <https://www.brookings.edu/wp-content/uploads/2016/06/0128_turkey_vaisse.pdf> (last accessed 26 November 2020).

Vergin, Nur (2004), 'Siyaset ile Sosyolojinin Buluşduğu Nokda', *Türkiye Günlüğü*, 76, pp. 5–9.

Wilks, Judith M. (1995), 'Aspects of the Köroğlu Destanı: Chodźko and beyond' (PhD dissertation, University of Chicago).

Yanık, Lerna (2016), 'Bringing the empire back in: the gradual discovery of the Ottoman Empire in Turkish foreign policy', *Die Welt Des Islams* 56 (3–4), pp. 466–88.

Yasamee, F. A. K. (1996), *Ottoman Diplomacy: Abdulhamid II and the Great Powers 1878–1888* (Istanbul: ISIS).

Yavuz, M. Hakan (1997), 'Political Islam and the Welfare (Refah) Party in Turkey', *Comparative Politics*, 30(1), pp. 63–82.
Yavuz, M. Hakan (1998), 'Turkish identity and foreign policy in flux: the rise of neo-Ottomanism', *Critique: Critical Middle Eastern Studies*, 12, pp. 19–41.
Yavuz, M. Hakan (1999), 'The matrix of modern Turkish Islamic movements: The Naqshbandi Sufi Order', in E. Özdalga (ed.), *The Naqshbandis in Western and Central Asia* (London: Curzon Press), pp. 129–46.
Yavuz, M. Hakan (2000), 'Turkey's fault lines and the crisis of Kemalism,' *Current History*, 99, pp. 33–9.
Yavuz, M. Hakan (2001), 'A preamble to the Kurdish question: the politics of Kurdish identity', *Journal of Muslim Minority Affairs*, 18(1), pp. 9–18.
Yavuz, M. Hakan (2001), 'Five stages in the construction of Kurdish nationalism in Turkey', *Nationalism and Ethnic Politics*, 7(3), pp. 1–24.
Yavuz, M. Hakan (2003), *Islamic Political Identity in Turkey* (New York: Oxford University Press).
Yavuz, M. Hakan (2008), *Secularism and Muslim Democracy in Turkey* (Cambridge: Cambridge University Press).
Yavuz, M. Hakan (2013), *Toward an Islamic Enlightenment: The Gülen Movement* (New York: Oxford University Press).
Yavuz, M. Hakan (2016), 'Social and intellectual origins of neo-Ottomanism: searching for a post-national vision', *Die Welt des Islams*, 56(3–4), pp. 438–65.
Yavuz, M. Hakan (2018), 'A framework for understanding the intra-Islamist conflict between the AK Party and the Gülen movement', *Politics, Religion & Ideology*, 19(1), pp. 11–32.
Yavuz, M. Hakan (2019), 'Understanding Turkish secularism in the 21st century: a contextual roadmap', *Southeast European and Black Sea Studies*, 19(1), pp. 55–79.
Yavuz, M. Hakan (2020), *Nostalgia for the Empire: The Politics of Neo-Ottomanism* (New York: Oxford University Press).
Yavuz, M. Hakan and Bayram Balci (2018), *Turkey's July 14th Coup: What Happened and Why* (Salt Lake City: University of Utah, 2018).
Yavuz, M. Hakan and John Esposito (eds) (2003), *Turkish Islam and the Secular State: The Gülen Movement* (Syracuse: Syracuse University Press).
Yavuz, M. Hakan and Michael M. Gunter (2001), 'The Kurdish nation', *Current History*, 100(642), pp. 33–9.
Yavuz, M. Hakan and Michael Gunter (2007), 'Turkish paradox: progressive Islamists versus reactionary secularists', *Middle East Critique*, 16(3), pp. 289–301.

Yavuz, M. Hakan and Mujeeb R. Khan (2015), 'Turkey asserts its role in the region', *New York Times*, 11 February, <https://www.nytimes.com/2015/02/12/opinion/turkey-asserts-its-role-in-the-middle-east.html> (last accessed 30 November 2020).

Yavuz, M. Hakan and Rasım Koç (2016), 'The Turkish coup attempt: the Gülen movement vs. the state', *Middle East Policy* 23(4), pp. 20–39.

Yavuz, M. Hakan and Nihat Ali Özcan (2006), 'The Kurdish question and the AKP', *Middle East Policy*, 13(1), pp. 102–19.

Yavuz, M. Hakan and Nihat Ali Özcan (2007), 'Political crisis in Turkey: the conflict of political languages', *Middle East Policy*, 14(3), pp. 118–35.

Yenigün, Halil İbrahim (2014), 'Hayrettin Karaman'la "Laik Düzende Dini Yaşamak" yahut Siyaset Fıkhının Sınırları', *Birikim Dergisi*, 303–4, pp. 203–10.

Yesilada, Birol (2002), 'The Virtue Party', *Turkish Studies*, 3(1), pp. 62–81.

Yeşiltaş, Murat (2013), 'The transformation of the geopolitical vision in Turkish foreign policy', *Turkish Studies*, 14(1), pp. 661–87.

Yıldırım, Ergun and Hayrettin Özler (2007), 'A sociological representation of the Justice and Development Party (AKP): is it a political design or a political becoming?', *Turkish Studies*, 8, pp. 5–24.

Yıldız, Ahmet (2003), 'Politico-religious discourse of political Islam in Turkey: the parties of national outlook', *Muslim World*, 93(2), pp. 187–210.

Yılmaz, Mehmet (2006), 'Amaç Orgeneral Büyükanıt'ı yıpratmak!', *Hürriyet*, 6 March.

Yılmaz, Turan (2001), *Tayyip: Kasımpaşa'dan Siyasetin Ön Saflarına* (Istanbul: Umit).

Yılmaz, Zafer (2017), 'The AKP and the spirit of the "New" Turkey: imagined victim, reactionary mood and resentful sovereign', *Turkish Studies*, 18(3), pp. 482–513.

Yücel, Dilek Mayaturk (2017), 'Inside and outside: on the 100th day of Deniz Yucel's imprisonment', *Deutsche Welle*, 24 May, <https://www.dw.com/en/inside-and-outside-on-the-100th-day-of-deniz-yucels-imprisonment/a-38961794> (last accessed 30 November 2020).

Zalewski, Piotr (2013), 'Protocols of the interest rate lobby', *Foreign Policy*, 27 June, <https://foreignpolicy.com/2013/06/27/protocols-of-the-interest-rate-lobby/> (last accessed 4 December 2020).

Zengin, Bahri (1995), *Özgürleşerek Birlikte Yaşamak* (Istanbul: Birlesik Yayıncılık).

INDEX

1453 (Fall of Constantinople), 89, 120
1908 revolution, 55, 78, 148, 173
2003 Iraq War, 149
2023 (Turkey Republic vision), 109, 197

Abbas, Mahmoud, 294
Abbasid (civilisation), 88
Abduh, Muhammad, 56
Abdulhamid II, 11, 62, 63–4, 66–9, 78, 81, 190, 201, 250, 255, 309
Ackerman, Xanthe, 92
Ağar, Mehmet, 142
AK Saray (White Palace), 33, 176
Akar, Hulusi, 230, 231–2, 235, 237, 238, 239, 240–6, 254, 256
Akdoğan, Yalcin, 114, 270, 279
Akkaş, Muammer, 193
AKP (Justice and Development Party), 4, 5–6, 7, 9, 15, 17, 20–2, 23–4, 31, 32, 33–4, 36, 60, 67, 78, 81–2, 92–5, 97–9, 100–1, 104–7, 108–9, 110–12, 139, 148, 149–52, 160–2, 165–6, 168–70, 173, 175–6, 177, 179–80, 182–3, 185, 187, 189, 193–6, 201–2, 206–7, 208–9, 212–13, 226–7, 229, 249, 250–2, 255, 259–61, 265, 268, 283, 285, 287, 289, 290–2, 296–9, 302–3, 309, 315–18, 320, 323
  closure case (2008), 156–8
  elections (2002), 129–37
  elections (2007), 152–6
  elections (2011), 164–5
  elections (2015), 197–200
  formation of party, 125, 128
  Gülenist alliance, 213–21, 254
  Gülenist clash and alliance breakup, 221–6, 232–6
  presidential crisis (2007), 141–6
  presidential election (2014), 196–7
al-Afghani, Jamal al-Din, 56, 309
Al-Aqsa mosque, 90, 313
al-Banna, Hasan, 58
Alevis, 4, 17, 102, 104–5, 106, 114, 163–4, 181–2, 185, 197, 251, 277, 322
Ali, Ben, 298

Alış-Veriş Merkezi (AVM), 175
Alparslan, 79, 121
Altınok, Selami, 193
ANAP centre-right party, 131–2, 138, 142
Anatolia, 1, 2–3, 15, 17–18, 27, 30, 31, 49, 50, 53, 56, 65–6, 77–8, 79, 82, 85, 88–9, 106, 121, 132, 137, 144–5, 153, 177, 183–4, 197, 227, 253, 261–2, 283–4, 307, 314, 316, 322
Ankara, 31, 33, 63, 82–3, 86–7, 122, 132, 143, 145, 150, 176, 182, 198, 217–18, 222, 224, 245–6
Annan Plan (2004), 287, 288, 310
Anti-Defamation League, 89
anti-Semitism, 53–4
Arab League Summit, 293
Arab Spring, 20, 26, 34, 80, 99, 162, 172, 183, 187, 258, 268, 272, 273, 292, 296–302, 306, 316
Arab world, 15, 289, 291–6, 297, 309
Arınç, Bülent, 20, 125, 126–8, 148, 156, 182–3, 315
Armağan, Mustafa, 69
Armenian–Turkish Protocols (2009), 291
Armenians, 64, 153, 169, 197, 262
Arvasi, Shaykh Abdulhakim, 48
Aslan, Süleyman, 192–3
Assad, Bashar, 99, 273, 293, 298, 300, 307, 312
Assyrians, 197
Asya Finance Bank, 238
Atalay, Besir, 267, 318
Atasoy, Yildiz, 3, 26
Atatürk, Mustafa Kemal, 1, 17–18, 30, 63–4, 69–71, 73, 79, 84, 87–91, 94, 105, 110, 123, 141, 143, 147, 148, 167–8, 173–5, 176, 178, 321

Augustine (*The City of God*), 93
authoritarianism, 8, 9, 16, 26, 37, 54, 68, 98, 149–50, 179, 207–8, 250–1, 253, 255, 283, 299, 305–6, 308
Ayalon, Danny, 295
Azerbaijan, 66, 286, 291, 307, 310

Babacan, Ali, 11, 70, 129, 140, 185, 200, 318
Bağış, Egemen, 193, 195, 286
Bahçeli Devlet, 97, 272, 274, 317
Bahrain, 20, 298
Balkans, 67, 68, 71, 87, 106, 121, 148, 177, 262, 290, 297, 307
Balyoz trials, 99, 158–60, 237, 316
Barzani, Masoud, 168, 268
Basbuğ, İlker, 147, 158–60, 167, 171, 227, 236, 256
başyüce (or başyücelik), 6, 51–2, 73, 136, 317
Batmaz, Kemal, 232, 233, 239, 245
Baykal, Deniz, 142
Bayraktar, Oğuz, 75, 192, 198
Ben Buyum (This is Me), 49
Besli, Hüseyin, 26, 45, 72, 74, 107–8, 137
Beştepe, 63
Beyefendi, 111
Beyoğlu, 22, 23, 39, 58, 111, 117–19, 170, 173
Binney, Horace, 19, 28
Bir Adam Yaratmak, 48
Bittner, Jochen, 30
Black Sea, 34, 35, 83, 109, 247
Black Turks, 15, 27, 29, 30, 32, 122, 137, 153
Blair, Tony, 61, 289, 311
Boehnermann, Jan, 81
Boran, Zulfikar, 92, 113

Bosnia, 14, 17, 34, 87, 266, 286, 307, 309
Bosporus Sea, 109
Boyner, Cem, 183, 203
Bulut, Yigit, 323
bureaucracy, Turkey, 19–21, 43, 106, 115, 122, 129, 142, 150, 155, 169, 212, 215–21, 224, 232, 242, 243, 261, 292
Burma, 309
Bush, George W., 291
Büyük Doğu, 48, 49, 72, 73
Büyükanıt, Yaşar, 142, 150–1, 157, 158, 167, 168, 169
Bylock, 244

Çağlayan, Kaan, 192
Calisir, Ekin, 92, 113
Çamlıca Hill, 109, 175–6
Camuroğlu, Reha, 169, 185
Can, Osman, 189, 204
Çandar, Cengiz, 270, 279
Cankaya Place, 63, 146, 246
capulcu, 183, 203
Çarkoğlu, Ali, 4
Caucasus, 1, 71, 87, 262, 297, 307
caudillismo, 10
Celikkol, Ahmet Oguz, 295
cemaat, 48, 134, 168, 208–9, 214, 226, 228
Chechnya, 307
CHP (Republican People's Party), 1, 49, 93, 129, 267, 309
China, 13, 322
Christian Social Union (CSU), 289
Çiçek, Cemil, 196
Cinisli, Rasim, 47
Clinton, Bill, 61, 62
Clinton, Hillary, 291
Close, David, 10

CNN, 8, 168, 189, 247
Cold War, 2, 47, 93
Committee of National Unity (1960), 149
Committee of Union and Progress Party, 55
Communalism, 208
constitution, Turkey (1982), 165, 248
Constitutional Court, 3, 4, 21, 23, 60, 99, 126, 127, 139, 141, 143, 152, 156–60, 167, 171, 194, 219, 229, 230, 316, 319
   (2007–8), AKP case, 21, 23, 139, 143, 152, 156–60, 171
constitutional referendum (2010), 23, 139, 160–2, 218–19, 268, 297
constitutional referendum (2017), 249, 257
Copenhagen Criteria (EU), 98, 142, 287
Copenhagen Summit (2002), 287
corruption, public and governmental, 6, 10–11, 12–13, 19, 21, 24, 34, 60, 75, 97, 112, 129, 133, 136, 138, 141, 176, 181, 188, 197–8, 200–1, 218, 219, 232, 249, 256, 277, 283, 286, 299, 305, 316–17, 322–5
corruption probe (December 2013), 172, 192–6, 212–13, 222–5, 229, 235, 238–9, 240, 255
Council of Higher Education, 141
COVID-19 pandemic, 11
Crimea, 1, 34, 307
Cyprus, 140, 165, 287–8, 289, 310

Daily Sabah, 68, 102
Dale, Roger, 41
dar al-harp, 43, 44, 72
Dardanelles Campaign, 54

Davutoğlu, Ahmet, 34, 70, 97, 168, 195, 198, 240, 286, 297–8, 312, 318
de Bellaigue, Christopher, 69, 75, 76
Demir, Mustafa, 192
Demirel, Süleyman, 2, 94, 127, 132
Demirören Holding, 102
Demirtaş, Selahattin, 196, 256, 270–1, 274
Democrat Party, 2, 78, 148, 188
Democratic Union Party (PYD), Syria, 296, 306
democratisation, 12, 100, 106–7, 11, 128–9, 141, 162, 263, 266, 317, 321
Derin Tarih (Deep History), 69, 75
Dersim, 104–5, 114, 164, 171, 259, 263
Derviş, Kemal, 39, 108
d'Estaing, Giscard, 288
Dilipak, Abdülrahman, 64, 75, 110
dindar, 124, 161, 171
Directorate of Religious Affairs (DRA), 94, 106
Directorate of Turkish Radio and Television (TRT), 141
Diriliş, 251
Dişli, Mehmet, 246, 257
Dişli, Şaban, 246, 257
Doğan Holding Group, 8, 27
Doğu Perinçek group, 181
Dolmabahçe Declaration, 270–1, 280
Dumankaya, 35
Duterte, Roderigo, 29
Düzce, 118
DYP centre-right party (True Path Party), 131, 138, 142

Ecevit, Bülent, 53, 108, 129, 136
Economist, The, 299

economy, Turkey, 4, 14, 16, 39, 97, 108, 129, 133, 138, 146, 165, 170, 176, 197, 287, 289, 293, 305, 308, 316, 323
  economic crisis (2001), 4, 14, 16, 39, 108, 129, 133, 138
  middle class, Turkey, 31, 79, 97, 131, 145–6, 184
Egypt, 12, 20, 21, 24, 49, 56, 58, 108, 111, 172, 190–2, 200, 203, 211, 291, 296, 307, 309, 313
  coup (July 2013), 12, 24, 108, 172, 190–2, 200, 203, 291, 296, 307, 309, 313
elections
  (1950), 2, 78, 132
  (1991), 118
  (1995), 121–2
  (2002), 4, 65, 129–33, 135
  (2007), 4, 152–3, 169
  (2011), 4, 162–5, 219
  (2014), 196–7, 256
  (2015), 4, 112, 196, 197–200, 261, 271–2
Enlightenment philosophy (Locke, Rousseau, Montesquieu and Constant), 100, 288
Erbakan, Necmettin, 2, 3–4, 39, 53–4, 58–61, 117, 119, 121–2, 122–3, 126, 127, 136, 188, 214, 303, 313
Erdoğan, Ahmet Burak, 60, 75
Erdoğan, Bilal Necmettin, 60, 75, 193
Erdoğan, Fatma, 35
Erdoğan, Hasan, 35
Erdoğan, Latif, 235
Erdoğan, Mehmet, 35
Erdoğan, Mustafa, 10, 34, 61
Erdoğan, Recep Tayyip, 3–22, 314–27
  education, 39–58, 90–1
  foreign policy, 282–313

Gülenist clash, 206–29, 267, 306, 315–16
imprisonment, 23, 85, 97, 105, 122–4, 125, 126
kleptocracy, 242, 250, 254, 318, 323, 324
Kurdish Question, 258–81
local politics, 116–20
mayor, Istanbul, 3, 4, 14, 23, 33, 38, 45–6, 83, 97, 106, 120–4, 126, 166, 265
nationalism, 197–200, 251–2
political career, early period, 58–62
political crisis (2007), 141–5
political period (2002–7), 129–37
political period (2010–11), 160–5
political period (2013), 172–96
political period (2014–15), 196–201
political period (2016–21), 248–55
populism, 12, 18–19, 27–8, 64, 103–4, 251, 324–5
Public Procurement Law (PPL), 324
reis (chief), 6, 29, 77, 108, 111
Respect for the National Will, 185, 188
'seduced' coup (15 July 2016), 230–48
Siirt, 47, 59, 85, 91, 120, 123–4, 120, 136, 265
Erdoğan, Tenzile, 35
Ergenekon case, 158–60
Ersoy, Mehmet Akif, 22, 41, 52, 55–8, 74
  Sebi-ül Reşat, 55
  Sırat-ı Mustakim, 55
Ertem, Cemil, 68
Erzurum, 135, 188–9
Eskişehir, 182
Etiler, 65
European Court of Human Rights, 161

European Customs Union, 293
European Union, 9, 208, 213–14, 221, 236, 252, 253, 261, 265, 286–91
Evren, General Kenan, 161
Eyub Lisesi High School, 40
ezik ruhlu, 56

Fanon, Frantz, 77, 89, 113
Faulkner, William, 81
  Requiem for a Nun, 81
federalism, 201, 258, 269–70, 275, 277
Felicity Party (SP), 4, 127
FETÖ (Fethullah Terrorist Organisation), 24, 171, 209, 240; *see also* Gülenist movement
Fidan, Hakan, 186, 222, 229, 235, 241–6, 256, 268, 279
Filkins, Dexter, 178, 311
Financial Times, The, 98, 324
Fırat, Dengir Mir Mehmet, 104, 112, 138, 162, 186, 259, 264–5, 275
foreign policy, Turkey, 94, 95, 191, 218, 221, 227, 229, 240, 253, 282–313
FP (Virtue Party), 4, 126, 157
  yenilikciler, 127
France, 93, 96, 144, 174, 289

Gallipoli Campaign, 54, 56, 74
Gates, Robert, 291
Gaza, 221, 292, 294, 295; *see also* Mavi Marmara
Georgia, 34, 34, 87, 266, 311
Germany, 236, 247, 269, 286, 305
Gezi Park protests, 24, 80, 98, 108, 172, 173–90, 202, 203, 204
Ghannouchi, Rached, 14, 27
Göle, Nilüfer, 184, 203
Great Britain, 174

Greece, 191, 289
Gül, Abdullah, 4, 20, 34, 70, 99, 101, 127, 128, 141, 166, 189, 228, 240, 267, 291, 294, 315, 318
Gülbaran, Emine, 59
Gülen, Fethullah, 123, 142, 231, 246, 256, 286, 324
Gülenist movement, 6, 12, 19, 20, 21, 24, 33, 88, 99, 108, 123, 126, 133–4, 142, 144, 146, 150–2, 157–9, 160–2, 166, 167, 168, 169, 170, 172, 178, 182, 185–6, 189, 192–6, 268, 324
  Nokta magazine, 152
  seduced coup (15 July 2016), 230, 231, 232–45, 247, 251–7, 308, 320
Güler, İhami, 14, 27
Gülerce, Hüseyin, 235
Gunter, Michael, 113, 273, 278

Hagia Sophia, 11, 63, 83, 89–90, 313
Halk Bank, 193
Halk TV, 182
Hamas, 292, 294, 311
Hatay territory, 294
  Orontes/Asi river, 294
HDP (People's Democratic Party), 99, 196, 271
Hearth of Ottomans, 252
Helsinki Summit (1999), 287
hemşerilik (hometown pride), 121
hizmet (service), 95, 106, 114, 134, 214, 231
Holt, William, 106, 114
Housing Development Administration of Turkey (TOKI), 175, 176, 192
Huduti, Adem, 243–4
Huntington, Samuel, 4, 285, 297

Hürriyet, 8, 75, 102, 113–14, 168, 170, 171, 203, 228, 255, 280, 311, 313
Hussein, Saddam, 291

Ihsanoglu, Ekmeleddin, 196, 256
Imam Hatip schools, 20, 22, 34, 37–47, 58, 59–60, 90, 92, 123, 124, 161, 171, 286, 320
İnönü, İsmet, 178
Intcen, European Union, 236
Internal Service Law of 1961, 147;
  see also military, Turkey
Iran, 149, 274, 291, 298, 300, 304, 307, 308
Iraq, 9, 26, 32, 99, 141, 146–7, 149, 168, 199, 262, 272, 274, 275, 287, 291, 299, 300, 306, 308, 309
ISIS (Islamic State of Iraq and the Levant), 9, 17, 199, 273, 296, 299, 300–1, 306, 307, 308, 317
Islamic identity, 1, 80, 92, 123, 127, 131–2, 161, 166, 248, 282, 284, 300, 304
  High Islam versus Folk (vernacular) Islam, 209
  seyfülislam (the sword and shield of Islam), 95
Islamic law (*seriat* or sharia), 15, 51, 130, 146, 192, 207, 303
Islamic revival, 1–2, 22–3, 40–5, 47, 56–8, 63–9, 72, 79–80, 82, 84–93, 119–20, 161–2, 209, 214, 303, 319, 321, 322
Islamism and Islamisation, 1–5, 6, 11–15, 17, 23–5, 27, 29, 30–2, 39, 45, 47–56, 58–61, 63–9, 74, 78–81, 84–93, 94, 97–101, 103, 107, 110, 112, 122–37, 140–1, 144–52, 153–6, 157, 159, 161–4,

166, 169, 184, 186–7, 190,
191–2, 201–2, 207–9, 213–14,
218, 220, 225–6, 227, 242, 248,
250–1, 252, 254–5, 259–60,
264, 265–6, 269, 275–7, 283–6,
293–4, 296–310, 316–17,
319–20, 323, 324–5
Islamophobia, 9, 30, 285
Islamo-Turkish nationalism, 47, 161,
271, 299
   medeniyet tassavvuru (civilisational
      perspective), 161
   umma, 162, 190, 304
   Ummayad (civilisation), 178
   yönetici sınıf (new ruling elite), 50
   zihniyet (synthesis), 50
Israel, 32, 85, 86, 172, 185, 192, 207,
214, 219, 221, 285, 287, 292,
294–6, 308, 312
Istanbul, 3, 4, 11, 14, 23, 32–4, 35,
38–9, 44–6, 48, 53–6, 59–61, 65,
67, 69, 82–3, 85, 89–90, 97, 106,
109, 116–17, 120–2, 132–3, 138,
159, 166, 173–90, 192–3, 217,
246–7, 265, 304, 312
Izetbegovic, Alija, 14, 27
Izmir, 109, 132, 145, 182

Jacobin model, 37, 58, 93, 174–5, 321
Jordan, 293, 295, 298

kabadayı (Erdoğan), 6, 63–6
Kafka, Franz, 36, 72
Kahl, Bruno, 236, 247
Kahraman, Ismail, 47, 67
Karaca, Osman, 244
Karaman, Hayrettin, 323, 327
Kashmir, 34, 309, 322
Kavakçı, Merve, 126–7
Kavala, Osman, 185, 203

Kayseri, 53, 135, 171, 185
Kazlıçeşme, 188
Kemalism, 2–5, 21, 25–7, 30, 37,
40, 42, 45, 47–52, 54, 64–6, 73,
77–9, 82–3, 88, 91, 94, 97–100,
110, 114, 122–5, 132, 134–6,
139–41, 144–6, 149–50, 152,
154–60, 166, 170, 174, 178–9,
182–3, 203, 212–14, 218–19,
237, 238, 248, 258, 259–65, 284,
287, 303, 314, 315–16, 318,
321–2, 325; *see also* secularism
Mekteb-i Mülkiye, 314
Kerry, John, 308
Khashoggi, Jamal, 234, 304
Kılıçdaroğlu, Kemal, 97, 105, 163,
164, 231, 239, 263, 309
Kinzer, Stephen, 100, 114
Kirkuk, 141
Kısakürek, Necip Fazıl, 14, 22, 41,
47–56, 64, 67, 73, 74, 79, 90,
119, 126, 227, 248, 259, 300
   hakimiyet hakkındır, 51
   Ideolocya Örgüsü, 51
   Ulu Hakan II, Abdülhamid Han, 64
Konya, 30, 135, 184
Köroğlu, 6, 63–6, 74, 75
Kosovo, 286, 307
Kotku, Shaykh, 46
Kouchner, Bernard, 291
Koza Ipek, 324
Küçükçekmece, 116
kulturkampf, 2, 37, 85–6, 177, 228
Kurds, 1, 4, 7, 9, 17, 18, 19, 25, 33,
34, 54, 64, 80, 87, 92, 93, 99,
104–5, 107, 114, 141–2, 145,
146–52, 154, 164, 168, 169, 181,
197, 198–200, 201, 216, 222,
229, 256, 258–81, 298–302, 312,
319, 322, 325

Kurds (*cont.*)
  Kurdistan Communities Union (KCK), 222
  Kurdistan Regional Government, 268
  Kurdistan Workers Party, 9
Kurtulmus, Numan, 60
Kutan, Recai, 127

Lausanne, Treaty of, 17, 90, 262
Lavrov, Sergey, 291
Lebanese war (2006), 294
Lebanon, 293
Levant Quartet, 293, 299
Libya, 11, 20, 191, 309, 310
Lincoln, Abraham, 19–20
Louis XIV, 318

Machiavelli (*The Prince*), 6, 82, 96, 113, 114
Macron, Emmanuel, 297
mahalle baskısı (neighbourhood pressure), 155, 163–4, 170
Manjib, 306
Manzikert (1071), 79, 316, 317
Maraniss, David, 61–2, 75
Mardin, Şerif, 5, 26, 73, 155, 170, 227, 228
Marmara Sea, 2, 109
Mas-kom-Ya, 53–4
Mavi Marmara, 221, 295, 316
mazlum (oppressed or the wronged one), 53, 65, 152, 153, 169
McGurk, Brett, 301
Mehmed the Conquerer, 317
Mehmet, Fatih, 81, 121
Menderes, Adnan, 2, 78, 100, 132, 134, 149, 188, 204
Merkel, Angela, 140, 289, 290, 297, 305, 311

Metiner, Mehmet, 101, 114, 276, 279, 281
MGH (National Outlook Movement), 22, 35, 53, 97, 119, 134, 135, 148, 152, 259, 303
MHP (National Movement Party), 17, 53, 97, 131–2, 138, 152, 156, 160, 164, 167, 196, 199, 200, 249, 256, 261, 272, 276, 280
Middle East, 34, 86, 88, 111, 161, 189, 191, 270, 284, 291–305, 307, 312
military, Turkey, 4, 12, 20–1, 23–4, 25, 30, 93, 98–9, 105, 107, 128, 130–2, 134–5, 136, 138, 141–52, 154, 157–60, 161, 165, 167–70, 195–6, 202, 205, 210–11, 213, 215, 223–4, 227, 229, 260, 264–5, 267, 271, 279, 284, 287, 288, 292, 294, 296, 301, 304, 311, 315, 316, 317–18, 326;
  see also military coups, Turkey
military coups, Turkey
  (1960), 2, 50, 99, 148, 149, 204, 263
  (1971), 99, 148, 263
  (1980), 99, 117, 148, 161, 233, 263
  (1997) (soft or 28 February process), 3, 23, 99, 102, 122–7, 134, 136, 148, 170, 188, 212, 233, 263
  (2016), 7, 149, 160, 204, 221, 225, 230–57
Milli Gazete, 42, 113, 138
milli irade (national will), 100
Milliyet, 27, 102, 113, 114, 124, 138, 168, 169, 170, 203, 279, 280
Ministry of Education, Turkey, 40, 89, 150, 161, 220
Mishal, Khalid, 294
Mısıroğlu, Kadir, 110, 259

MIT (Turkish Intelligence Service), 222, 244, 267, 279
modernisation, Turkey, 1, 5, 37, 41–2, 45, 67, 77–8, 88, 131, 135, 174, 287, 314, 321
Modi, Narendra, 13
Monde, Le, 288, 311
Moro Liberation Movement, 309
Morsi, Mohamed, 24, 108, 190–2, 200, 296, 309, 313, 316–17
MSP (National Salvation Party), 38, 53, 112, 116
MTTB student union (National Turkish Student Union), 34–5, 47, 50–1, 54–5, 59, 67, 74
Mubarak, Hosni, 298
Mudde, Cas, 18, 28
muhacir (post-Ottoman refugees), 1
Muhammed, Prophet, 56, 169
Muhteşem Yüzyıl (Magnificent Century), 177
Mumcu, Erkan, 142
Muslim Brotherhood (MB), 5, 44, 45, 58, 90, 162, 190–2, 221, 248, 259, 273, 296–8, 300, 302–8, 309, 312
Muslim world, 16, 29, 34, 57, 88, 95, 111, 250, 260, 285, 297, 303, 307, 309, 316, 322
Mussolini, Benito, 13
müşteri-odaklı siyaset (customer-oriented politics), 264
Myanmar, 34, 255; *see also* Burma

Naipaul, V. S., 314
Nakşibendi Sufi tradition, 46, 48, 58, 263; *see also* Sufism
National Education Law (Article 32, No. 1739), 40
national education system, 40–1, 220

National Pact of 1920, 82
national police, Turkey, 21, 99, 117, 130, 134, 150–1, 158–9, 170, 172, 180, 182, 183, 187, 189, 192–6, 203, 204, 210–13, 215–26, 227–8, 234, 238, 242, 252, 325
  Police Department's Financial and Anti-Corruption Unit, 192–3
National Unity and Fraternity Project (Kurdish Initiative, 2009), 260, 266
nationalism, Turkey, 2, 17, 23, 34, 47–9, 55, 61, 64, 78, 87–8, 91–2, 110, 147, 156, 167, 248, 260, 265, 267, 271, 300, 301, 317
  Nationalism and Social Communication, 88
  Turan (unification), 44
  ülkücüler, 45
NATO, 13, 253, 306, 307
Necipoğlu, Gülru, 73, 89
neo-Ottomanism, 26, 61, 68–9, 72, 81–3, 84–93, 109, 119, 120–1, 166, 189–90, 252, 255, 269, 275, 278, 282–312, 320–1
Netherlands, The, 81, 305
New Turkey, 5, 14, 23, 69–70, 116, 165, 197, 269, 270
New York Times, The, 15, 68, 100, 155, 236, 320
New Yorker, The, 178
Nuri, Ihsan, 263
Nursi, Said, 214, 219

Obama, Barack, 20, 61, 187, 292, 300, 301, 308, 312
Öcalan, Abdullah, 267, 268, 269–72, 274, 277, 280
O'Donnell, Guillermo, 10
Öksüz, Adil, 231–3, 239, 241, 245

Old Testament (The Bible), 85–6
Olmert, Ehud, 295
Öniş, Ziya, 125
Önsoy, Murat, 285
Operation Cast Lead massacre, 294
Operation Euphrates Shield, 301, 310
Organization for Security and Cooperation (OSCE), 249
Organization of Islamic Cooperation, 192, 196, 293
Osmanoğlu, Nilhan, 69
Ottoman Empire, 1, 2, 17, 26, 56, 64, 66–7, 68, 79, 81–3, 106, 113, 147, 149, 174, 175–6, 259–60, 261–2, 322
   Balkan Wars (1912–13), 55–6, 167
   Ottoman–Russo War (1877–8), 68
   Tanzimat Reforms (1839), 50, 51, 64, 72, 287
Ottoman Islamic heritage, 1, 2, 12, 16, 17, 31, 34, 42, 44–5, 49–50, 51–2, 53, 54, 68–70, 79–83, 84–93, 106, 109, 119, 120–1, 132, 135, 153, 175–6, 178, 189, 209, 259, 278, 314, 320–1;
   see also neo-Ottomanism
   pious generation (*dindar nesil*), 92, 161, 162, 320
   tarihdaş (sharing Ottoman history), 297
Öz, Zekeriya, 212, 227
Özal, Turgut, 2–3, 27, 78, 128, 132, 134, 145, 178–9, 188, 204, 234, 263, 284
Özen, Ergun, 182, 203
Özkök, Hilmi, 137, 149, 151, 169

Pakistan, 15, 49, 150, 309
Palestine, 34, 255, 304; see also Gaza, Mavi Marmara

parliament, Turkey, 4, 6, 21, 25, 67, 97, 99, 106–7, 112, 126–7, 129, 141, 142–4, 149, 152–3, 156, 160, 164–5, 167, 169, 188, 194–200, 202–3, 216, 217, 219, 229, 235, 248, 249, 252, 255, 256, 265, 267, 270–1, 291–2, 294, 318, 319, 326
People's Protection Units (YPG), Syria, 300–1, 312
Peres, Shimon, 85–6, 294, 296
Perwer, Sivan, 268–9
Philippines, 309
Pope, Hugh, 290
Popp, Maximilian, 236
presidential system and powers, Turkey, 6, 11, 25, 30–1, 52, 63, 64, 69, 78, 141–5, 155, 167, 196–200, 225, 248–55, 271, 272–4, 282–3, 317–18, 326
press freedom, 7, 249
public morality, 43, 44
public opinion (Turkey), 8, 12, 15–16, 125, 184, 196, 285, 286, 291–2, 299, 306, 308, 320
Pew Research Center, 8–9, 12–13
Pulur, Hasan, 86
Putin, Vladimir, 7, 13, 29, 286

Qatar, 172, 192, 302, 304, 305, 310
Qutb, Seyyid, 58

RP (Welfare Party), 3, 23, 59, 117, 265
Reis, Admiral Piri, 95
Rize, 22, 35, 91, 121, 266
Rose, Charlie, 292
Russia, 13, 17, 87, 190, 202, 234, 252, 253, 286, 291, 296, 298, 300, 301–2, 306–7, 310–11, 317

Salman, Mohammad bin, 304
Samanyolu, 158, 218
Sarıkaya, Ferhat, 151, 222
Sarkozy, Nicolas, 140, 289–90, 297, 311
Saudi Arabia, 190, 192, 293, 295, 297, 304–5, 322
Schmitt, Carl, 42
Second Republic, 154, 169
secularism, 3, 4, 25, 58, 59, 64, 93–5, 105, 107, 11, 125, 130, 135, 139, 141, 142, 145, 146–7, 154, 167–8, 174, 213–14, 254, 258, 259, 276, 290, 303, 316; *see also* Kemalism
Seljuk (civilisation), 31, 53, 70, 79–80, 81, 84–5, 88, 91, 113, 153; *see also* Ottoman Islamic heritage
Semdinli incident, 151
Şener, Abdullatif, 70, 127, 128, 129, 315, 318
SETA (Foundation for Political, Economic and Social Research), 298, 312
Sevket Pasha, Mahmut, 174
Sèvres, Treaty of, 16–17, 56, 261–2
Sezer, Ahmet Necdet, 141, 143, 155
Simmel, George, 209–10
Sisi, Abdel Fattah, 111, 191
Sofuoğlu, Ebubekir, 68–9
Solana, Javier, 291
Somalia, 34, 310
Sönmeztaş, Gökhan, 246
Sovereign Wealth Fund, 323–4
Soylu, Süleyman, 60
Soysal, Mümtaz, 86
Sözen, Nurettin, 122
Spiegel, Der, 169, 236
Stoiber, Edmund, 289
Sufism, 46–7, 58, 59, 132, 150, 178, 209, 262

Süleyman, Kanuni Sultan, 121
Sunnis, 2, 4, 32, 46, 78–9, 84, 91, 92, 93–4, 104–6, 110, 155, 163–5, 182, 201, 213, 283, 296, 299, 322, 325
Supreme Military Council (YAŞ), 232, 241
Sykes–Picot, 26, 34, 303–4, 308
Syria, 3, 20, 25, 26, 87, 99, 191, 199, 200, 211, 234, 258–9, 262, 263, 268, 272, 273–5, 291–6, 298–302, 305–6, 307, 309, 310, 312, 317
Syrian National Council, 298

Taksim Square, 173–90, 200, 203; *see also* Gezi Park protests
Talmon, Jacob, 100
Tan, Altan, 264, 274, 279
Tanyeri-Erdemir, Tugba, 89
Taşcı, Hasan, 151
Taşgetiren, Ahmet, 121, 138
Tatlıses, Ibrahim, 268
Toprak, Binnaz, 4–5, 15
Toynbee, Arnold, 88
Transparency International's Corruption Perception Index, 176
Trump, Donald, 186, 286, 301, 305
Tunisia, 14, 298
Türkeş, Alpaslan, 53, 199
Turkish Airlines, 177
Turkish Council for Scientific and Technological Research (TUBITAK), 178
Turkkan, Levant, 245
Turner, Victor, 15
TÜSIAD (Association of Turkish Industrialists and Businessmen), 145

Uighurs, 322
Ulusal TV, 182
Unification of Education Law No. 430, 40
United Arab Emirates, 172, 190, 304
United Nations Security Council, 293
United States, 11, 12, 17, 19–20, 38, 61–2, 83, 93, 146, 149, 174–5, 181, 214, 240, 253, 254–5, 285–6, 289, 291–4, 300–2, 306, 307, 308, 312
  US Civil War, 19–20
  US Congress, 19–20, 292
Ünsal, Faruk, 151

Venice Commission, 319

Wahhabi, 53–4, 305
War of Independence (Turkey), 17, 54, 70, 148, 202, 262, 278
Washington, George, 20
Western ideals and imperialism, 1, 3, 4, 9, 12–13, 15, 16–17, 19, 20, 29, 32, 34, 42, 45, 48–53, 56–8, 67, 68, 70, 72, 74, 77–81, 86–8, 90, 91, 98, 105, 110–11, 120, 135, 140, 145–6, 154, 173, 177–9, 187, 190, 192, 204, 214–15, 218, 225, 235–6, 254, 259, 283–6, 289, 297, 300, 304, 306–9, 314–15, 321–2

WhatsApp, 247
White Turks, 15, 24, 27, 29–30, 32, 65, 122, 137, 153
WikiLeaks, 83
Wolfowitz, Paul, 292
World Economic Forum (Davos, 2009), 85, 295
World War I, 16, 303

Yalçınbayır, Ertuğrul, 152, 169
Yasamee, F. A. K., 67
Yassin, Ahmed, 294
Yazıcı, Ali, 246–7
Yazidis, 197
Yemen, 20
Yenikapı Convention (2016), 317
Yıldırım, Binali, 247
Yılmaz, Mesut, 128–9, 132
Young Turk revolution, 52, 78, 148, 173–4, 263
Young Turks, 86, 127, 237, 278, 283
Yücel, Deniz, 286
Yüksekdağ, Figen, 274

Zaman, 19, 151–2, 158, 170–1, 218, 242
Zanjani, Babak, 193
Zarraf, Rezza, 193
Zengin, Bahri, 119, 137

EU representative:
Easy Access System Europe
Mustamäe tee 50, 10621 Tallinn, Estonia
Gpsr.requests@easproject.com

www.ingramcontent.com/pod-product-compliance
Lightning Source LLC
Chambersburg PA
CBHW050159240426
43671CB00013B/2182